Cambridge Medieval Classics 3

Johannes de Hauvilla
Architrenius

D1363541

Cambridge Medieval Classics

General editor

PETER DRONKE, FBA

Professor of Medieval Latin Literature, University of Cambridge

This series is designed to provide bilingual editions of medieval Latin and Greek works of prose, poetry, and drama dating from the period *c.* 350–*c.* 1350. The original texts are offered on left-hand pages, with facing-page versions in lively modern English, newly translated for the series. There are introductions, and explanatory and textual notes.

The Cambridge Medieval Classics series allows access, often for the first time, to outstanding writing of the Middle Ages, with an emphasis on texts that are representative of key literary traditions and which offer penetrating insights into the culture of medieval Europe. Medieval politics, society, humour, and religion are all represented in the range of editions produced here. Students and scholars of the literature, thought, and history of the Middle Ages, as well as more general readers (including those with no knowledge of Latin or Greek) will be attracted by this unique opportunity to read vivid texts of wide interest from the years between the decline of the Roman empire and the rise of vernacular writing.

Opening titles

1 Nine Medieval Latin Plays, translated and edited by PETER DRONKE
2 Hugh Primas and the Archpoet, translated and edited by FLEUR ADCOCK
3 Johannes de Hauvilla, *Architrenius*, translated and edited by WINTHROP WETHERBEE

Other titles in preparation

Prodromic Poems, translated and edited by MARGARET ALEXIOU and MICHAEL HENDY
Adelard of Bath, *Quaestiones Naturales* and *De Eodem et Diverso*, translated and edited by CHARLES BURNETT
Dante, *De Vulgari Eloquentia*, translated and edited by STEVEN BOTTERILL
Dante, *Monarchia*, translated and edited by PRUE SHAW
Digenis Akritas, translated and edited by ELIZABETH JEFFREYS
Nigel of Longchamp, *Speculum Stultorum*, translated and edited by JILL MANN
Dhuoda, *Liber Manualis*, translated and edited by MARCELLE THIÉBAUX
Gregory of Nazianzus, Autobiographical Poems, translated and edited by CAROLINNE WHITE
Peter Abelard, The Theological and Polemical Letters, translated and edited by JEAN ZIOLKOWSKI

Johannes de Hauvilla
Architrenius

TRANSLATED AND EDITED BY

WINTHROP WETHERBEE

Cornell University

CAMBRIDGE
UNIVERSITY PRESS

Published by the Press Syndicate of the University of Cambridge
The Pitt Building, Trumpington Street, Cambridge CB2 1RP
40 West 20th Street, New York, NY 10011-4211, USA
10 Stamford Road, Oakleigh, Melbourne 3166, Australia

First published 1994

Printed in Great Britain at the University Press, Cambridge

A catalogue record for this book is available from the British Library

Library of Congress cataloguing in publication data

Johannes, de Hauvilla, 12th cent.
[Architrenius. English]
Johannes de Hauvilla, Architrenius / translated and edited by Winthrop Wetherbee
   p.   cm. – (Cambridge medieval classics: 3)
Includes bibliographical references
ISBN 0 521 40543 2
1. Verse satire, Latin (Medieval and modern) – Translations into English.
I. Wetherbee, Winthrop, 1938–   .   II. Title.
III. Title. Architrenius.   IV. Series.
PA8360.J65A913   1994
873'.03–dc20   93–47336 CIP

ISBN 0521 40543 2 hardback

CE

Contents

Acknowledgments

Of the various people who have helped with this project, my greatest debts are certainly to Professor Paul Gerhard Schmidt, who gave his permission for the reprinting of his excellent text of the *Architrenius*, and Peter Dronke, the general editor of the Cambridge Medieval Classics, who went carefully over the entire translation to my great benefit. My mentor in twelfth-century matters, Professor Paul Piehler of McGill University, long ago showed me that the *Architrenius* was a poem worth studying. One Cornell colleague, Janet Durholz, did what could be done to help me grasp the poem's astronomy, and another, Danuta Shanzer, somehow found time to go over most of my translation, which is much the better for her scrutiny. At a late stage Dr. Charles Burnett of the Warburg Institute kindly reviewed the astronomical material and made several necessary corrections. My friend Sarah Carleton performed the cheerless task of transcribing the Latin text cheerfully and efficiently. Finally, there is hardly a day of my life when I do not have occasion to be grateful to a wonderful teacher, Mr. Theodore Wells of Milton Academy, to whom I owe most of what Latin I know, and a good deal of the pleasure I derive from it.

Introduction

The poem and its author

The *Architrenius*, a narrative satire in nine books and 4361 lines of Latin hexameter, describes the journey of its hero through a world which represents panoramically the ills of Church, court, and schools in the later twelfth century, and offers a remedy for these ills in the form of moral philosophy. Architrenius (the "Arch-Weeper") is a young man on the threshold of maturity who is shocked to find that all his thoughts and impulses, and those of the world around him, tend to vice. Convinced that Nature must be at fault, he resolves to seek out the goddess and confront her with the spectacle of his hapless state. His quest leads him to the court of Venus, the house of Gluttony, the schools of Paris, the palace of Ambition, the mount of Presumption, and the unnamed site of a battle between the army of the generous (led by King Arthur and Sir Gawain) and the forces of Avarice. Eventually he arrives in Tylos, a natural paradise where he encounters the ancient philosophers and receives a long series of brief lectures on vice, the vanity of worldly things, and the need for self-discipline. Finally Nature appears, responds to Architrenius' complaint with a lecture on the order of things, and proposes to remedy his condition by giving him the beautiful maiden Moderation as a bride. The poem ends with the celebration of their marriage.

The *Architrenius* was something new when it appeared toward the end of the twelfth century, but its distinctive features show the effects of developments in western European society over the preceding hundred years. Urban culture, commercial and professional in outlook, had become a steadily more important counterweight to the traditional dominance of aristocratic wealth and privilege. The bureaucratization of government and administration in Church and state had opened new avenues for social advancement and created new functions for educated men. At the same time higher education in the liberal arts had become increasingly the province of cathedral schools located in urban centers. Out of the growing organization and specialization of students and masters was evolving the institution of the university, one of many indications of a new sense of identity associated with the possession of knowledge.[1] The intellectual had emerged as a social type, a professional class increasingly defined by its role in a secular society, alert to the opportunities for advancement that education made possible, and possessed of the artistic skill to express its new social awareness in a range of new literary forms.

It is "clerks" of this type who composed the first vernacular romances, celebratory though often covertly critical of the courtly–urban culture of France and England. They produced works like the *Moralium dogma philosophorum* (*c.* 1150) attributed to Guillaume de Conches and the *Policraticus* (1159) of John of Salisbury, works in which classical ethical and political thought are brought to bear on twelfth-century social and political institutions. And in a bewildering range of Latin poetry, ranging from adaptations of vernacular animal fable to the most sophisticated imitations of classical models, they maintained a steady barrage of satire, aimed not only at the venality and greed of the rich and powerful, but at the avarice and ambition of men whose training and horizons were often essentially their own.[2]

It is largely for and about such "new men" that the *Architrenius* was written, and its author, Johannes de Hauvilla, to judge from what little we know about him,[3] is in many ways a representative of the type. He was a *magister* in the important cathedral school of Rouen. The *Architrenius*, his only known work, was dedicated in 1184 to Walter of Coutances, who was about to be installed as Archbishop of Rouen, and it contains an array of elaborate compliments to one whom Johannes

---

[1] For a good brief account of these developments, see Jacques Le Goff, *Les intellectuels au Moyen Age* (2nd edn, Paris, 1985), pp. i–x, 1–69.

[2] See Alexander Murray, *Reason and Society in the Middle Ages* (2nd edn, Oxford, 1985), pp. 71–77; John A. Yunck, *The Lineage of Lady Meed: The Development of Medieval Venality Satire* (Notre Dame, 1963), pp. 47–187; Claus Uhlig, *Hofkritik im England des Mittelalters und der Renaissance* (Berlin, 1973), pp. 85–91.

[3] For the evidence regarding Johannes' life and career, see the introduction to the edition of Paul Gerhard Schmidt (Munich, 1974), pp. 18–26. The *Architrenius* was complete around the end of 1184 (see n. 4 below). Johannes was not yet old (1.85–87), and so his birth may be placed around 1150 or shortly after. He was evidently a Norman, perhaps from the village of Hauville near Rouen. In 1184 he was presumably already teaching at Rouen, where the grammarian Gervais of Melkley was his pupil toward the end of the century, and "Magister Iohannes de Havilla" is named as witness in a cathedral document of 1199. Gervais in his *Ars poetica* (ed. Hans-Jürgen Gräbener. Forschungen zur Romanischen Philologie 17, Münster Westphalen, 1965) often cites the *Architrenius*, but always refers to his old teacher in the past tense, and thus we may suppose that Johannes was no longer living when the *Ars poetica* appeared, probably between 1208 and 1216.

doubtless viewed as a potentially valuable patron.[4] Much of the poem's satire engages themes already common in the Latin poetry of the period, and which often express the mere disgruntlement of what was becoming, in R. R. Bolgar's phrase, an "intellectual proletariat":[5] thus it has much to say about the lack of respect for scholarship among men of power, and the opportunism of those whose superficial learning gains them preferment in the schools or in the Church. But in the vast sweep of the *Architrenius* these become only the symptoms of larger problems and forces, for the most part only intuitively sensed and impressionistically rendered by the poet, but sufficiently recognizable to make plain his responsiveness to the fundamental transformations affecting his society. The thematic range of Johannes' narrative, and the persistence with which his satirist's instinct for detail reinforces his moral vision and counters the abstracting tendency of his allegory, show him effecting a difficult transition, redeploying the resources of "high" poetry, ancient and medieval, to focus with a new directness on the secular world of his own place and time. In both its occasional brilliance and its frequent awkwardness the *Architrenius* marks an important first step in the literary experiment that was eventually to produce the fully realized comic worlds of Jean de Meun, Boccaccio and Chaucer.

The *Architrenius*: form and theme

Moving as it does with disconcerting freedom between the worlds of visionary allegory and topical satire, the utopian peace of the ancient philosophers and the lower depths of Parisian student life, the *Architrenius* does not lend itself to categorization, and I will begin by trying to indicate what it is not. Despite its obvious debts to Bernardus Silvestris and Alan of Lille, it is not a philosophical or theological allegory, nor, though Hell and damnation are a recurring theme, and Architrenius is admonished by the philosophers of old concerning the fear and love of God, is it essentially religious. The gist of the *Architrenius* is in its social criticism, its representation of a world where the pursuit of wealth and

---

4 See *Architrenius* 1.100–74, which place Walter's birth in the context of Trojan and British history, and announce his imminent elevation from Bishop of Lincoln to Archbishop of Rouen. Pope Lucius III approved the conferral of the archbishopric in September or October of 1184, and the installation occurred on 24 February, 1185, so that the poem must have been finished during this brief period; see Schmidt, pp. 16–17. Unlike most such gestures, Johannes' lavish praise of Walter and his lineage is not confined to the dedication, but recurs at considerable length in the course of the narrative (see 5.384–480, 6.311–16).
5 *The Classical Heritage and its Beneficiaries* (Cambridge, 1954), pp. 178–88.

preferment is an all-consuming concern. The arrogance of power, its flaunting of wealth and abuse of patronage, and the ambition, greed and hypocrisy of the aspiring courtier or cleric are what bring Johannes' verse to life, and most of the lessons he seeks to teach center on the values that govern conduct in the secular world.

Much of Johannes' finest poetry is devoted to describing the material fabric of the life of those who have attained the heights of power in this careerist society. We learn at length of their elaborate style of dress (2.90–164; 4.284–300), their sumptuous and endlessly varied diet (2.184–263), and the lavishness of the construction and decoration of their homes (4.179–90, 214–321). Much of this description, considered in isolation, is seemingly admiring. The decoration of the Palace of Ambition includes costly materials of all sorts, and Johannes notes the way in which nature conspires with art to produce its splendor:

> fecunda bonorum
> Luxuriem largitur humus mundique nefandis
> Obsequitur votis, rerum tellure ministra
> Edificat securus homo; nam terra paratum
> Iurat in auxilium, quidvis Natura potentis
> Expedit ad nutum: lapides et ligna ligandis
> Edibus et, quicquid preciosior exigit usus.
> Exibet et gemmas, quarum fulgore diescit
> Sole suo contenta domus ...

The very earth, so productive of good things, bestows luxury, serving the base desires of the world; man builds confidently, when earth herself provides the means. And indeed she pledges her ready assistance. At the great man's nod, Nature delivers whatever he wishes, stone and beams for framing houses, and whatever else a more lavish undertaking may require. She proffers gems, in whose splendor the palace basks, content with its own sun ... (*Architrenius* 4.182–90)

This passage has a rich literary tradition behind it. It clearly invokes the theme of *homo microcosmus*, dear to Bernardus and Alan: Nature will appeal to Architrenius in similar terms at the end of the poem, declaring that the universe at large exists to mirror and fulfill the capacities of mankind. The lines express the aspirations of human art as Baudri of Bourgueil had expressed them a century earlier, in a long poem in which the bed-chamber of the Countess Adela of Blois, daughter of William the Conqueror, with its tapestries, painted ceiling, and intricately paved floor surrounding the elaborately carved bed, becomes an image of the universe, world history, and the arts which comprise philosophy.[6] The scope and grandeur of Baudri's project suggest a new sense of larger possibilities for medieval culture, and for the poetry that celebrates this culture. It marks the early stirring of the desire to integrate the role of the poet as celebrant of urban or courtly culture with the traditional ideal of the universally learned *poeta platonicus*, an ambition perceptible in Bernardus Silvestris and Alan of Lille, and central to the project of their contemporaries, the vernacular poets who produced the first romances.[7]

For Johannes, however, though he duly acknowledges the beauty and dignity of the artistry involved,[8] the magnificence he describes is suspect from the outset. Wealth and material splendor are consistently presented in the *Architrenius* as the object or reward of ambition or sheer greed, illusory in their appeal and treacherous to those who obtain them. The inveighings of Cato, Democritus, Pliny and Pythagoras against the excess and moral weakness to which wealth gives rise are already implicit in Johannes' tableaux of court life. There is no indication that the sumptuousness described is a code, a symbolic manifestation of coherent cultural or political achievement, or an idealized rendering of the life and prerogatives proper to nobility.[9]

Indeed one of the most striking features of the poem is the limited role played by the values of aristocratic society. The lines in which Johannes discusses kinship as a ground for preferment (3.454–62) suggest a grudging acknowledgment of aristocratic prerogative, and largesse in the form of *noblesse oblige* appears fleetingly in Sir Gawain's self-portrayal as one who has never withheld what he might bestow (6.4–8). The need for unstinting and enlightened patronage is a recurring theme of the long survey of the hardships of student life, and Democritus later centers on enlightened giving as the one really noble use to which riches may be put (6.286–316). But Johannes is concerned less with the occasions patronage affords for noble gestures than with its abuses, its function as part of the complex network of bribery and favoritism that organizes the careerist society of the poem. This is

[6] Baudri of Bourgueil, *Carmina*, ed. Karlheinz Hilbert (Heidelberg, 1979), No. 134, ed. Hilbert, pp. 149–85; see Gerald A. Bond, "'Iocus Amoris': The Poetry of Baudri of Bourgueil and the Formation of an Ovidian Subculture," *Traditio* 42 (1986), pp. 143–93.
[7] See Alfred Adler, "The *Roman de Thèbes*, a 'Consolatio Philosophiae'," *Romanische Forschungen* 72 (1960), pp. 257–76; Johan Huizinga, "Über die Verknüpfung des Poetischen mit dem Theologischen bei Alanus de Insulis," in *Mededeelingen der Koninklijke Akademie van Wetenschappen. Amsterdam* 74B, no. 6 (1932), pp. 154–59.
[8] See especially 4.272–81, and below, pp. xx–xxi.
[9] On the literary use of such codes see Jacques Le Goff, "Vestimentary and Alimentary Codes in *Erec et Enide*," in *The Medieval Imagination* (Chicago, 1988), pp. 132–50.

the "real" world of the *Architrenius*: Gawain and the traditional heroism he embodies exist on their own plane, at an uncertain remove from the main action of the poem.[10]

To the extent that a coherent rationale can be discerned for this displacement of traditional values, one of the most important factors is the role of money, at once the means and the all-consuming object of advancement for the *curiales* who infest the world of the poem. The desire for wealth is obsessive, to the point at which Johannes, here as so often taking his cue from Juvenal,[11] makes his gluttons literally consume the very gold that enables their indulgence and constitutes the basis for the claim to social status of which their feasting is the visible sign (2.248–56). Queen Money and her "ennobling" power were an established theme for satire by Johannes' day,[12] but it would be hard to find a text in which the coercive power of wealth and the horror of greed are expressed more powerfully than in the *Architrenius*, or one which makes clearer the degree to which they render social relations artificial and ambiguous. In the Palace of Ambition "an artful Liberality spreads its riches about; Money's cornucopia pours forth friendship; Pledges are sold into mutual bondage" (4.95–98). The courtier "bends the laws at every opportunity for gain, takes on whatever sort of work will make the purse grow fat, and trades his right to cast his vote for a cash reward" (4.340–43). The power of money seems to transcend human relations altogether: "They serve not at the bidding of men, but of wealth. It is from wealth that men's authority is drawn ... " (4.445–46). The Palace of Ambition, the Hill of Presumption, the rich man's hall infested by the Furies express Johannes' nightmarish sense that a larger force, rather than individuals and political functions, is the controlling factor in the court world he describes, and a series of lurid tableaux make plain its transformative power: When Presumption comes to court,

> regina Pecunia iuri
> Preminet, ausa suis astringere legibus orbem
> Quas racio nescit. sed ei devincta cupido
> Dictat et indicit avidi facundia questus
> Et loculos ardens discincte audacia lingue:
> Census censura fiunt iniuria iura,
> Pura minus pura, sacra littera sacra litura.

---

[10] Le Goff discusses this displacement of the traditional status of chivalry, "Warriors and Conquering Bourgeois: The Image of the City in Twelfth-Century French Literature," *Medieval Imagination*, pp. 151–76.

[11] Glossing this passage, Schmidt aptly cites Juvenal, *Sat.* 11.14–16.

[12] See Murray, *Reason and Society*, pp. 71–77.

Queen Money, the teeming mother of vice, dominating the throne itself with her oppressive yoke, takes precedence over justice, for she has boldly subjected the world to laws of her own, unknown to reason. Property performs the office of judgment, injustice does the work of justice, purity grows less pure, and and sacred tradition gives way to sanctifying forgery. (5.95–101)

Later Architrenius encounters the monster Cupidity,

> Mater Avaricie, sompni ieiuna Cupido,
> Eternam dampnata sitim producere, nullis
> Exsaciata bonis, lucri studiosa, rapinis
> Artifices factura manus, visura recessus
> Antipodum noctisque dies umbrasque sinistras,
> Ardentis secreta sinus . . .
>   . . . plena est discordia. questus
> Ardor ubi pugnat, studio concurritur omni
> Ad loculos; nam sola potest reverencia nummi
> Quodlibet ad libitum mundano quolibet uti.
> Hec vaga commutat solidis, quadrata rotundis . . .

the mother of Avarice, the fantasy of hungering Greed, condemned to produce an endless thirst that no material good can satisfy . . . her eyes see into the depth of night's Antipodes, the sinister shadows, the secret places of the heart's desire . . . She is full of discord. When the desire for profit asserts itself, all rush eagerly to man the money-bags; for only when money is revered can one enjoy whatever one wants as much as one wants and wherever one wants. She can change fluids to solids, make square things round . . . (5.244–49, 260–64)

The cumulative effect of such declamations is to make the workings of money appear as something organic, dominating and transforming human life. Finally this becomes explicit:

> Heret in ere sitis, habitis furit ardor habendi,
> Pullulat in questu questus amor. omnia nullum
> Pondus habent, nisi sint unum simul omnia pondus.

The thirst is inherent in the money itself, the fever of possession rages in the things possessed, the process of acquisition only spreads the love of acquiring. Nothing has value unless all things can be possessed at once. (5.289–91)

Money of course is only the catalyst of social process. The *Architrenius* could serve as a text-book illustration of the thesis by which Alexander Murray has explained the effect on European society of the development of a money economy. Money facilitates social mobility: the relations among and within classes and estates become "liquefied," and as traditional hierarchies and relationships dissolve, power, like cash value, is abstracted from individuals to institutions.[13] New social conditions generate new mental habits, and Murray singles out two such habits as fundamental:

> One was the habit of desiring more and more money, which medieval theologians usually called avarice. The other was the habit of desiring that power and dignity which society concentrates in its institutions. Despite some confusion, this usually went under the name of ambition.[14]

Johannes is the poet *par excellence* of the capitalist–careerist mentality Murray here defines. It would of course have been impossible for him or any contemporary observer to achieve so clear an analysis of the forces at work, and the traditional conception of service as a relationship between one man and another must have made even the growth of bureaucracy difficult to recognize as such,[15] but the quasi-monstrous powers whose inexorable and all-involving influence controls the world of Johannes' courtiers clearly embody the new forces that were transforming the workings of social power in his time.

It is the same sense of the court as a focus of strange, dark forces that emerges from the opening pages of the *De nugis curialium* of Walter Map, who probably began his compilation during the very years when Johannes was at work on the *Architrenius*,[16] and who opens it with a series of bizarre images aimed at capturing the effect of the new institution. The court is in a state of constant flux, in that its human components come and go, yet it is "constant in change," like Boethius' *Fortuna*. It is a giant with a hundred hands, clumsy but impossible for any Hercules to wholly subdue. Its populace is in one sense united in service to a single lord, yet their true "sovereign mistress" is Avarice, and their environment is a kind of hell, where their desperate pursuit of favor and position recalls the yearnings and strivings of Tantalus, Sisyphus, and Ixion.[17]

The *Policraticus* of John of Salisbury (1159), in broadest outline a treatise on statesmanship, also deals with the experience of the courtier, and has much to say about the pernicious effects of avarice, gluttony,

---

[13] Murray, *Reason and Society*, pp. 59–61, 81–109. For a brief, lucid account of the social context of this process in twelfth-century France and England, see Jean Dunbabin, *France in the Making* (Oxford, 1985), pp. 277–86.

[14] *Reason and Society*, p. 60.   [15] See Dunbabin, *France in the Making*, pp. 329–30.

[16] Much of the material in the *De nugis*, which was evidently completed in 1191, can be dated as early as 1181–82; see the introduction to the Brook-Mynors revision of the M. R. James edition (Oxford, 1983), pp. xxiv–xxxii.

[17] *De nugis* I. 1–5.

and especially the practice of flattery and adulation, which both alienate the courtier from his own individual character and destroy self-knowledge in his patron.[18] John is deeply troubled by the perversion of learning that results from the use of education as a stepping-stone to preferment,[19] and the *Policraticus* includes as well a long, powerful account of the forms and circumstances in which ambition manifests itself in civil and ecclesiastical contexts.[20] Like Johannes, John is capable of recognizing a certain pragmatic necessity for ambition in public life,[21] and he is willing to condone even flattery if it serves to combat the unjust authority of a tyrant,[22] but in the main his argument has less to do with practical politics than with the political and theological principles to which the ambition of unscrupulous men poses a threat. He is acutely aware also of the psychological aspect of ambition. His analysis begins *ab ovo* with the human susceptibility to cupidity, "the fountain of all evils," and shows how this leads to a false sense of freedom, pride, and the lust for power and glory. He conveys eloquently the attractive power of wealth and position and the terrible delusions to which they lead; and his discussion makes frequent reference to the divine power which the ambitious in their perversity ignore, the constant threat of divine judgment.

At such moments the *Policraticus* anticipates the many passages in the *Architrenius* that set the workings of ambition and presumption in an infernal or apocalyptic perspective. For both authors what is most terrible about greed and ambition is their power to blind and pervert human aspiration, driving their victims to submit themselves to a kind of self-damnation. The emphasis is clear in the following lines from the opening of the *Policraticus*, a passage that would not be out of place in the discourse of one of the ancient philosophers of Johannes' Tylos:

[18] On avarice, *Policraticus* 7.16–17; 8.3–4, 13, 15; on gluttony, 8.6–7; on flattery, 3.4–7, 14–15.
[19] The *Metalogicon* was written largely to reaffirm the true purpose of learning against such encroachments, and the *Entheticus maior* touches many of the same themes (see esp. the long speech which John puts into the mouth of an ambitious logician, 58–108); cp. *Architrenius* 3.401–30.
[20] *Policraticus* 7.17–21.
[21] See *Policraticus* 7.17, where the intolerability of the selling of preferment in the Church is contrasted with the relative openness of public life; in general, of course, John's ideal is the statesman who has no ambition for power, but lives his life in such a way as to be worthy of it (see *Policraticus* 5.1). For Johannes' view of the potential value of ambition, see *Architrenius* 4.111–45, esp. 133–37 (where, however, there is perhaps a measure of irony).
[22] See *Policraticus* 7.15.

Success, implacable foe of virtue, applauds its devotees only to harm them, and with its ill-starred prosperity escorts them on their joyous way to bring about their ultimate fall by first pledging them in cups of sweet wine and, when they are intoxicated thereby, mixing in the draught of deadly poison or anything conceivably worse. The more brilliant the success the denser the clouds that gather around their dazzled eyes. As the darkness thickens the truth vanishes, virtue withers with severed roots, and a crop of vices sprouts. The light of reason is extinguished, and the whole being is carried headlong into the abyss of destruction.[23]

It is in much the same tone that Johannes, having dwelt at length on the workings of presumption, reflects that wealth and power become a kind of hell for those who give themselves to them too completely:

> Tartareus iam civis homo, Stygis incola, mortis
> Non expectato laqueo venit, illa supremo
> Vis rapitur fato: mavult precedere liber
> Fatorum quam iussa sequi, iam tramite ceco
> Ad Styga rumpit iter, vivus venisse laborat,
> Quo defunctus eat . . .

For man is even now a citizen of Tartarus, and dwells in Stygian darkness. Hither he comes, seized by the unsuspected snare of death, his strength taken from him by all-powerful fate. He thinks to pursue freedom, rather than submit to the bidding of the Fates, but already, in blind career, he is forcing a path to the Stygian shore: it is his life's labor to arrive at the place whence he will depart when dead . . . (*Architrenius* 4.164–69)

The great exemplar of this folly is Lucifer, whose fall is described at length (5.177–219); Cato later provides a vivid account of the damnation of the rich man, beset by the Furies and demons of his own obsessive greed:

> . . . surgit cum divitibus factura Megera
> Colloquium notaque diu cum prole susurrat
> Et iacit amplexus et plaudit et oscula miscet,
> Incautoque doli ridenti arridet alumpno.
> Interdum Stygias attencius edocet artes
> Sollicitumque minus intorto verberat idro,
> Effusumque iacit Stygium per viscera virus,
> Quo nequeat non velle nefas scelerumque soporem
> Nesciat et numquam facinus succumbat honesto.

---

[23] *Policraticus* 1.1.19, tr. Joseph B. Pike, *Frivolities of Courtiers and Footprints of Philosophers* (Minneapolis, 1938), p. 11.

Megaera emerges to commune with the wealthy, whispers with her long-cherished progeny, bestows embraces and praise mixed with kisses, and smiles on the smiling pupil unmindful of her guile. As she carefully instructs him in her Stygian arts, she strikes him all unawares with a writhing serpent. Its bite spreads through his body a hellish poison, so that he is unable not to will evil; he knows no rest from wrongdoing, and honor cannot overcome his wickedness. (6.136–44)

Architrenius himself later provides the fullest and most eloquent expression of this overpowering worldliness, which has left him "dwelling inwardly in the darkness of night," haunted by images of hell (7.229–76). Repeatedly Johannes sounds the trumpet of apocalypse to warn of the judgment awaiting those whose power and wealth has driven them irresistibly to abuse these gifts and bred in them a false sense of self-sufficiency (5.164–76, 232–35; 6.180–96).

But while *Architrenius* and *Policraticus* are often strikingly close in tone and theme, the similarity is potentially misleading. John of Salisbury is a religious moralist. His political ideals are grounded in biblical and patristic injunction, as well as in the classical precepts and *exempla* on which his reputation as a humanist is founded. From the outset the message of the *Policraticus* is charged with reminders that our worldly conduct will ultimately be scrutinized by "the Angel of the Great Judgment,"[24] and that only divine grace can protect us from the consequences of our errors. He is concerned with the causes of these errors: the attainment of the right reason that he enjoins on his ideal statesman, like the *sapientia* which crowns human learning in the *Didascalicon* of Hugh of St. Victor, is repeatedly shown to depend on the recovery, enabled by grace, of the image of the Creator within ourselves which we have darkened and distorted through sin.[25]

There is nothing like this systematic religious purpose in the *Architrenius*. Though doubtless expressive of real conviction, Johannes' religious rhetoric, with its apocalyptic and infernal emphases, is more significantly part of his repertory as a satirist, and shows him concerned less with the causes of sin than with dramatizing its effects as vividly as possible. Throughout the poem the boundaries demarcating the earthly plane of the poem's action from its paradisal and infernal extensions are readily permeable: hell lurks in the depths of the rich man's household, and Elysium is an outward expression of the tranquillity of the philosopher. And though it seems to me to be going too far to suggest, as

[24] *Policraticus* 1. Prol. 18.
[25] See *Policraticus* 1.1, 2.20, 3.1. The theme recurs in John's writings on philosophy; see *Metalogicon* 1.23; 4.17, 40; *Entheticus maior* 219–324.

Jean-Charles Payen has done, that Johannes is simply unconcerned with questions of sin, grace, and *contemptus carnis*,[26] it is certainly the case that these tend to be dealt with as ethical, rather than religious issues. Even before Nature has introduced the sanctions of her own *religio nativa* as the remedy for Architrenius' misfortunes (9.242–49), the religious dimension of the poem has been largely reduced to questions of conduct. Christ is the prototype of generosity (5.68),[27] or of a "gentleness" which is explicitly discussed in both secular and religious terms (8.45–52). And this secular note grows steadily stronger as the poem approaches its conclusion, the wedding of Architrenius and Moderation, which is an unambiguously earthly affair from beginning to end. While attendants like "Reasonable Expenditure" (*expense ratio*, 9.441) bustle about, Fortune smiles on a union hallowed above all by practical good sense, and the poet ends with the wish that the divine limit imposed on their feasting may remain far off.

Humanism: the *Architrenius* and the ancient world

In addition to its prevailingly secular emphasis, there are moments when the *Architrenius* seems to set its satirical purpose to one side, and dwell on the merely human, rather than the moral significance of the worldly behavior it describes. A concern with what in another context would have to be called the tragic aspect of human life can surface unexpectedly. Thus in the course of his account of the Palace of Ambition, primarily an indictment of vanity and luxury, Johannes describes a tapestry beautifully worked with scenes from the fall of Troy. As he contemplates the death of Hector, the tears of Helen, Priam pleading before Achilles, he seems, like Vergil's Aeneas in the Carthaginian temple, to become distracted by the beauty of the stories depicted, and reflects that "it is sweet to feel sorrow at the sorrows of men, to grieve at their grief, to repay tears with tears, lamentation with lamen-

---

[26] Payen, "L'utopie chez les Chartrains," *Le Moyen Age* 90 (1984), pp. 390–93. It is only just to note that the late Professor Payen, for his part, considered me to have slighted the utopian aspect of the poems of Johannes and Alan of Lille in my *Platonism and Poetry in the Twelfth Century* (Princeton, 1972); see "L'utopie chez les Chartrains," p. 400.

[27] See also 7.328–31, where generosity is discussed in conspicuously Christlike terms, though Christ is not named. John of Salisbury cites Christ as an *exemplum* of secular virtue ("liberalissimus et civilissimus aut facetissimus paterfamilias"), *Policraticus* 8.9; see Peter von Moos, "The use of *exempla* in the *Policraticus* of John of Salisbury," in *The world of John of Salisbury*, ed. Michael Wilks (Studies in Church History: Subsidia 3, Oxford, 1984), pp. 251–54.

tation" (4.252–53). Later a remarkable passage in a similar vein compares the fallen Lucifer to Ovid's Narcissus:

> felix, nisi se tot fonte bonorum
> Lucifer agnosset! alter Narcisus et oris
> Dotibus et fati lacrimis. solacia concors
> Prebeat eventus, communis sarcina dampni
> Pondus utrumque levet. miser illc, sed ille, quod ultra,
> Quam liceat, temere speciem, quam vidit, amavit.

Happy Lucifer, had he not beheld his image in a well of such bounty! He was a Narcissus, in the rich beauty of his face, and in his tearful fate. Let their consonant ending be a source of solace, and the shared onus of self-destruction ease the burden for both. One is utterly miserable, but the other is so because he foolishly loved beyond measure the beauty he beheld in himself. (5.214–19)

What we see at such moments, I think, is a remarkable intuitive feeling for the humane element in classical Latin poetry, a sense of the *lacrimae rerum* capable of temporarily subordinating the impulses of the satiric moralist. At times the effect can be incongruous, as when Johannes makes Pittacus bestow on the fallen Lucifer a gentle Horatian valediction that associates him with the early kings of Rome (8.36–37), but it is clearly the result of intense and appreciative study, and it expresses itself both in the appropriation of themes and motifs and in the fidelity with which Johannes recreates the style of his chosen *auctores*. Predictably, Ovid is the source of far more borrowed phrases and formulae than any other author, and the influence of the *Metamorphoses* pervades Johannes' mythological and world-historical vision, but he is closer in spirit to Horace and especially Juvenal. Like any good satirist he is fascinated by temperament and idiosyncrasy: he can sketch a Terentian parasite in a few brief strokes (4.376–86), and his philosophers are not mere names linked to set speeches, but show themselves as angry and abrupt (Cato, 6.123ff.), self-absorbed (Crates, 6.396ff.), obsessive (Xenocrates, 7.146ff.), or avuncular (Thales, 7.277ff.). Stylistically, Lucan and Juvenal are his preferred models, though his "imitations" of them often involve expanding a pithy formulation to several times its original length.[28] Even when he achieves brevity he is all too apt to dilute it with repetition. But at his best he is capable of catching the tone of his *auctores* with a fidelity few twelfth-century poets can match. His survey of the workings of ambition in Roman history

---

[28] See Schmidt, pp. 54–55, for an analysis of Johannes' eleven-line recreation of Juvenal, *Sat.* 8.139–40, and a list of similar elaborations on formulae from Horace.

(4.116–31) has Lucan's biting energy, and like Juvenal he is capable of fantastic invention on the themes of wealth and greed, as when he shows his gluttons debating learnedly on sauces and modes of cooking (2.184–231), or describes their richly decorated goblets (4.307–17). Like Juvenal, too, he is unfailingly responsive to poverty, and aroused by the spectacle of its coexistence with great wealth. His inventory of the furnishings and cuisine of a student's lodgings (3.55–80) is vivid, precisely detailed, and unusually free of the mannerisms of school-poetry; and he can capture the giddiness of a poor man's wine-induced fantasy of status:

> Sortemque beatam
> Pauperis esse iubes et, qui servire steterunt,
> Consedere duces et Bacchi stante corona
> Surgit ad hos patere dominus septemplicis Aiax
> Anglicus . . .

You [Bacchus] decree that the poor man's lot shall become a happy one. Those who have stood in attendance sit at the feast like lords; for so long as they are crowned with the garland of Bacchus, the English Ajax himself, the lord of the sevenfold bowl, rushes to obey their orders . . . (2.300–5)

Johannes' engagement with the ancient world appears also in his frequent use of *exempla*, short historical narratives that illustrate a particular aspect of human conduct. Here again John of Salisbury was an important precedent: for both authors, stories drawn from compilations like that of Valerius Maximus, and designed originally to provide illustrative material for budding orators,[29] are an important means of incorporating ancient ethical ideas into their texts, and by this means making good the deficiencies of Christian and biblical tradition as a source of social and political wisdom.[30] They express the same impulse that leads Johannes to introduce ancient philosophers as characters in his poem, and to fill the discourse of these sages with doctrines drawn from Cicero and Seneca.

In general, it is clear that for Johannes, as for John of Salisbury, ancient literature is the repository of universal truths, good and bad,[31]

---

[29] See Hans Liebeschütz, *Medieval Humanism in the Life and Writings of John of Salisbury*, Studies of the Warburg Institute 17 (London, 1950), pp. 67–73, and von Moos, "The use of *exempla* in the *Policraticus*."

[30] See von Moos, "The use of *exempla* in the *Policraticus*," pp. 247–57.

[31] Johannes' view of the ancient world was not one-sided. Schmidt can speak of his "almost unlimited reverence" for the "nobler culture" of antiquity (p. 52), but as the disciple of Juvenal and Lucan, he draws negative as well as positive *exempla* from his classical sources. Just as the barriers between earth and hell are often hard to define in

concerning the basic tendencies of human nature and human history, and that the recovery of direct contact with the classical authors is an essential aspect of his project in the *Architrenius*. It is probably true as well that Johannes' devotion to pagan thought and literature as a unique and indispensable educational resource – the conviction expressed in Johannes' "omne bonum veterum labiis distillat" (8.1) – coexists, as it unquestionably does in John of Salisbury, with an orthodox conviction of the sole sufficiency of Christian truth. But where John deliberately and systematically juxtaposes pagan and Christian ideas, asserting the value of the one while maintaining the ultimate authority of the other, Johannes introduces Christianity only intermittently and seemingly at random. Christ and Christian ideals are unexpectedly invoked by the pagan moralists (e.g. 7.328–31; 8.41–44), but they remain loose ends, and are never placed in a coherent relation to the *religio nativa* of Nature. The vast body of moral teaching digested in the later books of the *Architrenius* has none of the consistency of that "praeter-Christian" perspective, complementary to the Christian vision but deliberately presented in philosophical rather than religious terms, that John of Salisbury had admired in Boethius;[32] and though the long exemplary tale of Polemo's renunciation of dissipation for philosophy (8.251–85) has a certain recapitulatory function and heralds the appearance of Nature, the conversion it portends never issues in a spiritual perspective on Architrenius' career.

Johannes de Hauvilla as a medieval poet

If the *Architrenius* testifies to the capacity of medieval humanism for appreciating the distinctive features of ancient culture, it is also a product of its place and time. For every line in which we hear the voice of Lucan, Horace or Juvenal there are dozens that could only have been produced by a twelfth-century rhetorician, a virtuoso practitioner of the *ornatus difficilis*. No moment is too solemn to afford an occasion for such virtuosity, which frequently disrupts the very passages in which Johannes comes closest to attaining a sort of classical gravity. There is a certain flamboyant charm in a paean which, perhaps briefly recalling the hymns of Ambrose, declares Bacchus to be more stellar than a star, or brighter than light ("sidus plus sidere, luxque / lucis . . ." 2.270–71).

Johannes' poetic universe, so past and present form a continuous historical reality, with no clear evidence of progress or decline.

[32] See *Policraticus* 7.15; and von Moos, "The use of *exempla* in the *Policraticus*," pp. 247–50, 254–56.

And at times the compulsive word-play has a certain blocky dignity of its own, as in the lines which describe the transformation of the Athenian rake Polemo by the teaching of Xenocrates:

> Succedente mora succedit gracia morum,
> Inque dies cedit Venus accedente venusto,
> Rectificatque virum declivem regula virtus,
> Philosophumque facit facundia philosophantis ...

As his resistance gives way, the appeal of morality takes its place, and Venus yields, day by day, as its charm gains the ascendancy. The rule of virtue rectifies the fallen man, the charm of philosophizing makes him a philosopher ... (*Architrenius* 8.281–84)

But even here we could certainly spare the last line, and too often such passages convey only a kind of stylistic hyperactivity. It is hard to see why so admirably concise a formulation as "ardua tollit / cras ruiturus homo" (4.201–02) should be followed immediately by four separate variations on the paradox expressed in *tollit* / *ruiturus*, or why, after Pliny has brought his grim account of a ruined life to the *optata quies* of death (6.382), he should be forced to add that in death "vulnus curatur vulnere, pena / pena, dolore dolor" (385–86).

But it is such passages as these, for many modern readers the least attractive feature of this type of poetry, that gained the *Architrenius* its great reputation. Johannes was famous above all as a stylist, a master in the deployment of the rhetorical figures prescribed by the *artes poeticae*. No less an authority than Geoffrey of Vinsauf could declare that the *Architrenius* surpassed all works of modern times in its use of complex figurative language (*tropicae locutiones*).[33] Gervais of Melkley, who complains of the poem's *durissimae translationes* (i.e. difficult metaphors), and cites examples that seem to him excessive,[34] nonetheless admired the *Architrenius* sufficiently to declare that to study the poem carefully was an education in itself.[35] (One thinks of Bede's gentle censure of the excessive parallelisms in the writings of his beloved Gregory.) Judgments regarding style, he acknowledges, are a matter of taste, and he cites a "man of discernment" who had declared that the

---

[33] Traugott Lawler, ed. *The "Parisiana Poetria" of John of Garland* (New Haven, 1974), prints excerpts from the longer version of Geoffrey's *Documentum de modo et arte dictandi et versificandi*, pp. 327–32; for Geoffrey's judgment on the *Architrenius*, p. 329.

[34] See *Ars poetica*, ed. Gräbener, pp. 8, 17, 84, 136–37.

[35] "Cuius quidem libelli sola sufficit inspectio rudem animum informare," *Ars poetica*, p. 3.

style of the *Architrenius* was *too* perfect – flawed (*vitiosum*) only in that its lines were wholly free of *vitia*.[36]

Among earlier medieval poems, Johannes clearly knew well the *Alexandreis* of Walter of Châtillon, which he frequently echoes, and perhaps also the *Frigii Daretis Ylias* of Joseph of Exeter. And it is clear that the intellectual content of the *Architrenius*, its extensive treatment of cosmological questions and the prominent role played by the goddess Nature, owe a great deal to the great allegorical poems of Bernardus Silvestris and Alan of Lille. Traces of Bernardus' *Cosmographia* (1147) and Alan's *De planctu naturae* (1160–70) and *Anticlaudianus*[37] (1182–83) appear on virtually every page of the *Architrenius*, and Schmidt considers the influence of the *De planctu naturae*, with its central motif of Nature confronting the fact of human sin, stronger than that of any other medieval text.[38] But Johannes' poem, as Marc-René Jung observes in comparing it with the *Anticlaudianus*, is of another kind.[39] Bernardus and Alan are philosophical and religious poets: cosmology and its theological implications, problems of language and epistemology, and the substance of the Liberal Arts are fundamental to the structure and meaning of their poems. Johannes is aware of these concerns,[40] but they do not inform his poem at a fundamental level. When he introduces "a few themes of each of the Liberal Arts" (3.137–76), they serve only to lend an authenticating touch to his account of Parisian student life. Later Nature herself spends some 300 lines discoursing to Architrenius, as to the dreamer-poet of Alan's *De planctu*, on celestial motion and the order of the universe (8.335–9.148). But her discourse in no way transforms or enhances the facts and formulae of the treatise from which the bulk of it is borrowed, the *Differentie* of the ninth-century Arab astronomer Al-Farghani, and it conveys none of the alertness of Alan's goddess to the moral and spiritual implications of her theme.

Even on the thematic level, the clear debt of the *Architrenius* to these forebears must be qualified. It is certainly true, as Schmidt argues, that Johannes owes to Alan his view of Nature as cosmic power and moral guide, and Schmidt sees in Johannes' narrative only a "further develop-

---

[36] *Ars poetica*, p. 8.
[37] In what follows I assume that Alan's *Anticlaudianus* predates the *Architrenius*, for reasons given in the Appendix to this Introduction.
[38] Schmidt, pp. 80–81.
[39] See Marc-René Jung, *Études sur le poème allégorique en France au Moyen Age* (Bern, 1971), p. 113.
[40] See, for example, 3.325–33, which summarize the vision vouchsafed by the Muses of scholarship in terms worthy of Bernardus Silvestris himself.

ment" (*Weiterentwicklung*) of the plot of the *De planctu naturae*, whereby Architrenius becomes the complainant and Nature is allowed to resolve the crisis posed by human sinfulness, which the *De planctu* had left unresolved. It seems to me, however, that the role of Johannes' Nature is less a development than a contradiction of the implication of Alan's use of the goddess. The *De planctu naturae* ends by emphasizing the *limits* of Nature's power to regulate the life of man, and the necessity for the intervention of a higher power, a project which provides the plot of the *Anticlaudianus*. In both of Alan's poems the crisis is finally theological in its implications. The *Architrenius*, by contrast, shows a remarkable unconcern with the theological implications of human sinfulness. That his Nature is able to resolve the crisis posed by Architrenius' dilemma is clear confirmation of Johannes' commitment to the ethical view of life.

But finally it is difficult to say how important even Nature is in Johannes' scheme. Though the hero's reunion with the goddess provides an obvious climax to the narrative, the episodes that lead up to it are disposed in no coherent order. It would seem reasonable to suppose that Architrenius' wanderings were in some sense intended to prepare him for the marriage which concludes his quest, and which apparently confirms his reconciliation with Nature, but I have been unable to discover evidence of any such systematic intention. Indeed it is difficult to know whether marriage with Moderantia is Architrenius' reward for having learned the lesson of his experiences or a last recourse on Nature's part, a final attempt to improve his otherwise desperate and incorrigible state. Even the climactic encounter with Nature herself has its anticlimactic aspect for a reader who comes to it with the work of Bernardus and Alan in mind. When Nature ends her cosmological discourse with a triumphant affirmation of her bounty, the arch-weeper's only response is that this was not what he wanted to learn: for him, and for Johannes, there is no longer a necessary connection between the lofty vision to which Nature had inspired the cosmological poets and the anxieties that have impelled him on his journey. What Johannes' Nature will refer to as *religio nativa* has been effectively reduced to a body of ethical precepts. It is as though the poet had introduced Nature and her cosmic lore only to dramatize the shift of emphasis that separates his work from its twelfth-century models.

Of Johannes' other medieval affinities, the most interesting is with Geoffrey of Monmouth's *Historia regum Britanniae*. The genealogy which links Walter of Coutances and his father Rainfroy to Geoffrey's mythical Trojan hero Corineus, the colonizer of Cornwall, must be at least partly based on family tradition of the sort that led other members of the

Norman nobility to claim Trojan ancestry,[41] but Johannes' fulsome elaboration of it is very much in the spirit of Geoffrey's own inventions in the *Historia*. If Johannes is responsible for the specifically Galfridian linkage to Corineus, his invention was tacitly acknowledged as *ben trovato* by Giraldus Cambrensis,[42] and may have provided a precedent for similar Geoffreyesque inventions in the *De nugis curialium* of Walter Map.[43]

Fortunae

The *Architrenius*, like the poems of Bernardus, Alan, and Walter of Châtillon, seems to have been recognized as the medieval equivalent to a classic text almost from the time of its appearance. Johannes was incorporated into the canon of school-authors in the *Laborintus* of Everardus Alemannus,[44] and the dozen surviving thirteenth-century manuscripts, together with the number of manuscripts that contain extensive glosses,[45] make it plain both that the *Architrenius* was widely read, and that it was appreciated for its considerable learning as well as for its style. Further evidence for the "classic" status of the poem is *La Bataille des set ars* (*c.* 1240), by the French poet Henri d'Andeli, written in response to the changing intellectual milieu of the early thirteenth century and the increasing specialization of the university curriculum, which seemed to allow too little scope to the humanistic pursuits that had flourished (or were wistfully recalled as having flourished) in the

---

[41] See Bernard Guenée, *States and Rulers in Later Medieval Europe* (Oxford, 1985), pp. 58–63.

[42] Giraldus Cambrensis, in the course of a brief account of the career of Walter of Coutances, declares that Walter was "de Corinei domo Cornubiaque natus, et nobili Britonum gente ac Trojana stirpe originaliter propagatus" (*Vita S. Remigii*, c. 25, in *Opera*, ed. J. S. Brewer, J. F. Dimock (Rolls Series 21), Vol. 7 (London, 1877), p. 38.

[43] See *De nugis curialium* 2.17–18; and the Brook-Mynors introduction, pp. xxxiv–xxxvi, xxxix–xlii.

[44] *Laborintus* 629–30: "Circuit et totum fricat Architrenius orbem, / Qualis sit vitii regio quaeque docet"; ed. Edmond Faral, *Les artes poétiques du xiie et du xiiie siècle* (Paris, 1962), p. 359. Everardus' treatise, which postdates the *Poetria nova* of Geoffrey of Vinsauf (*c.* 1208–13) and the *Doctrinale* of Alexander de Villa Dei (1212), was surely produced in the first quarter of the thirteenth century. On the medieval conception of canonical authors, see E. R. Curtius, *European Literature and the Latin Middle Ages* (New York, 1953), pp. 48–54; Elisabeth Gössmann, *Antiqui und Moderni im Mittelalter. Eine geschichtliche Standortsbestimmung* (Munich–Vienna, 1974), pp. 92–101.

[45] On the manuscripts see Schmidt, pp. 93–117. The two most extensively glossed manuscripts, both from the fifteenth century, are Oxford, Digby 64 (Schmidt's Q) and Rome, Vatican Reg. Lat. 1812 (x), cited as Q and x in my notes to the poem. I also cite glosses in Leiden, Rijksuniversiteit, Vulcanianus 94 (D) and Rome, Vatican Reg. Lat. 370 (v).

twelfth-century schools. In the course of a strange battle in which an army of poets and sages including Plato, Ovid, Martianus Capella and Bernardus Silvestris is routed by the forces of logic, "mon seignor Architraine / Un des barons de Normandie" is slain by "Parealmaine" (Aristotle's *Peri Hermeneias* or "On Interpretation").[46]

It is harder to discover evidence for the influence of Johannes' poem in the work of later vernacular poets. Even Jean de Meun, though his portion of the *Roman de la Rose* is much closer in spirit to Johannes than to the poems of Alan of Lille which both poets employ as a foil to their own more worldly concerns, may not have known the *Architrenius*.[47] What seems clear is that the poem's career was largely confined to the work of teachers and commentators. The fourteenth-century mythographer John Ridewall, in his *Fulgentius metaforalis*, quotes at length from the description of Architrenius' encounter with the monster *Cupiditas* and other passages on greed,[48] and the poem is cited in both the marginal glosses and the later prose commentary to the anonymous fourteenth-century *Echecs amoureux*.[49] The English antiquary John Pits reports the story of Hugo Legat, a monk of St. Albans in the early fifteenth century, who was so impressed by his reading of the *Architrenius* that he renounced all other books and devoted himself entirely to a commentary on the poem.[50] But further evidence of its use outside the schoolroom remains to be discovered.

In 1373 the aging Petrarch was provoked to compose an *Apologia* in response to a tract in which a French friar, Jean de Hesdin, had extolled French culture at the expense of that of Italy. Jean had quoted at length from the encomium on Paris which concludes the second book of the

---

[46] *La Bataille des set ars* 282–84; ed. L. J. Paetow, *Memoirs of the University of California* 4.1 (1914), p. 53.

[47] Edmond Faral, "Le Roman de la Rose et la pensée française au xiiie siècle," *Revue des deux mondes* 35 (Sept. 1926), pp. 449–52, takes for granted Jean's familiarity with the *Architrenius*, but cites only the two poets' common habit of invoking classical dicta and exempla at every turn.

[48] *Fulgentius metaforalis. Ein Beitrag zur Geschichte der antiken Mythologie im Mittelalter*, ed. Hans Liebeschütz (Leipzig, 1926), pp. 105–06.

[49] See Schmidt, p. 10, n. 11.

[50] John Pits ("Johannes Pitseus"), *Relationum Historicarum de Rebus Anglicis Tomus Primus* (Paris, 1619), p. 568; see also Kuno Francke, "Der Architrenius des Johann von Anville," *Forschungen zur deutschen Geschichte* 20 (1880), pp. 475–76. As Francke notes, the glosses most likely to be Hugo's are those in Rome, Vatican Reg. Lat. 1812 (Schmidt's x). John Bale, *Index Britanniae Scriptorum* (c. 1560), quotes a passage, apparently from Legat's commentary, in praise of Johannes' poetry, "quem tot vestiuit figmentis poeticis, tantis antiquorum purpurauit historijs, et tam arduis inuoluit scientiarum difficultatibus, ut vix nostra florentes etate nudam ipsius faciem perspicue potuerint intueri ..." (*Index*, ed. R. L. Poole, Oxford, 1902, p. 215).

Architrenius, and Petrarch's rejoinder includes a scathing attack on Johannes' poem as an impossibly tedious and laughably inept performance.[51] Later humanists were more charitable. Josse Badius Ascensius published the first edition of the *Architrenius* in 1517, though he did not hesitate to introduce new readings of his own in order to bring Johannes' grammar and prosody into conformity with humanist standards,[52] and Juan Luis Vives pronounced the poem exceptional for its age, the one bright spot in the dismal history of Latin poetry between Sidonius Apollinaris and Petrarch.[53] Konrad Gesner cited Vives' judgment approvingly, and Lilio Giraldi, though he complained of the barbarity of the *Architrenius*, considered it a poem one would regret not having read.[54] That is perhaps the appropriately grudging tone in which to praise the *Architrenius*, and it was virtually the last notice the poem would receive until the later nineteenth century, when Thomas Wright's edition and the appreciative study of Kuno Francke brought Johannes and his strange *summa* back to life.

The present edition

The Latin text which accompanies my translation is that of Paul Gerhard Schmidt. Here again, as in all aspects of this project, I owe a very great debt to Schmidt's excellent edition, and I have at least paid him a small portion of the tribute his tactful and astute editing deserves, in that there is no point at which I have found myself in disagreement with one of his readings. I have necessarily departed from strict fidelity to Johannes' Latin by reordering and redistributing phrases, turning participles to verbs, and other recourses aimed at obtaining coherent English equivalents for Johannes' syntax, but in all but one or two cases, duly noted, I have aimed to render the sense indicated by Schmidt's punctuation.

In the translation itself I have sought to offer coherent and reasonably graceful prose. I have not attempted to imitate Johannes at his own game, aside from an occasional bit of word-play or alliteration, and whatever *durissimae translationes* may have crept in are unintentional.

[51] For the passages from both writers that cite the *Architrenius*, see Schmidt, pp. 307–08; on the controversy, see Ernest H. Wilkins, *Petrarch's Later Years* (Cambridge, Mass., 1959), pp. 233–41.

[52] See Schmidt, pp. 110–11.

[53] *De tradendis disciplinis* 3.9: "Johannes Hantuillensis, qui *Architrenium* propter materiam scripsit, non omnino malus, certe melior quam pro seculo."

[54] See Francke, "Der Architrenius," p. 476; Max Manitius, *Geschichte der lateinischen Literatur des Mittelalters*, Vol. 3 (Munich, 1931), pp. 805–06.

Reading such things in Latin can be bracing and even fun, but to translate them, though at first one may take a certain pride in one's sheer ingenuity, is eventually to develop a kind of loathing for John's virtuosity. Where he is literal, I have tried to be equally so. When he tells us, in so many Latin words, that a girl's ear was cleaned by the finger of Nature, I have gritted my teeth and said the same thing in so many English words. But at certain points (the point of the lady's chin in Book One, for example) I have found myself unable to give anything but a general impression of what is going on.

Appendix: Did Johannes know the *Anticlaudianus*?

Despite the thematic differences discussed above, there can be no questioning the close connection between the *Architrenius* and the *Anticlaudianus* of Alan of Lille. Similarities include not only the obvious correspondences of theme and motif in the two poems' use of the goddess Nature, but also common structural features, and a number of striking verbal correspondences that can hardly be explained by anything but the direct imitation of one poet by the other. The traditional assumption, understandable in view of Alan's great eminence, has been that the *Anticlaudianus* was the earlier work. The *Architrenius* can be clearly dated to the end of 1184, and the *Anticlaudianus*, which alludes plainly to the *Alexandreis* of Walter of Châtillon, and hence must postdate the appearance of that poem,[55] has usually been assigned to 1182–83. This dating is endorsed by Charles Hutchings, who discovers allusions to contemporary history in Alan's poem, and whose article on the subject remains the sole attempt to argue the question of priority seriously. I agree with Schmidt (pp. 84–86) in finding Hutchings' historical arguments unconvincing, in part because they seem to have been prompted to a great extent by the prior assumption that the *Anticlaudianus* had influenced the *Architrenius*, and hence could only be placed between 1182 and 1184.

Schmidt, writing in 1974, considered that the question of priority must be left open in the absence of further historical evidence. Recently such evidence seems to have surfaced in the form of the convincing argument of A. C. Dionisotti that Walter's *Alexandreis*, usually assumed to have appeared in 1181–82, "was largely complete before 1176 and

[55] "L'Anticlaudianus d'Alain de Lille. étude de chronologie," *Romania* 50, 1924, pp. 1–13.

probably published in that year."[56] Alan's use of the opening words of the *Alexandreis* ("Gesta ducis Macedum," *Anticl.* 1.167) to identify the poem suggests that its appearance may have been a recent event, fresh in his readers' minds, and so a redating of Walter's poem would provide an argument for redating the *Anticlaudianus* as well, and strengthen the case for regarding it as a model for the *Architrenius*.

In any case I think that the internal evidence provided by the two poems, much of it pointed out by Schmidt, provides sufficient basis for assuming that Alan's poem is the earlier. Since this evidence bears on the literary character of the *Architrenius*, I would like to review some of its more significant features. Correspondences of phrasing provide an obvious point of comparison. In one of many passages that reveal his fascination with language, Alan praises the translations of Boethius, through which the *virtus* of logic forsakes its native language and "nostri peregrinat in usum" (*Anticlaudianus* 3.135), a phrase which evokes the theme of the *translatio studii* and the meditations on the shifting history of language in Horace's *Ars poetica*. When the same phrase appears in the *Architrenius*, it describes a gluttony which literally consumes gold, so that the metal itself grows soft and "epuli peregrinat in usum" (2.251). Again, when Alan's Prudentia returns from Heaven bearing the divine gift of a new soul for humankind, ". . . miratur in illo / Artificis Natura manum, munusque beatum / laudat" (*Anticl.* 6.486–88). Johannes, describing the luxury of the court, cites goblets so sumptuous that "miratur in illis / Artificis Natura manum, seseque minorem / Agnovisse pudet" (*Architr.* 4.303–305).

Many such contrasting examples can easily be discovered, but these will serve to suggest the essential contrast. In both cases, details which in the *Anticlaudianus* express an intellectual and spiritual coherence become, in the very different world of the *Architrenius*, symptoms of a bizarre and contentious materialism. The difference between the reverence of Alan's Natura and the envy that reduces Johannes' goddess to all-too-human size, or that between the translation of language and the transmutation of gold into food, seem to me to make far better sense if Johannes is seen as adapting to his own use motifs originally conceived by Alan, setting the selfishness and the shameless idolatry of his satiric

---

[56] A. C. Dionisotti, "Walter of Châtillon and the Greeks," in *Latin Poetry and the Classical Tradition*, eds. Peter Godman, Oswyn Murray (Oxford, 1990), pp. 90–96. For the traditional dating of the Alexandreis see Heinrich J. C. Christensen, *Das Alexanderlied Walters von Châtillon* (Halle, 1905), p. 10; Marvin L. Colker, ed. *Galteri de Castellione Alexandreis* (Padua, 1978), pp. xi–xv.

world in parodic contrast to the sacramental values that prevail in Alan's.

The same relationship between the two poems seems to me to be indicated in other areas of correspondence. As Schmidt notes, the epilogues of both poems broadly resemble the epilogue to Statius' *Thebaid*. In Alan's case, the links are direct and unmistakable, and the allusion to Statius forms an apt conclusion to a poem ostentatious in its appropriation of the trappings of classical epic to the purposes of a new and distinctly medieval poetic project. In Johannes' case, though the resemblance to Statius is plain enough, no such direct links occur. And his reference to his poem as "togati / ingenii proles rudis et plebea" (9.468–69), which seems deliberately to stress its un-epic character, seems to me to make far better sense if it is understood as contrasting the *Architrenius* with Alan's elaborately classicizing construct, rather than with the *Thebaid*, to which it bears no particular relation.

Both poems, too, are divided into nine books. But as Schmidt observes, the only principle governing Johannes' division seems to be to break the *Architrenius* into blocks of roughly equal size; there is so little concern for content that three times a speech or description is cut in two by the ending of a book. In contrast, the length of Alan's books varies widely, showing a concern for content, and every motif in the *Anticlaudianus* is fully rendered within the book in which it is introduced. One may add that there is a clear concern for drama (e.g. the expectation of the speech of Reason at the end of Book One, the outbreak of battle at the beginning of Book Nine) and structural symbolism (e.g. the shift from "natural" to "theological" language at the center of the poem in Book Five), and that Alan's obvious thematic debt to the nine books of Martianus Capella's *De nuptiis* is underlined by clear allusions at the beginnings of Books Three and Four. Alan's nine-book structure, in sum, is dictated by a variety of considerations specific to his purpose in the *Anticlaudianus*, whereas Johannes' division of his poem is best explained by a desire to invite comparison with Alan, perhaps in the interest of pointing up their strikingly divergent narratives, and emphasizing the resolutely horizontal course of his own quest-narrative as against the trajectory of Alan's celestial voyage.

Architrenius

Prologus[1]

Architrenius quidam, cum ad annos virilis roboris devenisset, recordationis stilo retroacti temporis actus colligit universos; secum quicquid egerit scrutabundus inquirit nec moribus unquam invenit esse locum. conqueritur igitur in Naturam. nam, que maiora poterat, et
5 illud utique potuisset, quod adversus scelerum motus et impetus inconsultos homo inquassabilis perduraret. post querelarum ergo lacrimas profusissimas "Queram" inquid "Naturam, ut odiis expurgatis indignacionis huius extergatur fermentum at amoris azimi[2] vinculo solidato optatum Architrenio subsidium conferatur."mundum igitur
10 pede circummeans vagabundo Venerem, Ambicionem, Avariciam, Gulam et mundi ceteras invenit meretrices, que fune multiplici ad rerum temporalium amplexus illicitos attrectant hominem et inclinant. Nature tandem invente genibus obvolutus, vie causam evolvit et porro quicquid postulat impetrato pro subsidii summa de Nature consilio
15 uxor Architrenio, Moderancia nomine, desponsatur. quos Deus coniunxit, homo non separet.[3] Architrenius iste ab eventu sic dictus est;[4] nam locis fere singulis peregrinacionis sue mundo compatitur sub viciorum fluctibus naufraganti, et lamentis animum et lacrimis oculum impluit et immergit. liber autem iste Architrenius nuncupatur; unde hic est titulus
20 "Ad Walterum Rothomagensem Archiepiscopum Architrenius incipit". Ex supradictis patet tam intencio quam materia. ex titulo collige, ad quem scribitur hoc opus. de quo autem aut quibus in libris singulis texatur oracio, posita in principio capitula te docebunt. lege igitur. de
25 actore si queras, dixisse sufficiat: Iohannes est nomen eius.

2

Prologue[1]

A certain Architrenius, when he had attained the years of manly vigor, compiled, with the pen of recollection, all his actions of earlier times. Carefully investigating all that he had done, he found that there had never been a place in his life for morality. Therefore he complained

5 against Nature, for she who had accomplished far greater things, could certainly have ensured that mankind be capable of enduring unperturbed the contrary motions and unexpected impulses of wickedness. Thus after copious weeping and lamentation he declared, "I will seek out Nature, so that when her hostility to me has been vented, and the ferment of this anger purged, a bond of uncontaminated love[2] may be established, and she may grant Architrenius the assistance he seeks."

10 Traversing the world with wandering steps he encounters Venus, Ambition, Avarice, Gluttony, and all those forms of worldly prostitution which seize a man with their many-stranded rope and make him long to know the unlawful embrace of temporal things. Discovering Nature he throws himself at her feet, and explains the cause of his journey. All that

15 he demands is granted, and at Nature's bidding, as the completion of her provision for him, a bride, Moderation, is married to Architrenius. Whom God has joined together, let no man put asunder.[3] This Architrenius is so named from his experiences.[4] For at nearly every stage of his pilgrimage he feels compassion for a world foundering in the seas of

20 vice, so that his heart pours forth laments and his eyes fill with tears. The book is also named "Architrenius," and hence its title is this: "Here begins the 'Architrenius,' dedicated to Walter, Archbishop of Rouen."

From what has been said the intention of the book, as well as its matter, will be clear. You may gather from the title to whom the book is written. What it is about, and in what several books the discourse is contained, the list of chapter headings placed at the beginning will tell

25 you. Therefore read on. If you are curious about the author, suffice it to say that his name is John.

Liber Primus

Cap. 1 De potencia laboris et ingenii et de impotencia desidie ·

Velificatur Athos, dubio mare ponte ligatur,[1]
Remus arat colles, pedibus substernitur unda,
Puppe meatur humus, pelagi Thetis exuit usum,
Salmoneus fulmen iaculatur, Dedalus alas
5 Induit: ingenii furor instat et invia preceps
Rumpit et artifici cedit natura labori.
   Languida Segnicies Veneris nutricia tractat
Ocia, dilatrix operum, dissuada laborum,
Venativa more, vix inceptura, quod ipso
10 Principio rumpit, hodiernos crastinat actus
Et quod preteritum, numquam facit, usque futurat,
Ausus attenuat, animos premit, illigat artus
Contemptusque luto defedat aromate morum
Pectus odorandum, fame secura, pudende
15 Assuescit vite, viciique paludibus herens
Sorde volutatur, oculoque improvida ceco
Mentis ab excubiis expellit inhospita curas
Sollicitosque metus, currentibus urget habenam
Ingeniis, fixoque modo conamina sistit, –
20 Torporisque iacet studii vigilancia sompno.
Difficiles aditus et, quo luctamine prono
Nitendum est, odit, non invitata labores
Laude coronanti nec, quo dulcescere sudor
Edidicit, lucro, gladios in bella trahenti
25 Facturoque leves freta, tela, pericula, cedes.
   Tedia Segniciem comitantur et invida letis
Tristicies, Luxusque vacans Lascivia pompis
Et Venus et renum cinctus Petulancia solvens,
Cognatusque Necis Sopor et precursor inhermis
30 Torpor Egestatis et amara Opprobia vultu

4

Book One

Ch. 1 The power of hard work and ingenuity, and the impotence of sloth

Ships sail over Athos, the ocean is spanned by a shaky bridge,[1] oars furrow the hillsides, the waves are subjected to walking feet, dry land is surveyed from the stern, Thetis has forsaken the deep. Salmoneus hurls
5 his thunderbolt, Daedalus dons his wings, a frenzy of ingenuity is upon us, bursting headlong into regions uncharted, and nature yields to the onslaught of art.

Languid Sloth, the nurse of Venus, draws out the idle hours, toying with any undertaking while discouraging real endeavor. Like one who,
10 having scarcely begun to hunt, breaks off the pursuit at the very outset, she puts off the day's duties until the morrow, and ever postpones the past obligations which she never fulfils. She wears down courage, oppresses the spirit, fetters the limbs, and befouls with the filthiness of her contempt any breast which retains the least scent of morality.
15 Heedless of reputation, she lapses into a shameful life, keeps to the swamps of vice, and sinks into the mire. Blind and reckless, she inhospitably banishes Care and anxious Concern from the outposts of the mind, gives rein to galloping Ingenuity yet stands immovable in the path of
20 Endeavor, till zealous Vigilance succumbs to sleepy Torpor. She shuns places difficult of access, and hates to bend her back in strenuous effort. She is attracted neither by praise, the crown of achievement, nor even by wealth, which makes exhaustion taste sweet, lures the swordsman
25 into battle, and makes light of the perils of the sea and of hostile arms.

The companions of Sloth are Boredom, and Melancholy, the foe of all pleasure; Lechery, and Wantonness, given over to revelry; Venus, and Lewdness, which loosens the girdle about the loins; Sleep, the brother of
30 Death, and Listlessness, the herald of helpless Poverty; harsh Detraction, with grim and livid face; Mockery, whose jests have the power to

Mesta verecundo, salibusque Irrisio mordens
Et Pudor et partes Infamia nuda pudendas
Et vaga propositi Levitas et nescia fixis
Mobilitas mansisse rotis et devius Error,
35 Votorumque vices crebro Inconstancia versans
Et fluitans Animus et non statura Voluntas,
Pigraque Mollicies et Inhercia parca laboris
Et fractus studii Languor, morbusque senecte
Debilitas, sterilisque brevi sub pondere manans
40 Sudor et abscisis titubans Ignavia nervis.

Cap. 2 De remocione arrogancie

At ne Desidia Muse michi sopiat ignes,
Nascitur et puero vagit nova pagina versu,
Propositique labor victorem spondet et audax
Grandibus inceptis studii constancia; verum
45 Inter Apollineas lauros fas esto mirice
Deiectis vernare comis, non precinit omnem
Ad digitum Phebea chelis, non novimus aures
Aonia mulcere lira, non pectinis huius
In plebem vilescit apex; hec gloria vatum,
50 Hoc iubar, hic titulus solos contingit Homeros.
Sufficiet, populo si suffecisse togato[2]
Hic poterit nostre tenuis succentus[3] avene.
In Cresi ne sudet opes privatus Amiclas![4]
Contentum proprio faciunt me tuta facultas
55 Angustique lares, modico me posse potentem
Metior ad multum, nec gutture rumpar hanelo
Sirenum insidias equasse et funus oloris,
Dum mea ieiuno michi sibilet ore cicada.
Non ago precipites sopire leonibus iras
60 Pectine vel rigidos mores mollire ferarum.
Hoc precor, hoc satis est, si nostra hec arida plebis
Aure sono tenui ieiunia solvat harundo.
Incola mergus aque madidis ne provocet alis
Surgentes aquilas lambentibus ethera pennis!

wound; Shame, and Infamy, exposed in shameful nakedness; Fickle-
ness, infirm of purpose, and Restlessness, incapable of maintaining a
35 fixed course, and wandering Error; Inconstancy, whose desires are
constantly changing; uncertain Purpose and unsteady Will; sluggish
Effeminacy and shiftless Idleness; Apathy, broken in spirit, the crippling
40 affliction of Age; Futility, its strength wasted in fruitless struggle; and
Faintheartedness, with its slack and shaky limbs.

Ch. 2 A disavowal of arrogance

But Idleness cannot quench the fires of my Muse: a new work is
born, and utters its first childish squallings. The difficulty of the task
befits a heroic spirit, and that constancy of mind that is emboldened by
45 great challenges; but amid Apollo's laurels, be it right that the myrtle,
too, flourish with its drooping boughs. The lyre of Phoebus is not suited
to every hand; we cannot all charm the ear with Aonian chords; such
50 high artistry does not yield itself to everyone. It is the glory of true bards,
a brilliance and distinction that belong only to such as Homer. It is
enough for us if the lower note[2] of our pipe find acceptance among
ordinary people.[3] A homely Amyclas[4] should not aspire to the wealth of
55 a Croesus. A sound mind and a humble dwelling content me; though
modestly endowed, I hold myself capable of accomplishing much, and I
will never become broken-winded from striving to rival the Sirens or the
dying swan, for my song is as the whispering voice of the cicada. I do
60 not propose to soothe the lion's unbridled wrath with music, or refine
the savage behavior of beasts. My prayer will be answered if the sound
of my pipe, however dry and meager, may ease the hard lot of common
folk. A water-dwelling gull should not challenge eagles, who rise
toward heaven on gleaming wings!

Cap. 3 Contra depravacionem veterum modernorum

65   O michi suspecta veterum mordacior etas,
   Acrius in iuvenes decorrosiva senectus!
   Ne preme, sed pressa meritorum nomina tolle,
   Que male tondenti decerpit forcipe livor;
   Dulcescat gravium maiestativa virorum
70   Lingua, nec invidie fuso crudescat aceto.
   Deucalioneum pelagus vel naufraga Pirre
   Secula non vidi vel, quas solaribus ardens
   Vector[5] equis radio sicienti sorbuit, undas;
   Non me preteritis iacto latuisse diebus
75   Meoniumque senem michi convixisse, nec evi
   Laucius intitulor senioris laude, modernis
   Maior, ab ignotis fame lucrosior annis.
   Sustineas quod me dederint hec tempora nec, si
   Videris auctorem, precio leviore libellum
80   Argue nec, si quem meruit, deperdat honorem.
   Non me limes Acin,[6] non barbarus edidit Athlas;
   non apud Arturi glaciem solemque Sienes
   Advena spectandos ordiri glorior ortus -
   Philosophum faciente loco soloque verendum
85   Externi terrore loci; nodosa meretur
   Nondum ruga coli, nondum veneranda senecte
   Albet olore coma,[7] non sum cui serviat auri
   Turba vel argenti, cui rerum copia mundo
   Plaudat adulanti, cui Serum purpura vatis
90   Attitulet nomen, cuius facunda smaragdus
   Disputet in digitis vulgique assibilet aures
   Attonitas gemmis; liber est, non libra,[8] Iohannes
   Quod canit et Cirre modicum de fonte propinat,
   Hiisque magis Phebus ciatis quam Bachus inundat.
95   Ha quod Alexander tetigit: decisor Homeri,
   Zoile, tu laudum cinicus, tu serra bonorum,
   Magna doles, maiora notas, in maxima sevis.
   Siste gradus solitos, odio tibi vapulo, libro
   Parce, nec auctoris in opus iactura redundet.[9]

Ch. 3 An answer to the perversity of the old men of our day

65   O suspicious and backbiting generation, old men so eager to judge harshly the deeds of the young! Do not attack, but rather seek to rescue the names of worthy men already under attack, names which the sharp shears of envy have cut down. Utter the sweet and ennobling speech of
70   just men, not words curdled by the acid of jealousy.

It is true that I did not witness the flood in the shipwrecking days of Deucalion and Pyrrha, nor those waters which the too ardent chariot-eer[5] subjected to the parching heat of the horses of the sun. I do not
75   claim to be a survivor from ancient times, a contemporary of the old Maeonian; I do not, on grounds of mere seniority, lay claim to a grander name, as if I were greater than modern men, more deserving of renown because of my unnumbered years. Accept the fact that modern times have produced me, and do not, because you have seen the author, value
80   the book more lightly or deny it whatever honor it may deserve. Neither far-off Acin[6] nor rough Atlas gave me birth; I am no prodigy who glories in a wondrous origin amid the Arctic ice or beneath the Egyptian sun, as if the place itself could make me a philosopher, one to be
85   regarded with awe by men who fear the unknown. As yet I show no venerable maze of wrinkles; my hair does not yet gleam with the downy white of reverend age;[7] I am not one whom a heap of gold or silver may advance, whose sheer wealth might commend him to an adoring world,
90   for whom robes of purple silk might gain a priestly dignity, whose eloquence the jewels on his fingers would declare, gaining ready access to the ear of a multitude dazed by their brilliance. Books, not balances,[8] provide the substance of Johannes' song; his modest libation is from the Cirrhaean fount, and it is Phoebus, not Bacchus, who fills the bowl.

95   How well Alexander said it: "Zoilus, you carp at Homer, you sneer at what is praiseworthy, you tear at the works of good men. What is well done causes you pain, you snipe at what is superior, and greatness drives you mad. Cease your posturing, I loathe your scurrility. Spare the book; let not the death of the author be extended to his work."[9]

Cap. 4 De ortu eius ad quem scribitur

100   Gloria Pergamee sepeliri gentis Achiva
       Non potuit flamma, stetit occursante ruina
       Indilapsus apex, pulsanti cedere fato
       Non cecidisse tulit; Danais Fortuna caminis
       Excoxit non seva Friges, maioraque bellis
105 Erudiit perferre viros, et diruta maior
       Stanti Troia fuit; non est incensa, sed igni
       Uberius lucrata iubar, radiosque Pelasge
       Dardanios auxere faces, nec palluit illo
       Sol Asie fumo; fines augusta potestas
110 Indignata breves, iam fastidiverat Ide
       Artari plebea iugis, mundique recessus
       Occupat et validis maiora supermeat ausis.
       Plenior imperii Romanis Pergama pensat
       Fascibus et, tanto si quid de culmine fati
115 Diminuit livor, virtus reparavit: et orbi
       Hic urbem rapuit, hec orbem reddidit urbi.
       Prodiga nec tandem niveis exhausta metallis,
       Utilium mater dulcique puerpera gleba,
       Absolvit Frigiis affusa Britannia Grecos.[10]
120   Immo Friges Frigius sanguis solatur, hanelos
       Exhilarat luctus, quem derivavit Iuli
       Postera maiestas nostroque insplenduit evo.
       Nec nisi nobilium medios intexuit ortus
       Ille Dei sedes, thalamus virtutis, honesti
125 Ortulus et morum, viciis impervia, Tempe
       Altera, quam nec hiemps nec fervor marcidat, Hibla.
       Ille procellosos innaufragus enatat annos,
       Inferius flantem scelerum premit altior Austrum,
       Nec mundi quatitur hac tempestate, malorum
130 Nubibus et ventis sublimior, alter Olimpus.
       Surgit et explicitos apices extendit in ortus,
       Crescit et in titulos maiores erigit Idam,
       Fulget et aureolo populatur sidere noctem,
       Gaudet et impluvium meroris siccat et imbres,
135 Vernat et hiberna Walterus[11] diluit, in quo
       Florida Troianum redimit Cornubia dampnum.
       Vix tanti ciatum pelagi delibo, licebit
       Solverer in quevis commendativa viroque

Ch. 4 The origins of him to whom the book is addressed

The glory of Pergama could not be extinguished by Achaean fire; its loftiness remained unfallen amid the general destruction, and though it yielded to the force of fate it did not wholly succumb. In subjecting the Phrygians to the heat of the Danaean forge, Fortune was not cruel: she taught them to endure greater things than war, and Troy destroyed became greater than Troy at its height. It was not consumed by fire, but instead its radiance attained a richer glow; Pelasgian torches only enhanced Dardanian brilliance, the sun of Asia was not dimmed by their smoke. Its august majesty, disdaining narrow confines and scorning to be basely contained by the ridges of Ida, reached forth to the ends of the earth, and overcame great obstacles through great daring. Augmented by the Roman fasces, the imperial authority of Pergama was all the greater, and though envious fate cast it down from the summit of power, virtue made good the loss: The one robbed the world of a city, the other repaid the city with the world.

Britain, richly endowed and freely giving, not yet drained of her supply of gleaming metals, mother of every resource, her soil rich and fertile, granted the Greeks a final absolution for the destruction of the Phrygians.[10] Indeed it was a man of Phrygian blood who solaced the Phrygians, who brought them joy after exhausting labor, whom the latterday majesty of the race of Iulus produced to lend its luster to our own day. For only among a noble people could there be born such a man – a temple of God, a bower of virtue, a garden of honor and good deeds, immune to vice, a second Tempe, a Hybla which neither winter nor the heat of summer can affect. He steers his course unharmed through an age of storms, like some higher power that stills the raging of wickedness. He is unshaken by the storms of worldly life, rising above the winds and clouds of evil like a second Olympus which raises its peak toward heaven, a new Ida made lofty by yet greater dignity. His glory robs the night sky of its starry brilliance, his smile dries the flows of dismal rain. Walter,[11] like spring itself, dispels the winter, Walter, in whom flourishing Cornwall makes good the loss of Troy.

Even if it were possible to pour myself forth in a flood of commendation and shower this man with praise, I would scarcely be drawing off

Impluerem laudes, nam morum prevolat alis
140 Curriculum laudis, solus capit omnia fame
Nomina: nec veris adventum percipit Ethne
Gloria, nec crescit Phebus face, mundus harena,
Secula momento, nimbo mare, linea puncto.

Cap. 5 De oblacione opusculi

O cuius studio, quo remige navigat estu
145 Mundanoque mari tumidisque exempta procellis
Linconie sedes, o quem non preterit equi
Calculus, o cuius morum redolencia celum
Spondet et esse nequit virtus altissima maior,
Indivisa minor, cuius se nomen et astris
150 Inserit et Fame lituo circumsonat orbem;
O quem Rothomagi sedes viduata maritum
Sperat et aspirat, solidisque amplexibus ardet
Astrinxisse virum, fragrantis odoribus uti,
Morum deliciis, virtutis aromate, sponsi
155 Pectore, quod Phebum redolet, quod Nestora pingit;
Vere novo thalami florere expectat et illos
Ascendisse thoros, ubi Virtus pronuba, Christo
Auspice, sacrati et sacre connubia firmet;
Optat ut Arthois infusum manna Britannis
160 Cedat et irriguum Normannis influat, urbis
Aridule deserta rigans, siciencia sacros
Linconie fontes et vix libata recentis
Gaudia prima favi, longum sperata brevique
Degustata mora; Revocat, quem misit, alumpnum
165 Depositumque petit et, quo videt Anglia, reddi
Poscit inoccidui commissum luminis usum;
Virgo virum, matura thoros, innupta maritum,
Orba patrem, mutilata caput, iactata salutem,
Ceca ducem, tenebrosa iubar, nocturna lucernam
170 Exigit et queritur tardanti mane, suumque
Eclipsata sitit rediturum Cynthia Phebum;
O michi Mecenas operis, tractique laboris
Expectata quies, rudis indubitata Minerve
Spes, adhibe ceptis oculi mentisque favorem.

140 a cupful from a vast ocean. For with wings of virtue he far outstrips the chariot of praise, and lays claim unaided to all the titles of renown. So glorious Aetna does not deign to notice the coming of spring, so Phoebus' light is hardly increased by a mere torch, the world by a grain of sand, time by an instant, the sea by a shower, or a line by a point.

Ch. 5 The dedication of the work

O you by whose zeal and guidance the see of Lincoln sails the
145 raging ocean of this world exempt from furious storms, you whom no accounting of justice can exclude, whose sweetness of spirit is a promise of heaven, a virtue so lofty that it cannot be made greater, an integrity
150 that admits no diminishment; whose name inscribes itself among the stars, and is echoed the world over by the trumpet of Fame; o you for whom the widowed see of Rouen hopes and yearns as husband, eager to clasp you in firm embrace as a lover, to enjoy your fragrance, the
155 delights of your character, the virtuous aroma of a bridegroom whose spirit is endowed with the vision of Phoebus, the judgment of Nestor. She waits, ready to come to flower in the springtime of the marriage bed, eager to enter that nuptial chamber where Virtue, with the sanction of Christ, will unite the consecrated bridegroom and sacred bride. She prays that the manna which has been showered on the northerly
160 Britons may now be poured forth on Norman fields, that the dry earth about the thirsting city may be watered with the sacred streams of Lincoln, and the first pleasure of this new nectar, long awaited and as yet barely tasted, be enjoyed without delay. She calls home the nursling
165 whom she had sent forth, seeks him whom she had assigned to another's care and, discovering him, demands that England restore the unquenchable light entrusted to it. The virgin desires a man, the woman a marriage-bed, the maiden a husband, the orphan a father, the maimed body a head, the fallen succor, the blind a guide, the shadowed
170 a light, the benighted a dawning. Cynthia, deprived of her luster, searches the early morning darkness, and longs for the return of Phoebus.

O thou Maecenas of my work, thou in whom my long labor finds its long awaited rest, unquestioned inspiration of my uncouth genius, grant to the work now begun the favor of your scrutiny and judgment.

Cap. 6 De invocacione ad Deum

175 O qui secretas homini metiris harenas
Et numero claudis dubium monstrancia fatum
Sidera; qui nosti, mundine intermina surgat
Area, nec Stigie noctis latuere recessus,
Et solus solisque modum luneque meatum
180 Scis, Deus, et celas incauto iudice visu
Astrorum excursus: fallitque et fallitur idem
Etheree venans oculus secreta Minerve;
O divum deitas, nusquam deflexa superni
Linea consilii, divine pagina mentis,
185 Qua nec desit apex nec iotha superfluat, una
Singula complectens, que dispertita quotannis
Evolvit series nulli mutanda sororum;
Cui Cloto, Lachesis deservit et Atropos: illa
Stamina dispensans fusis vitalibus, illa
190 Filla trahens operi, donec concluserit illa;
    O Cirre latices nostre, Deus, implue menti,
Eloquii rorem siccis infunde labellis
Distillaque favos, quos nec, dum Tagus harenis
Palleat aut siciat admotis Tantalus undis,
195 Horreat insipidos etas vel livor amaros.
Dirige, quod timida presumpsit dextera, dextram
Audacem pavidamque iuva, tu mentis habenam
Fervoremque rege; quicquid dictaverit ori
Spiritus aridior, oleum suffunde favoris.
200 Tu patris es verbum, tu mens, tu dextera: verbum
Expediat verbum, mens mentem, dextera dextram.

Cap. 7 Contra invidos

Hoc eciam votum facili bonitate secunda,
Hoc nostris superadde bonis, ne transeat istud
Ad limam livoris opus, ne senciat illam
205 iudicii formam, qua cancellatur honestum,
Suppletur vicium, que verba decentia radit,
Turpia subscribit, que prestantissima scalpro
Mordet et omne bonum legit indignante labello.
Dulcius expectat examen pagina, iustas
210 Pro viciis latura notas habituraque nomen

Ch. 6 An Invocation to God

175   O God, who measure out the moments of human life, and subject
to your harmony the stars that reveal our uncertain fate, you who
know whether the expanse of the universe is unbounded, and from
whom the recesses of Stygian night are not hidden; God, you who alone
180 know the course of the sun and the moon's wandering, and who
conceal from our uncertain vision the courses of the stars (for the eye of
man both deceives and is deceived when it pursues the secrets of
heavenly Minerva); O lord of all things divine, unalterable pattern of
185 supreme wisdom, scripture of the divine mind (where not a letter is
missing, yet not a dot is superfluous), embracing in one moment all
those single events which will be disposed over time by a serial law
which none of the Sisters may alter; you whom Clotho, Lachesis and
Atropos obey, one meting out thread for the spindles of lives, one
190 working the threads into a pattern which the third will bring to
completion.

O God, pure source of our Cirrhaean fount, infuse my mind, moisten
my parched lips with the dew of eloquence; distill sweet springs which
(though not so bright as the sandy stream of Tagus, or that stream so
195 close to hand for which Tantalus thirsts) may be not so tasteless that the
age will reject them, nor yet so bitter as to arouse their spleen. Guide the
work which a hesitant hand has dared to begin, sustain my bold strokes
and strengthen my faltering ones, be both the curb and the inspiration
of my thought, and suffuse with the balm of your grace what a too
200 barren spirit may have dictated. For you are the word, the mind, the
right hand of the Father: may that word, mind and hand sustain my
own.

Ch. 7 A prayer against envy

Favor this prayer in your gentle goodness, and add to my blessings this last: let this work of mind never come under the harsh gaze of
205 envy. Let it not know that type of criticism which dismisses simplicity
and promotes meanness; which crosses out seemly words and under-
lines dirty ones; which hacks and slices at genuine excellence, and reads
anything of merit with a condescending sneer. My work hopes for a
milder assessment. It is ready to undergo just censure for its faults, but
210 also to gain recognition, and even praise, for its merits, if indeed it

Pro meritis laudisque vicem, si forte venusti
Quid ferat, auditu dignum punctoque favoris.
Sit procul invidie suspecta novacula, solis
Ingeniosa dolis; procul hec sit vipera, nullo
215 Corruptura nisi rerum momenta veneno.

Cap. 8 De recordacione Architrenii circa opera retroacta, et ibi incipit narracio operis

Dumescente pilis facie, radioque iuvente
Obscuris pallente genis, cum mala viriles
Exacuit nemorosa rubos nec primula mento
Vellera mollescunt, virides quot luserit annos,
220 Respicit et, quicquid tenero persuaserit etas
Floridior, recolit memor Architrenius, imas
Pectoris evolvit latebras mersosque profunda
Explorat sub mente lares,[12] nec moribus usquam
Invenit esse locum, nec se virtutibus unum
225 Impendisse diem. "Mene istos" inquit "in usus
Enixa est Natura parens, me misit ut arma
In superos dampnata feram, divumque reatus
Irritent odium? legesque et iura meique
Preteream decreta Iovis? viciine potestas
230 Mortales eterna premit? facinusne redundat
Diis invisa palus? mater quid pignora tante
Destituit labi nec, quem produxit, alumpno
Excubat, ut nullis maculam scelus inspuat actis?

Cap. 9 De nature potencia

Illud enim supraque potest nullaque magistras
235 Non habet arte manus, nec summa potencia certo
Fine coartatur: astrorum flammeat orbes,
Igne rotat celos, discursibus aera rumpit,
Mollit aque speram, telluris pondera durat,
Flore coronat humum, gemmas inviscerat undis,
240 Phebificans auras, stellas intexit Olimpo.
Natura est quodcumque vides,[13] incudibus illa
Fabricat omniparis, quidvis operaria nutu
Construit, eventusque novi miracula spargit.
Ipsa potest rerum solitos avertere cursus,

possesses sufficient charm to be heard and favorably received. But let the slanderous razor of envy, keen only in treachery, remain far off, and far off too be that viper whose venom is harmful only to noteworthy
215 achievements.

Ch. 8 Architrenius reflects on his past conduct. Here the story proper begins

As his face becomes overgrown with hair, and the gleam of youth fades on his darkened cheeks, while his bushy jaws grow sharp with manly bristles, and the fleece of early youth is no longer soft on his chin,
220 Architrenius considers how many springtime years he has given to revelry, the things to which a too flourishing youth has enticed his weak will. With all of this in mind he delves into the shadowy depths of his heart and seeks out the ruling spirits buried in his innermost mind.[12] He discovers that there has never been a place there for morality, and that
225 he has never devoted a single day to virtue. "For such purposes as these did mother Nature give me birth?" he asks. "Has she sent me forth to wage impious war against the gods, that my guilty acts may arouse their hatred? Am I to ignore laws and statutes decreed by Jove? Does sin
230 have power to oppress human life eternally? Is our guilt like some boundless swamp, hateful to the gods? Why has my mother abandoned her charge to such peril? Why does she not keep watch over the child she has borne, so that his actions may remain untainted by guilt?

Ch. 9 The power of Nature

235 "Nature can do all of this and more. There is no art that her hand has not mastered, and her supreme power knows no limit. She kindles the starry orbs, makes the heavens revolve by her vital heat, stirs the air with conflicting movements, makes the watery region fluid and hardens the bulk of the earth. She decks the land with flowers, plants precious
240 gems in the deep, imbues the air with Phoebus' light and adorns the firmament with stars.

"Whatever you behold is Nature;[13] she labors at her all-creating forge, creates at will whatever she pleases, and spreads abroad a miraculous array of new products. She has power to alter the normal
245 course of events, and prodigally litters the world with huge and mon-

245 Enormesque serit monstrorum prodiga formas,
     Gignendique stilum variat, partuque timendo
     Lineat anomalos larvosa puerpera vultus.

Cap. 10 De monstruosis[14]

     Mascula Graccorum tribuit gestamina matri;
     Malleolosque ferens duplici cum folle viriles,[15]
250 Coniectura fuit gemini Cornelia sexus.
     Nubit Aristonte mulier modo,[16] nubitur illi
     Permutatque thoros ea vir modo, federe fedus
     Rumpit et efficitur illa ille, marita maritus:
     Passaque tritorem rursus terit area, ducit
255 Femina, sulcus arat, fodit ortus, malleat incus.
     Curio natalas armato dentibus ore
     Exiit in luctus; acuit pro dentibus ossis
     Continui massam Prusie filius; ossa
     Ligdamus extersis habuit concreta medullis,
260 Qui tulit ad Siculos victoris premia laurum,
     Quam dedit Herculei ludi servator Olimpus.
     Ethiopum naso facies non surgit et oris
     Planicie strata, non delibantur odores
     Naribus aut cerebrum lacrimosa foramina purgant.
265 Sunt quibus excludit lingue iactura susurros,
     Eloquiique vices digiti facundia tractat,
     Interpresque manus animi secreta retexens,
     Obsequium vocis signis affabilis equat
     Et tacite rixans imitatur garrula lites.
270 Sunt quibus ora brevi coeunt obnoxia rime,
     Qua bibulis stomacho cibus inspiratur avenis,
     Vixque trahit cannis extorta liquamina Maurus,
     Quem dapis irrigua mediatrix lactat harundo,
     Dum calami rores angusta mamillula plorat.
275 In pede bis binos digitos duplat accola Nullo.
     Est qui monoculo vultu contentus et uno
     Crure potens cursus, plantam resupinat ad ignes
     Solis et erecti spacio pedis efficit umbram.
     Gens Libre vicina,[17] carens cervicibus, inter
280 Supremos humeros oculorum concavat orbes.
     Sunt qui bis binis pedibus, sunt qui ore canino
     Degenerant: homines specie, sed monstra figuris.

strous forms. The style of her conceptions is ever changing, and the fearful labor of her fantastic fertility gives shape to abnormal creatures.

Ch. 10 Strange creatures[14]

"Nature assigned the actions of a man to Cornelia, the mother of
50 the Gracchi, and it was held that she was bisexual, possessing the little hammers of a man in their double pouch.[15] Arescon first entered into marriage[16] as a woman, then entered the marriage chamber again, now as a man, and another was married to her. One bond was broken by means of another: she became he, the wife a husband. Having endured the thresher, she worked a threshing floor of her own; the
55 woman took a wife, the furrow did the plowing, the garden spaded, the anvil hammered.

"Curio was brought forth by the pangs of childbirth with his mouth fully armed with teeth, while the son of Prusia displayed, in place of
60 teeth, a mass of solid bone. The bones of Ligdamus, who brought to Sicily as a token of victory the laurel which Olympus had first bestowed on beholding the Herculean games, were drained of their marrow as they took shape. An Ethiopian's face has no projecting nose; because of the flatness of its surface no odors are inhaled by the nostrils, and no
65 tear-ducts provide purgation for the brain. There are those whom lack of a tongue prevents even from whispering, so that a witty finger must serve in place of eloquence and the interpreting hand unfold the secrets of the mind. Courteous gesture performs by signs the office of the voice, while aggressive pointing, silently brawling, garrulously mimes a
70 quarrel. There are those whose mouths tend naturally to form a narrow slit, through which food is drawn into the stomach by a drinking straw; indeed the Moor, to whom a reed, suckling like a nurse, conveys liquid food, can scarcely take in even liquids strained through a tube, and the straw, like a tiny teat, weeps little droplets for him.

75 "Those who dwell on Mt. Nulo have two sets of four toes on each foot. There is a race content with a single eye in their faces, and capable of moving swiftly on one leg; when lying down they turn the sole of one foot toward the sun, and by keeping it elevated provide themselves with shade.

80 A race who dwell beneath Libra[17] have no necks, and their eye-sockets appear between their upraised shoulders. There are people disfigured by two pairs of feet, or a dog's face; though human in kind, they have the form of monsters. There is a people whose hair grows

Est cui cana comam puerilis liliat etas,
Maturusque putrem vetulam deliliat annus.
285   Staturam cubitis septem distendit Horestes;
Bis senis Frigios potuit movisse ruentis
Gemagog arduitas, Corinei[18] fracta lacertis.
In bis quinque pedes produxit Gabbarus artus;
Aucta ter undenis cubitis mensura Metellum
290 Terruit, et Flacci tenuit mirantis ocellos
Corporis humani plus quam Titania moles.[19]
     Gens Scita spectatu geminis oculata pupillis
Ledit et irata Bitia, quocunque rotatur,
Enecat intuitus, oculis inserpit inurens
295 Ira, peremptivi radiis interfica visus.
     Non est passa levi Crassum mollescere risu,
Antoniam Drusi sordente madescere sputo,
Fumida Pomponii solvi ructatibus ora,
Fulmine Fortune Socratis pallescere vultus
300 Aut miseris letos rigidum flexisse tenorem.
     Felices et pene dei, quos educat aura,
Quam pomi premellit odor: fragrancia genti
Panis agit potusque vices, hic Bachus in eius
Est ciatis, hec corbe Ceres, sic Gangis alumpno
305 Vivitur et redimunt oris ieiunia nares;
Non effusa gule, non ventris tabida luxu
Nacio: nec sordet utero, nec gutture peccat.
     Duricia Psillum sic loricavit, ut atris
Integer eludat pugnantes morsibus angues,
310 Solaque pro muri cutis est insaucia vallo.
Parma veneniferi iaculis impervia dentis.
     At me pestiferis aliis exponit inhermen
Anguibus et tortis viciorum deteror idris.
Non michi pacifico nudum latus asperat ense,
315 Non Calibum plumis lorice recia nodat,
Non surgente caput animosum casside cristat,
Non clipei telis obtendit menia: nec, quos
Det Natura, timent scelerum Stimphalides arcus,
Nec furtim lesura nefas deterret harundo.

lily-white in childhood; mature years deflower its whiteness with the aspect of decrepit age.

285 "Orestes stretched to a height of seven cubits. The towering height of Gemagog's twelve cubits, rushing upon them, was enough to terrify the Trojans, until he was overthrown by the strong limbs of Corineus.[18] The limbs of Gabbarus ended in five pairs of feet. The more than Titanic mass 290 of a human body grown to a length of thirty-three cubits terrified Metellus, and held the wondering gaze of Flaccus.[19] A Scythian tribe whose eyes are equipped with double pupils have the power to kill by staring, and when the Bithian is angry her look is deadly wherever she 295 turns her face; burning wrath creeps into her eyes and transmits death through the beams of her lethal gaze.

"Nature did not allow Crassus to relax in a gentle smile, nor could Antonia, the daughter of Drusus, perform the coarse act of spitting. The steaming face of Pomponius could find no relief by belching. Socrates' 300 countenance did not grow pale at Fortune's blows, nor alter its unvarying expression even when faced with misery.

"How happy, how godlike is that people sustained by a mere breeze laden with the sweet scent of fruit. This fragrance serves them in place of both food and drink: it is the Bacchus in their goblets, the Ceres on their 305 board. Such is the life of those who dwell on the Ganges, satisfying the hunger of their mouths through their nostrils. This people are not dissipated by excess, nor consumed by a lust to eat, but remain immune to the sins of throat and belly.

"Austerity so steeled Psyllus that he escaped unharmed from ser- 310 pents menacing him with their black jaws. His skin alone, unscathed, served as a protecting wall, a shield impervious to the darts of their poisonous fangs.

"But Nature has left me unarmed amid poisonous vipers of another kind, for I am ensnared by the twisting hydra of my vices. She has not armed my body with the menace of a sword which might pacify them, 315 nor bound my plumed corselet with a mesh of steel, crowned my head nobly with a lofty helmet, nor offered me the protection of a shield. Those whom Nature so favors do not fear the Stymphalian darts of sin, and the arrows of sinfulness that wound by stealth do not dismay them.

Cap. 11 De proposito Architrenii

320   Quid faciam novi: profugo Natura per orbem
Est querenda michi. veniam, quacumque remotos
Abscondat secreta lares, odiique latentes
Eliciam causas et rupti forsan amoris
Restituam nodos, adero: pacemque dolorum
325   Compassiva feret et subsidiosa roganti
Indulgebit opem, flecti pacietur, hanelas
Hauriet aure preces et mentis verba medullis
Blanditiva bibet, lacrimisque pluentibus udas
Siccabit mansueta genas, ad vota parentem
330   Filius inducet" – spes solativa timorem
Eicit et ceptis favet et temptasse repulsa
Nil metuit peius – "ibo properancius, ibo
Ocius et, que sit miseris fortuna, videbo."

Cap. 12 De itineracione eiusdem

Rumpitur ergo more sterilis dilacio, ceptum
335   Promovet, urget opus, mundi circummeat axes
Et pcde sollicito terit Architrenius orbem:
Montibus insudat, metit egro poplite valles,
Languet in abruptis, in planis prevolat auras;
Ardua morbificant, relevant devexa laborem;
340   Sicca pedum curru, manuum legit humida remo,
Sese navicule, sese vice remigis utens;
Nec suspendit iter, scopulos si planta queratur,
Crura rubus fodiat, faciem ramalia cedant,
Dumus aret vultus, Boree furor ora flagellet,
345   Ardeat ad radios cutis, extinguatur ad imbres,
Sub Phebo siciat, pluviis adaquetur amictus,
Seviat aut estus aut frigoris ira, caputque
Alba ligustret hiemps, nigra quod vacciniet estas,
Et face sol Maurum faciat, nive bruma Britannum.

Cap. 13 De domo Veneris

350   Iamque fatigato Veneris domus aurea, rerum
Flosculus, occurrit, monti superedita, qualem
Cantat odorifero Philomena poetica versu,

Ch. 11 Architrenius proposes to act

320   "I know what to do: I must seek out Nature by roaming the world. I will discover that far-off place, wherever it be, where she dwells in secret, bring to light the hidden causes of her hostility, and perhaps repair the broken bond of love. When I appear before her she will be
325   compassionate and resourceful, soothe my grief and grant the aid for which I plead. She will allow herself to be swayed, lend an ear to my breathless appeal, draw my affecting words into the depths of her mind, and in compassion dry these cheeks now wet with flowing tears. A son will induce a parent to grant his prayer."
330   Consoling hope drives out fear and encourages his plan; he fears no worse result than to have tried and failed. "I will set forth at once, travel swiftly, and see what fortune may await the wretched."

Ch. 12 His journey

The fruitless hesitation of delay is interrupted forthwith; Archi-
335   trenius sets about his task, presses forward, and sets off around the world. He wears out the very earth with his troubled wandering, toils up mountainsides and crosses valleys on shaking legs. He moves wearily up the crags, but outstrips the wind on level ground; steep
340   places wear him down, but descending eases his labor. His feet serve in place of a chariot on dry land, and on the water his hands serve as oars; he himself is his only vessel, he himself is his oarsman. He does not break off his journey though his feet complain of the rocks, brambles gouge his legs, branches lash his face, thorns dig into his cheeks, and
345   the raging north wind stings his lips; though his skin burns with the sun's rays, or is drenched with rain, though he is parched by Phoebus, while storms turn his very garments to water; whether cruel heat or raging cold assail him, whether winter strew his head with white or summer stain it black, whether the sun give him the face of a Moor or the hoar frost that of a Briton.

Ch. 13 The house of Venus

350   At last Venus' golden palace, the flower of creation, presents itself to the weary traveller, set high on a mountain, the very place of which the poetic nightingale sings in scented verse – Philomela who, to

Que, quibus intorsit odii certamina livor,
Rufinum viciis, Stiliconem moribus armat,
355 Alternansque stilos istum premit, erigit illum,
Neutrum describit, tacet ambos, fingit utrumque.[20]
Hic dea virginibus roseum cingentibus orbem
Presidet et rudibus legit incentiva puellis,
Inque viros faculas accendit et implicat hamos.
360 Ex quibus una, loci specie pictura, choruscat
Stelligero vultu plus quam Ledea, Dione
Altera, que lunam maiori prevenit astro,
Et quam subradiat Phebi minus emula Phebe.

Cap. 14 De descriptione puelle

Verticis erecta moderatum circinat orbem
365 Sperula, nec temere sinuato deviat arcu,
Non obliqua means, ubi nec tumor advena surgit,
Nec vallis peregrina sedet; lascivit in auro
Indigena crinis, nec mendicatur alumpnus
Pixidis, exter honos, nec nubit adultera ficte
370 Lucis imago come: non exulat arte capilli
Umbra, nec aurifero ferrum sepelitur amictu.
Hec capitis preciosa seges nec densior equo
Luxuriat, iuncto descensu prona, nec errat
Limite turbato, nec divertendo vagatur
375 Transfuga, nec cedit alio pulsante capillus.
A frontis medio tractu directa superne
Verticis ad centrum via lactea surgit aranti
Pectine, cuius acu geminas discessit in alas,
Et tandem trifidum coma cancellatur in orbem
380 Divisoque prius iterum cohit agmine crinis.
Liber apex frontis nitidum limante iuventa
Tenditur in planum: trito radiosa politu
Et bysso, quo prima cutem vestiverat etas,
Candida, nec macule nevo nubescit, oloris
385 Emula, nec recipit vaccinia mixta ligustris.
Qua propior naso frons ultima vergit, aperto
Parvula planicies spacio nudatur, utrimque
Luna supercilii tenui succingitur arcu,
Nec coeunt medio distincta volumina fine:
390 Gracius alternos prohibent divorcia tactus,

describe the conflicts which splenetic hatred provoked, arms Rufinus
55 with vices, and Stilico with virtues, varying her style to put down the
one and exalt the other, yet describes neither one accurately, keeps
silent about the true nature of both, creates a false image of each.[20]

Here the goddess presides over a rosy world, surrounded by maidens;
60 she teaches the inexperienced girls her enticements, kindles their
torches and baits their hooks for men. The beauty of one among the
maidens is an image of the place itself, her face fairer than the Ledaean's
in its starry glow, a second Dione who surpasses the moon in radiance
so that Phoebe, no longer imitating Phoebus, seeks to borrow her light.

Ch. 14 A description of the girl

65   The small globe of her head, held high, has the form of a sphere;
there is no random deviation from its continuous arc, no divergent
contour, for there is neither unwelcome bulge nor intrusive depression.
Her hair luxuriates in its natural gold, and there is no need for those
external adornments produced by the cosmetic case. She does not
70 submit her locks to an adulterating appearance of false radiance; there
are no dark strands for art to banish, nor is any iron grey veiled by a
mantle of gold. This precious crop of her head is luxuriant but not too
dense, is easily drawn together as it falls, and does not resist confine-
75 ment or stray rebelliously in all directions, and no strand must submit to
the tugging of another.

From the center of her forehead a milky way rises straight upward to
the crown of her head, defined by the furrowing comb, whose edge
divides her hair into twin companies, and it is then arranged in a
80 threefold coil, as the locks whose ranks had been divided draw together
again.

From its peak her forehead opens out into a smooth surface, glowing
with a youthful radiance born of careful scrubbing and set off by the
linen headdress with which she has decked her youthfulness. The
85 swanlike whiteness of her skin is not clouded by any mark or blemish,
and its white bloom has received no admixture of the juice of berries.

Where the lower portion of her forehead tapers toward the nose, a
little level space is exposed; on either side the crescent shape of an
eyebrow is defined by a delicate arc. Separated by this middle ground,
90 the two curves do not commingle; a tactful divorce prohibits one from
touching the other. Thus the common highroad is not thicketed over; no

Communisque rubo via non silvescit, eamque
Non operit mentis pilus accusator amare,
Nec clausi loquitur fellis nemorosa venenum.[21]
    Tortilis auricule nodosaque cellula gyrum
395 Explicat et tornata brevem complectitur orbem,
Mundaque Nature digito purgata, latenti
Nusquam sorde rudis; scabros inculta recessus
Erubuisse nequit verborum semita, planum
Libera sternit iter; fruticoso calle, lutosis
400 Non odiosa viis, susceptam nuncia menti
Portatura notam, vocisque domuncula, cuivis
Semper aperta sono, tersisque penatibus hospes,
Murmura vel timidos non exclusura susurros.
    Excubie lampas faculis ignescit ocellus
405 Sidereis, in quo saphyri flammata diescit
Gemmula, quam rutili mediam circumligat auri
Torquis, ad extremos tractus ardente beryllo.
    Prima pudicicie testis mansuescit ocelli
Simplicitas, mentisque foris iuratur honestas,
410 Promittitque fides oculi sincera Sabinam.
    Egreditur nasi brevitas producta, magistro
Permittente modo, quo precurrente tumentis
Ardua colliculi non dedecet aggere, turpes
Excursus aquila nescit vel sima recursus;
415 Dirigitur iusto spacio librata, venuste
Tracta nec alterutro declinans regula: nasum
Non procul extendit refugove reciprocat arcu.
    Naris odorate redolet thymus, intimus extra
Non celatur honos, gemino dulcescit aroma
420 Thuribulo spirans, letum fragrancia pascit
Aera vicineque lares imbalsamat aure,
Et vacuos implent absencia cinnama tractus.
Non ibi lascivis riget importuna pilorum
Silvula, nec naris tenui crinitur arista
425 Munda, nec interius rudibus dumosa capillis.
    Ebriat aspectus, animum cibat; omne tuentis
Delicium facies et predo, cupidinis hamo
Piscatura viros; hec Nestoris esse timori
Iam gelidis annis, hec sollicitasse Catonem
430 Recia vel laquei vel pulmentaria possent.
    Hic color exultat placituro sedulus ori

bristling hair obstructs it, bearing witness to bitter thoughts, nor does a dense thicket proclaim the poisonous gall concealed within.[21] The
395 twisting channel of her finely turned ear ends in a little gnarled chamber shaped to shelter a small circular opening. Unblemished, and cleaned by Nature's own finger, it is never defiled by any hidden impurity. The path of speech is never allowed to grow red and rough with lurking sores, but
400 maintains an open and level course, never rendered unpleasant by overgrown or muddy stretches; it is like a messenger ever ready to convey to the mind the tidings it receives, a little dwelling-place for voices, ever open to any sound whatever, a hospice with well-swept chambers from which even murmurs and timid whispers are not excluded.

405 Like the lantern in a watch-tower the pupil of her eye shines with starry fire. At the center a little blazing gem of sapphire shines like the light of day; it is surrounded by a band of ruddy gold, while the outer rim is glowing beryl. The first evidence of her purity is the gentle simplicity of her glance, which outwardly attests her honorable
410 thoughts. The sheer good faith expressed in her eyes is a guarantee of her Sabine purity.

The modest length of her nose is drawn forth with a masterfully controlled indulgence, which prevents its gently swelling prominence from reaching an unseemly size. It is neither the eagle's jutting beak nor
415 the receding snout of the ape. Charmingly fashioned, it follows its carefully defined course to the proper extent, its straightness deviating neither to one side or the other; it neither extends too far nor turns up too abruptly.

The scent of thyme is diffused from her perfumed nostrils; the special quality within is not concealed from those without, for a sweet aroma
420 breathes forth from these twin censers. A fragrance enriches the happy air, and imbues the passing breeze with its perfume, while imagined spices are spread abroad. No unruly little forest of bristles riots in her
425 nostrils; their openings are not fringed with fine hairs, nor is there an undergrowth of rough stalks within.

Her appearance is intoxicating; her beauty both feeds the mind of the beholder with pleasure and preys upon him, enticing men with the baited hook of desire. Such nets, such snares, such delicacies might
430 trouble a Cato, or disturb the chilly old age of a Nestor. Lively color flourishes in her charming face; a natural rosy heat, set off by the

Incola flamma rose, quam circumfusa coronant
Lilia, candentes vultus accendit et ignes
Temperat et parcit faculis et amicius urit
435 Blandior extremi fusa nive purpura limbi.
    Hec rosa sub senio nondum brumescit et oris
hic tener in teneris puerisque puellulus annis
Flosculus invitat oculos et cogit amorem
Mentibus illabi stupidis, Venerique ministrat
440 Arma suasque faces, lunatque Cupidinis arcum
Pectoris in vulnus. glacie contracta senecte
Non ibi languet hyemps, illuc inserpere ruga
Non presumit anus, subito circumvaga passu
Et faciem longo pede signatura viatrix.
445 Vernanti minio suffusa labellula, nullo
Vulgari pictore rubent, nec protrahit Artis
Obsequium, quam sola dedit Natura, rubricam.[22]
Non morsu solito[23] – parcenti dente – labelli
Extorquetur honos et, quo suprema loquendi
450 Ianua vestitur, non huius texuit ostrum
Artificis pecten, orisque accensa gemello
Limine sardonicis, native prunula candet.
    Divite precingit vallo redolencia lingue
Atria dentis ebur, qui nec livescere morbo
455 Erubet aut putris olida ferrugine sordis;
Nec male radicum solidata sede minuto
Agmine rarescit nec, dum comes improbus instat
Proximus, urgenti cedens extrarius errat,
Nec minor est speciem merito vicinia fine,
460 Nec linguam reserat foribus distancia ruptis,
Aut clausos aperit spacii cesura penates.
    Colle tumens modico convexi argentea menti
Area descendit, quantum studiosa venusti
Nobilitas forme decreverit, omnia iusto
465 Philosophata modo; pretenditur ordine lecto
Meta, nec effusum pregnanti porrigit alvo
Curvatura sinum, teretisque licencia clivi
Non nimis ausa brevi sinuatur fine, decenti
Monticulo surgens, humili lascivula dorso.
470 Ningit in albenti mansura pruinula collo,
Nec quatitur ventis, nec hanelo carpitur estu
Verna, nec hiberno Boree cessura tiranno,

surrounding lily whiteness, creates a warm light in her cheeks, but its
35 fire is tempered, and the softer red which suffuses the snowy white of the
rest of her face has a gentler glow.

This rose has not yet been blighted by the chill of age. It is just this
tender and girlish bloom that lures the eye to boys of tender years as
well It is this that causes love to infiltrate spellbound minds, provides
40 Venus with her weapons and torches, and bends the wounding bow of
Cupid. Here is no sluggish winter, no cramped and chilly age; no old
woman's wrinkles have yet dared to insinuate themselves, those wide-
ranging travellers who will so soon inscribe her countenance with their
tracks.

45 Her lips, suffused with flourishing vermilion, owe their redness to no
common painter, for one whom Nature herself has marked with her
rubric[22] has no need for the services of Art. The beauty of her lips is not
attained at the price of making her teeth forego their normal exercise,[23]
50 and no artisan's hand has woven the purple with which the outermost
portal of speech is decked.

The shining redness of her mouth is made brighter by twin rows of
natural sardonyx. The ivory whiteness of her teeth surrounds the
sweet-smelling chamber of the tongue with its sumptuous rampart,
55 which is never embarrassed by feverish distemper or the stinking odor
of decay. Set solidly on the foundation of their roots, her teeth form no
straggling rank: none allows itself to be forced out of line by the
importunity of a disorderly companion who has drawn too close, and
none shows less well than its neighbor by virtue of the space assigned to
60 it. Her tongue is not allowed to move far abroad when the gates are
opened, nor does a gaping aperture reveal the inner chambers.

Modestly swelling, the silvery surface of her well-rounded chin
descends in accordance with the most scrupulous standard of graceful
65 and noble form; every detail expresses a philosopher's ideal of order. The
tip of the chin conforms to this careful standard; its roundness does not
protrude like the out-thrust swelling of a pregnant womb, but the
freedom of its rounded curve, modestly bold, quickly turns back on
itself, like a graceful little hill that entices by its gentle rising.

70 Perpetual snow gleams on her white neck; its vernal purity is never
assailed by winds, nor sullied by the hot breath of summer; it does not
yield to the wintry tyranny of Boreas, nor fears the roar of the lordly

Nec metuens Parthi dominum latrasse Leonem,[24]
Cum fumante furit, timor anni, Sirius arcu.
475   Gutturis illimi speculo contendit ad unguem
Tersa superficies, cupidos vix lubrica tactus
Sustinet, ut possit digito labente repulsam
Erubuisse manus; non hic montana thorosos
Multiplicat pinguedo gradus, testata gulosam
480 Finitimis clivosa iugis; non proxima nudos
Gutturis orbiculos cutis exprimit, ossibus arto
Nubilis amplexu, paulo placitura recedit;
Nec, carnis medie quod epentesis addit, avare
Sincopat exertis macies ingloria nervis.
485 Omnis in hac una species consedit, ubique
Inseritur, nusquam declinativa, modumque
Iactitat in quovis spacio librasse venustum.

Parthian Lion[24] at that fearful season when Sirius rages in the blazing
sky.
75   The surface of her throat, polished to perfection, rivals a spotless
mirror. Its softness seems hardly capable of enduring a wanton caress;
one's very hand might blush to have its straying fingers repulsed. No
mountainous fleshiness compounds its firm contours, no surrounding
80 hills give evidence of gluttony, yet the skin is not so tight, so intimately
wedded to the bones of her neck, as to expose the protrusion of the
gullet, but maintains a pleasing distance. There is no need to reduce the
effects of bodily excess by stingy and ignoble starving, which exposes
85 the underlying sinews. A uniform beauty, all-pervading and unvarying,
informs her, proclaiming that the standard of grace has been observed
in every detail.

Liber Secundus

Cap. 1 De residuo descriptionis puelle

Uritur et cecum fovet Architrenius ignem,
Spectandoque faces acuit, vultuque ruentes
Inserit intuitus; facies presencior estum
Asperat et tandem visu sibi pestifer omni
5 Mollibus ad partes alias divertit ocellis.
　　Parcior attollit diffusio pectus: amarum
In muliere sapit membrorum sarcina, dulce
Virginis est animo, non corpore, pondus; honorem
Attenuat, pugiles quicquid densatur in artus.
10 Est brevibus maior, magnis minor, omne recidit
Stature vicium medio statura venustas.
　　Consuluit Natura modum, cum sedula tantum
Desudaret opus, ne qua delinqueret; utque
Artificis digitos exemplar duceret, ante
15 Pinxerat electi spacii mensura puellam,
Ne male Pygmea sedeat, Titania surgat.
　　Circumcisa, brevis, limata mamillula laxum
Non implet longeva sinum, puerilibus annis
Castigata sedet, teneroque rotundula botro
20 Pullulat et nondum lacrimante puerpera lacte
Clauditur et solidum succingit eburnea nodum.
　　Bina mamillarum distinguit pomula planum
Vallis arans sulcum, descensu libera, donec
Ventriculum tollat spacii cautela, brevemque
25 Obvius enodis uteri tumor erigat arcum.
　　Qua teres astricti mediam domat orbita cinctus,
Contrahitur flexo laterum distancia lumbo,
Plenior ad pectus, tenuatur ad ilia, donec
Luxuriet renum gremio crescente volumen.
30 　　Invius excluse Veneri, secrecior ortus
Flore pudicicie tenero pubescit; ibique

Book Two

Ch. 1 The rest of the description of the girl

Architrenius is consumed by a hidden fire, and feeds it, for the torch burns more sharply as he looks, fixing his eager gaze on her face. But at length the too vivid impression of her beauty causes him pain; his very
5 powers of sight become a disease, and he diverts his too sensitive eyes to other parts.

The swell of her bosom is restrained: a large body is an unpleasant thing in a woman. A maiden's gravity should be charming, a matter of spirit, not bulk, and whatever makes for brawny limbs detracts from her
10 dignity. Too tall to be called short, she is yet less than tall; her very middling height, by avoiding both extremes, becomes a source of charm. Nature deliberated carefully, eager though she was to produce such a work, so that nothing should be lacking. To ensure that her fashioning hand conformed to the ideal pattern, she first designed the
15 girl by carefully calculating her height, so that she would neither crouch like a lowly pigmy nor rise to Titanic heights.

Her breasts, small, restrained, and clearly defined, do not overflow her bosom like those of an old woman, but hold their position with a
20 firmness proper to her tender years. Each little sphere puts forth a tender bud. This, since there is as yet no infant for whom it must weep milky tears, remains closed, a tight little node set in ivory. A valley divides the twin fruits of her breasts like a straight and level furrow, descending
25 unhindered until a nice sense of proportion gives rise to her stomach, and the modest swell of her smooth womb ascends to meet it. Where the circling girdle draws tight about her middle, the width of her flanks narrows down to the supple loins. Fuller at the breast, her body narrows, until the loins swell sumptuously to accommodate the full curve of her womb.

30 Below, in a place inaccessible to Venus, a secret garden puts forth the tender bloom of chastity. Here a still unravished modesty flourishes, not

Vernat inattritus nec adulto saucius evo,
Nondum preda, Pudor, vacua qui regnat in aula,[1]
Solus habens thalamos, ubi non admittitur hospes.
35   Temperat innocuas iuvenilis flamma favillas,
Nec Venus intrudit, quo mores pruriat, ignem,
Nec divertit Amor ad inhospita tecta Pudoris,
Nec nocet hic vel ea: mater face, filius arcu.
Improba non aperit vicii presumptio clausas
40   Clavigera virtute fores, adamante ligatur
Ianua, quam voti gravitas infracta sigillat.
Pro foribus lanugo sedet, primoque iuvente
Vellere mollescit, nec multa in limine serpit,
Sed summo tenuem preludit margine muscum.
45   Subtiles patula digitos manus extrahit, unguem
Cesilis urbano premordens forcipis usu.
Lenta verecundos amplexus brachia spondent,
Nata puellares collo suspendere nexus.
Plena, tenella, teres surarum pagina leves
50   Pumicis attritus refugit,[2] non indiget huius
Auxilio lime, tactum non decipit isto
Morsa diu scalpro, non hoc sentosa pilorum
Turba timet rastrum, fruticum radice revulsa,
Hanc meliore polit nativa novacula cultu.
55   Orbiculum tollit communis fibula crurum
Surarumque, genu, nec, quem internodia lunant,
Angulus incurvi corrugat poplitis arcum.
Non distorta rudi procedit tibia torno
Recta, nec agricolam meminit male nata parentem.
60   Sublimata brevem cogit pedis area calcem,
Articulosque ligans tersis decet unguibus ordo.
Incisiva cutem scabies non asperat; illic
Nullus inhorrescit scopulus, nec ledit acuto
Exterretque manus caro limatissima rusco,
65   Nec simulat sparsa cristatam cuspide rannum.
Hec oculis partim notat Architrenius et, quos
Non videt, a simili visorum conicit artus,
Nudaque pro speculo velate gracia servit.
Hec placet, hanc voto, quod vix respiret, hanelat,
70   Cernendique favum cupidis delibat ocellis,
Nec sitis infuso minor est idropica melle.

yet disturbed by maturity, an inviolate Purity that rules over an empty court,[1] in sole possession of that chamber to which no guest has been admitted. The warm glow of youth tempers its harmless fires; Venus has not yet infected her with the flame that awakens desire, nor has Love sought to enter this unwelcoming refuge of Modesty. As yet the mother's torch and the son's bow do not trouble her. No basely presuming vice can open portals locked by the key of virtue; the doors are as if bound with iron bands, on which the unfailing power of a vow has set its seal. Soft down spreads about the portals, soft with the first fleeciness of youth. It does not stray in profusion over the threshold, but confines its mossy carpet to the outer borders.

Her open hand reveals delicate fingers, the nails trimmed by the graceful exercise of the keen scissors. Her slender arms lend themselves to modest embraces, ready to entwine themselves girlishly about one's neck. Full yet delicately rounded, the skin of her calf shuns the light rasping of pumice,[2] and has no need of such polishing. It does not deceive the touch by virtue of long scraping with a razor, and no bristly tangle of hairs resists plucking, like some thicket torn up by the roots. Natural refinement, superior to any razor, makes her skin clear.

A joint in the form of a little sphere brings together shin and calf, and the bending of the knee does not mar with wrinkles the arch formed by its tendons. The shin extends straight, undistorted by any bending, and no innate flaw recalls peasant parentage. The finely arched sole of her foot requires a small shoe, whose confinement sets off her toes with their well trimmed nails.

No scar or scab roughens her skin, no mole with menacing bristles; her complexion, perfectly smooth, harbors nothing painful or irritating to the touch, no scattered stalks that suggest the sharp thorn or bristling bush.

Architrenius takes note of those parts that are visible, and deduces what he does not see from the evidence of things seen; the grace of what is exposed serves as a mirror of what is veiled. Pleased, he pants out a scarcely whispered prayer that he may feed his avid eyes on this honeycomb, and thirsts no less feverishly for the honey stored within.

Cap. 2 De studio Cupidinis

At vagus intuitu flexo miratur Amoris
Suggestus alios: iuvenum dum pectore fraudes
Implicat Idalias, non maiestate sedendi
75 Quam deitate minor, teneris tener ille magister
Discipulis, pharetram nunc sumit, cuius aperto
Carcere vulnificum numerando colligit agmen.
Quid declive meet oculo monstrante, sagittas
Dirigit et cote mucronibus asperat iras,
80 Cuspidibusque minas acuit, quasdamque recisis
Aligerat pennis, filique superpolit orbes,
Unde maritatur volucri teres hastula plume.
Nunc stat et obsequiis genuum cessantibus arcum
Lunat et accedit humeris, flexisque recedit
85 Renibus, inque latus levam preporrigit ulnam,
Obliquoque pedes spacio diducit et – ecce! –
Cornibus ad coitum nitentibus effugit arcus
Ex oculis, ad quos retrograda serpit harundo
In digitis, nervo mox progressiva relicto.

Cap. 3 De vestitu eiusdem

90 Aliger – et nullos alias dignatus amictus –
Purpureo vestis ardebat sole; stupetque
Omnia, sed cultum magis Architrenius: in quo
Succincte medio solee diffusior ante
Et retro forma sedet. solee substringitur arcu
95 Calceus obliquo, pedis instar factus, ut ipsos
Exprimat articulos, cuius deductior ante
Pinnula procedit, pauloque reflexior exit
Et fugit in longum tractumque inclinat acumen.
Exterior lateris paries coit integer, intra
100 Calceus admisso spacio discedit, et ambas
Alterno laqueus morsu complectitur horas.
Artatur calige descensus ad infima, donec
Plenior occurrat pedis area. porcio summa
Fluxior assurgit, caute crescentibus illa
105 Indulget spaciis; crurum magis ampla tumori
Pars facit et – posset offendi poplitis arto
Curvatura sinu – longo sub poplitis arcu

Ch. 2 Cupid's occupation

But his roving gaze is soon struck with wonder by other enticements.
For as his youthful spirit is drawn in by the deceptive arts of Venus,
75 Love, a god whose divinity is commensurate with his majestic dwelling
place, the soft master of soft disciples, takes up his quiver, and releases
from its depths a carefully chosen array of arrows. Keeping an eye on
whatever passes below, he aligns his arrows, sharpens their fierce
80 points with a whetstone, and adds barbs to the shafts; some he wings
with trim feathers, and finishes them neatly with coils of thread, so that
the round shaft is inseparably bound to the winged plume.

Now he rises from his knees, strings his bow, thrusts his shoulders
85 forward, draws back at the waist, and pulls his left arm back against his
side. Setting his feet at an angle, he draws the string taut, and lo! as the
polished horns are on the point of meeting, the bow springs away from
the eye, and the retreating arrow slips through the fingers, quickly
gaining speed as it leaves the string.

Ch. 3 Cupid's costume

90   The winged god, disdaining garments of any other kind, is resplendent in a robe of brilliant purple. Architrenius, astonished by all he sees,
marvels most at his adornment. The form of his thonged sandal is such
that it projects a little forward and behind. The boot, bound to the
sandal across the arch, conforms so closely to the shape of his foot that
95 one can trace the very toes. A little projecting wing extends slightly
forward, then curves abruptly and retreats backward, tapering to a
100 point. The surface of the boot is unbroken on the outer side, but the
inner side is split, leaving an open space, and a lacing, crossing back
and forth, draws the two edges together. The boot is close fitting as it
descends to meet the broader surface of the foot, but the upper portion
105 grows looser as it ascends, making careful allowance for an increasing
fullness. There is ample space for the swell of the calf, and since the
bending of the leg might have been inhibited by its gathering, the rest of
the boot is caught and bound just below the long hollow behind the

Stringitur excursu calige pars cetera, presso
Tensior amplexu, ne, si spaciosior amplos
110 Porrigat amfractus, intus vaga fluctuet, extra
Turpiter assurgat rugarum tibia dorso.
   Gracior irrugat ritu lascivia braccas
Teutonico, crispatque sinus amplexibus artis
Balteus undantes, teneros dum mollia surgunt
115 Suppara per renes, oculis factura repulsam
Archanosque virum prevelatura recessus.
   Prodigus in latum nec castigatus avaro
Forcipe procedit tunice discursus, et idem
Peccat in interula vestis modus: omnia luxus
120 Ignavus provisor agit, sola exit in artum
Luxuries manice, summa castracior hora.
   Multiplici laqueo manice mordetur hiatus;
Artificis qua cessat acus, pars cautius illa est
Sutrici neglecta manu, nam colligit horas
125 Fibula distantes nodoque extrema maritat,
Ut manus artanti manice iunctissima nubat.
   Ilia substringens spaciosum cinctus amictum
Contrahit et ruga tunicam depingit anili,
Rugarumque togam senio iuvenescere cogit.
130   Qua toga laxat iter capiti, qua nobile pondus
Pectoris erigitur collo confine, choruscant
Gemmarum radiis stellata monilia, noctis
Sideree mentita diem, flammatur in auro
135 Pectus et ardenti dulcescunt fulmina collo.
   Ne coma liberior erret, ventoque feratur
Importuna genis, vultusque exire volentis
Celatura iubar, succedit circulus alto
Incumbens capiti, cedit statura comarum
Mobilitas, cedit servire licencia pressis
140 Orbe coacta comis, vultusque erumpit aperta
Gracia, dum gemina suspenditur aure capillus.
   Mollibus exultat spoliis tunicata, suaque
Lascivit manus ipsa toga, que a pollice tractis
Decurrens spaciis media plus parte lacerti
145 Induit et summum cubitum delibat,
Clausa iacens; ipsaque manus scribente figuram,
Certius in digitis nodi numerantur et ungues,
Quos male tornatos incudi reddit amictus

110 knee – caught in a tight embrace lest its increasing fulness spread too
freely, the inner part flapping loosely, the outer swollen by an unseemly
ridge of wrinkles.

His breeches, gathered together in the Teutonic manner, are of a
more becoming looseness. A belt draws together the billowing folds
115 with its close embrace, while soft linen is drawn over his tender loins, to
thwart the gaze and veil the place where his manly parts are concealed.
His long robe flows in profusion, unchecked by the miserly shears, and
120 the blouse beneath luxuriates in the same fashion. Here excess has been
idly generous; sheer extravagance is expressed in the cut of the sleeve, a
fulness that is cut off only at the wrist. The open side of the sleeve is
made fast by elaborate basting. The work of the needle leaves off at a
certain point, a deliberate omission by the artful seamstress, for a
125 brooch draws together the sundered edges, and joins them in a knot at
the wrist, so that the hand is intimately united to the confining sleeve. A
belt, drawn about the loins, draws the voluminous robe together,
inscribing the garment with an old woman's wrinkles, though the
youthful cut of the robe is set off by these very marks of age.

130 Where the robe ceases its ascent toward the head, and the noble
mass of the chest rises toward the base of the neck, necklaces gleam
with the starlike brightness of gems, a starry night creating the illusion
135 of daylight. The breast is aflame with gold, and its lightning flashes
enhance the beauty of the gleaming throat.

Lest his hair stray too freely or be continually blown about his cheeks
by the breeze, hiding the brightness of a face eager to be seen, a circlet
imposes itself on the lofty head, and the restless locks consent to remain
still; once subdued, their freedom of movement confined to this narrow
140 circle, they submit to servitude, and the fairness of his face shows itself,
while the hair falls over his two ears.

The god rejoices in his sumptuous finery; even his hand sports a
garment of its own which is drawn over the fingers and extends its
145 length to cover more than half of his arm before closing loosely around
the elbow. It defines the shape of his hand so exactly that the joints may
be counted, and its tight fit restores an ill-trimmed nail to its proper

Pressior et forme vicio mendicat honorem.
150   Crimina surgentis uteri, Si quasque tumoris
Desidior Natura notas incauta reliquit,
Has nova providit industria demanicatis
Occultare togis, quarum contracta supremos
Artat forma sinus, humerisque angustior herens
155   Crescit et inferius spaciosos exit in orbes.
Ultima lascivit luxu clamis ebria, dextrum
Dedignata latus, humero iurata sinistro.
    Arguit exterior animum status, intimus extra
Pingitur affectus, levitas occulta forensi
160   Scribitur in cultu, cultu monstrante latentis
Copia fit mentis; habitus, qui cetera velat,
Pectora develat, aperitque abscondita morum
Garrulus interpres et – mentem veste loquenti –
Predicat exterior internas pagina leges.

Cap. 4 De ingluvie

165   Hec stupet et, cepti memor, Architrenius inde
Transit, et – ecce – locus visum ferit obvius, in quo
Affectus varios hominum trahit una colende
Sollicitudo gule, molli studiosa palato
Deliciis lactare cibos, varioque paratu
170   Extinctas animasse fames, dispendia noctis
Producto breviasse mero, longasque dierum
Corripuisse moras, Bacho vigilante dolores
Et sensum sopire malis, mentisque labores
Fallere, ieiuno redituras pectore curas.
175   Hic ieiuna modi, transgressus ebria, ventris
Ingluvies humiles fastidit prodiga mensas
Privatosque lares vel, quod pre fascibus ipsis
Fabricius[3] morderet, olus, trabeatus aratro
Serranus[4] posito riguis fovisset in ortis.
180   Nescit, ut humane redimat dispendia vite,
Quam modicum Natura petat: producere vitam
Sola Ceres Nereusque potest, illudque beatum
Vivere, quod foliis rudibusque innititur herbis.

shape, creating an illusion of grace by its very gaudiness.

150 Should Nature have grown lazy, and carelessly left traces of the scandalous swell of a bloated belly, modern industry has made provision for concealing them by means of sleeveless robes, whose narrow cut clings closely to the upper body, and more closely still to the
155 shoulders, but grows fuller as it descends, and ends in capacious folds. A final outer garment revels in its sumptuous purple; it scorns to cover his right side, and is fastened to his left shoulder.

His exterior condition declares his mind; the inner disposition is
160 painted on the surface, the public display tells of a concealed frivolity and suggests what the inner resources amount to. A costume which conceals everything else unveils the mind, providing an all too garrulous account of the hidden flaws of his character. The clothes proclaim the man, like a page of writing that gives outward expression to the laws which rule within.

Ch. 4 On Gluttony

165 Architrenius is astonished by it all, but mindful of his undertaking he passes on. And lo, a place presents itself to view where one preoccupation governs the desires of every one: a concern to cater to gluttony, and nurture the tender palate with delicacies, to revive extin-
170 guished appetites by strange means, to make the long nights short and speed the slow pace of day by protracted drinking, to lull pain and the sense of misfortune to sleep with Bacchic vigils, and to evade burdensome thoughts, cares that will nevertheless return with the return of hunger.

175 Here prodigal gluttony, starved of moderation, drunk with sheer excess, scorns the humble board, the modest dwelling, such simple fare as Fabricius[3] would eat with the fasces before him, or such as Serranus[4] raised in a well-watered garden, even after he had abandoned the plow
180 to don the robes of state. Gluttony does not know how little Nature needs to make good the expense of human life. Ceres and Nereus are sufficient by themselves to ensure longevity, and it is a blessed way of life that is sustained by simple herbs and vegetables.

Cap. 5 De questionibus ventricolarum

Inter ventricolas versatur questio, pisce
185 Quis colitur meliore lacus, quis fertilis aer
Alitibus, que terra feras effundat edules,
Quos assare cibos, quos elixare palati
Luxuries discincta velit, que fercula molli
Iure natent,[5] que sicca gule trudantur Averno,
190 Quo iuris iactura meri redimatur in unda,
Quot capiat fartura modos, quo federe nodet
Oppositos mixtura cibos, quo frixa paratu
Exacuant gustus, que corpora cura nepotum
Dictet aromatico panis mandare sepulcro;
195   Que novitas adiecta cibis epulonis acutum
Commendet studium, nam quevis prima voluptas
Delicias novitate capit, nam gracia rebus
Prompta novis preciumque venit, precepsque bonorum
Gloria temporibus recipit fragmenta favoris;
200   Quid prosit variare dapes possitve cadentem
Erexisse famem, nam prona paratibus isdem
Occurrit sacies, recipit fomenta ciborum
Alteritate fames, diversaque fercula gustus
Invitant, similesque creant fastidia mense;
205   Quis precio leviore cibus, quis plure refertos
Emungat loculos, nam condimenta palato
Plus sapiunt, que pluris emis, preciumque paratus
A precio sumit; refert, quo vivitur, asse
Veneat an libra; mense spectatur in ere
210 Nobilitas, censuque sapor maiore iuvatur;
Que raro molles exornent fercula mensas,
Namque voluptates offendit copia, raris
Accedunt momenta bonis, convivia raro
Sumpta iuvant, rarusque venit iocundior usus.
215   Distat utro piscis, an dulci ventre palatum
Plus iuvet an tergo; tenero quis crure, quis ala
Ingluviem plus ales alat, que prima ferarum
Nobilitas mensis veniat pictura potentum,
Exceptis excepta viris, non Baccidis[6] olle,
220 Non Codri[7] sperata case, convivia regum
Delicat et numquam mense popularis ad usus
Degenerat, nullique toge partitur honorem,

Ch. 5 The gluttons' disputation

85   A debate is going on among the belly-worshippers: what lake breeds the finest fish, what climate is best for birds, what lands are rich in game animals; which foods the unbridled appetite prefers roasted, which boiled; what dishes, according to the law of taste, should swim,[5] which
90   ones should be plunged still dry into the Avernos of the gullet (and how the deprivation imposed in the latter instance can be made good with a flood of wine); how many forms stuffing may take; what rules enable one to mix different kinds of food; what way of preparing a fricassee is most tempting; in what cases piety decrees that the corpse be consigned to an aromatic tomb of bread.

95   What new way of preparing a dish will commend it to the keen discernment of the feasters? Any form of pleasure is delightful at first because of its novelty; gratitude and reward are ever ready to greet what is new. The glory of good works is fleeting, and after a time it earns
200   only scraps of favor. What will serve to lend variety to a banquet and revive the flagging appetite? Surfeit is the likely response to menus that are ever the same, and hunger is stimulated by different kinds of food. An array of dishes appeals to the taste, while familiarity breeds a distaste for dining.

205   Which foods cost least, and which inveigle the most from the well-stuffed purse? For those dainties are sweetest to the taste which cost you the most; the feast derives its value from its price. Whether one's sustenance costs a penny or a pound is an important matter. The
210   splendor of the feast is computed in cash, and its taste is enhanced by a greater expenditure.

What dishes adorn the gourmet's table most rarely? Ready availability detracts from enjoyment. Rare delights are esteemed more highly; goods rarely consumed are pleasing; the rarer pleasure is the more enjoyed.

215   Opinion varies as to whether the plump belly or the tender back of a fish is most tasty; which birds' legs offer the glutton most, and which birds' wings; which beast, by virtue of its nobility, should come forth first to adorn the tables of the great. These privileges of the privileged,
220   undreamt of in the kitchen of Baucis[6] or Codrus' cottage,[7] grace the feastings of kings, and are never found in lowly service at common people's tables. Such honors are not imparted to the humble toga; what

Quem proprium pretexta rapit, sublimis ad aulas
Convolat et sese raro committit Amicle.
225   Par labor et studium, quo fercula fine parata,
Quo frustrata modo, qua scissa libidine possint
Ardorem fudisse gule, nam forma paratis
Delicias preciumque parit, multumque tenetur
Materies forme, nam, si labor improbus assit,
230 Materiam superabit opus, opibusque paratus
Addet opes, acuetque gulis ardentibus ignes.

Cap. 6 De sollicitudine circa salsas

Amplius in salsis labor amplior, ambiciosas
Facturis avidasque fames, maioraque magno
Laturis momenta cibo: properatur ad Indos
235 Ardentemque polum secretaque sidera strati
Etheris, ut toto cogantur aromata mundo
Et condimenti surgat lascivia mensis
Auctior et calido subsidat flamma palato.
    Curritur ad Macedum fines Nilique recessus
240 Et nudam sub sole Pharon, qua sidera Memphis[8]
Non oculo languente videt, dum cuncta sereni
Libertate legit, qua semper utrumlibet axem
Vel neutrum demergit Aren,[9] qua dirigit ortus
Occasusque pares oculorum meta colurus.[10]
245 Itur ad Eoas species messemque perusti
Axis odoriferam, ventris devellere toto
Nititur orbe dapes et condimenta libido.

Cap. 7 Contra vescentes auro

O furor inque nefas egressa licencia mense
Prodigiumque gule! labor est in prandia quamvis
250 Flectere naturam, mollis fit cena metallum,
Ingenitusque rigor epuli peregrinat in usus,
Principibusque cibum mentiri cogitur aurum.
    Ergo aurumne gule vivendi protrahit auram
Et Crasso[11] concludit idem? Crassosne iuvabit
255 Et Crasso nocuit? absit! pudeatque pudorem,
Quod vicium surgat, quo virtus corruit, auro.

robed dignity claims as its own flees to the halls of the great, and rarely
bestows itself upon an Amyclas.

225   An equally grave concern is the design with which each dish is
prepared, how it is served and how the enticing appearance of each
serving may serve to quench the burning of greed. For it is the style of a
banquet that creates the effect of pleasure and expense, and the actual
230   ingredients are valued largely as they are presented. If one works at it,
the effect can be made to transcend the means; a lavish presentation can
compound the effect of sumptuous ingredients, and so intensify the
ardent appetite.

Ch. 6 The importance of sauces

Still more effort is expended on those sauces which turn simple
hunger to ambition and greed, and make grand dishes still grander.
235   They send to India, to the south pole, to the most remote star in the vast
heavens, and gather every aroma in the universe, so that the stimu-
lation of spice may enhance the feast and ease the palate's burning
desire. They send to distant Macedonia, and the upper reaches of the
240   Nile, and sunburnt Egypt, where Ptolemy[8] gazes on the stars with
unblinking eye, and ponders the nature of things in the freedom of a
tranquil mind: where Aren[9] continually sees one of the two poles, or
neither one, sink below the horizon; where the colural band, marking
245   the limit of our vision, balances the risings and settings of the sun.[10]
They send to the beauteous Orient, and the sweet-scented fields of the
torrid south; from every corner of the world the lust of gluttony labors to
draw spices for its banquets.

Ch. 7 Against those who feed on gold

This madness in feasting goes beyond mere licence and becomes
250   monstrous and sinful. It seeks to transform all natural things into food;
even metal becomes soft and edible, and its inherent hardness is drawn
into the service of the feast. Gold is compelled by princes to masquerade
as food.

Will gold, then, prolong the life of the glutton? Did this prove true for
255   Crassus[11]? And will that benefit other Crassuses which was so harmful
to Crassus himself? God forbid, and let the gold that gives rise to such
wickedness, that so corrupts virtue, be rejected as something shameful.

Cap. 8 De vini optimi quesicione

Sudor et attrite superest vigilancia cure
Excoctusque labor studiumque, quod occupet omne
Ingenium, quesisse merum; nam gracia mensis
260 Absque mero decisa venit, nec plena voluptas
Est mense, que fundit aquas, facinusque receptis
Naufragium fecisse cibis: solempnia mense
Bachus agit, mestos animi devellit amictus.

Cap. 9 De commendacione Bachi

"Bache, corymbiferis Frigie spectabilis aris,
265 Quem Iove maiorem Thebe venerantur alumpnum
Parnasusque deum, cunctis deus inclyte terris,
Quam bonus es! meliusque sapis, plus sole sereni,
Plus splendoris habes auro Pheboque nitoris,
Plus auro Pheboque potes, tu cetera pleno
270 Obnubis radio, sidus plus sidere, luxque
Luce, diesque die, plausus seris, ocia tractas
Et tiasis tirsisque iuvas, tibi meror et omnis
Cedit hiemps, vernusque venis, lugubris amaram
Pectoris abstergis lacrimam, sepelisque sepulcra
275 Leticie, curas; refoves felicius egro
Pectus hebes luctu, per te tranquillior omnis
Intima luxuriat pax expirante tumultu.
Pretimidos audere facis, leporique leonem
Inseris et nervis animos ut vina ministras,
280 Imbelles in bella vocas, animosque iacentes
In Martem mortemque rotas, Mavortis in usum
Invalidos Mavortis agis, dextramque trementem
Sub senio vinoque regis, tuus ensis in enses,
In galeas galea quemvis rapit, ignis in ignes.
285 Fecundo fecunda mero facundia surgit
Et vino verbisque fluit, sic lingua Lieum
Mercuriumque sapit, gemina sic estuat unda
Eloquii torrens, eciam prudencia vino
Uberior fervet. exurgis, Bache, caputque
290 Et linguam pectusque moves: capitique Megera,
Pectoribus Nestor, linguis inserpit Ulixes.
Tristibus oppressos animos in leta relaxas,

Ch. 8 The search for the finest wines

There is still hot work, and the sleeplessness of gnawing anxiety to be endured, for an exhausting task remains, a problem demanding the
260 utmost ingenuity – the quest for wine. For the charm of dining is cut in half without wine. The feast at which water is served cannot be fully enjoyed, and it is a crime to consign one's food to a watery grave. To Bacchus belong the rites of the feast; it is he who plucks the mantle of sorrow from the mind.

Ch. 9 In praise of Bacchus

265   "Bacchus, proclaimed by the ivy-laden altars of Phrygia, whom Thebes reveres as a god greater than Jove, and whom Parnassus acknowledges as a divine foster-child, thou god renowned in every land: good as you are, your taste is better, more radiant than a clear sky, richer than gold, brighter than Phoebus. For you are more potent than
270 gold or Phoebus, your brilliance casts these others into darkness, stellar beyond any star, more luminous than light, a fairer day than ever dawned. You are the source of rejoicing, the lord of idleness, the patron of the Bacchic dance and the Thyrsis. Grief and winter's chill give way before you, your coming is like the spring, wiping away the bitter tears
275 of the heavy hearted and burying care beneath a heap of pleasure. You revive the spirits of the sick man grown dull through suffering; through you men revel in a surpassing inner peace, as the tumult of the world fades away.

"You endow the timid with daring, imbue the hare with the spirit of
280 the lion. The wine you proffer stiffens men's resolve, summons the unwarlike to war, makes the craven spirit rush to face death in battle. You impel those unfit for martial strife to the service of Mars, you steady with wine the hand that trembles with age. Your wine is the sword of those whom you urge against the foe, their armor and their valor.

285   "When wine is flowing wit flows as well; the tongue becomes a stream of wine and words, Bacchus and Mercury conspire to produce a torrent of eloquence. Wine makes even the wise more full of wisdom.
290 Your influence, O Bacchus, governs thought, speech and spirit; Megaera infests the brain, Nestor claims the breast, and the tongue becomes a Ulysses.

"You grant to spirits oppressed by sorrows the freedom to be happy.

Meroris tumidam curas ydropisin, egro
Peoniis animo medicina potencior herbis.
295 Languores languere facis, sensumque doloris
Cogitur ipse dolor posuisse, malisque malorum
Eripis effectum, relevas servire parate
Paupertatis honus; tociens quod sensit, egestas
Dediscit sentire iugum, felicia fata
300 Et rerum momenta creas, sortemque beatam
Pauperis esse iubes et, qui servire steterunt,
Consedere duces et Bachi stante corona
Surgit ad hos patere dominus septemplicis Aiax[12]
Anglicus et calice similis contendit Ulixes."
305   Hec ibi funduntur Bacho preconia, tales
Multiplicat plausus plebes devota, refertis
Incubuisse cifis, erroris prodiga, mente
Saucia languenti, racionis dedita sacrum
Extinxisse iubar, rapido submersa Lieo.

Cap. 10 De potu superfluo

310   Ergo vagante cifo, discincto gutture "wesseil"
Ingeminant "wcsseil"; labor est plus perdere vini
Quam sitis, exhaurire merum studiosius ardent
Quam exhaurire sitim, commendativa Liei
Est sitis et candens calices iterare palatum
315 Imperiosa iubet, ad Bachi munera dextras
Blandius invitat, pluris sunt pocula, pluris
Ariditate sitis, Bachusque ad vota peruste
Candentisque gule recipit crementa favoris.
    Non modus est calicis, nisi sarcina sumpta redundet
320 Et primum repetatur iter, data nausea reddit
Altera vina cifis: luteo corrupta veneno,
A venis in vasa venit, sua munera Bacho
Indignata refert, reditumque urgente palude,
Bache, retro properas, verseque recurritis unde.
325 Sic male libratos castigat nausea sumptus
Et fugat excessus nature parca voluptas.
    Non satis est haurire satis, se credere citra
Naufragii discrimen aquis, pede summa profundi
Carpere nec mergi; rerum gula preterit usus
330 Improba felices, ieiunia sustinet egre

You minister to the swollen dropsy of grief with a medicine more
295 efficacious for the diseased spirit than any of Paeon's herbs. You make
faintness grow faint, cause pain itself to lose the sense of pain, rob our
evils of their evil effects, and ease the burden of a poverty resigned to
serfdom. Those in need, when they feel your effect, lose all sense of their
300 burden. You make our fates seem blessed, and lend an importance to
dull lives. You decree that the poor man's lot shall become a happy one.
Those who have stood in attendance sit at the feast like lords; for so long
as they are crowned with the garland of Bacchus, the English Ajax
himself, lord of the sevenfold bowl,[12] rushes to obey their orders, and
Ulysses, his equal as a drinker, vies with him in service."
305   Such are the tributes poured forth to Bacchus, such the praises that
rise, again and again, from his worshippers. They recline with brimming goblets, full of confused thoughts, stricken with a dulness of mind,
committed to extinguishing the sacred light of reason in the swift
Lyaean flood.

Ch. 10 On drinking too much

310   Then, waving the goblet about, shouting unrestrainedly, they cry out
"Wassail!," and again "Wassail!" Wine, not thirst, is what they strive to
banish; they are far more eager to exhaust the supply of wine than to
ease the pressure of thirst. Thirst is Bacchus' ambassador, and delivers
315 his imperial decree that the tingling palate taste repeated draughts. It is
thirst that graciously bids the hand take up Bacchus' gifts, gifts that
seem more valuable when parching thirst enhances their appeal.
Bacchus is never more venerated than when he answers the prayer of a
dry and burning throat.
     But now there is drinking without limit, until the bellyful taken in
320 overflows, and retraces its original journey. The gift of nausea restores
the wine again to the cups. Streaked with yellow bile it comes forth from
the belly into the bowl, restoring to Bacchus those gifts which the dank
abyss within obliges the drinker to reject – but you are quick, o Bacchus,
325 to turn the tide again. Thus does nausea punish ill-considered indulgence, for Nature's pleasures are temperate and she rejects excess.
     It is not enough to have drunk enough so that one feels one's self just
short of sinking beneath the waves, to tread the surface of the abyss yet
330 not to be submerged. Reckless gluttony must always go beyond pleasure, can scarcely endure privation, and will never submit to the dictates

Nec librante modo novit deponere, rebus
Utitur ad penam, dum ventrem copia iusto
Plenior attollit, dum parcius esse beatus
Vellet homo, dampnatque suas habuisse faventes
335 In sua vota manus; gula, quas Natura creavit,
Delicias tormenta facit, sumptusque minores
Pauperis absolvit: heu numquam sobria, numquam
Nacta modum, recipit ieiuna et plena flagellum.

Cap. 11 De exclamacione in gulam

Ha gula, que mundum penitus scrutatur et usus
340 Torquet in illicitos Terre predulcia matris
Pignora, que gremio defovit blandius, ipsis
Egregio factura deis miracula partu.
　　Ha gula, que mundum modico concludit in utre,
Omnia detrudens stomachi ferventis in Ethnam
345 Vivendique lares, nature vile sepulcrum
Tabificansque rogus et edulis funeris urna.
　　Ha gula – delicias cuius perferre quis equa
Mente potest? – cunctis opibus circumflua mundi,
Tot non posse dolet uno concludere ventre.

Cap. 12 De statu gulosi in commestione

350 　Fercula metitur ventrisque palacia, tantis
Invenisse studet capientem rebus abyssum.
Gutturis ergo vias latebrosaque viscera tendit.
Est sacius rumpi quam mense parcere, ventrem
Distraxisse cibos quam non consumere dulces.
355 Increpat angusta ventris presepia, monstrum
Ventre licet sit homo, stomachi piget esse recessus
Tam modicos et ea Nature dampnat avaras
Parte manus; reliquo Pygmeus corpore mallet
Ventre fuisse Gigas, augeri cetera ducit
360 Membra supervacuum, mallet se cetera nano
Plenius augmentum ventris pigra sarcina penset.
　　Respicit ergo dapes, circumfusosque paratus
Iam votis oculisque vorat, circumspicit omnem

of moderation. Its enjoyments become punishments when its excessive providing swells a man's belly, so that he longs to have been blessed more sparingly, and curses his hands for having so willingly responded to his desire. Gluttony turns to torment what Nature created to give delight, and spares only the modest consumption of the poor. Alas, never sober, incapable of restraint, she feels the pains of both want and surfeit.

Ch. 11 An outcry against Gluttony

Such is gluttony, which endlessly ransacks the world and perverts to forbidden uses the beloved offspring of Earth, their mother, whose bosom provides tender nurture to miraculous forces, and can give birth to prodigies and even gods; gluttony; which holds the world shut up in a wineskin, and thrusts all creation into the seething volcano of the stomach, so that the sanctuary of life becomes the foul burial-place of nature, a pyre of decayed matter, an urn filled with the remains of the feast; gluttony whose pleasures none can endure untroubled, who founders in a sea of worldly goods, yet whose only regret is that a single belly cannot contain it all.

Ch. 12 How the glutton feels as he eats

He first measures the dishes before him against the palatial expanse of his belly, painstakingly seeking a hollow that can accommodate so many things. To the same end he stretches open the channel of his throat and the shadowy caverns below. For it is preferable to burst than to stint at the feast, to tear the belly asunder rather than fail to consume some delicacy. Now he inveighs against the narrow confines of his belly, even though it be of monstrous size, feels shame that the recesses of his stomach are so small, and curses Nature for her stinginess in this regard. Though the rest of his body be that of a Pigmy, he wishes to possess the belly of a Giant, and considers it unnecessary that his other limbs should have been allowed to grow. He would gladly be a dwarf in other respects, if this were balanced by a greater increase in the sluggish bulk of his belly.

Thus he looks over the banquet, already devouring the array spread before him with wishful thought and glance, and takes in every sump-

Luxuriem mense; sed cum non possit ad omnes
365 Suffecisse cibos, nescit gula, nescit, an istis
Irruat aut istis, sed et illis ardet et illis.

Cap. 13 De statu eiusdem post saciem

Ut satis est ventri, nec iam vacat angulus, escis
Invita parcente gula, longumque momordit
Versavitque diu, pleno cogente repulsam
370 Gutture, iam veniam fessis poscentibus egro
Dentibus attritu, nec plus datur esse facultas,
Iam cumulum capiente cibo, cum postulat equam,
Ne vergat dapis unda, gulam, tunc cogitur esse
Tandem larga manus, partitur, si qua supersunt,
375 Convivis conviva satur, transferre necesse est,
Quod retinere nequit; cui non licet, ut sit avarus,
Cogitur, ut largus; trahitur dare dextera, dando
Penitet et sequitur redeunti munera voto.

Cap. 14 De sobrietate alborum monachorum

Hec indignatus et abhorrens omnia secum:
380 "O sancta, o felix, albis galeata cucullis,[13]
Libera paupertas, nudo ieiunia pastu
Tracta diu solvens nec corruptura palatum
Mollicie mense: Bachus convivia nullo
Murmure conturbat nec sacra cubilia mentis
385 Inquinat adventu, stomacho languente ministrat
Solempnes epulas ventris gravis hospita Thetis
Et paleis armata Ceres; si tercia mense
Copia succedat, truncantur oluscula, quorum
Offendit macies oculos pacemque meretur
390 Deterretque famem pallenti sobria cultu.

Cap. 15 De sobrietate Fabricii et Baccidis

Hec sunt, Fabricius que legit, oluscula, quorum
Asperitas modico sale fracta et simplice limpha,
Rustica non novit molli mansuescere cultu.
Consulis hee dulces epule lautique paratus,
395 Quasque probat Natura, dapes. o terque quaterque

65 tuous detail of the feast. But since he cannot possibly deal with the entire
meal, his greed is suspended, uncertain whether to pounce on this dish
or that, but lusting equally for both.

Ch. 13 His condition after he has had enough

When the belly has had enough, and no cranny remains empty,
when gluttony has reluctantly drawn back from its meal, still chewing
70 and rechewing what the surfeited gullet is compelled to reject, while the
exhausted jaws beg for a respite from their now feeble grinding, since no
means of consuming more presents itself; when the massive accumu-
lation of food demands a corresponding effort from the glutton to keep
the feast from pouring forth again; then at last his hand is compelled to
75 become generous; sated with feasting, he shares whatever is left with his
fellow feasters. What one is incapable of retaining must be given over;
he who can no longer be greedy must perforce become generous. But
though his hand is coerced into giving, the gesture pains him, and he
follows each gift with a prayer for its return.

Ch. 14 The sober life of the White Monks

80 Angered and revolted by it all, Architrenius cries out: "How blessed,
how happy and free is that poverty, helmeted by the white cowl,[13]
which breaks its long-protracted fasts with simple food and never fills its
mouth with the corrupting delicacies of the feast. Bacchus does not
disrupt their communal meals with noise, nor by his intrusion pollute
85 the sacred chambers of the mind. When the stomach grows weak with
hunger, Thetis, stern housekeeper, and coarsely clad Ceres provide
sober meals. If a third course follows, it is a head of cabbage, the spare
90 austerity of whose pale covering offends the eye, but keeps hunger at
bay and achieves an inner peace.

Ch. 15 The sobriety of Fabricius and Baucis

"These are the simple foods that Fabricius preferred, country food
whose coarseness, tempered by a pinch of salt and fresh water, was not
of a kind to be subjected to delicate preparation. Such were the rich
meals and sumptuous banquets of a consul, feasts such as Nature
95 herself commends.

Baccida felicem sociumque Philemona lecti
Pauperis et mense, cuius pes tercius impar
Equa subinducta tenuit mensalia testa.
Ille beatorum cene modus, illa beata
400 Mensa viris optanda fuit, quam larga profudit
Fecundo Natura sinu mundoque paravit,
Ingenio contenta suo, non indiga victus
Artifices quesisse manus, sollercior artes
Respuit humanas; preciosa Philemonis illa
405 Fercula, que Baccis studio tractavit anili.

Cap 16 De mensa Baccidis

Panis triticea de messe siligine mixta,
Quam volvente manu mola rustica fregit, et illum
Baccis sub tepida coxit studiosa favilla,
Detersitque sinu, digitoque abrasit adusti
410 Corticis extremam, quam pruna momorderat, horam.
Pro vino miscentur aque, quas putris avene
Corrupteque solo turbatas pulvere primum
Coxerat et lutea mox fermentaverat olla.
Addit olus, quod item cum ruris edulibus herbis
415 Legerat et calidis rigidum defregerat undis
Imbueratque bovis, riguo quam paverat orto,
Lacte novo, pinguique suis condiverat osse.
Caseus accedit vetus et, quem fiscina nuper
Miserat, et sinum qui nondum liquerat infans
420 Et tener et tepidi servans cunabula sini
Et qui flere gena nondum desueverat uda.
Additur agresti contractum lance butirum
Quodque superducto solidi curvamine lactis
Continuoque sinu clausit sollercia maior
425 Seduliorque manus rurisque urbanior usus.
Dulcia succedunt nivei libamina lactis
Idque, quod extorta solide pinguedine masse
Exeso macies vultu viridavit, et illud,
Tempore quod tracto solidatum reddit aceto
430 Rustica cognatum. quid plura? beacior omni
Dlvite pauper anus lactis genus omne ministrat.
Addit apis quas fudit opes, ancilla potentis
Sedula Nature, dat mella, et coniuga cere,

"How manifold were the blessings of Baucis and Philemon, companion of her bed and of that poor table whose uneven third leg was kept steady by a tile slipped beneath the board. Such are the feastings of the saints; such blessed meals are what men long for, meals which generous Nature pours forth from her fertile womb and offers to all the world. Content with her own native skill, she requires no artful preparation for the food she provides; her resourcefulness disdains mere human art. Precious indeed, then, are those dishes which Baucis, with an old woman's care, prepared for Philemon.

Ch. 16 Baucis' cuisine

"Her bread was made from the flour of ripe wheat which a rude millstone, turned by hand, had ground. She baked it slowly, under a low flame, wiped the loaf on her apron and rubbed off with her finger a charred edge of crust which the coals had nipped. In place of wine there was water, clouded only by the dust of dry and decayed oats, which she had first boiled and then fermented in an earthen jug. There was cabbage, too, which she had picked along with the edible herbs of the countryside; she had softened it in warm water, then steeped it in the fresh milk of the cow she had fed from her well-watered garden, adding the fatty bone of a sow for flavoring.

"Aged cheese was provided; and cheese newly emerged from the basket; infant cheese which had not yet forsaken this place of nurture; and cheese so new and soft that it was still confined to the cradle of the cool vat, and had not yet learned to make its cheeks damp with weeping. There was also butter, piled on a rough dish; first drawn out as a twisted lump of congealed milk, it was then quickly enclosed in a mold; such are the resourcefulness, the assiduity, the more than urbane practicality of country folk.

"Sweet libations of snow-white milk come next, and also milk to which the thinness of its pinched face gives a greenish pall, after the rich fatty mass has been churned away, and milk which, as it congeals over the course of time, the countrywoman turns into something close to vinegar. Why should I say more? The poor old woman, more blessed than any rich man, serves milk of every kind.

"She adds those riches which the bee produces, that eager handmaid of powerful Nature: she offers honey still united with its wax casing, and

Et viduo iam passa favi divorcia lecto;
435 Ovaque largitur tepidis admota favillis
Et versata diu – partim submollia pruna
Parcius urenti, partim solidata favilla
Acrius ignita – digito que morsa superne
Corticibus ruptis iterantis pollicis ira
440 Sordescente salis lapidosi fragmine Baccis
Sparserat et tandem festuce fixa rigentis
Cuspide premorsa, lauti ieiuna paratus,
Sponso non alio luxu placitura propinat.
Mille modos cultus recipit tractabilis ovi
445 Mollicies, sed eos – uno contenta – cucullis
Parca voluptatis senio vergente reliquit.
    Poma dat, et mellis et aceti proxima, poma,
Quorum verna genis prime lanugo iuvente
Texitur, et poma, que filia ruga senecte
450 Exarat, intorta senio nodante cicatrix,
Utraque corticibus tunicata: nec ille nec illa
Cesilis ingenio ferri devellit amictum.
Ultima tornato pomi devellere giro,
Non fortuna case, non ruris curia novit.
455   Dat pira, dat tenero corna inflammata rubore,
Dat ficus, dat pruna, rose que purpura velat,
Et, que pallidior blando crocus induit auro,
Et, quibus exterius ferruginis enatat umbra,
Et, que nature studio mixtura colorum
460 Gracior et dulcis oculo discordia pingit.
    Nux datur, et nemorum que dumos incolit, et nux
Puniceo nuclei peplo generosior et nux
Nobilior gustu, quam gessit amygdalus, et nux
Exteriore toga pallentibus ebria succis
465 Mansuramque diu digitis factura lituram.
    Has inopis mense dat opes et cetera – pleno
Cetera si qua dedit orti sacra Copia cornu –
Liberiore manu Baccis dedit omnia, si quo
Plenior arrisit autumpni gracia mense
470 Tempore, nam multis opibus Natura parandis
Tempora multa parat et rerum temperat usus
Tempore non uno, variat successio tractu
Successus vario, nec sic parit ista, quod illa
Nil veniat paritura dies, felicia reddit

honey that has already been divorced from the now barren bedchamber of the comb.

35   "She offers eggs that have been placed close to a warm fire and turned for a long time, eggs that are partly soft within, where the coals have scorched them lightly, and partly hard, where the heat has been more intense. When the top has been broken by a finger, and the shell
40 torn off by a ceaselessly aggressive thumb, Baucis sprinkles it with a bit of rough salt, and then, having impaled it on a stiff straw in lieu of a serving dish, and taken a preliminary bite, she offers it to her spouse, whom no delicacy could better please. The soft and adaptable egg lends
45 itself to a thousand kinds of preparation, but the old woman, having contented herself with one, leaves the rest in their shells, grown frugal in her pleasure with the onset of age.

          "She brings fruits whose taste is close to both honey and vinegar, fruits whose cheeks are covered with the fresh down of youth, and
50 fruits furrowed with wrinkles, daughters of time, the twisting scars of gnarled old age. Each fruit is still clad in its rind, and neither he nor she plucks away this garment by the artful use of a sharp knife. To divest a fruit of its outer covering in a single twisting spiral is not a cottager's lot; the rural courtier has no such arts.

55   "She offers pears, cornel-cherries flushed with a delicate red, and figs. She brings plums, some clad in rosy purple; some imbued with a yellow more delicate than white gold; some over whose surface float shadows of rusty red; and some which Nature in her zeal has painted with a
60 variety of colors, a charming discord pleasing to the eye.

          "Those nuts are served which are found in woodland thickets; those whose high birth is attested by the purple cloak of the kernel; those, nobler in taste, which the almond tree bears; those whose outer cloak is
65 a drunken red, and whose pale juice will leave a long-lasting stain on the fingers.

          "All these things, the riches of a poor man's table, she offered, and if the bounteous horn of divine Abundance bestowed other things on her garden, or if the harvest season graced her table more bountifully than
70 usual, Baucis would generously offer these fruits as well. For Nature, in disposing her many rich gifts, disposes many seasons as well, to ensure that all her resources are not deployed at any one time. The changing year produces changing results. No single time of year produces so much that another time produces nothing at all. The benevolence of the

475   Tempora distincto superum clemencia cultu.
    O Deus, humanis circumspice, frena palato
    Pone modumque cibo, mundum Lascivia maior
    Exeat, haut alio dispenset Copia cornu.
    Parcius effusam tractet Moderancia mensam
480   Admissusque pati venter doceatur habenam.''

Cap. 17 Quod Architrenius Parisius venit

    Hec fatus lacrimas non ultra continet, illo
    Devenisse dolet, alio festinat. eunti
    Exoritur tandem locus: altera regia Phebi,
    Parisius, Cirrea viris, Crisea[14] metallis,
485   Greca libris, Inda studiis, Romana poetis,
    Attica philosophis, mundi rosa, balsamus orbis,
    Sidonis ornatu, sua mensis et sua potu,
    Dives agris, fecunda mero, mansueta colonis,
    Messe ferax, inoperta rubis, nemorosa racemis,
490   Plena feris, piscosa lacu, volucrosa fluentis,
    Munda domo, fortis domino, pia regibus, aura
    Dulcis, amena situ, bona quolibet:[15] omne venustum,
    Omne bonum, si sola bonis Fortuna faveret!

75 gods blesses each season with its own occupation.

"Oh God, look down on humankind: set a curb on appetite, a limit on consumption. Free the world of this vast excess, and let Nature's cornucopia be our only source. Let Moderation govern feats more 80 frugally disposed, and may the belly grow submissive and be schooled in restraint."

Ch. 17 Architrenius arrives in Paris

Having spoken thus, he restrains his tears no longer, grieving that he should have encountered all this, and making haste to leave. At length a place appears before him: Paris, the second palace of Phoebus, Apollo-85 nian in its citizenry, Chrysaean[14] in its wealth, a Greece in its libraries, an India in its schools, a Rome for poets, an Attica for philosophers; the flower of the world, balm of creation, a Sidon in its splendor, its feasts and its drinking. The land is ideal for farming, its soil rich, its vineyards productive, its harvests abundant, yet still covered with copses and 90 shaded by groves; game is plentiful, the lakes are full of fish, many birds haunt the streams. Its houses are handsome, its barons bold, its rulers godly, its air fresh, its situation delightful;[15] it is ideal in every respect, endowed with every grace, every good – if only Fortune favored the deserving!

Liber Tertius

Cap. 1 De miseria scolarium

At diis paulo minor plebes Phebea secundos
Vix metit eventus, quicquid serat, undique tortis
Vapulat adversis. gemit Architrenius agmen
Palladis a miseris vix respirare, beatos
5 Pectore philosophos, Fato pulsante, flagello
Asperiore premi, nulla virtute favori
Divitis annecti, studio sudante malorum
Continuare dies, senium prohibentibus annis
Precipitare malis, pubisque urgere senecte
10 Dampna rudimentis, dum vite abrumpit egestas
Gaudia, dum tenuem victum Fortuna ministrat
Ad modicum torpente manu. ruit omnis in illos
Omnibus adversis: vacui furit aspera ventris
Incola longa fames, forme populatur honorem
15 Exhauritque genas; macies pallore remittit,
Quam dederat Natura, nivem, ferrugine texit
Liventes oculos, facula splendoris adustam
Extinguit faciem; marcent excussa genarum
Lilia labrorumque rose, collique pruina
20 Deicitur livore luti; mestissima vultu
Mortis imago sedet; neglecto pectinis usu
Cesaries surgit, confusio crinis in altum
Devia turbat iter, digito non tersa colenti
Pulverulenta riget, secum luctamine crinis
25 Dimicat alterno; non hec discordia paci
Redditur, intortum digito solvente capillum.

Cap. 2 Quod egestas a corpore cultum amoveat petulantem

Non coluisse comam studio delectat arantis
Pectinis, errantique viam monstrasse capillo.

Book Three

Ch. 1 The wretched life of the scholar

But this people, though all but gods in their Phoebean wisdom, reap little reward; the seed they sow is blown about by hostile whirlwinds. Architrenius weeps to behold the ranks of Pallas all but exhausted by their misfortunes. Philosophers blessed with wisdom are beaten down by the cruel lash of unrelenting Fate. For all their great merit, they obtain no favor from the wealthy. Their very zeal for study prolongs their days of misfortune, hastens the onset of old age despite their years, and drives them to abandon their youth to this early schooling in age. For poverty deprives them of the joys of life, and Fortune's listless hand provides only a bare sustenance.

Evils rush upon them from every quarter. The empty belly is end-lessly infested by raging hunger, all grace of body is laid waste and the face grows lean. Hunger substitutes its pallor for the snowy white which Nature had bestowed, and traces lines of rust on the inflamed eyes; every spark of brightness is extinguished in the seared face; the blighted lilies of the cheeks and the roses of the lips grow withered, the whiteness of the neck is defiled by spots of dirt, and the face assumes the ghastly appearance of death.

Since the task of the comb has been abandoned, the hair bristles; random confusion makes it stray into an upward path. Untouched by any grooming hand it grows stiff with dirt; the locks struggle in battle among themselves, and the discord is not reduced to peace by the fingers that might unsnarl the tangled hair.

Ch. 2 How poverty does away with artful grooming

Poverty takes no pleasure in tilling the hair by applying the furrow-ing comb, and so defining a path for the straying locks. When a poor

Languenti stomacho nitidi non sentit egestas
30 Cultus delicias, dissuada libidinis odit
Pectinis arte coli, forme contenta venusto,
Quod Natura dedit. maior depellere pugnat
Sollicitudo famem, graviorem gentis Erinim,
Que, Thetin[1] ore bibens, animo bibit ebria Phebum.

Cap. 3 De tenuitate vestitus

35 Quem scopulum mentis – scopulo quid durius? – illa
Horrida non flectat logicorum turba? rigorem
Quis non excuciat et toto pectore dulces
Derivet lacrimas, quociens occurrit honesta
Philosophi fortuna minor? defringitur evo,
40 Qua latitat, vestis; etatis fimbria longe
Est, non artificis; ipsa est, que abrumpit amictum
Portandique labor, quodque omnibus unus adesse
Cogitur obsequiis, varios dampnatus ad usus.
Respirasse dies nullo sudore meretur,
45 Quem dederint noctes, venti suspirat ad ictus:
Litigat ad Boree flatus, assibilat Euris
Mollibus et Zephiri clementes ridet ad auras
Lecior, et madidis eadem lacrimatur ab Austris
Penula, tot lassata malis, propiusque senecte
50 Forcipe tonsa pilos; aut si qua est gloria cultus,
Exit ad aspectum, veris pretexitur umbra
Intima vestis hyemps, ledit minus abdita claustro
Divite paupertas, oculos deludit amictus,
Dum tenui Cresum prescribit imagine Codrus.

Cap. 4 De indigencia rerum familiarium et cibi maxime

55 Parva domus, res ipsa minor! contraxit utrumque
Immensus tractusque diu sub Pallade fervor
Et logices iocundus amor, tenuisque laboris
Emeriti merces et quod de more sophistas
– Miror qua invidia Fati – comitatur Egestas.
60 Pauperies est tota domus. desuevit ad illos
Ubertas venisse lares, nec visitat egrum
Copia Parnasum, sublimior advolat aulas,

30   man is faint with hunger he does not know the delights of being neatly groomed; one who feels no inclination to pleasure repudiates the hairdresser's art, content with that bodily grace which Nature provides. His graver concern is with the struggle to fend off hunger, the besetting Fury of all those whose lips taste Thetis,[1] while their minds grow drunk on the arts of Phoebus.

Ch. 3 Their threadbare clothes

35   Are there minds of such rocklike hardness (and what is harder than rock?) that the plight of this shaggy horde of logicians would not sway them? Who would not abandon severity and open his heart in floods of tender weeping at the spectacle of the philosopher's ignominious fortune?

o   The cloak in which he covers himself is ravaged by time. Its fringe is more the work of age than of craft. This it is that has torn the garment, this and the labor of enduring all the duties this one garment is compelled to perform. Condemned as it is to such a variety of uses, it can

5   never gain a day of rest by any amount of effort. This same cloak sighs at the buffetings of the wind which the night brings with it, and protests at the blasts of Boreas; whispers gently in the soft eastern breezes, smiles happily at the touch of Zephyrus' gentle breath, and is reduced to tears by the rainy wind from the south. Assailed by so many ills, its threads

10   are too soon sundered by the shears of old age, and if any trace of style remains, it is all on the surface: the wintry chill within is veiled by the springlike appearance of the garment. Poverty is less painful when concealed in a rich enclosure: so long as the garment deceives the eye, a Codrus may outwardly proclaim himself a Croesus.

Ch. 4 The lack of household goods, especially food

5   The house is modest, the furnishings still more so. Both have been reduced by vast and long-protracted effort in the service of Pallas, by the sweet love of logic; for the reward of such worthy work is meager, and Poverty, through some malicious quirk of Fate, is the long- standing

o   companion of the man of learning. The house is utterly impoverished: Plenty is unused to enter these chambers. Abundance does not visit a stricken Parnassus, but flies on lofty wing to the court, ignoring such

Hiis ignota casis, ubi pauca annosa supellex,
Languida sordet anus, admoto murmurat igni
65 Urceolus, quo pisa natat, quo cepe vagatur,
Quo faba, quo porrus capiti tormenta minantur,
Quo rigidum pallescit olus, quo fercula festo
Atriplices libanda die, quo vilior orti
Ieiunam expectat quevis farrago Minervam.
70   Hic unde assiduo conflictu litigat unda,
Hic coxisse dapes est condivisse. libido
Mense nulla venit, nisi quod sale sparsa rigorem
Esca parum flectit. solo fit amicior usu
Cenula, luctanti minus obluctata palato.
75 Maior in angustis si accedit copia, mense
Gloria solempnis, aries truncatur et olle
Maiorique minor unde mandatur, ut uncte
Asperitas mansuescat aque, mox carnibus esis
Suppleat hausta cibum, panemque absorbeat atrum,
80 Ardua dum pleno superet structura catino.

Cap. 5 De vilitate serviencium

Nudus in annoso tunice squalore ministrat
Geta[2] dapes, dum vile meri libamen in urbe
Birria[2] venatur, precio vestitus eodem,
Muricis eiusdem, luteus, macer, horridus, ore
85 Languidus exangui, plumarum squameus hirtam
Agmine cesariem, festuce extantis in altum
Cuspide cristatus. crinis silva intima denso
Pulvere pressa iacet, sed et hiis peiora latere
Suspicor, attritum digito scrutante capillum,
90 Nescioquid facilem dum sepe adducit ad unguem.

Cap. 6 De cubilibus

Sobria post mense tenuis convivia – frenum
Suscipiente gula, saciem quod prevenit ante
Dimidiasse famem – scabra farragine strati
Contrahitur macies, quo vix depressior infra
95 Area descendit, ut ferrea pene iacentem
Proxima frangat humus. illic pugil improbus heres
Sudat Aristotilis, oculum mordente lucerna;
Dum pallens studio et marcens oleo ardet, utroque

houses as this, where a feeble old serving-woman sits in squalor amid a
few ancient furnishings, and a little pot murmurs at being set so close to
65 the fire. Within, a few peas swim, and an onion wanders; while beans
and leeks threaten violence, a stiff cabbage leaf grows soft and pale. A
few herbs may be added as a special gesture on feast days, but it is the
70 humblest sort of vegetable stew that awaits starving Minerva. In such
circumstances, when the very water seethes with hostility, to prepare a
meal is to render it barely edible. No pleasure attends the meal, unless
when a pinch of salt makes the food give up a little of its harshness. Only
through habit does such a paltry meal become agreeable, or at least less
intolerable, to the embattled palate.
75   If an increase in resources should occur in these narrow circumstances, a small sheep is slaughtered to grace the great occasion, and
entrusted to the pot with a greater amount of water, so that the water's
brackishness may be softened by its fat and then sopped up with black
80 bread as an extra course, after the meat has been eaten, when all that
survives from the full platter is the gaunt skeleton.

Ch. 5 The low condition of the servants

Geta,[2] all but naked in the ancient squalor of his shirt, serves the
banquet, while Birria[2] hunts up a measure of cheap wine in town, clad
in robes of equal value and of the same splendid color; he is dirty, lean,
85 unkempt, his face dull and pallid, his scabrous head bristling with an
array of plumage, a crest of straw standing stiffly upright. The dense
forest of hair is covered over with thick dirt, but I suspect, from the
finger that scratches at the sparse scalp, that worse things lurk within,
90 since the deft fingernail readily draws forth I know not what.

Ch. 6 The scholar's bed

After the sober cheer of the meager feast, when the appetite has been
curbed in a way which forestalls satiety before hunger has been cut by
half, the thin pallet is burdened by the weight of a meal of coarse stew,
95 that pallet than which the floor itself is scarcely lower, so that the
ground, as hard as iron, almost breaks one's bones. Here the embattled
bastard heir of Aristotle toils, while the lamp devours his eyesight. Pale
from study, his eyes made weary by the light of the oil lamp, he is yet
eager for both; weary as he is, and with eyes and mind in need of sleep,

Languidus, insompnis et ocello et pectore, noctes
100   Extrahit alterutro vigiles, oculusque lucerne
Pervigil et lippit et lippum torquet ocellum.

Cap. 7 De nocturno studio

Imprimit ergo libris oculi mentisque lucernam,
Et libro et cubito dextreque innixus et auri,
Quid nova, quid veterum peperit cautela, revolvit.
105   Omnia, Castaliis pede que sudaverat antris
Pegasus, exhaurit oculis et mente fluenta:
Nunc oculo, nunc mente bibens, nunc haurit utroque,
Illo plus illaque minus; nunc lecta camino
Decoquit ingenii, memorique in pectore nodo
110   Pressius astringit; nunc delibata reducto
Preterit affectu non invitancia pectus,
Deliciosa minus alteque in scrinia mentis
Digna venire parum; nunc, que minus ardua parcunt
Reptanti ingenio, facilis transcurrit aperta
115   Planicie clivi; nunc, quod nodosius obstat
Ingeniumque tenet, ne tollat in altius alas,
Instanti rodit studio, conamine toto
Pectoris exertus, pronisque ignescit ocellis
Immergitque caput gremio, longumque volutat
120   Precipites reserasse vias, cursumque negantes
Oppositas fregisse fores, oculumque reducit
Sepius ad librum digitique et mentis acumen,
Inque diem limat tenebras. decrescit ocelli
Angulus in rugam, reliquam ferit obvia silvam
125   Silva supercilii, vario frons ignea sulco
Monticulosa cohit, studio crispatus in altum
Contrahitur nasus, anime luctamen hanelum
Pressa labella iuvant. sese procedere toto
Dimicat, obicibus ruptis suspiria tractim
130   Proicit et gemitus efflat, vultumque cruentat
Ignibus, ambustis oculis, totusque furore
Effluit, ingenii tandem studiique ruenti
Fulmine cogit iter et liber in ardua figit
Intuitum, totumque iubet sibi cedere celum,
135   Immensumque probat, quo mundus clauditur, orbem,
Si, quod nulla ligat mete orbita, dicitur orbis.

100 he imposes nocturnal vigils on each of them, until the eye of the watchful lamp becomes blurred, and strains his own blurred vision.

Ch. 7 His nights of study

Thus he applies the light of eye and mind to his books, attaches his elbow to the page and his hand to his ear, and ponders what the wisdom
05 of modern and ancient times has produced. He gulps with eyes and mind all those streams that the foot of Pegasus caused to issue forth from the Castalian cave, drinking now with the eye, now the mind, now both together, yet more with the former than the latter. Now he boils down what he has read in the furnace of thought, and consigns it,
10 securely bound, to the vault of memory; now he passes over things which, having been skimmed less attentively, did not delight or engage him, and so were not deemed worthy to enter the storehouse of the mind. At one moment he glides smoothly along on open and level ground which asks little of the mind as it creeps ahead. At another he
15 gnaws in intense concentration at a knotty passage which resists his efforts and ensnares the understanding that seeks to spread its wings. He exerts the utmost power of his mind, until his eyes grow inflamed with concentration, then buries his head in his arms and ponders at
20 length how to clear the steep path and break open the hostile doors that deny him access. Repeatedly he returns his eye to the page, with finger and mind pointing the way, and strives until dawn to clear away the shadows. The corner of his eye becomes wrinkled; one bushy eyebrow
25 strikes against the other; his burning, furrowed brow contracts into a series of ridges; the bridge of his nose, wrinkled by concentration, contracts; and pursed lips express the effort of the panting mind. He
30 strives to advance with his whole being, pours forth long-drawn sighs and groans as the barriers are broken, brings the hot blood to his face, and puts forth his uttermost effort, while his eyes blaze in frenzy.

At last the swift thrusts of insight and knowledge force a way and he is free to survey the steep path he has climbed. Now he bids the heavens
35 yield to him, and explores the vast sphere by which the universe is enclosed – if that which no circling path can encompass may properly be called a sphere.

Cap. 8 De singularium arcium liberalium capitulis paucis

Ethera directe cernit, contraque reniti
Quamlibet oblique stellam, solisque rotari
Orbe paralello, que sidera fixa vocavit
140 Segnior occursus. aperit, que forma, quis ordo,
Que natura latens, que vis distorqueat axes
Sideris errantis; fixis que musica cursus
Vincla[3] paralellent, eadem que perficit etas
Annosusque dies et in ordine firmat eodem,
145 Qui situs est idem; nunc mente et pulvere circos
Lineat et speras et, quod quadrangulus orbem
Quadruplet, evolvit, laterum qui ductibus exit
Et quibus hoc cingit mediumque hoc dividit orbem,
Quodque orbem spere maiorem quadruplet eius
150 Curva superficies, stupide sollercia menti
Nobilior monstrat; nunc elimasse laborat
Pressius Euclidis numeros cogitque, quod esse
Linea non possit numeri divisa secundum
Extrema et medium, quodque est asimetra coste
155 In duo quadratum partita diametrus aut est
Par impar numerus;[4] nunc ad miracula limam
Rethorice flectit reserans, qua molliit Orpheus
Rethore dura cheli, quanto facundia lingue
Robore Treicii defregit roboris agmen,
160 Qui fit, ut hanc vite populus fastidiat auram
Seque sibi mortis pugilem spontaneus armet
Et rupto gladium fatalem sorbeat alvo,
Dum nocuas in luce moras mundique retractat
Begesias luctus, contempnendumque perorat
165 Hoc Lachesis munus et apertum pestibus orbem,
Penarum pelagus, scelerum mare, cladis abyssum,
Fetoris puteum, viciorum sorde palustrem;[5]
Nunc, quo vera latent scrutatus scrinia,[6] cecis
A latebris vellit, quid verum semper idemque
170 Semper erit falsum, nec corpus corpore plures
Tenditur in partes, nec harena maius harenam
Partibus excedit; nunc pessum figit acumen
Grammatice cunis[7] et vocum circuit apta
Federa, mensus ubi geminum constructio rectum

Ch. 8 A few themes of each of the Liberal Arts

He observes that the etherial sphere moves in a direct path, and that the planets move obliquely in an opposite direction; that those stars which an imperfect understanding has termed "fixed" are borne in an orbit parallel to that of the sun. He discovers what form, what order, what underlying natural principle or force diverts the orbit of a "wandering" planet, and what musical bonds[3] ensure the parallel courses of fixed stars – laws which a power unchanging through time, a day embracing all the years, has ordained, a power that is itself unmoved, and maintains all things in an unchanging order.

Now he draws circles and spheres, in his mind and in the sand, and proves that a rectangle has four times the area of a circle when formed with sides whose lengths correspond to the circumference and the diameter of the circle. Now a heroic feat of concentration reveals to his dazed mind that the surface area of a sphere is four times that of the plane of its circumference. Now he strives to refine more precisely the formulas of Euclid, and proves that a line cannot be divided according to the ratio of extreme and mean; and that the diagonal which divides a rectangle into two equal parts must be incommensurable with the side of the rectangle, or else be at once an even and an uneven number.[4]

Now he scrutinizes the wonders of rhetoric, and discovers how Orpheus' eloquent lyre made harsh things grow soft, by what power the Thracian's charming words caused the oaks to break ranks. He learns how it came to pass that a people grew contemptuous of this life, willingly took up arms to wage deadly war against themselves, and thrust the deadly sword into their own torn bodies; for Hegesias spoke repeatedly to them of the hardships of the world and the perils of lingering in this life, concluding that the gift of Lachesis must be repudiated, that the world is a place of sickness, an ocean of pain, a sea of wickedness, a maelstrom of slaughter, a pit of decay, a foul swamp of vice.[5]

Now he probes to where the annals of truth lie hidden,[6] and plucks forth from the dark shadows both what will always be true and what is always false: that no one body is amplified by more dimensions than any other body; not even one grain of sand can exceed another in this respect.

Now he directs his probing mind to the cradle of grammar,[7] and traces the proper ways of connecting words, studying constructions in which two nominatives are bound together in a transitive relation, just

175 Transicione ligat, sicut contraria recto
    Obliquum racio sine transicione maritat.[8]
        At si quid studium celat caligo, retusam
    Elidens aciem, clivoque relangueat ardens
    Cursus in ascenso, desperantemque relabi
180 Arduitas cogat, id sola mente – vel illa
    Et calamo currente – notat clausumque reservat,
    Crastina quod maior possit reserasse Minerva.
    Et menti et calamo rerum velamina mandat,
    Que develanti possint venisse magistro
185 Mentis in aspectum, cum Phebi auriga fugabit
    Lutea purpureo stellas Aurora flagello.

Cap. 9 De sopore scolaris studio fatigati

        Talibus insudans olei librique lucerna
    Tabidus illanguet, toti nupsisse Minerve
    Sedulus ardet amor, dum strato Phebus ab axe
190 Antipodum surgat et paucis distet ab ortu
    Iam gradibus; tenui tum primum spargit ocellos
    Nube quies sompni, calamumque et cetera laxis
    Instrumenta rapit digitis – declive libello
    Suscipiente capud; sed in illa pace soporis
195 Pacis eget studii labor insopitus et ipso
    Cura vigil sompno: libros operamque ministrat
    Excite sompnus anime, nec prima sopori
    Anxietas cedit, sed, que vigilaverat ante,
    Sollicitudo redit et maior summa laboris
200 Curarum studiis insompnibus obicit ydram.

Cap. 10 De vexacione eiusdem in dormicione per sompnia

        Nulla quies sompnus! nec enim cessura quieti
    Cura soporatur, nec nulla potencia sompni,
    Cum, quod in astrictis rerum perplexio nodis
    Torserat, evolvit; quod non speraverat ante
205 Segnior intuitus vigilantis, multa magistro
    Nox aperit sompno: cum strati corporis extra
    Sarcina dormitet, vigilant in pectore sensus.
        Disputat oppresso strepitu, clausoque tumultu

as a contrary rule joins a word in an oblique case to a nominative without such a transitive link.[8]

But if a cloud should obscure what he seeks to grasp, resisting the dulled keenness of his mind, so that his eager rush up the steep path is
80 slowed, and difficulty makes him fall back in despair, he merely makes a mental note, or perhaps quickly jots it down, but allows to remain closed what tomorrow's greater Wisdom may be able to unfold. In such brief thoughts and jottings, too, he records obscure matters which may
85 become accessible to his mind through the master's exposition, when golden Aurora, Phoebus' charioteer, has put the stars to flight with her purple lash.

Ch. 9 The sleep of a scholar exhausted by study

Toiling at such tasks, by lamplight and by the light of learning, he grows faint with exhaustion, yet burns with eager love to make Minerva wholly his own. Only when Phoebus has arisen from the
90 low-lying Antipodes, and drawn within a few paces of the horizon, does peaceful sleep first spread its gentle mist over his eyes. Now he holds his pen and other tools with slack fingers, while the open book receives the
95 weight of his drooping head. But even in the peace of slumber the unceasing labor of the student finds no peace. Care remains wakeful even in the midst of sleep, and the sleeper's anxious mind is still proposing books and projects to itself. This abiding anxiety never succumbs to sleep; instead the preoccupations that had earlier kept him
100 awake return, and the vast amount of work to be done presents itself like a Hydra of troubles to his restless cogitations.

Ch. 10 The student is troubled by dreams as he sleeps

It is sleep without peace, for care will not let itself be calmed. Yet sleep is not wholly without effect, since it opens up what his earlier perplexity had twisted into tight knots. Night reveals through the tutelage of sleep
105 many things of which the flagging insight of the waking mind had despaired. While the bulk of the sprawling body is outwardly asleep, understanding is awake within. He disputes soundlessly, throws out

Argumenta iacit, tacitoque instancius ore
210 Et digito levam ferienti clamat, utroque
Garrulus immoto; nec numquam lingua loquenti
Temptatam seriem titubanti murmure turbat,
Nec nexu explicito sompno ligat ebria voces
Et sompni meminit cunas infancia[9] lingue.
215   Nec minus et digiti suspecta audacia leve
Surgere conatur, sed deside pressa soporis
Mole retardatur et solum palpitat icto
Aere vel libro, nam libro inversus inheret,
Exanimisque iacet sub mortis imagine, sompno.
220   Sic varia pectus ambage insompnia vexant,
Sollicitumque trahit curarum turba, soporis
Indepasta fame; iamiamque Aurora diei
Nunciat adventum, cum Phebo previus ortum
Lucifer explorat, primumque excerpere rorem
225 Mane novo sudante parat, ne semita Phebi
Polluat uda togam clamidisque elidat honorem.

Cap. 11 De excitacione eiusdem a sompno

Ecce sopor, Phebo vigili cessurus, ocellis
Philosophi cedit, sompno nutantibus astris
Iam vigilante die, stellis citus insilit hospes
230 Hospite mutato; miser ecce excitur ocellus,
Luciferi clamante tuba, dampnoque lucerna
Ardet adhuc, extincta die celique sepulta
Lumine, non oleo summam aspergente papirum
Obsequiove manus vasi revocantis olivum,
235 Post alios pastus se depascente papiro.

Cap. 12 De preparacione eiusdem ad studium profecturi

Excutit ergo capud vultuque assurgit, et ora
Turbidus et crines, digitorum verrit apertam
Pectine cesariem, sompnoque madencia siccat
Summa labella sinu, noctisque laboribus ore
240 Respirante gemit, oculosque in fece natantes
Expedit a nodis cilii texentibus umbram
Extricatque manu, partesque effusus in omnes

arguments in silent excitement, cries out vehemently with silent lips,
10 and strikes his index finger against his palm, running on amid total
silence. Often his tongue, with a faltering murmur, disrupts the intended
order of his speech, and drunkenly assigns words to his sleeping
thoughts in a wholly incoherent way; the mute babbling[9] of the tongue
15 seems to recall the cradle of slumber. So too the censorious boldness of
the index finger struggles to reach the left hand, but is held back,
burdened by the dull weight of sleep, and only taps the air, or the book
(for he still sits slumped over his book in a sleep that is the image of
death).
20   Thus strange apparitions trouble his wandering mind, and a throng
of cares continue to worry him even amid his unsatisfied craving for
sleep. Already Aurora announces the advent of day while Lucifer,
25 Phoebus' precursor, explores the horizon and prepares to sweep away
the dew of the fresh early dawn, lest a wet path stain Phoebus' tunic and
mar the glory of his robe.

Ch. 11 How the scholar is aroused from sleep

Behold sleep, giving way to wakeful Phoebus and withdrawing from
the philosopher's eyes, while the stars nod off to sleep at the awakening
of day, and the sun, like a swift traveller, forsakes his lodging and rushes
30 forth into the heavens. Now a wretched eye is jarred open by Lucifer's
clamorous horn. To his ruin, the lamp still burns, though dimmed and
finally eclipsed by the light of day; since no oil keeps the wick moist (for
no attendant hand has replenished the supply of oil in the bowl), the
35 wick, having consumed this other meal, now feeds on itself.

Ch. 12 The scholar prepares to set out for school

And so he shakes his head and looks around, his face and hair alike
in a state of confusion. He sweeps back his uncovered hair with the
comb of his fingers, dries his lips still moist from sleep, on the edge of his
40 tunic, and groans with a mouth still panting from his night-time labors.
He clears his eyes, still swimming with dross, and with his hand frees
them from the tangled lashes that still keep them in shadow, and while
his gaze moves quickly forth in all directions, he gropes for words

Undique discurrit oculus, dum tempore digna
Nomina deprendat. et, ubi dinovit ad ortum
245 Surgere Solis equos, queritur dispendia sompni
Plus iusto traxisse moras, nimiumque citato
Axe diem raptam, precessurusque magistrum
Precessisse timet et iam pro parte diurna
Intonuisse tuba fontisque secunda propinet
250 Pocula Cirrei, domitos torporibus artus
Increpat et mestos ire indignacio risus
Excutit et tumidos flammato pectore questus
Evomit, in lacrimas tandem vergente querela.

Cap. 13 De amatore qui amice pactus est accessum de nocte

Sic Veneris miles furtivum pactus amate
255 Postibus accessum, cum Luna retorserit ignes
Fratris ad occasum, Veneris minus apta rapinis
Lascivisque dolis, dum nocti infuderit umbram,
Anxius expectat, tandem titubancia sompnus
Lumina furatur dubiisque inserpit ocellis.
260 Quos ubi torporem Venus indignata vigilque
Sompno extorsit Amor, et iam tenet ultima celi
Coniuga Luna solo, sternitque cubilia fessam
Susceptura Thetis, umbramque extendit in ortus
Pressa soror Phebi, rabie crudescit amator,
265 Deside deludi sompno ratus; irrita languet,
Quam facit hora ratam, modicis spes saucia causis.
    Increpat excubiis oculi se credere, iurat
Dampno preterite quod vota fefellerit hore,
Quodque semel lusa numquam pociatur amata
270 Seque suique pudet, Veneris se intrudere castris
Degenerem dampnat; stimulos tamen invenit et spem
Consolatur Amor, et amans ad limen amate
Ocius igne volat rapiturque Cupidinis alis,
Suspiciensque simul terras metitur et astra,
275 Has pedis, hec oculi cursu. quod sole prematur
Signum, quod medium teneat sublimius orbem,
Mens oculusque vident; quantum est de nocte relictum,
Ethere scrutatur et cuncta loquentibus astris.

45 worthy of the hour. Realizing that the Sun's horses are approaching the
horizon, he laments that time spent in sleep has caused him to delay
unduly, that the day has been carried too far in its swift chariot. Eager to
arrive at school before his master, he fears that the other has arrived
already, that he has already sounded the horn for the daily lesson, and
50 is now proffering a second round of Cirrhaean libations. He curses his
body for succumbing to fatigue; indignation evokes a sneer of bitter
anger, and he spews forth the complaints that swell his burning bosom,
lamentations that bring him at last to the point of tears.

Ch. 13 The lover who has arranged to visit his beloved by night

It is thus with the soldier of Venus who has arranged to come in
55 secret to his mistress' door at nightfall, when the Moon casts back her
brother's reflected flames, a time ill-suited to the thefts and wanton
stratagems of Venus: he waits anxiously while she steeps the night in
darkness, but meanwhile sleep steals away his faltering vision and seeps
60 into his wavering eyes. When Venus, indignant at such slothfulness,
and wakeful Love snatch him from slumber, the Moon has already
reached the edge of the sky and is ready to reunite with the earth, and
Thetis has prepared a bed to receive Phoebus' weary sister as she
descends, casting long shadows toward the eastern horizon. Now the
65 lover grows fiercely angry, knowing himself idly mocked by slumber.
That hope which the naming of the hour had made real has proven vain
and futile, blighted by such small setbacks. He curses himself for having
trusted his eyes to keep watch. He declares that his prayers have been
rendered vain by the loss of the hour now past, that his beloved, once
70 deceived, may never be enjoyed. He grows ashamed, and condemns
himself as one unworthy of admission to the camp of Venus.

Yet even now he finds inducements: Love revives hope, and now the
lover flies, swifter than fire, to the beloved's door. Borne along by the
wings of Cupid, he gazes about him, and takes the measure of earth and
75 heaven, the one with his hastening feet, the other with sweeping gaze.
He sees and takes note of which sign is dominated by the sun, which one
has attained the zenith. From the sky and the all-revealing stars he
discovers how much of the night remains.

Cap. 14 De transitu scolaris ad scolam

Non secus et miles Phebi ad loca pacta Minerve
280 Discendique lares properat luctamine toto
Et pedis et mentis, Aurore ad limen eundo
Sepius aspectans, oculisque amplectitur ortus
Et pedibus terras; quantumque Aurora superni
Etheris ignito clamidis succenderit ostro
285 Et quantum a Phebo declinet linea Libre,[10]
Hoc oculis, hoc mente legit, devellit ab illis
Que mora, dum Thetios medius superenatet arcum
Sol, ubi philosophis est ianua prima diei.

Cap. 15 De statu eiusdem in magistri presencia

Ut ventum est, Pallas ubi micior agmina Cirre
290 Armat et est studii mens sudatura palestram,
Suscitat ingenii flammas, conamina mentis
Contrahit, exacuit animam, totusque coacti
Pectoris incumbit oculis, riguaque magistrum
Aure et mente bibit, et verba cadencia prono
295 Promptus utroque levat, oculique et mentis in illo
Fixa vigilque manet acies, aurisque maritat
Pronuba dilectam cupida cum mente Minervam.
Hanc sitit, hanc ardet studii Venus altera, maior
Alter hanelat Amor; totumque impendit acumen
300 Expenditque diem, dum Phebi roscidus orbis
Crescit in occasu, sublataque redditur astris
Flamma suusque dies, cum limina sole fugato
Et noctis reserat et lucis vespera claudit.

Cap. 16 De compassione rerum sevissimarum erga scolares

Hoc studii pondus, hec est congesta malorum
305 Philosophis moles, cui compassura quiescat
Monstrorum rabies: scopulus Scironis[11] amico
Degeneret fletu, veniat clemencia preceps
In Diomedis equos, Busiridis ara cruorem
Compluat humanum lacrimis, curvata recursum
310 Haut Scenis[12] arbor agat, dirumpat vincula carcer

Ch. 14 The scholar's journey to school

In the same way the soldier of Phoebus, exerting feet and mind to the
280 utmost, hastens to the precincts of Minerva, the sanctuary of learning,
continually glancing at the horizon as he proceeds, spanning the
horizon with his eyes, and the earth with his feet. He gauges with his eye
how much of the upper sky Aurora has set aflame with her glowing
285 purple mantle, and with his mind how far the line of Libra[10] has
withdrawn from Phoebus, and thereby determines how long it will be
before the Sun shows forth from amid the swell of Thetis – the starting
point of the philosopher's day.

Ch. 15 His behavior in the presence of the Master

290 Having arrived where gentle Pallas arms Apollo's host, and the mind
prepares to exert itself in the gymnasium of study, he stirs up the fire of
apprehension, musters his powers of mind, sharpens his wits, and gives
himself wholly to the perceptions of his attentive mind. He drinks in the
master's words with open ear and mind, hastily gathering up the words
295 that fall all about him, while eyes and mind remain alertly focused on
the teacher, and the attentive ear performs the marriage of the eager
mind with its beloved Minerva. It is for her that the Venus of study
makes him thirst and yearn, for her that he pants with a desire other
and greater than that of Cupid, devoting to her all his energy and the
300 entire day, until the world grows dewy again at Phoebus' setting, and
the withdrawal of his fires restores to the stars their own proper day,
while Vesper and the departing sun open the portals of darkness and
close those of daylight.

Ch. 16 Some sympathy for scholars and their harsh lot

305 Such are the burdens of study, such the mass of evils heaped upon
the philosopher, that the monsters' roars would fall silent in compassion
with him; Sciron's rocks[11] would dissolve in friendly weeping; kindly
feelings would suddenly seize the horses of Diomede, and the human
blood on the altars of Busiris be washed away by tears; Sinis' bowed
310 trees[12] would recoil no longer; Sulla's dungeons would burst their iron

Ferrea Sillanus, vinctis minus uda Neronis
Parceret ebrietas, Phalaris[13] pietate iuvencus
Mugiat, et pacis sit Cinna et Spartacus hospes.
    Auderent Stygii canis obmutescere fauces,
315 Mutaret Cochitus aquas aliisque maderet
Fletibus et Flegeton clementi aresceret igne.
    Que feritas illis non esset inaspera? talem
Redderet absenti Laberintus Thesea filo,
Sterneret intortos orbes mansueta Caribdis
320 Nec lesura rates, placidum cessante latratu
Scilla susurraret, et libertate profundi
Micior innocuis premeret vada Sirtis[14] harenis.

Cap. 17 Quod sciencia favorem potentum diminuat

    Cedere duriciem scopulis et in obvia flecti
Naturam hiis spero, quibus est immota potentum
325 Pectoris asperior rupes. non subsidet illis,
Quod veri extergunt tenebras rerumque retrusas
Altius effodiunt causas, nec preterit illos
Uncia totius orbis vel, si quid ab orbe
Cedit in immensos tractus, nec sufficit arto
330 Pectore diffusi clausisse volumina mundi,
Quin procul a superis acies admissa nec ullo
Limite fracta volet, surgatque relinquere mundi
Ausa supercilium: nulla hec suffragia Musis
Subsidiique ferunt fomenta, sciencia nullo
335 Robore flectit opes; sed et hec novisse favorem
Divitis elidit et risu morsa sciendi
Gloria lesa iacet, laudisque sciencia dampnum
Ludibriosa dolet, et in aula maius habetur
Ignorasse magis; risu ledente notatur
340 Grandiloquis fame titulis incognita virtus.
    Premia, que Davus[15] recipit, meruisset Homerus!
Ipsa sibi virtus odium parit. aulica rodit
Serra virum mores et laudis eclipticat astrum
Livor et in tenebris ingloria pallet honestas
345 Et virtus titulos, sua mater pignora, perdit.

fetters; Nero would become less sodden in drink and spare his victims; the bull of Phalaris[13] bellow in pity, and Cinna and Spartacus be joined in a bond of peace. The jaws of the Stygian dog would dare to fall silent; Cocytus' waters would reverse their flow and brim with tears of another kind; the plain of Phlegethon would burn with a milder fire.

What savagery would not give over its harshness for their sake? The Labyrinth would release such a Theseus though he had no thread to aid him; Charybdis would grow mild, calm her tormented waters, and cease to destroy ships; Scylla would cease howling and utter peaceful murmurs, and a milder Syrtis,[14] as free of access as the open sea, would heap up harmless shoals around its shallows.

Ch. 17 To possess knowledge is to be less favored by the great

I pray that rocks may lose their hardness, and the course of Nature be altered in favor of these philosophers, toward whom the hearts of the great remain harder still. It gains them nothing that they bring forth truth from darkness, and unearth the deeply hidden causes of things; that not an atom of the entire world eludes them, nor whatever exists withdrawn from the world in the immensity of the heavens. It is not enough to have enclosed within the confines of the breast a voluminous knowledge of the vast universe, or indeed that their soaring vision, unchecked by any obstacle, has gained them access to the realm of higher powers, and rises undaunted to transcend the scornfulness of the world. They gain no favor for the Muses, and no substantial assistance. All their learning has not the power to sway the wealthy; indeed to possess such knowledge is to lose the favor of the rich man. The glory of learning is wounded by mockery and cast down; science, an object of scorn, bemoans its poverty of praise. At court the greater ignorance is considered the more noble. A virtue that is not made known by high-sounding claims to renown is scathingly mocked and censured.

Thus Davus[15] receives the rewards that Homer had deserved. Virtue even brings hatred upon herself, for the sawteeth of the courtier gnaw at men's characters, envy eclipses the star of praise, honor languishes in shadowy ignominy, and mother virtue is deprived of those tributes which are her proper offspring.

Cap. 18 Quod artes a divitibus approbantur saltem in consciencia

Forsitan ad laudes lingue contraria sentit
Pectus et occulto rerum sub iudice Cirres
Exaltatur honos: foris os condempnat et intus
Divitis absolvit melior mens testis, et ore
350 Proditor accusat, animo commendat honestum.
     Non adeo tenebras serit ignorancia, mitre
Et solii morbus, ut tante transeat illos
Prosperitatis odor, lateatque incognitus aule
Sol melior mundi, fallatque altissima tantos
355 Lux oculos, – maiorque dies sidusque lucernam
Preradiat, vincuntque faces fulgore favillas.
     Absit ut hec lateat sceptratos gloria: fusum
Non cohibet lux tanta iubar, quin splendeat aule
Limine; sed que sunt studiis aliena potentum,
360 Sunt et eis famosa parum. diversa professos´
Rarus amor nectit, contempnitur obvia cure
Cura, favorque minor studiis discordibus exit.

Cap. 19 Quare qui artes noverint sint divitibus odiosi

Forsan inaccessis lux hec splendoribus aule
Mollibus occurrit oculis, et lumina lumen
365 Elidunt maiora minus, visusque reflectit
Impetus excursum, tantumque ingloria solem
Aulica celatur acies, carumque putatur
Vile, sed ignotum; laudis iactura beatis
Imminet occultis, bona commendantur operta
370 Parcius, et meritam premit ignorancia famam.
     Forsan et ex illis aliquis laudare veretur,
Quod nescire pudet, vel quo reptasse facultas
Libera nulla datur, dum torpidus illigat artus
Desidie Languor, et segnis in ocia vires
375 Pectoris egrescunt, studiique in mollibus ardor
Stinguitur, et plenis inserpit Inhercia rebus.
     Desidiam cornu mutato Copia fundit,
Ingenii tensum laxat Opulencia nervum.

Ch. 18 That the rich preserve a respect for learning at least in their hearts

Do such minds perhaps harbor thoughts that contradict the praisings of the tongue, and is the honor of Apollo more highly esteemed in their secret determinations? Does the voice outwardly condemn what the inner witness of the rich man's better judgment absolves? Does he
350 betray by his accusation those whom in his heart he considers honorable?

Surely ignorance, the besetting ill of bishops and kings, has not spread such darkness that the philosopher is denied even the scent of prosperity: can the world's true sun remain hidden, unknown to the
355 court? Can so great a light, so bright a day, go unperceived by noble eyes? A star shines brighter than a lamp; the light of a torch surpasses a mere spark.

Far be it that such glory should remain hidden from majesty; so great a light does not so curb its radiance that it may not shine before the
360 throne. But whatever is not at one with the activities of the great is too little esteemed by them. Scant love is bestowed on those who profess different ideals; concerns at odds with their concerns are scorned, and little favor attends divergent pursuits.

Ch. 19 Why those versed in the Arts are hateful to the rich

Does the light of learning perhaps strike the too feeble vision of the
365 court with an unapproachable splendor, so that its greater splendor effaces the lesser? Does its impact cause the gaze of the beholder to recoil, and does the glory of the courtly company appear mean and obscure in respect to such radiance? What is costly is often devalued because unknown. Precious resources are deprived of praise if they
370 remain hidden, concealed goods are sparingly recommended, and ignorance suppresses deserved renown.

But perhaps there are some at court who fear to praise what they are ashamed not to understand, matters in which they have been denied the capacity even to grope their way. Since the dull lethargy of sloth fetters
375 their limbs, and the powers of their sluggish minds have lapsed into idleness, all zeal for learning is extinguished in these effete creatures, and their abundance is infected by inertia. The horn of plenty pours forth mere dissipation, and opulence slackens the taut sinews of intellect.

Forsan et est mentis tumide suspectus in aula
380 Palladis hic miles, ne sit felicibus equo
Altius elatus, faciatque incauta bonorum
Moribus offensam deiuncta superbia Musis.

Cap. 20 De remocione elacionis a philosophis

Forsan id innocuam Cirren accusat. at illam
Insita philosophis absolvit et excipit omnem
385 Mansuetudo notam: pax est cognata Minerve
Et iocunda quies et frenum passa voluntas
Et lacrimis rorans pietas et prona fideles
Amplecti sincera fides et conscia recti
Dulcedo, facilisque bonis clemencia flecti.
390 Non datur exactum fame decus, omne venustum
Creditur elatum, sine limo gloria nulli
Affluit, immeritis aliena superbia culpe est,
Summaque Luciferi Boreis afflata putatur
Nobilitas, virtusque venit suspecta tumoris.
395 Hac macula tanti non delibatur honoris
Integritas, ubi verus honos, ubi cognita Phebo
Maiestas et fervor inest, ubi pocula Musis
Consecrata bibit verus conviva Minerve,
Veraque Cirreum perhibent insignia numen,
400 Commendatque datam mens Phebi conscia laurum.

Cap. 21 Contra superficiales philosophos

At sunt philosophi, qui nudum nomen et umbram
Numinis arripiunt, qui vix libasse Minervam
Exhausisse putant; tenuisque sciencia pectus
Erigit, et properata pudent insignia Musas,
405 Raptaque temporibus nubit – sed adultera – laurus
Hii sunt, qui statue veniunt statueque recedunt,
Et Bachi sapiunt non Phebi pocula, Nise[16]
Agmina non Cirre, Bacho Pheboque ministrant:
Hoc pleni, hoc vacui; puer intrat Delia miles
410 Castra, recessurus dicta sumptaque salute
Et dicto sumptoque 'vale', temereque magistri
Precipitatur honos, rudibus presumptio Musis
Insilit, et primos audacia decipit annos;

80 Perhaps too the court suspects the knight of Pallas of a presuming mind, as though he were excessively vainglorious about his endowments, and his thoughtless and unbridled pride in the Muses were an affront to good morals.

Ch. 20 Philosophers are far removed from vainglory

It may be that such an accusation is brought against unoffending
85 learning, but the inherent mildness of the philosopher absolves her, and protects her from all censure. Peace is Minerva's kinswoman, and happy repose; will submissive to restraint, and pity, brimming with tears; untainted honor, ever ready to embrace honorable men; the sweetness of conscious rectitude, and mercy, readily moved by good-
90 ness. Yet the well deserved honor of reputation is not granted. Every grace is deemed a vanity, and glory comes to no one without some taint. Pride is alien to these blameless men, yet their high nobility is presumed to be puffed up with the winds of Satanic arrogance, and their virtue is presumed to be conceit.
95 But the integrity of their great distinction is not diminished by this taint when it is true distinction, when the dignity and zeal that Phoebus acknowledges are present; when the worthy guest at Minerva's feast drinks from goblets consecrated to the Muses; then true tokens bear
100 witness to the Delian god, and the mind that acknowledges Phoebus' power justifies the awarding of the laurel.

Ch. 21 Against superficial philosophers

But there are philosophers who snatch at the bare name and shadow of this power, who suppose that to have tasted of the cup of Wisdom is to have drained it. A little learning puffs out their chests, and their hastily
105 acquired titles bring shame on the Muses. Stolen laurels lend a false grace to their brows. Such students arrive as mindless as statues and depart in the same state. They drink from Bacchus' cup, not Phoebus', for they are of the company of Nysa[16] rather than Cirrha, and though they serve both gods they are full of the one, untouched by the power of
110 the other. The boy-soldier enters the Delian camp only to depart again when he has given and received a greeting and given and received a farewell. The title of "Master" is hastily thrust upon him, and he presumptuously sallies forth inspired by coarse Muses, deceived by the

Iamque in bella venit imbellis, inhermis in arma.
415   Haut ea sunt fame Zephiris mandanda, nec aule
Hunc ego commendo, nam se maioribus equat
Contempnitque pares indignaturque minores,
Nulli iocundus, gravis omnibus, omnia preceps
Imperiosus agit, et pacis nulla tumoris
420 Fulmen habena premit. modico, quod novit, in astra
Conscendisse ratus, alienum scire labello
Progrediente notat et coniventis ocelli
Invidia mordet et, quod tetigisse veretur,
Laudibus attenuat pressis oculoque susurrat
425 Subridente notam, livoris cuncta veneno
Conspuit, ipse suis avidus laudator in actis,
Et librata diu, sed turgida, verba loquendi
Maiestate trahit et gutture tracta tonanti
Excutit, et linguam digito gestuque loquaci
430 Adiuvat, et vultus animo maiora fatetur.

Cap. 22 De venia divitum ab auctore postulata

At super hiis aule veniam peto, supprimat ire
Impetus excursum, frenoque modestia pacem
Imperet adducto. Cirreas scimus ad aulam
Divertisse deas, totumque infundere Phebum
435 Pluribus, et geminum contingit regia solem.[17]
Criminis unius hos colligit, excipit illos
Linea, paucorumque nota non tangimus omnes:
Hos cum declinet vicium, declinat ad illos.
Hos vel eos tetigisse licet, veniamque peroret
440 Excepisse bonos, redimatque exceptio culpam.

Cap. 23 Que sint cause dandorum redituum

Et tamen admiror, quam dandi ceca potentum
Sit reditus sparsura manus; nam prodiga fundit
Immeritis et avara tenet. cui larga tenetur?
Ad data prona datis, pollutaque munere munus
445 Restituit munusque putat, quod munere vendit.
Expectata bonis rapiunt bona prona cupido
In precium precio, nullique incognitus aule
Ambitus et laterum falerato multus in ore

boldness of youth. Unschooled in armed warfare, he takes up arms and
goes to war.

415   Such things ought not to be consigned to the breezes of rumor. I
cannot recommend this youth to the court, for he equates himself with
his superiors, scorns his equals and utterly disdains his inferiors, is
pleasant to no one, gruff to everyone, acts always in an abrupt and
420 haughty manner, and no restraining gentility curbs the thunder of his
bombast. Convinced that the little he knows has gained him a place
among the stars, he condemns the learning of others with outthrust lip,
while squinting envy gnaws at him. He belittles with faint praise things
425 which he would have feared to attempt, muttering censure while his eye
continues to smile. He sprays all others' work with the venom of his
envy, though eager in praise of his own achievements. With majestic
eloquence he draws forth words, long pondered but still turgid, emitting
them slowly from his sonorous throat, and aiding the tongue with
430 eloquent gestures of the finger, while his expression speaks far more
grandly than his mind.

Ch. 22 The author begs the indulgence of the wealthy

But in speaking of such matters I beg the indulgence of the court:
may it resist the impulse to act in anger, and may restraint, plying the
reins, impose peace. We know well that the Cirrhaean goddesses have
435 visited the court, and that the power of Phoebus has inspired many; the
court has come to acknowledge a double sun.[17] The crime thus defined
includes some and excludes others. In censuring a few we do not seek to
implicate all. The vice avoids some, though it adheres to others, and
though it should happen that this person or that be implicated by it, yet
440 it may claim in its behalf that it has exempted the good; let that
exemption redeem any error.

Ch. 23 The reasons for giving rewards

And yet I wonder at how blindly the hand of the rich man strews its
rewards; for it pours them forth prodigally on the undeserving, and yet
remains avariciously retentive. Toward whom does it show generosity?
Toward those willing to give in return for what they are given, those
445 who, corrupted by gifts, offer gifts in return, and consider gifts what
they buy with gifts.

Thus good men are robbed of their long awaited reward by greed,
ever ready to exchange reward for reward; by ambition, with which no

Tullius et celso cumulus speratus honori
450 Et furtim mitrata Venus, scelerisque minister
Conscius, imperiique metus viteque nocenti
Histrio suspectus et adulte gloria laudis,
Dando non meritis, nimiumque alterna potentum
Gracia, cognatusque movens precordia sanguis,
455 Consimilesque ligans animorum fibula mores,
Impliciteque dolis venundata copia lingue.
    Nec noto, quod sanctum Nature lege propinquis
Astringatur amor, truncique a robore ramus
Robora derivet, surgatque in sanguine sanguis
460 Idem in eodem; ortusque sui Natura memento.
In genus est proclivis amor, maiorque minores
Tollat honos, generisque genus sub sole diescat.
    At – quantum liceat – libeat, tollantque propinqui
Dona propinqua modo, reditusque in parte relinquant
465 Philosophis: unum capiant, qui cuncta merentur!
    Detur; et hoc aule fateatur Pallada munus,
Significentque data solium novisse Minervam,
Et studii quedam consorcia dona loquantur.
Impigra sit dandi meritis manus. infima laus est
470 Cuncta dari, cum nulla bonis; quas sorbet in hora
Histrio[18] dantis opes, logicus delibet in anno.

court is unacquainted; by the Cicero who abounds in the ornate speech
450 of faction; by the treasure given in hope of lofty dignity; by the Venus
who wears the mitre in secret; by the minister who condones wrongdoing; by fear of power; by the actor suspect for his vicious habits; by
the glory of fulsome praise; by gifts to the undeserving; by the too-
455 uncertain favor of the great; by kinship, which stirs the affections, and
unites the souls of men of like character; and by wealth, corrupted by
the wiles of a serpentine tongue.

I do not censure what is sanctioned by Nature's law, the love
contracted between kinsmen. The branch derives its strength from the
460 trunk; the same blood flows in the veins of men of the same stock; let
Nature be mindful of her origins. Love is responsive to the bond of
family. Let the greater glory sustain the lesser, and the descendents bask
in the glorious sun of their ancestry. But though this be granted, insofar
as it is right, let kinsmen carry off only the fruits of kinship. Let them
465 leave some small reward for the philosophers, that they, who deserve
much, may at least receive something.

Let this much be granted: let this gift be the court's tribute to Pallas;
let the giving attest that the court acknowledges Minerva, and the gift
declare some familiarity with study. Let the hand be unwearied in its
470 gifts to the deserving. That all has been given away deserves only a
mean sort of praise if nothing has been given to the virtuous. The
largesse that an actor[18] gulps down in an hour a logician would sip at
for an entire year.

Liber Quartus

Cap. 1 Compassio Architrenii super scolarium egestate

Lilia Castalii veris marcencia Fati
Sub Borea brumante gemit Nisamque negantem
Subsidium Cirre. verum presencia ledunt
Fortius adversa, contra distancia sensum
5 Diminuunt pene, nec compassiva dolendi
Tot stimulos lamenta ferunt et segnius urit
Fax admota minus; igitur meroris in unda
Naufragus inde meat alibi siccandus ocellus.

Cap. 2 De monte Ambicionis

Mons surgente iugo Pelleam despicit urbem,[1]
10 Astra supercilio libans, lunaque minorem
Miratur longe positam decrescere terram.
Sideribus vicinus apex, ut sepe meantem
Ocius offendat, cum cursu est infima, lunam
Augis in opposito,[2] cum visu maxima pessum
15 Vergit in orbe brevi, mediumque aspectibus offert
Quadratura iubar;[3] partem directior omnem
Vix aliqua vergit, facilemque admittere nescit
Arduus ascensum.[4] sola hic latus omne pererrans
Ambicio reptat predilexitque colendum
20 Pro laribus montem, Zephiris ubi succuba Tellus
Veris alumpnat opes passimque intexit amara
Dulcibus: et fruticum nodis armantur olive
Et laurus cristata rubis suspectaque dumis
Quercus et horrenti crudescit coniuga rusco
25 Esculus et rigidis spine vallatur aristis
Astra comis abies superum concivis inumbrans.
Hic, quecumque virum fit gloria crinibus arbor,

Book Four

Ch. 1 Architrenius' compassion for the students' poverty

Architrenius mourns to see the lilies of the Castalian spring withering beneath the wintry blasts of Fate, since Nysa denies sustenance to Cirrha. But it is those misfortunes that are present to us that wound us
5 most severely, and as they become more remote the sense of pain is diminished: compassion and lament cause us less anguish, and as the fire is withdrawn it burns less keenly. So, foundering in a sea of grief, Architrenius departs to dry his eyes elsewhere.

Ch. 2 The Mount of Ambition

From its lofty height a mountain looks scornfully down on the
10 Pellaean city.[1] Its brow touching the stars, it wonders that the earth, lying far below, grows smaller than the moon. So near the stars does it rise that its peak often obstructs the swift-moving moon at the low point
15 of her orbit, the perigee,[2] when, as she moves downward in her brief course, she appears largest, and her quartered surface presents only half of her radiance to the sight.[3] One face of the mountain does not rise more sharply than another, and its steepness affords no easy ascent.[4] Only Ambition creeps about here, roving over every slope, for she has
20 chosen this mountain as her abode.

Here the Earth, offering herself to Zephyr, provides sustenance for the fruits of Spring, and intersperses bitter and sweet at random: olives grow amid dense thickets; the laurel is crowned with thorns, the oak with menacing spines; the winter-oak becomes the rough bride of the
25 bristling broom; and the fir, fellow-citizen of the gods, shading the stars with its boughs, is fortified with stiff clusters of spikes. Whatever tree may serve to adorn the brows of men has a place in the mountain's

Gracia montis habet et, si qua audacius alto
Vertice diis certat; ibi nulla licencia presse
30 Arboris, ut surgat, montique assurgere nano
Crine mirica timet, steriles ibi verberat auras
Infecunda salix, riguisque libencior alnus
Ascendisse vadis, eternaque testis amorum
Populus Oenones,[5] platanusque et, si qua neganti
35 Natura haut recipit partus ingloria fructum.

Cap. 3 De quibusdam montis illius arboribus et floribus

Hic pinus graciles succingitur alta capillos,
Palmaque centennis tardante puerpera fructu,
Et preciosa rogos fumo condire cupressus,
Et meliore libro cinomolgi[6] cinnamus hospes,
40 Et lacrima felix nostre sacra balsamus are,
Et ficus geminis depingens floribus annum,
Et bina nucleum que claudit amygdalus archa,
Et siciens Bachi primevum pessicus imbrem,[7]
Et tunicata croco germanaque coctanus auri,
45 Et rugosa genam producto dactilus evo,
Et pirus,[8] huicque sacrum tituli dat Regulus omen,
Et pirus, hancque vole plenus denominat orbis,
Et pirus, huicque dedit matrina angustia nomen,
Et pirus, Augusto que patrinante vocatur,
50 Et pirus, hec nota est et filiolata Roberto,
Et pirus, est huius alius baptista Iohannes,
Et pirus a quovis precio signata, vel oris
Cena vel aspectus; coit uno quelibet arbor
Ambiciosa sinu, quo picte prodiga forme
55 Rumpitur in vernos montis lascivia risus.
    Gratus ibi livor viole, dulcique rosarum
Flamma cruore natans, terre devinctior auras
Mulcet odore crocus, et notus amantibus hospes
Exequasse nivi presumit lilia Pallor.
60   Floribus egregiis solum pubescit, ut absit
Gloria pauperibus ortis, vilesque ligustra
Ornatura rubos et, que certasse ligustris,
Nigra licet, cogit Zephyrus vaccinia pingens.[9]

favor, and any that is so bold as to challenge the gods with its lofty crest.
30 But low growing trees are not allowed to flourish here; the myrtle with
its tiny leaves is afraid to grow on these slopes. Here the barren willow
sways in the sterile breeze; the alder, which prefers to grow on well-
35 watered banks; the poplar, eternal witness to Oenone's love;[5] the plane,
and all those inglorious trees to which Nature has denied the power to
bear fruit.

Ch. 3 Some trees and flowers that grow on the mountain

Here the tall pine wreathes itself in graceful boughs; here is the palm,
pregnant a hundred years with its slow-growing fruit; the cypress,
prized for steeping the pyre in its scent; the cinnamon, with its even finer
40 bark, home to the cinnamolgos;[6] the balsam, blessed in the tears which
hallow our altars; the fig, which adorns the year with twin flowerings;
the almond, which encloses its kernel in a double coffer; the peach,
45 thirsting for the rain of Bacchus;[7] the quince, jacketed in a yellow that is
almost gold; the date, its skin wrinkled as if by great age. And there are
pears:[8] that on which Regulus conferred the sacred token of his own
title; and that round fruit which is named for the hollow of the palm;
that to which the narrow passage of motherhood gives its name; and
50 that for whose naming Augustus stood as godfather; that which was
acknowledged and christened by Robert; that one whose baptizer was a
second John; and pears distinguished by all sorts of attributes, whether
of taste or of appearance. The ambitious tree generates any and all kinds
55 in its single womb, so that a wanton profusion of bright shapes bursts
forth into the merry springtime of the mountain.

The violet's purple stain adorns this place, and the flaming red of the
rose, swimming in sweet gore; the crocus, kept close to the ground,
sweetens the breeze with its scent; and the lily's pallor, so familiar to
lovers, presumes to rival the whiteness of snow.

60 The mountain produces only unusual flowers. There is no place for
those glories of humble gardens: privet, which beautifies the rough
thorn hedge, and those berries which, black though they are, Zephyrus
compels to compete with the privet.[9]

Cap. 4 De rivulo in eius apice demananti

In planum descendit apex, variusque superne
65 Rivulus exultat, conflictantisque susurrat
Ludus aque, ripasque ioco pulsante lacessit.
Solis unda vacat preciis, haut ulla profundo
Vilis harena sedet lapidumque ignobile vulgus.
   Dicia luxuriant ridentibus ima metallis,
70 Exundatque iubar lapidum generosa propago,
Ut gelidus mixtis delectet in ignibus humor.
   Illic illimes bysso candencius undas
Liliat argentum, partimque argenteus auro
Amnis inauratur, gemmarum turba nitore
75 Auget aque radios, hic iaspidis, hic ametisti
Gloria lascivit, iacincti cerula plaudunt,
Et precium prebet nutricibus unio conchis,
Et fruitur viridis eterno vere smaragdus.

Cap. 5 De incolis eiusdem montis

Hic vaga discurrit, animi gravis incola, numquam
80 Cura soporis amans, Cureque annexa parenti
Anxietas, tacitique Metus et vota Voluntas
Dissimulans et Spes dubio vicina Timori,
Donaque nobilior populis sparsura Cupido
Et sceptri secretus Amor, nimioque vacillans
85 Credulitas voto, soliique occulta casarum
Laudativa Sitis, et honorum sedula plausus
Muneribus pavisse Fames, audaxque favores
Alternos emisse Favor, fameque sititor
Impetus expense, donataque Gracia gratis,
90 Sed reditura datis, vultusque Modestia raro
Gracior arrisu, Gravitasque affabilis oris
Non animi plausura ioco, mansuetaque lingue
Canicies, verbique virum testata Venustas.
   Hic Promissa volant, discursant Dona, Fidesque
95 Pollicitis proclivis adest, dandique Facultas
Libera spargit opes, plenoque Pecunia cornu
Fundit amicicias, emiturque in mutua Nexus
Federa, venalique datis succumbitur aule.
   Hic fictus virtutis Odor, fabricataque vultus

Ch. 4 The stream that descends the mountain

65   The slope descends steeply into a plain, and a winding river leaps
down from above. The play of its turbulent waters creates a murmur as
it dashes with playful force against its banks. The water admits only
precious things: no lowly sand lies at the bottom, or a base throng of
70 pebbles. The rich depths revel in bright metals, and the noble family of
jewels diffuse their brightness, so that the chill waters delight in their
mingled fires.

    Silver, whiter than fine linen, gleams through the clear waters, and
the silvery stream is gilded here and there by gold, while a host of gems
75 enhance the water's radiance with their gleam: the glory of jasper and
amethyst is flaunted here; sapphires display their deep blue; the pearl
gives value to the shell that gives it nurture; and the emerald rejoices in
the green of an eternal spring.

Ch. 5 Those who frequent the mountain

    Care, who infests the troubled mind, and has no love for sleep,
80 wanders restlessly here, and Anxiety, clinging close to Care, her parent;
unspoken Fears, and a Will that keeps its wishes hidden, and Hope that
is close to timid Fear; the Greed that ennobles itself by strewing largesse
among the people; a well-hidden Love of royal power, and the too-high
85 hopes of uncertain Credulity; the Thirst for a throne that conceals itself
in praise of the simple life; Hunger, eager to feed on the gifts of honor
and applause; Favor that boldly seeks to buy the favor of others;
Recklessness, still thirsty for the reputation it has squandered; Good
90 Will, bestowed at no expense, but sure to be repaid with gifts; a Modesty
of demeanor set off by rare smiles; Gravity, pleasant of speech, though
not of thought, in commending another's jest; a well-practiced Vener-
ability of speech; and a Charm in speaking that claims to express the
man.

95   Here Promises flit about, Gifts speed back and forth, while Trust gives
ready credence to assurances; an artful Liberality spreads its riches
about; Money's cornucopia pours forth friendship; Pledges are sold into
mutual bondage, and rendered subject to the dealings of a mercenary

100 Religio, clausoque tumens Elacio vento
   Et recti mendax Species et simia morum
   Ypocrisis neglecta genas, aucepsque favoris
   Eloquium, vernusque rudis Facundia cause
   Flosculus et turpem redimens Sollercia vitam.
105   Hic in amicicias hostem complectitur hostis,
   Blanditur Feritas, Odium favet, Ira salutat,
   Sevicies palpat, Libertas servit, obedit
   Imperium, premitur Maiestas, Gloria languet,
   Cedit apex, omnique via reptatur ad aulam,
110 Omnique Ambicio saltu venatur honores.
   Hic puer imperii cupidus ludebat, alumpnus
   Martis, Alexander, sceptrique infudit amorem
   Ambicio nutrix, totumque armavit in orbem
   Precipites animos, tenerisque induruit annis
115 Bella pati, votumque duos extendit in ortus.

Cap. 6 Quod ex Ambicione bella ortum habuerint

   Primos Ambicio remos et prima furori
   Vela dedit ventosque rudes, Martique volanti
   Cum sole et luna primas innexuit alas.
   In Magni iugulos animavit Cesaris enses
120 Corrupitque fidem soceri, pavitque Philippos
   Sanguine civili, pugnavitque hostibus hostis,
   Et Romana leves iuverunt prelia Parthos,
   Instantesque fuga supplerunt pila sarissas.
   Hac duce sunt Lacii totum diffusa per orbem
125 Vulnera: Penorum subsedit gloria Rome
   Fulminea pulsante manu bibuloque cruoris
   Hannibal ense furor, mundumque doloribus emit
   Cesareumque iugum Rome defessa iuventus
   Ambicionis acu, gaudensque laboribus omnes
   Indolis extorsit titulos, fuditque furore
130 Martis et Herculeo nitentem sanguine Pirrum.

Cap. 7 In quo genere hominum Ambicio conversetur

   Hinc hommum tortrix, Allecto maior, Erinis
   Summa, potestates urget violencius, ardor
   Arduus, Ambicio, soliteque accendere corda

court. Here are the odor of feigned Virtue; a contrived Religiosity of
manner; Self-Esteem puffed up by a bellyful of wind; the False
Semblance of rectitude; Hypocrisy, aping virtuous behavior un-
blushingly; Eloquence, laying its snares for favor; Glibness, the spring
flower that adorns an awkward appeal; and that Cleverness which
redeems the shameful life. Here enemy embraces enemy in friendship,
Savagery grows mild, Hatred is kind, Wrath is courteous, Cruelty
caresses, Freedom is submissive, Command obeys, Majesty is oppressed,
Glory fades, Authority yields. Ambition creeps toward the court by
every path, and stalks preferment behind every bush.

Here there played a boy, greedy for dominion: Alexander, the ward of
Mars. Ambition, his nurse, instilled the desire to rule, armed his impulsive spirit against all the world, steeled his tender youth to the
hardships of war, and stretched his aspirations to the two horizons.

Ch. 6 How wars originate from Ambition

It was Ambition that first gave oars, sails, and the rough winds to our
madness, and provided the wings that first enabled Mars to fly with the
sun and moon. She drove Caesar's sword against the throat of Pompey,
caused a father-in-law to break faith, and steeped the plain of Philippi in
civil bloodshed. In waging war against Rome's enemies she was herself
an enemy: Roman campaigns were a boon to the swift Parthians,
whose fleeting javelins served them in place of menacing pikes. At
Ambition's urging, Latian blood was shed throughout the world. The
glory of Carthage, Hannibal, and the fury of his bloodthirsty sword
submitted to the thunderously pounding arm of Rome. Driven to
exhaustion by the goad of Ambition, the youth of Rome reduced the
world to the yoke of the Caesars by their sufferings. Rejoicing in their
hardships, they exacted tribute from all as if by natural right, and
destroyed even Pyrrhus, who fought with the fierceness of Mars and of
his ancestor Hercules.

Ch. 7 The sort of men in whom Ambition resides

Then this tormentor of men, this greater Allecto, this arch-Fury
asserts her power still more violently. For Ambition is a lofty passion, a
torch that tends naturally to inflame noble hearts, an intense heat that

135 Nobiliora faces, indignatusque caminus
    Degeneres animos timidosque invadere votis,
    Integrum imperium summamque capessere mundi
    Et diis esse pares superumque instare favori,
    Fortuneque sequi tollentis in ethera dextram.
140   Contentos habitis submissaque pectora spernit
    Et votum, quod serpit humi; nam prodiga voti
    Sperat in immensum nullique indulget habene
    Ambicio, secura modi. spes ardua sola est,
    Que timuisse facit et hanelans summa voluntas
145 Et desiderii sicientis sceptra libido.

Cap. 8 De aula in montis eius vertice constituta

    Huc nova visurus fastigia surgere fessis
    Luctatur pedibus et iam superatur Olimpus
    Tertius, alter Athlas, et adest que sidera dorso
    Culminis aula quatit. contendit in ardua celo
150 Invidiam factura domus, sublimis in altum
    Ad modicum statura volat, transcendit et auras
    Et pacem, quam summa tenent, seque inserit astris
    Sollicitatque deos, iteretne prelia Flegre.
    Haut aliter celestis homo[10] suspecta minanti
155 Arduitate Iovem repetita in fulmina cogit,
    Armatusque manus hominum securus et arces
    Despicit et terre digna scelus expiat ira.
        Tollitur alta solo regum domus aula deumque
    Sedibus audaci se vertice mandat; at umbras
160 Fundamenta premunt, regnisque silentibus instat
    Ultima Tartareos equans structura recessus.
    Radices operis, ne verticis ardua preceps
    Sarcina subsidat, Stygias demittit ad undas.
    Tartareus iam civis homo, Stygis incola, mortis
165 Non expectato laqueo venit, illa supremo
    Vis rapitur fato: mavult precedere liber
    Fatorum quam iussa sequi, iam tramite ceco
    Ad Styga rumpit iter, vivus venisse laborat,
    Quo defunctus eat. descendit ad infima mundi
170 Centro fixa domus medioque innititur axi.
        Explicat aula sinus montemque amplectitur alis[11]
    Multiplici latebra scelerum tersura ruborem,

disdains to infuse mean spirits, or those too timid in their hopes. She
seeks to claim absolute dominion, supreme worldly power, to be equal
to the gods and enjoy the acclaim of divine beings, to follow the hand of
40 Fortune that points the way to the heavens. She scorns those who are
content with their lot, submissive spirits and the prayer that creeps
along the ground. For Ambition squanders prayers, her hopes are vast
and her recklessness accepts no restraint. Nothing causes her anxiety
45 but the loftiness of her own hope, a will that pants to gain the heights,
and the goad of a thirsting desire to rule.

Ch. 8 The court established at the top of the mountain

Architrenius, his feet grown weary, labors to ascend the hill and
behold new heights. At last this third Olympus, this second Atlas is
conquered, and a hall stands before him which strikes the stars with its
50 rooftree. The building thrusts itself to a height so lofty as to breed envy
in heaven, so sublimely high that it seems almost to soar. It transcends
both our atmosphere and the peace which the upper air maintains,
installs itself among the stars, and troubles the gods with fears of a
renewal of the battle of Phlegra. In the same way a sky-born race,[10] the
55 menace of whose great height bred mistrust, once drove Jove to hurl
repeated thunderbolts; but Jove thus armed is proof against the power of
men; he looks down on their towers, and his just wrath expiates the
world's guilt.

This royal dwelling, this hall rises high above the earth, and claims
for its audacious towers a place amid the homes of the gods. But its
60 foundations encroach on the realm of the shades; it is set above the
realms of silence, and its lowest supports are as deep as the depths of
Tartarus. Lest the towering bulk of the roof come crashing down, it
sends down its roots to the very waters of Styx.

For man is even now a citizen of Tartarus, and dwells in Stygian
65 darkness. Hither he comes, seized by the unsuspected snare of death, his
strength taken from him by all-powerful fate. He thinks to pursue
freedom, rather than submit to the bidding of the Fates, but already, in
blind career, he is forcing a path to the Stygian shore: it is his life's labor
to arrive at the place whence he will depart when dead. Thus his house,
70 rooted in the earth's very core, fast bound to the center of things, shows
the way to the lower depths.

The palace contains many chambers, and its corridors spread over

Ipsa loco factura nefas, erroribus umbram
Ceca parat noctisque vices, oculique verendas
175 Decipit excubias, pereuntis sepe pudoris
Celatura notas Venerisque accommoda furtis;
Nam tenebras, qui peccat, amat, latebrisque pudorem
Excusat, noctemque facit velamina culpe.
  Marmor et, attriti quicquid splendore politus
180 Aspectum pavisse potest aut nobile reddit
Et fame commendat opus, preciosa domorum
Materies laudisque venit. fecunda bonorum
Luxuriem largitur humus mundique nefandis
Obsequitur votis, rerum tellure ministra
185 Edificat securus homo; nam terra paratum
Iurat in auxilium, quidvis Natura potentis
Expedit ad nutum: lapides et ligna ligandis
Edibus et, quicquid preciosior exigit usus.
Exibet et gemmas, quarum fulgore diescit
190 Sole suo contenta domus, sed gloria paucas
Hec visura moras, cursum felicibus aufert
Temporis occursus, letis venit obvia fati
Ianua, summa dies, metuenda potentibus hora.

Cap. 9 Exclamacio Architrenii in eos qui opes edificando consumunt

Hoc fatui celum mundi videt inque dolentes
195 Excutitur risus: "Heu que demencia tantis
Erexisse domos studiis, tantosque labores
Perdere, tot census! quod crastina diruat etas,
Instruit instanter labor irritus. ocius ista
Ocia tollantur, ad inania mundus hanelat.
200 Deflectatur iter totusque in seria sudet!
Nam risu aut digito quid dignius? ardua tollit
Cras ruiturus homo. furor est sublimibus uti
Sedibus ad lapsum properanti, improvida montes
Accumulat casura manus, nam sufficit unam
205 Contraxisse casam morituro, cum irrita surgant,
Que Fati pulsante manu fastigia nutant.
  Hec tamen et, quicquid auget ludibria vite,
Sunt desperantis anime solacia; fati
Postera deterrent dubie presagia mentis.

the mountain,[11] providing countless hiding-places to efface the shame
of wrongdoing. Indeed the very nature of the place gives rise to crime,
Its darkness, like night itself, provides a veil for error, and deceives the
75 wary sentinels of sight, concealing many a tale of the loss of purity even
as it lends itself to the secret acts of Venus. For the sinner loves shadow,
denies his shame by concealing it, and makes night a cloak for his guilt.

80   Marble is at hand, and whatever else may feast the eye by the
splendor of its well-polished surface, whatever creates a noble appearance and demands notice, whatever makes for a sumptuous dwelling
and lavish praise. The very earth, so productive of good things, bestows
85 luxury, serving the base desires of the world; man builds confidently,
when earth herself provides the means. And indeed she pledges her
ready assistance. At the great man's nod, Nature delivers whatever he
wishes, stone and beams for framing houses, and whatever else a more
lavish undertaking may require. She proffers gems, in whose splendor
90 the palace basks, content with its own sun. But this glory will know
only a brief sojourn: the onslaught of time checks the course of happy
mortals, and amid their bliss there appears before them the fatal
gateway, that final day so fearful to the great.

Ch. 9 Architrenius inveighs against those who squander their wealth on mansions

Architrenius beholds this, the paradise of a foolish world, and breaks
95 into grim laughter: "Alas, what madness to take such pains to build a
house, to squander so much labor, so much wealth! It is a fruitless
endeavor to build with such care what another generation will destroy:
for such idle pleasures are swiftly swept away as the world pants after
00 new vanities. Would that it might change its course, and work at
serious things!

For what could be more deserving of laughter and derision? Man
builds tall, though he himself will be brought to ruin tomorrow. It is
madness for one rushing toward disaster to claim so grand a dwelling,
for a creature so ill-provided and unstable to heap up mountains. A
05 simply fashioned hut should suffice one who is condemned to die, and
those high roofs are raised in vain which totter at the powerful blows of
Fate.

"And yet these things, and whatever else may increase the foolish-
ness of life, are the comforts of the despairing spirit, and allay the dire

210 Crastina celamur, hodiernis utimur, iram
    Iudicis expectat incauti audacia mundi,
    Conscia delicti; suadet presencia clausos
    Expositura metus series occulta futuri."

Cap. 10 De pictura auleorum

    Hic auro Parias honerant aulea columpnas:
215 Nobile surgit opus, levius quod torsit Aragnes
    Pollice Lida manus et vestibus impluit aurum,
    Pectinis ingenio nulli cessura, licebit
    Pallas anum simulet. Hermi saciatur harena
    Gloria picture, florum lascivia ductu
220 Pectinis accedit et veris gracia maior
    Vestibus arridet, series depingitur anni
    Temporis excursu vario distincta, sed illic ·
    Aurea vernat hiemps et item Saturnius annus
    Ver habet eternum, picture clausula quevis
225 Secula clausa tenet, annosaque tempora vestis
    Colligit una dies, cuius brevis explicat ordo
    Omnia: nascentis ibi mundi vagit origo
    Et iam cana redit teneris infancia rebus,
    Preteritumque Chaos iterum puer induit orbis.[12]
230   Nec minus horrescit mundum clausura suasque
    Asperat hora minas et adusto murice candens
    Purpura iudicii supremum ventilat ignem.
        Temporis expressus medii pretermeat ordo,
    Ut vero videas succedere secula tractu
235 Nec spacio confusa brevi. pictura labores
    Antiquos meminit: Danaos ibi Pergama fleres
    Diruta flere dolos, lacrimis dum purpura sudat,
    Dum latus Hectoreum maior fodit Hector Achilles
    Succumbitque Paris Greca Venerisque sagitta
240 Et Venus Atride gladios iramque ministrat.
        Hic fletus teneros Priami vomit uda senecte
    Ariditas, redditque dolor, quod perdidit etas,
    Hectoreos casus morte ausa; hic sensus Ulixis,
    Hic Pirri gladius pugnat, conatibus ille
245 Pectoris, ille manus; hic flet Ledea nec oris
    Gloria diluitur lacrimis, sed fletibus ipsis

10 presages of the troubled mind. We refuse to confront the morrow as we
revel in today's pleasures. But even in its reckless boldness, the world is
aware of its wickedness and awaits the wrath of the judge. Though the
present seduces us, the unknown course of events to come will bring our
hidden fears to light."

Ch. 10 Designs in tapestry

15 Tapestries heavy with gold adorn the Parian columns. A noble work is
displayed, which a Lydian hand more delicate than Arachne's has
woven, showering the cloth with gold, a hand whose subtlety in
weaving would be unsurpassed though Pallas herself should play the
old woman once again. The glory of the pattern is amply set off by the
20 sands of Hermus: a riot of flowers appears at the needle's bidding, and a
beauty beyond that of spring radiates from the cloth. The cycle of the
year, marked by the changing sequence of the seasons, is depicted; but
here the gilded winter shines springlike, and again a Saturnian age
enjoys perpetual spring.

25   The enclosed space of the pattern holds captive all the ages; the
tapestry draws together in a single day the years of time past, and its
brief design unfolds it all. Here it begins, with the squalls of the
new-born universe,[12] now the ancient infant state of budding creatures
is restored, and the shape of the young world imposes itself once again
on a Chaos that has passed away.

30   The ending of the world, fraught with terror, is likewise shown; the
terrifying final hour presents its threats, and purple dye, flashing forth
from its dusky shell, quickens the fires of the ultimate judgment.

    The procession of intervening time is presented in due order, so that
35 one may observe the ages joined in sequence, not at all disordered by
the limited space. The imagery recalls ancient sufferings. Here you
might shed a tear for fallen Pergama, itself reduced to tears by Danaean
guile; kingly robes are drenched with weeping as that greater Hector,
Achilles, pierces the side of Hector, as Paris is overcome by the darts of
40 Greece and those of love, and Venus herself lends arms and fierce
courage to Menelaos. Here the withered old age of Priam, reinfused with
moisture, pours forth helpless tears, and his grief restores to him what
was lost to the world when death dared to visit itself upon Hector. Here
both the astuteness of Ulysses and the sword of Pyrrhus make war, the
45 one by feats of mind, the other by strength of arm. Here Leda's daughter
weeps: her glorious beauty is not dimmed by her tears, and indeed the
grace of her expression is enhanced by the very act of weeping. Here the

Vultus ridet honor; hic Greca, hic Dardana pubes,
Illa stat, illa cadit, tractantur bella, sed inde
Ensibus, inde fuga; et dum respirantibus armis
250 Consulit in dubios Atrides Nestora casus,
Ille vir, ille senex Frigio iuvenescit in auro.
Dulce virum luctus lugere, dolere dolores
Et lacrimis lacrimas, planctu rescribere planctum.
Dulcius est oculo dulci decurrere casus
255 Fortuneque vices, Veneris quas alea versat,
Et pasci lacrimis, quibus invitantur amantum
Gaudia, dum tenero dulcescunt oscula fletu
Et lacrimis inserpit amor miserisque fovetur
Maior in adversis. intextos pecten amorum
260 Exprimit eventus: ibi serum Piramus ense
Vindicat egressum, Tisbe lugubria fati
Pondera morte levat, tua non formidat ad umbras,
Pirame, fata sequi, sequiturque dolore dolorem
Et gemitu gemitum, producit funere funus.
265   Hic patris amplexus usurpat Mirra, noverca
Gracior ipsa sibi; Biblisque sororia fratri
Gaudia mentitur; Iolen ibi mollis amictu
Induit Alcides rigidoque et pensa stupenti
Pollice turbat opus, ausus latus ardua doctum
270 Edocuisse colos, fuso meminisse cadenti
Cogitur Alciden positamque resumere clavam.
   Hec et, si qua iuvant oculos, pictura iubenti
Pectine producit, homines et bruta creanti
Pollice tela parit, operis laudisque magister
275 Omnia doctus arat, Nature cuncta potentis
Induit ille manus: vigilant ibi sidera celo,
Equora piscis arat, vario discurritur aer
Alite, terra feris, nostrique superbior oris
Maiestate parit homini quod serviat, omni
280 Obsequiosa bono quovisque iuvantibus usu
Sedula deliciis; ibi leta et tristia spargit
Ambigua Fortuna manu, fati exitus omnis
Texitur et tenui dependent omina filo.

Cap. 11 De luxu vestium

   Luxuriem cultus nullo modus ordine, nullo
285 Limite metitur. luxus non claudit honestas

youth of Greece stand firm while the Dardanians fall back; both are
waging war, but on the one side with weapons, on the other by flight.
250 And when, during a lull in the combat, Agamemnon consults with
Nestor about their uncertain situation, both the mature man and the
elderly grow young again, set off in Phrygian gold.

It is sweet to feel sorrow at the sorrows of men, to grieve at their grief,
to repay tears with tears, lamentation with lamentation. Sweeter still to
255 survey with tender gaze the fatal errors and shifts of Fortune to which
the hazards of Venus give rise, to indulge oneself with those sorrows
which enhance the joys of love: for kisses are made sweeter by tender
weeping, and love mingles itself with such tears, cherished all the more
260 by unhappy lovers in their adversity. The weaver's art sets forth
embroidered tales of love. Here Pyramus pays with the sword for his
lateness in setting forth, and Thisbe by her own death eases the sorrowful burden of fate; fearlessly she pursues a fate like yours, O Pyramus,
even unto death, matching grief with grief, compounding mourning
265 with mourning, your funeral with her own. Here Myrrha usurps the
love of her father, preferring to play the role of her own step-mother,
and Byblis dissembles to her brother her sisterly pleasure. Here an
effeminate Alcides wraps Iole in his own cloak, and botches with stiff
and clumsy fingers the other's task of spinning. Though he strives to
270 teach his hard-schooled limbs to ply the distaff, the scattered yarn forces
him to recall that he is Alcides, and to take up again the club he had laid
aside.

These scenes and whatever else may please the eye are imaged forth
at the weaver's bidding. Under the guiding hand the tapestry gives birth
to men and beasts. The skilled master inscribes his work with every
275 mark of industry and excellence, and assumes the role of all-creating
Nature: here stars keep watch in the sky, fish furrow the sea, the air is
traversed by many-colored birds, the land by beasts. The earth, made
proud by the majesty of our human presence, brings forth whatever
280 may be of use to man, attentive to his every need and eager that delight
may attend all his occupations. Here too Fortune's equivocating hand
scatters joy and sadness; all the workings of fate are woven here, and
great consequences hang by a slender thread.

Ch. 11 Sumptuous dress

285 Moderation exercises no control, sets no limit to the lavishness of
apparel here, no sense of decency bars the way to luxurious excess.

Pretereuntis iter. precium quesisse laborant
Vestibus uda Thetis et fecundissima Tellus,
Mater opum: calido tenuis mandatur ab axe
Carbasus, et Pharii linum de litore Nili
290　Tollitur, ut nudam gemat Isida nudus Osiris.
　　　Vellera dant Seres, studiique Britannia maior[13]
Ingeniique potens, quocunque vocaverit usus,
Ausa dedisse manus, raptique paracior ala
Fulminis, ut precio queat exequasse laboris
295　Altera Naturam Natura, Minerva Minervam.
Fervescit Tirius sudor fudisse cruorem
Muricis, equoream penitus scrutatus abyssum,
Ut falli facilis roseo flammata veneno
Vellera miretur oculus mundumque beari
300　Sic putet, interius animam torquente reatu.

Cap. 12 De pictura vasorum

　　　Divitis ingenio picture gaudet et auri
Gloria vasorum rutilo pallore choruscat,
Nec precii nec laudis egens. miratur in illis
Artificis Natura manum seseque minorem
305　Agnovisse pudet; nam gracia surgit in auro
Plenior et quevis facies ornacior exit.
　　　Blandius invitat ad pocula vasis in imo
Stans hominis signum, Bacho superante futurum
Naufragio felix, nisi quod gula sepe paratis
310　Subvenit auxiliis hominemque urgentibus undis
Humanum servasse putat, volat ebrius ales
Inferius tardante mero, serpente bibenti
Innocuus conviva bibit, bibit angelus uda
Sanctificans dextra, blandum fremit ira leonis
315　Poture tranquilla gule, mansuescit in unguis
Pace minax ursus, Nerei mutasse profundum
Piscis amat, Bachique lacus et litora servat.
　　　Gracia picture picturaque gracior, aurum
Gemmarumque dies, Bachum latura favoris
320　Nectare vasa replent. vasis pictura decorem
Exibet ornatus, decus aurum, gemma nitorem.

Watery Tethys and the teeming Earth, mother of riches, strive to gain the prize for raiment. Fine flax is sent from the hot south, and linen is
290 borne away from the banks of the Egyptian Nile, so that a naked Osiris bemoans his naked Isis. The far east provides wool. Thus does Britain,[13] "great" in learning and richly inventive, presume to extend her grasp wherever opportunity may beckon, swifter to strike than the winged
295 thunderbolt, so that a second Nature may equal Nature herself in the fruits of her industry, a new Minerva rival the old. The Tyrian, ransacking the depths of the sea, sweats in his eagerness to pour out the bloody dye of the murex, that the eye, so easily deceived, may wonder at woolen robes inflamed by this bright poison, and imagine that the world
300 is a blessed place, even as the mind within is racked with guilt.

Ch. 12 Painted vessels

A glorious array of drinking vessels rejoices in the skill of their sumptuous decoration, and gleams with the ruddy pallor of gold, unsurpassed in costliness and quality. Nature herself wonders at the
305 artisan's handiwork, and is ashamed to realize herself inferior, for a richer beauty than hers resides in gold, and whatever shape it assumes appears more elegant.

The image of a man, standing in the bottom of the bowl, cheerfully bids us drink, happy at the shipwreck that Bacchus' powerful effect
310 portends for him; but gluttony is usually at hand with ready aid, thinking to save a fellow mortal from the whelming tide. A bird hovers drunkenly, as the force of wine retards its flight; another banqueter drinks unharmed while a serpent shares his drink; an angel drinks,
315 blessing the board with his dripping hand; a raging lion roars softly, remaining calm while gluttony drinks; a fierce bear draws in his claws in peace; fish gladly forsake the Nerean depths and frequent the lakes and shores of Bacchus.

The beauty of the images, and gold and brilliant gems, more beautiful still, have already filled these vessels designed to convey Bacchus with
320 the nectar of their charm. The images on the vessel set off the beauty of the handiwork, the handiwork sets off the gold, and the gems catch its gleam.

Cap. 13 De accidentibus aule et eius incolis

Illic ingluvies, illic Venus effluit, illic
Texitur occulto studio dolus, emula veri
Fabula prevelat fidei periuria peplo.
325 Pacis habent vultus odii secreta, venenum
Fraudis amiciciam tenui mentitur amictu.
Occulit immanes animos clemencia vultus.
Pectoris asperitas, risu pretexta sereno,
Interius fervens laqueos innodat et hamos
330 Curvat in insidias, rabiemque in pectore fixam
Armat in omne nefas. non est, quod abhorreat aule
Incola, delictum: facie describit amicum,
Hostem mente premit; linguam dulcedine lactat,
Mentis amara tegens; animo blanditur operto,
335 Ledit in occulto; presenti parcit amico,
Vulnerat absentem; quicquid presencia pacis
Spondeat, a gladio non est absencia tuta.
    Nulla fides aule, nulla est reverencia, nullus
Committendo modus. viciis indulget, honestum
340 Ambicione premit, equum declinat in omni
Materia lucri, studio quocunque laborat,
Ut loculus crescat, lingue suffragia vendit
Ad precii libram, rapiunt maiora patronum
Munera nec numquam partitur puncta favoris
345 Partibus adversis, unum promittit utrimque
Obsequium, neutrumque iuvat, qui utrique tenetur,
Proditor amborum; nam vel bellator utrimque
Arma negat, vel utrique favens utrique minatur.
    Prodigus eloquii, vultu non mente serenat
350 Aulicus affatum. Zephiro vernancior oris
Lilia verborum cuivis largitur et omnes
Nectar amicicie redolenti pace salutat.
Quid doleas, quid non, quid dulce, quid utile, quid non
Sollicitus querit et tantum verba daturus
355 Singula promittit, crescentibus omnia spargit
Pollicitis, sed nulla manu. spem mandat inanem
Pectoribus dextreque nichil, spes credula fallit
Pectora, verba manum. sese ligat aulicus omni
Omnia facturum largoque enititur ore
360 Quilibet ut speret. sic imminet ardua multis

Ch. 13 What happens at court and who resides there

Here gluttony and lechery abound, here deceit is wrought by secret arts, falsehood strives to resemble truth, and perjury shrouds itself in the mantle of good faith. Lurking hatred wears a face of peace, and the poison of fraud disguises itself in a thin cloak of friendship. A humane countenance hides inhuman thoughts. The cruel spirit, veiled by a serene smile but seething inwardly, sets its snares and barbs its hooks for treachery, and the madness that infests the bosom is ready for any wicked action. There is no crime that the courtier shuns: he presents the face of a friend, burying enmity in his heart, imbuing his tongue with sweetness to conceal the bitterness of his mind. His outward expression offers a caress, but he wounds in secret, and though he spare a present companion he will attack an absent one. Whatever pledges of peace one gains in his presence, in absence one is not safe from his dagger.

There is no trust at court, no reverence, no limit to what can be done. It indulges vice, and keeps down integrity in favor of ambition. The courtier bends the laws at every opportunity for gain, takes on whatever sort of work will make the purse grow fat, and trades his right to cast his vote for a cash reward. It is the greater gift that obtains patronage, and sometimes the mark of favor is bestowed on two opposing factions; a single service is promised to both but helps neither; he who is committed on either side betrays both. For he will either refuse to take up arms in either cause or pose a threat to each side by supporting the other.

Lavish of fine words, the courtier makes his speech fair by his expression, not his thoughts. A breath more springlike than Zephyrus bestows verbal flowers on all alike; the nectar of his friendliness greets one and all with the sweet scent of peace. Solicitous, he asks why you are sad, or why not, what may please or serve you and what will not. Though words are all he has to offer, he promises anything, bestowing it all by way of expansive promises, but presenting you with nothing. He bestows vain hope on the spirit, but puts nothing in your hand: hopeful credulity betrays the spirit, vain words the hand. The courtier pledges himself to perform all things for all men, and strives by his generous speech to keep them hoping. Thus a grave crisis looms for those whose

Sarcina, dum verbis temere fiducia surgit,
Dum spes ceca iacet, subiti secura flagelli.
Heu facinus! multos in summa pericula misit
Naufragioque fuit lingue tranquillior aura.

365   Mobilis et nullos solide complexus amicos,
Mente vagus dubia, nullis nisi fedius uti
Federibus novit, odiis alternat amores,
Mutat amicicias, has exuit, induit illas,
Quosque minus constanter amat, constancius odit.

370 Vagit amicicie teneris infancia cunis,
Gracior ad veteres numquam perducitur annos
Nec senii matura sapit; fastidia ferret,
Si senio marceret anus. dum spirat odorum
Primicias, expirat amor. sic aula diurnos

375 Eligit et tractos ultra fastidit amicos.

Cap. 14 De adulatoribus aule

     Principis ad nutum servi inconstancia nutat.
Quodlibet ad votum didicit versare favorem
Clausus adulator: ad quodvis 'nolo' paratum
'Nolo' relaturus et, si 'volo' dixerit ille,

380 Reddet et ille 'volo'; semel hinc 'non' dicitur, inde
Ingeminatur 'non'; semel hinc 'ita' dicitur, inde
Ingeminatur 'ita'; quicquid laudaverit, illo
Nil melius, quicquid animo non sederit, illo
Nil visum est peius; si quid iubet acrius, ipsum

385 Iuratur licuisse nefas, si micius, ipso
Tollitur ad superos melior Iove; quicquid agatur,
Id bene, dii melius! hic est, qui pulvere nullo
Excuciat nullum[14] cauteque absolvere querat
Crimen, ubi non est, suspectam sordis amictus

390 Mundiciam reddens, ut quo placet, inde mereri
Debeat offensam. servi manus illa ministrat
Non reprimit culpam, domino male sedula servit
Obsequio ledens. hic est, qui adversa volenti
Prospera diffinit, dominoque in fata ruenti

395 Iurat in eventus dextros, laudatque sinistri
Augurium fati; quicquid Fortuna minetur,
Mentis pace ferens, placeat modo. pauca dolorem
Altius infigunt. hic est, qui gaudia mente

confidence rises foolishly at mere words, whose hope remains blind, unmindful of the lash about to strike. Alas, such false dealing has cast many into extreme peril, and words, like a too-favorable breeze, have led to shipwreck. Fickle, embracing no one in sincere friendship, inconstant in his anxiety, the courtier has no use for promises unless to debase them; he shifts from love to hatred as he changes friendships, shaking off one to put on another, and though his love is inconstant, he is constant in hatred. His friendship is like a feeble infant that squalls in her cradle, never so favored as to survive to later years, or attain the ripeness of age. Should she become an old woman, withered with age, she would incur his contempt. Even as it inhales the scent of its first fruits, love expires. So too the court prefers friendships of a day, and scorns those that endure longer.

Ch. 14 The flatterers at court

Servile inconstancy nods at the nod of the great man, for the flatterer in his bondage has learned to adapt his assent to whatever wish is expressed. To every "I will not" he returns a ready "I will not"; if the master has said "I will" he replies "I will." The moment "nay" or "yea" is uttered on the one side, "nay" or "yea" is repeated on the other. If the master has praised something, there is nothing finer; if it has not struck his fancy, nothing worse has ever been seen. Should he issue an overly cruel command, the wicked act is declared to be lawful; if he is lenient, a greater than Jove himself is exalted to the heavens. Whatever he does is right.

May the gods preserve us from him who, where there is no dust, sweeps away that dust,[14] who takes pains to absolve guilt where none exists, bringing a clean robe under suspicion of being soiled. When he pleases most, he is most deserving of censure. His servile hand accommodates guilt rather than reproving it, and his very attentiveness serves his lord badly, wounding by obsequiousness. For he calls circumstances favorable which are against his lord's interest, swears that the master is prospering and approves the omens of impending ruin even as his lord rushes toward disaster, bearing with tranquil mind whatever fortune may threaten, so long as he himself may remain in favor. Few things affect him deeply enough to cause pain. He suppresses the joy in his

Supprimit, ore gemit; et rursum gaudia vultus,
400 Pectus habet gemitus. vultus accomodat omni
Fortune domini, nusquam vestigia mutans
Solvitur in risus, in quos se solverit idem,
Ore pluit lacrimas, animo quas pluverit idem.
    Cum dominus tali facinus committit amico,
405 Ille doli vulpes domuique domesticus hostis
Omne domus vicium mordenti ridet ocello
Et pede vel cubito socios et crimina tangens,
Quod lingua reticet, loquitur pede; cuncta loquentis
Garrulitate pedis domini commissa revelat
410 Et fidei fracto reserat secreta sigillo.

Cap. 15 De potentum impotencia et cecitate

    Has aliasque notas notat Architrenius, ergo:
"Heu! quem divicie, quem mundi vana loquuntur
Gaudia felicem, viciique ancilla beatum
Gloria mentitur! gladiis linguisque suorum
415 Ceditur ipse, manus non evasisse ministras
Forcior ipse potest, non extorsisse latentem
Perfidiam novit, animo non prendit apertum
Crimen adulantis, oculo quod prestat et auri,
Non oculo non aure videt, popularibus auris
420 Auribus assurgit, leta preconia vulgi
Dulcia mente bibit, circumfusisque favorem
Plausibus indulget nec laudibus artat habenam,
Sed sibi iam melior et maior laude videtur.
Ipse nefas totusque nichil, se credit ad omnes
425 Esse satis laudes, preciumque in laudibus esse
Concipit, at nescit: precium non laude meremur,
Sed precio laudem; nescit quod turpibus ipsa
Laus dampnosa venit, cum sit derisio pravis
Laus, pictura bonis, ipsa est que exultat honestis,
430 Insultat viciis, illis arridet et illa
Caucius irridet; nescit, dum lingua redundat
Laudibus, omne malum mentis secreta loquuntur.
    Non aperit clausura dolos facundia servi,
Quo prosit domino, sed quo delectet. ad aures
435 Verborum cum melle venit nec pectore librat
Utile suspenso, domini securior usum

mind and weeps outwardly, or, again, preserves a joyful countenance
00 while grief possesses his heart. He adapts his face to every shift of his
master's fortunes, never deviating from his footsteps. He is seized by the
very laughter to which the master gives himself, and sheds outwardly
the tears which the other sheds from the heart.

Should the master entrust to such a friend the punishing of wrong-
05 doing, this stealthy fox, this enemy of the house in which he dwells
laughs with mocking eye at all the misconduct of the household,
nudging his cronies and their misdeeds with foot or elbow. What his
tongue withholds, his foot declares: by the chattering of his eloquent
10 foot he reveals his lord's commission, and lays bare his secret orders by
breaking the seal of trust.

Ch. 15 The impotence and blindness of great men

Architrenius takes note of these bad signs, then cries, "Alas for him
whose wealth, whose vain worldly pleasures proclaim him happy!
whom glory, the handmaid of vice, falsely calls blessed! He is wounded
15 by the swords and tongues of his own household; for all his power he
cannot escape the hands of his servants, nor force lurking treachery to
show itself, nor grasp with his mind the barefaced guilt of the flatterer,
though it is plain to his eyes and ears. Indeed he does not truly see or
20 hear, but pricks up his ear to the windy voice of the people, happily
drinks in the sweetness of popular acclaim, bestows his favor on those
who surround him with applause. He sets no limit to their praise of him,
and indeed seems to himself a greater and more virtuous person because
25 of it. Though he be utterly base and empty, he imagines himself worthy
of the highest praise, supposing such praise to be the measure of his
worth. He does not realize that merit is not attained through praise, but
praise through merit. He does not see that even praise is destructive
when it is visited on unworthy objects. (For though praise is an adornment to virtue, the praise of depravity is a kind of mockery. It is the
30 nature of praise to delight in honor and scorn vice, to make merry with
the one, while laughing inwardly at the other.) He does not realize that
while the tongue pours forth praise, the hidden meaning is utterly
malicious.

"The charming speech of the servant is a keep whose hidden
resources are never brought forth to serve his lord, but to gratify him.
35 He visits the lord's ears with honeyed words, but since no thought of
being useful burdens his shifting thoughts, he ignores the lord's interest
without concern. The lord's good will is kept secure by a rampart of

Preterit. eloquii vallo, ne capta recedat,
Gracia munitur; verbo vallante favorem
Claudere fervescit et, dum sua tuta ferantur
440 Linthea, precipiti domini non subvenit alno.
  Vulgus ad obsequium numquam dominantis honestas
Invitat, sed dantis opes; servire minores
Maiori non suadet amor, sed cogit egestas
Imperiique timor et in aspera prona cupido.

Cap. 16 Quod opibus non hominibus deservitur

445 Non hominum votis, sed opum servitur; ab illis
Imperium mendicat homo, famulantis ad illas
Servus hanelat amor et, cui devinctior heret,
Vellet, ut exiguo dominum mutaverit ere;
Iuranti licet ore neget, testatus et ipsam
450 Horrendam superum fidei Stiga, quelibet ausus
Testanti factura fidem, – periuria venti
Non reditura ferunt, aura rapiente recursu
Non lesura volant. non est, cui lingua minorem
Postponat dominum, quicquid mens obvia lingue
455 Liberior dictet, quicquid suppressa susurret
Libertas animi, nullius passa tyranni
Imperiosa iugum nulloque absterrita monstro.

Cap. 17 Quod adversitas adulatorum detegit falsitatem[15]

Si lingue ad faleras, si detur ad omnia verbi
Condimenta fides, domino nil maius in ipsis
460 Excellit superis, nec habet preciosius illo
Area Fortune; malletque et luce carere
Et se quam domino – Fortune ad vota fruenti
Uberiore bono. sed si modo dando solutam
Contrahat illa manum raptamque in tristia verso
465 Urgeat orbe rotam, dominum quem multa ministri
Turba loquebatur, servus modo pocula fati
Solus amara bibit; sibi soli applaudit amico,
Qui premitur fato. sepelit, quos leta creavit,
Mesta dies fati, servi celaverat ante,
470 Nunc aperit fraudes. domus extunc cogitur omnem

eloquence, lest having once been captured it should escape again. He works furiously to imprison favor with a wall of words, and while his 140 own sails bear him safely along, he does not seek to aid the careening vessel of his lord.

"It is never the integrity of the man of power that draws the common people to his service, but his power to bestow wealth. Love does not compel the lowly to serve the great: it is need that compels them, and the fear of authority, and greed, ever ready to endure harsh treatment.

Ch. 16 Service is given not to men, but to wealth

145 "They serve not at the bidding of men, but of wealth. It is from wealth that men's authority is begged, and wealth that the attendant's servile love strives to gain, even though he would be willing to trade for a meager sum of money the master to whom he clings so closely. Of 150 course he would deny this with a mouthful of oaths, calling to witness Styx itself, which the very gods fear to swear by, and fearlessly naming whatever might lend credibility to his testimony. But the winds bear perjury away, never to return; they float off on the swift breeze, and will not damage him by returning. There is none to whom his tongue would 155 acknowledge his master inferior, however much his franker thoughts might oppose his words, however he might mutter in the suppressed freedom of his spirit, that haughty spirit which will never endure the tyrant's yoke and remains unafraid in the face of terror.

Ch. 17 Adversity unmasks the falseness of flatterers[15]

If one give credence to the embellishments of the flatterer's tongue, and all the spices of his speech, there is none more excellent than his 160 lord among the gods themselves; the domain of Fortune holds nothing more precious than he, and one would rather be denied the light of day, or lose one's very self, than this lord – for so long as Fortune decrees that this lord enjoy her goods in abundance. But should Fortune close that 165 hand now generously open, seize her wheel and drive it around its circle into sorrow, then he whom a great throng of servants now call master will become a slave himself, and drink the bitter cup of fate in solitude. He whom fate has cast down has no friend to acclaim him but himself. A sad day sees the funeral of those friendships to which happier times gave 170 birth. A happy day had concealed the servant's falsehoods, but now they appear openly. Henceforth the house is compelled to lay bare all its

Exeruisse dolum, dominum non decipit ultra.
Mundi nulla fides! et que latuere secundis,
Cernit in adversis. hominem quid prospera celet,
Asperior Fortuna docet, felicia fati
475 Excecant animos: distinguere nescit amicos,
Qui fruitur letis; Fortune quicquid ab alto
Sidere despectet, unum celatur amari."
    Ut satis est visum, viso indolet, intimus exit
Exclamatque foris gemitus, solitumque recurrit
480 Meror ad impluvium, positumque resuscitat imbrem
Vivus item luctus et pectore rivus aquoso
Enatat et notis oculorum spargitur undis
Alveus et gemina lacrimarum rumpitur urna.

deceptions: the lord can be deceived no longer. He no longer puts his trust in the world, and he perceives in adversity what had been hidden from him in happier times. Adverse Fortune teaches a man what 75 prosperity had concealed; fate's blessings make us blind. He who enjoys a happy life cannot distinguish his true friends. Whatever he may see as he gazes down from Fortune's starry realm, bitterness alone is concealed from him."

Having seen enough, Architrenius grieves over what he has seen; his inner sorrow emerges and proclaims itself openly. Again his grief has 80 recourse to the accustomed cistern, and fresh weeping renews the sunken water-level. A stream flows down his dripping bosom, and the basin is splashed with the eyes' familiar streams as the double vessel of tears is unsealed.

Liber Quintus

Cap. 1 De colle Presumptionis

Transit ab aspectis nondum rorancia siccus
Lumina nec tersus oculos merore palustres.
Nec mora, finitimo tractu Presumptio collem
Stringit et insolido nitens pede sarcina pessum
5 Nutat, ubi testudo volat, fastidit in alto
Mergus aque sedes, aquila cessante ministrat
Arma Iovi milvus, spolio contendit olori
Corvus, id est ferrugo nivi, strepit anxius anser
Acteam vicisse lyram, cecusque pererrat
10 Bubo diem nisumque fugat torpentibus alis,
Dum mendicata sequitur cornicula penna.[1]
Hic lepus insurgit animo pallente leoni,
Simius, humane nature simia, vultus
Despuit illimes,[2] bubali bos cornua cornu
15 Prevenisse putat, admissam tigrida barri
Segnicies inflexa fugat,[3] lupa nupta Molossis
Iactitat insignes thalamos, Licaonis ausa
Coniugii rupisse fidem; contraque leenam
Pardus, asellus equam presumpto federe lecti
20 Ducit et hircus ovem, solioque pudendus adulter
Semimari partu Pasiphen taurus honustat.

Cap. 2 De quibusdam presumptionis exemplis

Hic Niobe multa Latonam prole lacessit
Ardua, sed numerum tam Sol quam Cynthia pensat.
Surgit in aurigam, dum Phebi sanguine Pheton
25 Nititur et nitido temere confidit in ortu,
Errantemque diem mundo nimis obvius urit,
Miraturque citum Boreas ardere Boeten,[4]
Indomitosque regi spargens auriga iugales

Book Five

Ch. 1 The Hill of Presumption

Architrenius turns away from the spectacle, still unable to dry his
brimming eyes or clear their standing pools of sorrow. Immediately he
sees Presumption assailing a nearby hill, struggling upward with
5 uncertain tread and staggering backward under its burden.

Here tortoises fly; the diving gull disdains its home in the depths of
the sea; the kite bears the arms of Jove while the eagle gives place; the
raven competes with the swan in plumage, rusty brown with snowy
white; and the anxious squawk of the goose seeks to excel the Grecian
10 lyre. The blind owl wanders abroad in daylight, and drives away the
hawk with its sluggish wings, while the crow, in borrowed plumage,[1]
gives chase. Here the faint-hearted hare rises up against the lion; the
ape, aping human nature, disdains an unbemired countenance;[2] the
15 cow imagines her horns to surpass those of the buffalo; the unbending
sluggishness of the elephant puts to flight the eager tigress;[3] the
she-wolf, mated with the Molossian hound, boasts of her illustrious
marriage bed, boldly breaking her wedding-vow to Lycaeon; con-
versely, the panther claims the lioness, the ass the mare, the goat the
20 ewe, in presumptuous union, while the adulterous bull, disgracing the
throne, burdens Pasiphae with her half-human progeny.

Ch. 2 A few examples of presumption

Here haughty Niobe taunts Latona with her numerous progeny, but
the Sun-god and Cynthia together even the score; Phaeton, glorying in
25 the blood of Phoebus, takes over his chariot, foolishly trusting in his
glorious origin. Passing too close to the earth, he leaves a fiery trail
across the day. Boreas is amazed to see burning Bootes move so swiftly,[4]
while the charioteer, having allowed the uncontrollable team to scatter,

Precipiti fato meriti mercede laborem
30 Claudit et in patria tandem se novit habena.
    Amplexus Cereris dulces avellit opaci
Insipidus Plutonis amor; regique Molosso[5]
Ideum dat preda thorum; Nessusque biformi
Alciden deludit equo; celique litura,
35 Lennius, innupte connubia Palladis ardet.
    Hic furit in superos Tellus armasse Gigantes
Et nivibus montes galeatos Ossan, Olimpum,
Pelion et scopulis populosa cacumina pacem
Tollit in etheream, securaque fulminis instat.
40   Hic sibi rethoricos Theodentis gloria flores
Deputat,[6] auctorem titulo mentitus inani;
Assumptumque note mens conscia dampnat honorem,
Nec meritam laudem maiestas nominis equat.
    Ardua Pierides ineunt certamina Musis,
45 Sed rapitur rapto laurus cum nomine; laurus
Ornat et in memori victoria nomine vivit
Eternumque negat laurum marcescere nomen.
    Persius in Flacci pelago decurrit et audet
Mendicasse stilum satire, serraque cruentus
50 Rodit et ignorat polientem pectora limam.

Cap. 3 De presumptione personarum ecclesiasticarum et magistrorum

    Hic puer insolidus et mente et corpore, lese
Indolis, et teneris animo nervoque solutus,
Quem renum senior lascivia mollit et evi
Ardescens novitas, emptas in devia preceps
55 Ecclesias auriga rapit, superumque regenda
Suscipit innumera lactandus ovilia pastor.
Omnibus ecclesiis haut contraxisse veretur,
Centigamusque novo superis de iure ministrat
Presbyter, in sponsi spolio preclusus adulter.
60 Moribus insipidus nostri Iovis inquinat aram
Accessuque notat, Veneris Bachique sacerdos,
Numen utrumque sitit: lumbosque et guttura solvens
Sedulus hiis servit. liceat scelus esse locutum,
Quod fit inoccultum, vicium facit ipsa loquendi
65 Materie sordes, ire furor imperat ori,

30 concludes his undertaking in a fitting manner with a fatal plunge, and
learns at the last what it is to take on his father's duties. The unappeal-
ing love of Pluto steals away the beloved child of Ceres, and theft
bestows an Idean bride on the Molossian king;[5] Nessus, in his semi-
equine form, deceives Alcides; and Lemnian Vulcan, a blot on the
35 pantheon, burns to possess unwedded Pallas.

Here Earth labors madly to arm the Giants against the gods, and
thrusts up the snow-capped peaks and rock-strewn slopes of Ossa,
Olympus and Pelion to menace the peace of the heavens, forgetful of the
40 thunderbolt in her defiance. Here the vainglory of Theodectes claims for
itself the flowers of rhetoric,[6] feigning authorship on the strength of an
empty name; but the mind that recognizes the distinctive character of
the work condemns this assumed distinction, and the grandeur of title is
no equivalent for praise well earned. The Pierides engage in desperate
45 competition with the Muses, but the laurel is denied them, together with
the title they had sought to claim. For the laurel trophy and the victory
itself live on in the name that recalls them; when the name is eternal the
laurel can never fade. Persius plunges into the great sea of Horace, and
50 dares to counterfeit the satirist's manner. Bloodthirsty, he hacks away
with his saw, and knows nothing of the file that gives polish to the
mind.

Ch. 3 The presumption of churchmen and teachers

Behold a giddy boy, his natural endowments of mind and body
ruined, slack and feeble in thought and action, one whom the wanton
desires of an old man and a young man's burning love of novelty have
55 utterly dissipated. In his lurching chariot he descends abruptly on
churches he has purchased and, though scarcely weaned himself,
undertakes to be the guiding shepherd of countless flocks of God. This
centogamous priest would not hesitate to plight his troth in every
church in Christendom, for he serves the gods by a new dispensation, an
60 adulterer wrapped in the despoiled robe of the Bridegroom. A moral
weakling, he defiles the altar of our Jove and defames it by his presence.
He is the priest of Venus and Bacchus, and thirsts to know the inspiration of both, eagerly giving over his loins and gullet to their service.

Be it lawful to speak of crimes that are practiced openly; though the
65 foulness of the subject matter turns speech itself into something vile, yet
the force of wrath governs my lips, and indignation evokes words less

Circumcisa minus movet indignacio verba.
Pauperibus dandos reditus inviscerat et, qui
Cuncta dedit, nulla contingit porcio Christum,
Emungitque bonis ara ventris numinis aram,[7]
70 Cuius delicias uteri deperdit in utre,
Dum, quod in ore sapit, stomachi corrumpit Averno.
    Hic vulgus cathedras – rapta deitate magistri –
Insilit et vacua de maiestate tumorem
Concipit, impubis et mento et mente, virenti
75 Crudus adhuc succo, iuvenem solidosque viriles
Preveniens culmos nec maturata senecte
Precipiti lauro non expectasse veretur
Hos ego pretereo tactos sine nomine; nosque
Preterit ignotus, insania nota, magister.
80   O rabies sedisse rabi, dulcique Minerve
Intonuisse tuba, nondum pacientibus annis!
    Hic in philosophos ausa est sevire flagello,́
Mortis alumpna, Fames, animoque potencia Phebi
Pignora Pauperies curarum verberat ydra.

Cap. 4 Quod presumptio est Senectutis ad regem Anglie divertisse

85 Hic ubi delegit summam Presumptio sedem,
Inserpit festina comis crispatque Senecta
Henrici faciem, quem flava Britannia regem
Iactat, eoque duce[8] titulis Normannia ridet
Et belli et pacis, totumque supermeat orbem
90 Indole, quam belli numquam fregere tumultus,
Dedidicitque virum gladio matura Iuventus.
Hiis vernare genis eternum debuit evi
Flosculus et nulla senii marcescere bruma.
    Hic vicii fecunda parens soliumque domanti
95 Imperiosa iugo, regina Pecunia iuri
Preminet, ausa suis astringere legibus orbem
Quas racio nescit. sed ei devincta cupido
Dictat et indicit avidi facundia questus
Et loculos ardens discincte audacia lingue:
100 Census censura fiunt iniuria iura,
Pura minus pura, sacra littera sacra litura.

carefully restrained. He gorges himself on offerings intended for the poor, and no portion is assigned to Christ, who bestowed it all. The pigsty of the belly defrauds the altar of God,[7] and the fruits of this womb are abandoned to the bladder, for what is sweet to the taste is destroyed in the Avernos of the stomach.

Here too anyone may clamber into the teacher's chair, usurping the divine title of "master," and become pregnant of bombast by this empty dignity. Though both chin and mind are beardless, though he is still a mere green sapling taking precedence over strong and mature timber, he does not hesitate, decked in his hastily bestowed laurels, to lay claim to rewards held in store for age. But having touched on such as these I will leave them unnamed; let the "master" pass unknown, though his madness is known to all. For it is madness to have sat as teacher and sounded the clear clarion of Minerva before one was of sufficient age.

Here too Hunger, the foster-child of Death, has dared to wield her lash against the philosophers, and Poverty assails the strong-spirited disciples of Phoebus with a hydra of woes.

Ch. 4 How Age has presumed to visit the King of England

Here where Presumption has established her principal dwelling, premature Age has crept into the hair and wrinkled the face of Henry, whom golden Britain proudly calls King, while Normandy rejoices to name him her Leader[8] in war and peace. He surpasses all the world in ability; the violence of war has not broken his spirit, and his mature Youth has unlearned the role of the warlike man. The youthful bloom should have flourished on his cheek eternally, and the winter of age should never have sullied it.

Here Queen Money, the teeming mother of vice, dominating the throne itself with her oppressive yoke, takes precedence over justice, for she has boldly subjected the world to laws of her own, unknown to reason. Greed, her inseparable companion, instructs her, while the glibness of the eager bargainer and the unbridled impudence of the fortune-hunter make her eloquent. Property performs the office of judgment, injustice does the work of justice, purity grows less pure, and and sacred tradition gives way to sanctifying forgery.

Cap. 5 De Superbia

Vicinos germana lares attollit et astris
Invidet inferior cognata Superbia, terris
Impaciens habuisse parem celoque priorem.
105   Surgit in articulos, summos descendit in ungues,
Crure stat inverso, renes obliquat in arcum,
Ventre parum cedit, suspendit ad ilia levam,
Educit cubitum, flexam procul arduat ulnam,
Tenditur in pectus, declives vergit in armos,
110   Grandiloquum guttur et garrula colla supinat
Et, nisi pro voto respondent omnia, vultu
Candet et ignitis oculis pronosticat iram
Et digito nasum ferienti magna minatur,
Sed lesura parum, solo nocitura tumultu.
115   Ortu sidereo sublimis, proxima celo
Hec dea nobilium mandat se mentibus, illas
Adventu dignata suo. torquentis Olimpum
Sedibus orta Iovis, patrio desuescit ab ortu
Degenerare, casas vix intratura minores.
120   Sic sublime volat sceptrisque domestica reges
Incolit, hiis pugnat iaculis, hoc militat ense.
Et tamen interdum claustris invecta, potentum
Atria commutat casulis illicque profanam
Continuat sedem, sanctis illapsa cucullis.

Cap. 6 De monacho elato

125   Ecce supercilium monachi lunatur in altum,
Sublimis rapitur vultus declivis, ocellus
Surgit in obliquum, ventremque Superbia festo
Plus epulo tendit: duplex sic regnat Erinis
Interius, venterque Notho turgescit utroque.
130   Quid, cum turbatur animi pax intima? verbis
Intonat, ardescit oculis vultuque minatur.
Quid, quociens pastor erranti publica monstrat
Vel privata gregi iuris vestigia? nonne
Dictat in oppositum tumide presumptio mentis
135   Et leges alias decepte immurmurat auri?
Quid, quociens morbos ovium nocuosque tumores
Subsecuisse parat? reliquum pacienter ovile

Ch. 5 Pride

Her sister Pride has raised her dwelling nearby, and repines at being lower than the stars, refusing to acknowledge that anyone on earth is
05 equal to her, or closer to heaven. She rises on the balls of her feet, and walks on tiptoe; stands with her leg turned in, arches her loins, draws her stomach in a little, rests her left hand on her thigh, thrusts out her elbow, and holds her bent arm away from her body, pushes her breast
10 forward, draws her shoulders down, pulls back her high-sounding throat and gooselike neck – and then, if all does not conform to her wishes, her face grows hot, and her flashing eyes give notice of her anger. A finger tapping on her nose threatens terrible things, but little harm will come of it; her menace is no more than bombast.
15 Proud of her sidereal lineage and proximity to heaven, this goddess appeals to the minds of the nobility and honors them with her company. Born in the palace of Jove, who holds sway over Olympus, she is not used to descending from her high birthplace, and rarely visits humble
20 cottages. She soars aloft, and dwells as a familiar in the halls of kings. Scepters are the javelins and swords with which she wages war. Sometimes, however, she is brought into the cloister, and exchanges the great man's hall for a little cell. Here she maintains her profane way of life, though reduced to the cowl of holy poverty.

Ch. 6 Monkish Pride

5 See how the eyebrows of a certain monk are drawn upward, how his submissive gaze is raised up, and his eye looks this way and that. It is Pride, even more than the festive board, that swells his stomach. A double Fury rages within him, his belly is swollen by two kinds of wind.
10 What is it that resounds in his words, flashes from his eyes and makes his face seem threatening when the inner peace of his mind has been disrupted? What happens whenever the abbot seeks to give pastoral instruction to his erring flock on the patterns of public and private conduct? Does not the presumption of this monk's puffed-up
15 mind speak out against him, and deceive the listener by insinuating advice of another kind? Why is it that when the abbot seeks to cure his sheep of diseases and harmful growths, the rest of the flock patiently accept the chastisement of the shepherd, and remain quiet under his

Pastoris sequitur virgam pacemque flagellis
Exibet ut monitis; sed claustri hec belua, de qua
140 Fabula narratur, mansuescere verbere nullo
Sustinet aut verbo, domitores odit et instat
Asperior virgis, oculisque vomentibus iram
Fulminat et monitus fumanti despuit ore.
Hic, quarum vita est humili deiecta cuculla,
145 Spernit oves et eas audet presumerc de se
Delicias, in quem precium tocius ovilis
Confluat et solus virtute supernatet omnes.
Si quando careat baculus pastore, suoque
Rege vacet sceptrum moniale, hec belua sedem
150 Iam sibi sortitur viduam, dextramque maritat
Absenti baculo, vacua iam regnat in aula,
Iam subiecta iubet, omni se concipit unam
Imperio dignam, vacuam spem figit in alto,
Presumitque sibi baculum, quem perdere virtus
155 Et vicium rapuisse solet. iam fulgurat astri
Alterius radiis, iam tollit in ardua mentem,
Iam Iovis alterius ruituro pectore fulmen
Tractat et alterius animo prelibat honores,
Induiturque prius animus quam dextera sceptrum.
160 Sic fit apud claustrum; ventosque Superbia preceps
Velis prerapidos nigris infundit et albis,[9]
Mundanique maris rapto per inania cursu
Naviculam scopulis perituram mandat acutis.
      Ut, cui nota domus famuletur, novit: "O" inquit[10]
165 "O vicii radix primeva! novissima Christum
Accedit visura Deum, sed prima recedit;
Nativumque sibi propriumque hunc deligit usum,
Ut non unanimes faciat, quos inquinat una.
Magna quidem molles animos ligat unio, magna
170 Conciliat cupidas pacis clemencia mentes,
Pax quoque firma leves animos amplectitur, immo
Pax alios vite sumptos communiter usus
Nectit et unus amor studiis inservit eisdem;
Verum par tumidis venit indignacio preceps
175 Mentibus, alterno factura tonitrua vento
Discordesque secat morum concordia mentes.

40 blows and admonitions, while this cloistered monster whom my tale concerns cannot bear to submit to words or blows, but hates his superiors and resists all the more fiercely for having been beaten. While he fulminates, his eyes pour forth anger, and he spits out his menace from fuming lips.

45 Such a monk spurns those sheep whose life is shrouded in the cowl of humility, and dares to indulge delightful thoughts of becoming himself one to whom the charge of the whole flock might flow, so that he might rise above them all in power. Should the staff ever be in need of a shepherd, should the scepter of admonition lack its proper king, this 50 monster imagines claiming the widowed throne for himself. Already he embraces with his hand the absent staff of office, already he rules over his phantom court, already gives orders to subjects. Imagining himself uniquely worthy of absolute authority, he fixes his empty hopes on lofty 55 objects, and presumes to lay claim to that staff which virtue is all too apt to lose, and viciousness ever ready to usurp. Already he seems to glow with the radiance of another's star, already his mind ascends on high, already in precarious thought he wields the thunderbolt of a second Jove, and enjoys in his mind another's dignity. His mind assumes the 60 scepter long before his hand. Such things come to pass in the cloister. Pride fills sails both black and white[9] with her eager winds, and drives in headlong flight through the world's vast sea little vessels that sharp rocks are bound to destroy.

As he realizes to whose service this familiar house is devoted, Archi-65 trenius cries out:[10] "Oh most ancient root of vice! The last age is at hand, the age that will behold God in Christ, but the first age has grown distant. For the world has embraced pride as a thing natural and proper to itself, and there can be no unanimity, where this one sin defiles all mankind.

"There is to be sure a great unanimity among degenerate spirits; a 70 great mutual forbearance brings greedy minds into harmony. A common purpose draws unstable spirits together, and those who have chosen to pursue this common way of life; a single love informs their common pursuits. But a single indignation will descend headlong on 75 these arrogant minds, creating storm and thunder of another kind, and the community of the just will reject discordant spirits.

Cap. 7 De casu Luciferi

Hoc animi fulmen solio detrusit ab alto
Luciferum, Iovia dum se miratur in aula
Partitusque polos superum sibi destinat axem
180 Devexumque Iovi, sua cui decreta vel astris
Mandet suppositis; igitur rapturus ad Arthon
Imperium, fatuo conceptis pectore regnis
Affigi Boream iubet, indignatus ad Austrum
Sub pedibus regnare Iovis.[11] sed gloria cecis
185 Fidit in auguriis et amara superbia dulces
Vix habet eventus, melior prudencia fastus
Irritat et rigidus lentescere cogitur arcus.[12]
    Ecce novos flatus et prima tonitrua pacis
Etheree strepitusque rudes et semina belli,
190 Primicias odii, fraudis cunabula, mortis
Primevam faciem, vite nova funera, mentis
Iupiter archano circumspicit et periture
Compatitur proli. celo iunctissima culpam
Excusat Pietas manifestaque crimina velo
195 Palliat erroris, vindictam fixa superne
Sanctio iusticie dictat iustamque reatum
Evocat in penam, nec enim Iove maior ad axes
Imperet astrigeros; velit ipsa Superbia tantum
Non voluisse gradum, caveat suspecta ruine
200 Summa deum sedes. igitur sentencia pene
Cum nequeat flecti, Pietas secedit et iram
Iupiter induitur et hanelos concutit axes,
Fulmineisque manum iaculis armatus et ira,
Precipitat tonitrus, penamque in fulmine mandat
205 Et superum patriis civem deturbat ab astris.
    O miserum civem, cuius sub fulminis ictu
Detumuit flatus! o gloria dulcis amaras
Eliciens lacrimas! o lux augusta profundis
Pallescens tenebris, solii pictura superni,
210 Delicie celi, precio solidata perhennis
Materie proles, omni circumflua forme
Imperio, Flegetontis aquis assatur, Averni
Fundamenta tenens, Cochiti sorbet abyssum
Luctificam. felix, nisi se tot fonte bonorum
215 Lucifer agnosset! alter Narcisus et oris

Ch. 7 The Fall of Lucifer

"This same spiritual thunderbolt drove Lucifer from his lofty throne,
even as he wondered at finding himself in a Jovian court of his own: for
80 he had divided the heavenly realm, and assigned himself a region
withdrawn from Jove, where he might impose his decrees on the
subordinate stars. Then, preparing to seize dominion over the Pole,
having imagined such a kingdom in his foolish spirit, he commanded
that the northern realm be seized, for he disdained to rule the south
85 beneath the feet of Jove.[11] But vainglory trusts in blind auguries, and
bitter pride rarely enjoys sweet success: a superior wisdom provokes
him to scorn, and his rigid bow is forced at last to grow slack.[12]

"Behold Jupiter, surveying in the secret depths of his wisdom new
storms, thunder for the first time disturbing the peace of heaven, rough
90 clamor and provocations to war, the first effects of hatred, the birth of
deception, the original face of death, a grim new end to life. Jupiter,
reflecting in the secret depths of his mind, feels compassion for the
offspring of his who must perish: Pity, inseparably joined to the divine
95 nature, excuses the guilty act and seeks to clothe crime in the mantle of
error. But the unalterable ordinance of divine justice decrees vengeance,
and summons the guilty one to a just punishment. For none greater
than Jove may govern the star-bearing heavens: let Pride itself wish
never to have wished for so lofty a place, and the high realm of the gods
00 beware the threat of ruin. Since, then, the punishment decreed cannot
be averted, Pity withdraws; Jupiter puts on his wrath and shakes the
terrified heavens; armed with bolts of lightning and armed with wrath,
05 he hurls down thunder, makes lightning express his will, and casts out a
citizen of heaven from his starry home.

"O wretched citizen, whose swollen pride shrivelled at the blast of the
lightning-bolt! That the sweet love of glory should give rise to such bitter
tears! O noble radiance, o vision of a lofty throne and heavenly delights,
10 now growing dim among the deep shadows! A creature sustained by
the gift of eternal substance, enveloped in the utmost dignity of form,
now broils in the waters of Phlegethon, lurks in the depths of Avernos,
drinks the bitter waters of Cocytus. Happy Lucifer, had he not beheld his
15 image in a well of such bounty! He was a Narcissus, in the rich beauty of

Dotibus et fati lacrimis. solacia concors
Prebeat eventus, communis sarcina dampni
Pondus utrumque levet. miser ille, sed ille, quod ultra,
Quam liceat, temere speciem, quam vidit, amavit.[13]

Cap. 8 Invectio in superbiam

220   O celi scabies, terre contagia, mortis
Iniciale malum, ventosa superbia, cuius
Flatu fletifero pax est excussa superne
Et superis extincta dies! o prima reatus
Clausula, prima deum confusio, prima dolendi
225 Ianua, vas vacuum, pondus leve, robur inane,
De facili turgens animi vesica, potentum
Addita sevicie pestis, corrumpere vatum
Pectora prompta lues, facilisque inserpere plectris
Dulcibus et teneris preceps dare cornua Musis.
230 O abies, que nunc peregrino ad sidera ramo
Serpis et abiectum fugis indignante comarum
Maiestate solum! preceps hanc imminet hora
Suppressura fugam, non hec pede gloria firmo
Nititur, invalidis truncus radicibus heret,
235 Exiguum Boree subito casurus ad ictum."

Cap. 9 De monstro Cupiditatis

Dixit et extrema lacrimis immersit et imbre
Detumuit ventus, quem lingue intorserat ira.
Iamque pererrato – per plana, per aspera – mundo
Parte tenus magna, monstrum reperitur, eunti
240 Insolitus terror; nam celum vertice pulsat
Et patulis terre digitis superoccupat orbem
Et Phebe medium fraternos amovet ignes
Et Christi radios melioraque lumina tollit,
Mater Avaricie, sompni ieiuna Cupido,
245 Eternam dampnata sitim producere, nullis
Exsaciata bonis, lucri studiosa, rapinis
Artifices factura manus, visura recessus
Antipodum noctisque dies umbrasque sinistras,
Ardentis secreta sinus mollesque Sabeos
250 Et rigidos sine sole Getas primevaque Phebi

his face, and in his tearful fate. Let their consonant ending be a source of solace, and the shared onus of self-destruction ease the burden for both. One is utterly miserable, but the other is so because he foolishly loved beyond measure the beauty he beheld in himself.[13]

Ch. 8 An outcry against Pride

"O blight on the heavens, earthly plague, first of deadly evils, stormy Pride whose grief-bearing blast drove peace from heaven and extinguished the light of day for heavenly creatures! O first act of crime, first disruption of the life of the gods, first gateway to sorrow, empty vessel, weightless burden, hollow force, a quickly swelling blister on the mind, a disease that increases the cruelty of the great, a plague ever liable to corrupt the hearts of bards; it creeps over us like soft music, then suddenly endows the gentle Muses with trumpets.

"O tree, now inching upward toward the stars with venturesome limbs, rejecting the lowly earth in the disdainful majesty of your foliage, the hour is at hand that will suddenly curb this flight: there is no solid basis for this striving after glory, the tree is held up by infirm roots, and will suddenly fall at the lightest blow from Boreas."

Ch. 9 The monster Cupidity

He spoke, drenching himself in a final shower of tears, and eased the swollen storm-wind which his angry words had stirred up. And now, when he had traversed the hills and plains of a great part of the world, a monster appeared, a terror hitherto unknown to the traveller. Its head strikes against the sky, and it overspreads the surface of the earth with its broad claws, deprives Phoebe of her brother's fires, and obscures as well the beams, the truer light of Christ. It is the mother of Avarice, the fantasy of hungering Greed, condemned to produce an endless thirst that no material good can satisfy. Zealous for gain, she teaches the skillful hand to steal; her eyes see into the depth of night's Antipodes, the sinister shadows, the secret places of the heart's desire. She visits the effete Sabaeans, the sunless land of the rough Getae, and the rocky threshold where the young Phoebus first appears, lands from which

Limina cum scopulis, quibus exulat ultima Tyle,
Ut varias rerum species emungat, avari
Orbis opes animi longo sudore secuta,
Ut tandem modico loculis deserviat ere.

Cap. 10 Quid de cupidate Architrenius senciat

255   Horruit et, noto quid erat, suspexit et inquit
    "Hec Stigie superis infelicissima noctis
    Filia fas abolet, cancellat iura, resignat
    Federa, pacta movet, leges abradit, honestum
    Dampnat, amicicias rumpit, divellit amorem
260 Succinditque fidem: plena est discordia. questus
    Ardor ubi pugnat, studio concurritur omni
    Ad loculos; nam sola potest reverencia nummi
    Quodlibet ad libitum mundano quolibet uti.
    Hec vaga commutat solidis, quadrata rotundis,
265 Solvit amicicias veteres iterumque renodat,
    Quas prius abrupit. alternos gracia nodos
    Vix recipit, nisi quos alterna pecunia nectit.
        Dulcia sunt cupido lucrosa pericula: dulci
    Eolus armatur horrore, Ceraunia fluctu,[14]
270 Blanda Caribdis aqua, Phorcis cane,[15] Syrtis harena.
    Emollit scopulos lucri dulcedo, diurnas
    Absolvunt hiemes lucri momenta, labores
    Expiat innumeros lucrum breve, sarcina lucro
    Fit levis, et rutilo sudor siccatur in auro.

Cap. 11 Quod cupidus nullis habitis sit contentus

275   At licet Hesperie fluvios[16] Bessique meatus,
    Vincula Macrobii,[17] Crises vada, lina Neronis,
    Hesperidum ramos, Martis penetralia, Danes
    Impluvium, Bachi tumulum,[18] Phariique tiranni
    Naufragium,[19] tenerosque Iovis spoliaverit annos
280 Et Phebi tulerit, sapientum premia,[20] mensam
    Et geminos axes una congesserit archa,
    Cura tamen numquam residet suspensa soporis
    Pace, nec alternam requiem delibat avarus.
        Inter opes mendicus opum: non temperat unda,
285 Qua natat ipse, sitim; semper post parta laborat

far-off Thule is exiled, that she may defraud them of their various resources; and she devotes long and exhausting thought to the pursuit of the riches of the greedy world, so that she may at last be able to provide her coffers with a little money.

Ch. 10 Architrenius' views on Cupidity

55 Architrenius, gazing at the monster in horror and, realizing what it was, exclaimed, "This is that most ill-fated daughter of Stygian night who destroys right in heaven, nullifies justice, rescinds promises, alters agreements, cancels laws, repudiates honor, breaks up friendships,
60 severs the bond of love, and subverts trust. She is full of discord. When the desire for profit asserts itself, all rush eagerly to man the money-bags; for only when money is revered can one enjoy whatever one wants as much as one wants and wherever one wants. She can change
65 fluids to solids, make square things round, destroy old friendships and reunite again those whom she had sundered. Rarely can favor attend an exchange of affection unless an exchange of money has reinforced it.

"To the greedy the perils of the quest for money are sweet; there is a
70 sweet terror in the power of Aeolus, the Ceraunian waves[14] and the waters of Charybdis are pleasant, Scylla with her dogs[15] and the shoals of Syrtis. The sweet love of money makes the hard rocks soft; money's motive power reduces a winter to a single day; a little money makes good unnumbered labors; any burden is made lighter by money, and the ruddy glow of gold dries the sweating brow.

Ch. 11 Nothing he possesses will content the greedy man

75 "But though he should visit the Hesperian stream,[16] and the winding Hebrus, look on the Macrobian's chains,[17] the shoals of Chryse or the nets of Nero, the trees of Hesperus' daughters, the sanctuary of Mars, or the shower of Danae, the tomb of Bacchus,[18] the shipwreck of the Egyptian tyrant,[19] though he should despoil the world that saw the
80 infancy of Jove, carry off the table that was Phoebus' reward to the wise men,[20] and place the god's twin axle-trees on his heap of treasure, even then his anxiety can never be quieted by the peace of sleep; the greedy man never enjoys an interval of rest. Amid his wealth he is still a
85 beggar: the flood in which he wallows cannot ease his thirst. After every

In partus alios, nulloque retunditur ere
Mentis acus cupide. loculo vix sufficit uni,
Quicquid Fabricius sprevit Crassusque probavit.
Heret in ere sitis, habitis furit ardor habendi,
290 Pullulat in questu questus amor. omnia nullum
Pondus habent, nisi sint unum simul omnia pondus.

Cap. 12 Quod sola morte cupiditas terminatur

Infelix cupidis omnis fortuna, sitimque
Nulla levant, que cuncta sitit; sed meta malorum,
Mors, sola innumeras curas expellit et una
295 Falce metit, varii quicquid peperere labores,
Et bene de cupido tandem mors sola meretur
Cum longo vigiles sompno suffundit ocellos.
Vix tamen a questu studium subducitur. ipsum
Mortis ad imperium sensus vigilancia census
300 Eternum meminit, loculis in morte cadentes
Assurgunt oculi, tenero super omnia voto
Dilectus suprema rapit suspiria nummus.
Iamque Stigis medium perlabitur umbra memorque
Nunc eciam questus, in carnis claustra reverti
305 Nititur, ut nummo rursum potiatur amato
Et loculum loculo superaddat, Pelion Osse,
Colliculum monti, fluvio vada, flumina ponto.
At nullos reditus regis dispensat opaci
Sanctio. sic dominam saltem suspirat ad archam
310 Extremumque 'vale' Stigiis mandatur ab undis:
        'O loculi dulces, iocunda pecunia, nummi
Delicie, Sirenes opum, Philomena crumene,
Cuius ad aurate vocis modulamina cedit
Orpheus, fastiditur olor, delirat Apollo.'
315   O geminos solis ortus amplexa cupido
Alterutrumque diem, cuius radicibus omnis
Perplexatur humus celumque cacumina terrent.
Ve terre! superis cum sis suspecta nec eius
Diviciis contenta, vocas Titanas in astra
320 Sollicitasque Iovem superosque in monstra resolvis,
Dum petitur celum per Pelion, Ossan, Olimpum.
        Heu sortis misere, quibus est angusta bonorum
Porcio, sol oculis quicquid metitur, habere!

increase he labors to generate still more, and no amount of money can
dull the keen edge of his greedy mind. All that Fabricius scorned and
Crassus tasted are scarcely enough for his one purse. The thirst is
inherent in the money itself, the fever of possession rages in the things
190 possessed, the process of acquisition only spreads the love of acquiring.
Nothing has value unless all things can be possessed at once.

Ch. 12 Cupidity comes to an end only with death

"All luck is bad luck to the greedy: nothing can relieve the thirst of
one who thirsts for everything. Only death, the terminus of evil, ban-
195 ishes his infinite worries, reaping with a single sweep of its scythe all
that his manifold efforts had produced. And in the end only death shows
kindness to the greedy man, by suffusing his watchful eyes with lasting
slumber. Yet scarcely even then is he drawn away from his eagerness
for gain. On the very threshold of death's realm, his still-wakeful
200 thoughts dwell endlessly on his property, and as he dies his drooping
eyelids open to gaze on his moneybags. It is his beloved money most of
all that draws his last breaths into a feeble prayer. And even as his shade
is borne through the Styx, even then it recalls its possessions, and
205 struggles to return to its fleshly prison, that it may once again enjoy the
money it loves, and add yet another bag to the heap, a Pelion to the
Ossa, a knoll to the mountain, a brook to the river, a river to the ocean.
But the decree of the shadowy king admits of no returnings, and thus he
210 can only sigh for his beloved coffer, and send forth a last farewell from
the Stygian depths: 'O sweet treasury, o charming money, delightful
coin, o Siren-like wealth, nightingale purse, at the sweet sound of your
golden voice Orpheus yields, the swan is scorned, Apollo seems to rave.'
215 "O Greed, encompassing the two sunrises and both daytimes, every
soil is infested by your roots, and for your sake mountains menace
heaven. Alas for the earth! For you are not content with her wealth, but
220 threaten the very gods; you bid the Titans assail the stars, harass Jove
and reduce the gods to monsters, reaching for the sky from Pelion, Ossa,
and Olympus.

"Alas for those ill-fated ones whose lot it is to possess only that
meager portion of the world's goods which the eye of the sun encom-

Indepulsa manent cupide ieiunia mentis,
325 Quam non exsaciant uno minus omnia, pontum
Exhausisse, nisi bibulas emungat harenas.
Heu, pugnaturos plus quam civiliter enses
Alterneque necis gladios accincta Cupido
Mille modos leti rerumque pericula tractat,
330 Ut mundi lacrimas loculi transfundat in usus.

Cap. 13 Exclamacio in prelatos

O utinam sanctos hec citra viscera patres
Ecclesie pupugisset acus, ne vilior auro
Ara foret, sed libra libro, sed numine nummus.[21]
Non Davo caderet morum censura, Catonis
335 Limatum tociens temere morsura rigorem;
Non partiretur – consulto Simone – Petri
Curia vel baculos Christi vel cornua; virtus
Surgeret excessus circumcisura, beatos
Illustres factura viros; librasset honores
340 Ad meriti libram, nec ea sub iudice possent
Iura peroranti loculo succumbere; numquam
Birria sufficeret, ubi defecisset Homerus."

Cap. 14 De bello inter largos et avaros

Fine dato verbis, subitos bibit aure tumultus
Et ruptas gladiis Martisque tonitribus auras
345 Haurit et, horrisonis qua litigat ictibus aer,
Flectit iter stupidum, dubiisque allabitur ausis,
Mars ubi sevus agit, gladius necis eliquat imbres,
Sidera texuntur iaculis, superosque sagitta
Territat et densa noctescit harundine celum.
350 Gemmis vernat apex galee, lorica nitoris
Ridet in argento, mucro splendore minatur
Reptat in umbone leo flammeus, igneus aurum
Ventilat in hastis volitans draco, mortis odore
Cuspis inescatur, ignes equus arduus efflat
355 Sanguine crudescunt falere, spumescit habena
Indignata regi, freni natat ardor in ira,
Ungula summa volat, raptos iuba verberat armos,
Pectoris excussus aries terit obvius hostem,

325 passes! The hunger of their greedy minds can never be banished: all
things are not enough for them if any one be missing; it is not enough to
have drunk an ocean unless they may also loot the thirsty sands. Alas
for Greed, girded with the weapons of a conflict worse than civil war,
the swords of mutual slaughter; it conducts its perilous affairs in a
330 thousand deadly ways, conducing the stream of the world's tears to the
service of its treasury.

Ch. 13 An outcry against prelates

"O would that a needle had punctured the bellies of the holy fathers
of the Church before this; the altar would not now be less precious than
gold, but wisdom would be preferred to wealth, godhead to greed.[21]
335 Moral judgment would not stoop to condone a Davus, while daring to
carp endlessly at the tempered discipline of a Cato. The court of Peter
would not dole out Christ's staffs and miters on the advice of Simon.
Virtue would prevail, curbing excess and ensuring that men of holy life
340 were rewarded: honor would be weighed on the scale of merit. These
laws, moreover, would not be subject to reinterpretation on the appeal
of wealth: never would a Birria succeed where a Homer had failed."

Ch. 14 The war between the generous and the greedy

As he finished speaking, his ear was greeted by a sudden tumult.
345 Hearing in the wind the clash of swords and martial thunderings, he
made his astonished way to where the air teemed with the terrible
sound of blows, and approached with faltering courage a place where
Cruel Mars was at work, creating a rainstorm of blood with his sword,
while the very stars were crisscrossed by javelins, arrows menaced the
gods, and the sky grew dark with the dense flight of weapons.
350 The crown of the god's helmet is adorned with gems, his breastplate
rejoices in gleaming silver, his sword arouses fear by its sheer brilliance.
A flame-red lion crouches on his shield, while on his spear a fiery
dragon beats the golden air with its wings. His spearhead is steeped in
355 the odor of death. His bold steed, its trappings caked with blood,
breathes fire and froths at the mouth, disdaining to be ruled by the
bridle. Impatient of restraint, it seems to fly in its rage and speeds along
on the tips of its hooves. Its mane is hung with captured arms, and its
chest strikes against the enemy with the impact of a battering ram.

Celum Marte tonat, gladii face fulminat aer.
360   Sanguine luget humus, eadem mare purpura vestit,
Morte natantur aque, terram bibit unda cruoris,
Aera mugit equo, lituo sinus etheris hinnit,
Ictibus exclamat gladius, conflictibus umbo;
Turbine saxa fremunt, tede igni, tela volatu;
365   Subticet adventum plumbi impetus, ala sagitte,
Et nec funda neces nec vulnera precinit arcus.
Insilit arma Furor, acies Discordia nodat,
Terror agit currus, Feritas auriga iugales,
Efferat Ira viros maiorque Audacia Martis
370   Filia, vexillumque ferens Demencia belli.
Mucroni gladius occurrit, harundo sagitte,
Cornipedi sonipes, lateri sinus, ungula cornu,
Umboni clipeus, lituo tuba, missile telo,
Lorice torax, galee iuba, fraxinus haste.
375   Mars in morte natat, feriens Furor inserit enses,
Dumque fodit, fede cedis cadit unda redundans.

Cap. 15 Sermo Walgani ad Architrenium de Corineo[22]

Quod metuit, vidisse iuvat, novitasque videndi
Affectus et vota facit, miratur et – ecce –
Improvisus adest miranti miles, hanelo
380   Pulverulentus equo. dantur redeuntque salutes
Pace relativa. quis sit, quo tendat, uterque
Discit, uterque docet. tamen Architrenius instat
Et genus et gentem querit studiosius; ille:
"Tros genus et gentem tribuit Lodonesia, nutrix
385   Prebuit irriguam morum Cornubia mammam,
Post odium fati Frigiis inventa smaragdus.
Hanc domitor mundi, Tirynthius alter,[23] Achillis
Atrideque timor, Corineus, serra Gigantum
Clavaque monstritera, socie delegit alumpnam
390   Omnigenam Troie, pluvioque faviflua lacte
Filius exilio fesse dedit ubera matri.
A quo dicta prius Corineia, dicitur aucto
Tempore corrupti Cornubia nominis heres.[24]
Ille Giganteos attritis ossibus artus
395   Implicuit leto, Tirreni litoris hospes,
Indomita virtute Gigas non corpore, mole

The sky resounds with the noise of battle, and the air is bright with
360 the flash of swords. The earth seems to weep tears of blood, and adorns
the sea with the same purple. The waters teem with death, and a tide of
blood soaks the earth. The air echoes with the whinny of horses, and the
depths of the sky are full of the clarion of their neighing. The sword
resounds as it strikes, and the shield as it receives the blow. Rocks in
their whirling flight give off a low roar, the torches roar as they burn,
365 and spears as they fly. The lead shot and the winged arrow give no such
notice of their coming; neither sling nor bow foretells the wounds and
deaths it inflicts. Madness rushes to arms, Discord firms up the battle-
lines, Terror drives the chariot forward, Savagery is the charioteer who
guides the team, Wrath lends fierceness to the troops, and Boldness,
370 elder daughter of Mars, and Folly, bearing the standard of war. Sword
clashes with sword, bowman with bowman, hard-hoofed steed with
loud-hoofed steed, side to side, hoof to hoof. Shields, war-trumpets,
375 missiles, armor, helmets, spears join in conflict. Mars wallows in death,
Madness lends force to the blows of swords, and at their deep cut a
copious stream of gory death pours forth.

Ch. 15 Gawain's speech to Architrenius concerning Corineus[22]

Though the sight is fearful, it pleases Architrenius to behold it, and
the unfamiliar spectacle elicits sympathy, desire and wonder. And lo, as
380 he gazes, a knight suddenly appears, covered with dust and on an
exhausted steed. Greetings are exchanged in mutual good will, and each
learns from the other, and explains to him, who he is and where he is
going. Yet Architrenius eagerly and earnestly asks the other's nation
and lineage, and he replies: "My people are Trojan, and London gave
385 me birth. Cornwall, that gem discovered by the Phrygians after the cruel
fate of Troy, was the nurse whose flowing breast sustained my upbring-
ing. It was this place that Corineus – the world-conqueror, the second
Tyrinthian,[23] the terror of Achilles and the Atrides, the cutter-down of
390 giants and batterer of monsters – chose as the all-producing nursery of a
new Trojan society; thus did a son offer to a mother worn out by exile
breasts flowing with milk and honey. Hence the place, at first named
Corineia, over the course of time assumed the corrupted name of
Cornubia.[24]

"Sojourning on the shores of Italy, Corineus destroyed the limbs of
395 giants with a bone-crushing embrace. He was himself a giant, not in
body but in his indomitable heroism. Though confined to medium

Ad medium pressa, nec membris densior equo
Sarcina terrifico tumuit Titania monte.
    Ad Ligeris ripas Aquitanos fudit et amnes
400 Francorum pavit lacrimis et cede vadoque
Sanguinis ense ruens saciavit rura, togaque
Punicea vestivit agros, populique loquacis
Grandiloquos fregit animosa cuspide fastus.
Integra, nec dubio bellorum naufraga fluctu,
405 Nec vice suspecta titubanti saucia fato,
Indilata dedit subitam Victoria laurum.

Cap. 16 De adventu Bruti et Corinei in Angliam et de Gigantibus

    Inde dato cursu, Bruto comitatus Achate,
Gallorum spolio cumulatis navibus equor
Exarat et, superis auraque faventibus utens,
410 Litora felices intrat Totonesia portus
Promissumque soli gremium monstrante Diana,
Incolumi census loculum ferit Albion alno.
    Hec eadem Bruto regnante Britannia nomen
Traxit in hoc tempus, solis Titanibus illo
415 Sed paucis famulosa domus, quibus uda ferarum
Terga dabant vestes, cruor haustus, pocula trunci,
Antra lares, dumeta thoros, cenacula rupes,
Preda cibos, raptus Venerem, spectacula cedes,
Imperium vires, animos furor, impetus arma,
420 Mortem pugna, sepulcra rubus; monstrisque gemebat
Monticolis tellus, sed eorum plurima tractus
Pars erat occidui terror, maiorque premebat
Te furor, extremum Zephiri, Cornubia, limen.
    Hos avidum belli Corinei robur Averno
425 Precipites misit. cubitis ter quatuor altum
Gemagog Herculea suspendit in aera lucta,
Antheumque suum scopulo detrusit in equor;
Potavitque dato Thetis ebria sanguine fluctus,
Divisimque tulit mare corpus, Cerberus umbram.

stature, and with limbs not disproportionately thick, he seemed to
assume a Titanic stature, massive and terrifying. On the banks of the
,oo Loire he routed the Aquitanians, and fed the rivers of France with tears.
Wreaking havoc with his sword and steeping the countryside in
carnage and streams of blood, he decked the fields in a purple robe,
humbling the haughty eloquence of a loquacious people with undaunted arms. A complete and decisive victory, undamaged by the shifting
,o5 tides of war, untroubled by any reversal and marred by no vacillation of
fate; earned him hasty laurels.

Ch. 16 The arrival of Brutus and Corineus in England and an encounter with Giants

"Pursuing his destined course, accompanied by Brutus, his Achates,
Corineus plowed the waves, his ships laden with Gallic booty. Favored
10 by gods and winds, and guided by Diana to this destined corner of the
world, he enters safe harbor on the Cornish coast at Totnes, and, with
his vessels unharmed, comes ashore in that rich treasury Albion.

"This same land has retained the name of Britain, from its ruler
15 Brutus, to the present time. In those days it provided a home only for a
few Titans, whose garments came from the damp bodies of wild beasts,
who drank blood from goblets of wood, who made their homes in caves,
their beds out of brush, their tables from rocks. Hunting gave them food,
rape served for love, slaughter was their entertainment. Brute strength
20 was their law, madness their courage, impulsive violence their warfare.
Battle was their death, and thickets were their tombs. The whole land
complained of these mountain-dwelling monsters, but they were for the
most part the terror of the western region, and their mad ravages most
afflicted you, Cornwall, uttermost threshold of the west wind.

"It was the might of Corineus, ever ready for battle, that drove these
25 creatures headlong into Avernos. In a Herculean struggle he lifted
Gemagog, twelve cubits tall, on high, then cast his Antaean enemy from
a rock into the sea. Drunken Thetis drank the stream of blood he gave
forth. The sea scattered his limbs; Cerberus received his shade.

Cap. 17 De conceptione Arturi et ortu eius ad quem scribitur

430   Nobilis a Frigie tanto Cornubia gentem
       Sanguine derivat, successio cuius Iulum
       In generis partem recipit, complexa Pelasgam
       Anchiseque domum. ramos hinc Pandrasus,[25] inde
       Silvius[26] extendit, socioque a sidere sidus
435   Plenius effundit triplicate lampadis ignes.
          Hoc trifido sole Corinei postera mundum
       Preradiat pubes, quartique puerpera Phebi
       Pullulat Arturum, facie dum falsus adulter
       Tintaiol irrumpit nec amoris Pendragon estum
440   Vincit et omnificas Merlini consulit artes
       Mentiturque ducis habitus et rege latenti
       Induit absentis presencia Gorlois ora.
          Ecce furor lucis![27] maiori sidere quintus
       Enituit Phebus, ad cuius lumina quivis
445   Sol alius Saturnus erit. splendore planetas
       Vesperat: obscuro brumescit Falcifer igne
       Cecus ea sub nocte senex, Iovis erubet astrum,
       Marte verecundo, peplo Venus occulit ora,
       Mercurius mitra; Phebe ferrugine vultus
450   Ethiopes odit faciemque intersa lutosam
       Plena latet nodo, germanaque turbida fratrem
       Et modicum lucis vocat et causatur avarum.

Cap. 18 De Ramofrigio[28]

          Hunc Ramofrigius mundo intulit, anchora iuris
       Impaciens nutasse ratem; se Tidea bello
455   Exibuit, se pace Numam, scelerumque procellas
       Propulit infracto securus navita clavo,
       Quem precessiva Racio dedit, excuba tanto
       Cum socia Virtute viro. se moribus ipsis
       Prebuit exemplum nec honesti flexit habenam
460   Alter – sed melior – hic Nestor, Nestore primo
       Annis inferior, par pectore, celsior actis.
          De genitore fidem genitus facit: optimus ille
       Extitit, existit superoptimus ille, bonorum
       Maximus absque gradu. non est quo surgat honestum

Ch. 17 The birth of Arthur, and the origins of him to whom the book is addressed

"Thus noble Cornwall traces its ancestry to the blood of the Phrygians, whose descendants, recognizing in Iulus their claim to this
heritage, joined the royal house of Anchises to that of Greece. Pandrasus[25] extended the royal line in one direction, Silvius[26] in another,
and the star derived from this union of stars poured forth the fuller
radiance of a triple light.

"The later progeny of Corineus spread the radiance of this triple sun
over the world, and the bringing-to-birth of a fourth Phoebus produced
Arthur, when the adulterer under a false appearance broke into Tin-
tagel. For Pendragon could not overcome the strength of his love, and
appealed to the versatile arts of Merlin. He assumed the appearance of
the duke, and, hiding his kingly identity, assumed the outward appearance of the absent Gorlois.

"Behold a frenzy of light![27] A fifth Phoebus gleams with a yet greater
brightness; any other sun is a Saturn in comparison. Its splendor
eclipses the planets. The aged Scythe-Bearer dwindles to a faint glow,
hardly visible in this darkness. Jove's star blushes, Mars grows shy,
Venus conceals her face with her robe, Mercury his with his helmet.
Phoebe, grown as dusky as an Ethiopian, loathes her appearance. Full,
but unable to cleanse her tarnished face, she hides in eclipse: the
distraught sister appeals to her brother for a little light and complains
that he is stingy.

Ch. 18 Ramofrigius[28]

"Ramofrigius, an anchor of rectitude who would not allow the vessel
of justice to go astray, introduced this sun to the world. He proved
himself a Tydeus in warfare, a Numa in time of peace, a steadfast sailor
who thrust forward through the storms of a wicked world with that
helm unbroken which foresighted Reason provided – Reason who had
long kept watch, with her companion Virtue, for such a man. He proved
exemplary in character, and never swerved from the path of honor, a
second and greater Nestor, inferior to the first in years, but equal to him
in wisdom and superior in deeds.

"The offspring gives clear evidence of his progenitor: if the one
excelled, the other is superexcellent, great beyond any measure of
achievement. Having attained the highest level honor can rise no

465 Supra summa situm, nec novit linea morum
Infinita gradum. reliquus sic orbis ab uno
Exsuperatur, uti, quem contingencia curvat,
Angulus a recto. numquam descendit ad Austrum
Articus et pleno radiat fulgore dieque
470 Integra sol iste superlativus et illo
Pro gemma voluit mundi teres anulus uti.
Hoc aurifrigio tellus redimitur, eoque
Stellea Rothomagi lascivit palla sabelo,
Gemmescitque novo Christi sacra nupta monili.
475 Hic sinus hos, hominum rosulas et lilia, vernat.
Regula: nil gignit olidum Cornubia. partus
Expolit illimes et ab ubere pignora tersis
Morigerat viciis et plus quam cetera scabram
Limat avariciam, que nostre sepius Artho
480 Institit et gelidum violenta lacessiit orbem.
At nos pro patria semper pugnavimus, armis
Elidendo minas; Laciumque repellere monstrum[29]
Cura laborque fuit. et adhuc, ne tanta nepotes
Belua subvertat, pugili sudamus in ense;
485 Reppulimusque suas acies hucusque, necesque
Fudimus innumeras. set adhuc cum multa supersint
Milia, non prono rapitur victoria cursu.

Cap. 19 De ducibus castorum Avaricie

Marte potens miles, nimbo populosior, illis
Semper agit castris, et ea de parte magistri
490 Bellorumque duces sunt, quos eterna notabit
Et notat illa lues: Parthorum victima, Crassus,
Septimulusque[30], suo qui Gracco pretulit aurum,
Et loculis donans ne tutus Cassius[31] esset,
Quique necis proprie Ptolomeus[32] rettulit hosti
495 Premia, ne census ageret divorcia pontus
Naufragioque daret dilecta pecunia penas.

higher, and no scale can define an infinite degree of virtue. The rest of
the world is surpassed by this one man, just as a right angle is greater
than an angle of contingence. This Pole Star never descends to the
70 south, this supreme sun shines with the full brilliance of a perfect day,
and the world is glad to make him the jewel in the ring of its circling
course. The world derives a new value from this orphrey, the rich
vestments of Rouen luxuriate in this sable, and the sacred bride of Christ
is resplendent in this new necklace.

75   "Such are the men the rich spring of this small place produced, the
roses and lilies of humankind. Take it as a law: Cornwall can produce
nothing rank. She gives birth to flawlessly fashioned creatures, and at
her breast imbues her progeny with character, rendering them free of
vicious habits and above all cleansing them of avarice, which has too
80 often infested our northern wind, and assailed the world with its chilling
blast.

     "But we have always been at war for our country, resisting threats
by force of arms. To drive back the Latian monster[29] has been our
anxious labor, and even now we must wield the sword of war lest this
85 terrible beast overthrow our descendents. Thus we have repelled her
attacks until now, and have produced countless slaughter, but when so
many thousands still survive, the path to victory is not easy.

Ch. 19 The leaders of the forces of Avarice

     "A powerful army, a throng more dense than a storm cloud, is
90 always on duty in their camp, and the strategists and generals of their
campaign are those who bear and will bear forever the mark of this
disease: Crassus, the victim of the Parthians; Septimuleius,[30] who
valued gold more than his own leader Gracchus; Cassius,[31] who enriched his treasury rather than ensure his own safety; and Ptolemy,[32]
95 who presented the rich reward of his own death to his enemies, rather
than let the sea divorce him from his property and allow his beloved
money to suffer shipwreck.

Liber Sextus

Cap. 1 De Arturo, Ramofrigio, Walgano in Avariciam dimicantibus

Ex alio belli cuneo sumus: alter Achilles,
Arturus, teretis mense genitiva venustas,
Et Ramofrigius, dandi non unda sed equor,
Et Walganus ego, qui nil reminiscor avara
5 Illoculasse manu. non hec mea fulgurat auro
Sed gladio dextra; recipit, quod spargat, et enses
Non loculos stringit. nec opes incarcero miles
Degener et cupide cumulato rusticus ere.
At me bella vocant et te tua forsitan urget
10 Sollicitudo, vale." non expectatus eunti
Reddidit ille 'vale' meditativusque recedit
Corde querelanti, quod scrutativus et Austrum
Viderit et Thetide miranti merserit Arthon,
Effusoque vagus oculo perlegerit orbem,
15 Nullaque propositi datur exoptata facultas.

Cap. 2 De transitu Architrenii in Tylon[1]

Intimus ergo tumet vultusque superfluit ira,
Purpureisque furor animi coquit ora caminis.
Nec mora, dum fervet nec tempore temperat ignem,
Floridulum mundi thalamum Verisque penates
20 Advenit usque Tylon, ubi numquam labitur – absque
Preterito presens – plus quam perfecta venustas.
Perpetuatur honos rosulis, intacta senecte
Lilia pubescunt, senium nec bruma nec estas
Advehit et veris eternativa iuventam
25 Floribus ipsa loci deitas nativa perhennat.
Hic, ubi planicies patulum lunatur in orbem,
Philosophos serie iunctos circumspicit; in qua

Book Six

Ch. 1 Arthur, Ramofrigius and Gawain wage war against Avarice

"We are an army of another kind: Arthur, that new Achilles, the source and glory of the Round Table; Ramofrigius, not a stream but an ocean of largesse; and I myself, Gawain, who can not recall consigning
5 anything to my purse with stinting hand. The gleam in this right hand of mine is not gold, but a sword. It receives only what it deals out, and it strikes, not at purses, but at weapons. I am no base knight who hoards his wealth, no villain greedily acquiring money. But battle calls me, and
10 perhaps cares of your own draw you away. Farewell."

Architrenius returned a "farewell" which the departing one did not wait to hear, and then went on, deep in thought, inwardly complaining that in his wanderings he had searched carefully through even the southern regions, seen the Bears sink beneath the waters of an astonished Thetis, and cast his sweeping gaze over the whole world, yet had not found an occasion for the task he hoped to perform.

Ch. 2 Architrenius' entry into Thylos[1]

Thus he seethes within, and anger suffuses his visage; the rage in his heart steeps his face in its purple flames. But soon, while he still rages
20 and time has not yet reduced the fire, he arrives at Thylos, the world's flourishing bower, the abode of Spring, whose more than perfect beauty, unaffected by the passage of time, never fades. Here the rose is perpetually in its glory, lilies bloom yet remain untouched by age; for neither withering frost nor the heat of summer intrudes, and an eterniz-
25 ing power, a deity native to the place, ensures the perennial flowering of its youthful spring.

Coming to where the open plain formed a broad circle, he saw around him an ordered array of philosophers. In their midst Archytas[2]

Architas[2] varios excessus explicat ire
Et docet, hac mentem Furia vexante, labores.

Cap. 3 Oracio Archite de ira

30   "Ira malum deforme viris, quo pectus acescit,
Sensus hebet, languet studium, sollercia lippit,
Cecatur racio, pietas tepet, alget honestas,
Macrescit virtus, vicium pinguescit, inundat
Livor, adest facinus, lex nutat, norma vacillat,
35   Pax titubat, surgit odium, clemencia vergit,
Cedit amor, crescit hostis, rarescit amicus,
Insidie serpunt, ruit impetus, evolat ardor,
Bella fremunt, Bellona tuba, Mars intonat ense,
Vita fugit, viteque sopor mors ultimus instat.
40   Ira malum, quo non aliud velocius alas
Urget in errorem pennasque in devia versat.
In faciem surgit et pectore nascitur ira,
Interiusque cremat et vultibus exilit ardor,
Precipitesque furor animos rotat, ora perurit.
45   Hic rogus, exterius celari nescius, urit,
Accensoque labor animi vulgatur in ore,
Nec tacet archanum mentis facundia vultus.
Imperat hec dextris rabies natosque parentum
Immergit iugulis, contraque in pignora patres
50   Efferat et fratris frater bibit ense cruorem.
Cognatas acies alterno sanguinis haustu
Polluit et gladio nature federa rumpit.
Cedibus accedunt cedes, et ceca nefandis
Implicat in facinus pugiles audacia sensus.
55   Ire fida manus cladesque ancilla ministrans
Surgit et exilium pacis molitur iterque
Rumpit in omne nefas: Rabies germana Furoris,
Pronus in arma Furor, stricto vagus Impetus ense,
Indocilis flecti Feritas et cognita sceptris
60   Sedicio cecusque Tumor regnique Tirannis
Et soror et coniunx, et belli semina, Lites
Litigiique tube, crudoque Insania vultu,
Rixarumque Faces et Iurgia plena cruoris,
Cedeque Sevicies Ire clausura tumultus.
65   Ira iuventutis solitus calor, ardor amantum

was expounding the disruptive effects of anger, and showing the hardships with which this Fury assails the mind.

Ch. 3 Archytas' oration on anger

30 "Wrath is an ugly quality, through which the heart grows bitter, understanding fails, alertness lapses, apprehension becomes sleepy, reason is blinded; loyalty grows weak, honor fails; virtue starves while vice grows fat; envy floods the mind and gives rise to crime, while law 35 and moderation falter; peace trembles at the emergence of hatred; mercy wanes and love recedes; hostility thrives and friendship dies away; creeping treachery, impetuous violence and soaring passion appear; war rages, as Bellona's trumpet and the sword of Mars resound; and life is banished by the onset of death, the final slumber.

40   No other evil flies so quickly into error as Wrath, beating its wings and flying about at random. It is born in the heart and wells up into the face. It burns inwardly and its heat bursts forth through the face; its 45 madness stirs up the impulsive spirit, and causes the face to burn. The flames of its great fire cannot be concealed from outward view, and the labor of the spirit is manifested in the blazing face. The eloquent expression of the face does not conceal the hidden state of mind.

This madness controls our actions, makes sons pierce the throats of 50 parents and causes fathers to act savagely against their children, a brother's weapon drink a brother's blood. It defiles the blades of kinsmen with reciprocal bloodshed, and severs the bonds of nature with a sword. Slaughter is added to slaughter, and a boldness blind to its own wickedness leads the warring senses into guilty actions.

55   A faithful retinue stands ready to serve Wrath with violent acts, striving to banish peace and force a path to every kind of wrongdoing: Frenzy, the sister of Rage; Rage herself, ever ready to take up arms; Violence, rushing about with drawn sword; incorrigible Savagery; 60 Sedition, the familiar of kings; blind Pomp; Despotism, the sister and wife of royal power; Dispute and loud Litigation, the seeds of open war; Madness with bloody face; Strife with her torches, and bloody Quarrel; and Savagery, which makes angry quarrels conclude in slaughter.

65   Wrath is present in the accustomed heat of youth, the ardor of a lover

Acrior in penas stragique paracior ense,
Maturasque neces laqueo, face, cuspide cogens,
Cum Veneris voto contraria ludit amantes
Alea, nec motus animi Fortuna secundat,
70 Nec ferit ad libitum voti quo tenditur arcus.
Ira parens Odii, quod proles tercia Livor
Subsequitur, pestis utriusque diucior heres."
    Audit et incinerat gelidis fornacibus ignes
Et sepelit vivam prius Architrenius iram.
75 Pascitur auditis, propius sedet, erigit aurem,
Cor patulum solvit; etenim sermone carenti
Gloria precessit. sequitur Plato verba secundans.

Cap. 4 Oracio Platonis de livore

    "Ecce furor livoris acus maiorque Megera
Invidie, fame cumulum raptura beatis.
80 Non pudet in mundos maculas iurasse, notatis
Adiecisse notas. Herebum fastidit Erinis
Maternamque Stygen, nostras peregrinat in edes
Hospita dente gravis, didicit revocasse favores,
Exacuisse dolos, clausos aperire reatus.
85 Ipsa scelus fictura nefas, tortura flagello
Pervigili mentes, successibus egra, sinistros
Ad casus lugubre canens, lacrimosa secundis,
Gavisiva malis, ideo merore serenum
Et risu lacrimans fatum comitatur amaro.
90   Livori assistunt Rabies animosa, Tumultus,
Pax armata dolis, suspectum Fedus, amoris
Umbra, latens Odium, gladio Mars igneus, 'arma,
Arma, viri' Bellona tonans et pronuba belli
Sedicio, primumque ferens Discordia pilum.
95   Livor in insidias et in ebria tela veneno
Irruit et varia cumulantur pocula morte
Exundantque neces, nec inexpugnabile prestant
Divicie vallum, sed vino purpura cedit
Mortibus hamato, dampnique incauta potestas
100 Illud easque bibit; aliudque infunditur ostro
Quam Tyrium virus: hoc enitet, enecat illud;
Erigit hoc fastus, illosque ulciscitur illud.
Detulit a superis radicem Livor et ortu

keen to brave pain and ever ready for a duel. It is Wrath that imposes untimely deaths by hanging, fire, or the sword, when at Venus' whim a contrary throw of the dice mocks a lover, and his Fortune does not
70 conform to the shape of his desire, nor the arrow strike in response to the hope with which it was aimed. Wrath is the parent of Hatred, from which a third offspring, Envy is descended, a disease that long outlives either of the others."

As Architrenius listens, the fires in his cold furnaces are reduced to
75 ashes, and he extinguishes his once active wrath. He feeds on what he hears, draws closer, pricks up his ears and opens his heart, for the surpassing glory of the discourse leaves him speechless. Plato follows, and conforms his words to the previous speech.

Ch. 4 Plato's oration on Envy

"Behold the raging of malice, the goad and greater Megaera of Envy, who seeks to snatch away the rewards of those blessed with a good
80 name. She is not ashamed to bear false witness against the blameless, adding her aspersions to their known qualities. This Fury disdains Erebus and her native Styx, and journeys abroad to our own halls, a sharp-toothed guest who has learned to retract gifts, incite treachery,
85 and lay open guilty secrets. In her wickedness she invents wicked acts, tormenting our minds with her ceaseless lash. She is made wretched by our successes, and mournfully celebrates our failures, weeping at good fortune, rejoicing at misfortune; thus she is complacent in the face of sorrow, and responds to occasions of grief with a bitter smile.

90 "Envy's attendants are unremitting Frenzy and Agitation; Peace armed with guile and the untrustworthy Covenant; the appearance of love and lurking Hatred; fiery Mars with his sword, Bellona thundering "To arms! to arms!"; Sedition, sponsor of war, and Discord who hurls the first spear.

95 "Envy is quick to prepare ambushes, and weapons drunk with poison; her goblets are full of death and overflow with slaughter. Even wealth does not provide an impenetrable rampart, for the great man, too, succumbs to wine barbed with death; in all his might, with no
00 thought of danger, he drinks down the one with the other. It is the taint of something other than Tyrian dye that infuses his purple splendor: the one is noble, the other deadly. The one breeds arrogance, the other avenges it.

"Envy traces her origin to heaven. Being of such lofty birth she

Summus summa petit, superisque simillima pulsat,
105 Certamenque deis plus quam civile minatur.
　　　Divitis et celo redolentis lilia fame
Livoris decerpit hiemps, insultat honori,
Extenuat laudes, adimit virtutis odorem
Nariculis Fame, superos fragrancia morum
110 Balsama delimat, virus inspirat et atro
Polluit afflatu, dens improbus omnia carpit
Nec sibi depercit, in cetera Livor et ipsum
Sevit in auctorem, roditque et roditur idem.
　　　Livor opem pressis et opes sublimibus aufert
115 Provectumque bonis, meritis infesta Celeno,
Eternum fornax odium coctura noverce.
Et puto philosophis laterum livore potentum
Tollitur accessus metuendaque gracia sceptri;
Nam livor titulum, quem non habet, odit haberi."

Cap. 5 Invectio Catonis contra divicias

120　　Ut modus est verbis, subeunt partita favorem
Murmura, nec serpunt vacui livore susurri.
Nec mora, dum linguis immissa licencia fandi
Materias versat, iuvat exclamasse Catonem:
　　　"O inopes virtutis opes! o gloria paucos
125 Productura viros, celoque invisa potestas,
Nec loculis factura deos! felicia molles
Seducunt animos, nec sunt commercia regnis
Cum Iove, nec mitra superis accedis; inopsque
Plus anime quam dives habet, levioribus alis
130 Pauper in astra volat, dulcique pecunia mole,
Quos aluit, lesura premit, nec Cresus in auro
Fata fugit, perdensque deos non perditur umbris.
　　　O Herebi descensus, opes, et maior Averni
Introitus mortisque fores, quas Cerberus alter
135 Ambitus extruxit medioque erexit in orbe,
Qua surgit cum divitibus factura Megera
Colloquium notaque diu cum prole susurrat
Et iacit amplexus et plaudit et oscula miscet,
Incautoque doli ridenti arridet alumpno.
140 Interdum Stygias attencius edocet artes
Sollicitumque minus intorto verberat idro,

frequents lofty places, strikes at those who most resemble the gods, and threatens something worse than civil war against the gods themselves. In the heavenly world of wealth, Envy is like winter, blighting the lilies of sweet-smelling renown, reviling honor and belittling praise. She removes the sweet scent of virtue from the nostrils of Fame, deprives her betters of the fragrant balsam of good character, infusing her poison and polluting everything with her black breath. Her wicked tooth snaps at everything, and does not spare herself: she is cruel to others, and cruel to those in whom she grows; as they bite at others, they themselves are gnawed by her.

"Envy begrudges aid to the oppressed, wealth to the great, preferment to the good. She is a Harpy in her cruelty toward merit, a furnace that glows with a stepmother's undying hatred. And I think it is through Envy that philosophers are denied access to the company of the great, and the awesome favor of the crown. For Envy is furious when any distinction is granted that she herself does not possess."

Ch. 5 Cato's inveighal against wealth

As the speech ended, it was met by murmured expressions of approval, and no hollow, envious whispers insinuated themselves. Without delay, even as the opportunity for speaking was giving rise to various topics, Cato was moved to cry out: "O riches poor in virtue! O glory that advances so few! O power hateful to heaven! Your wealth cannot make men into gods; your joys entice our weak wills, but your kingdom can have no commerce with Jove, nor your mitred ones enter heaven. The poor have more spiritual treasure than the wealthy. A pauper soars aloft on light wings, while the cherished mass of money proves an injurious burden to those whom it has enriched. Croesus amid his gold cannot elude his fate: though he squander his "gods," he cannot escape the world of the shades.

"Wealth is the way to Erebus, the main passageway to Avernos and portal of death, whose circles a second Cerberus has reconstructed in the midst of our world. Here Megaera emerges to commune with the wealthy, whispers with her long-cherished progeny, bestows embraces and praise mixed with kisses, and smiles on the smiling pupil unmindful of her guile. As she carefully instructs him in her Stygian arts, she strikes him all unawares with a writhing serpent. Its bite spreads

Effusumque iacit Stygium per viscera virus,
Quo nequeat non velle nefas scelerumque soporem
Nesciat et numquam facinus succumbat honesto.

Cap. 6 De transitu Megere et Mortis ab inferis in potentes

145 Hac solitum decurrit iter totumque Megera
Advehit infernum; quicquid Plutonius axis
Educat immundum, viciorum turba, sinistra
Progenies noctis, matrem complexa feruntur
Emerguntque sinu, bibulasque paludibus aulas
150 Aspergunt Stygiis, propiusque vocantur et omni
Assunt consilio. verum cum sorde fluenti
Polluti satis est et fuse lacius orbem
Afficiunt macule – nec Ditem evadere dites
Dant delicta fidem – , Mors ecce, extrema dierum
155 Vespera, pallenti subito procedit amictu
Accensamque tenet sicco Flegetonte cupressum,
Que decisa rogis pigmentet odoribus auras,
Divitibus supremus honos. prenuncia Fati
Noctua precedit, properanti Morte propinquos
160 Occasus infausta canens, buboque sinistri
Augurii vates; evumque in dulcibus annis
Atropos abrumpens Fati comitatur euntis
Indivisa vias, Lacrime Planctusque sequuntur
Et Gemitus, fletuque madens Decisio vultus,
165 Funeribusque comes Ululatus et horrida crinis
Arduitas, scissoque come Iactura capillo,
Diruptique Sinus et meste vestis Honestas
Et manuum presso coeuntes pectine Nodi.
    Inserit ergo manum trabeis gremioque reducto
170 Exuit, et dextre sceptrum, diadema revellit
Crinibus, et Stygie spoliatum mandat harene,
Funebrique tuba victrix circumsonat aulam
Et superis vindex clangoribus ethera pulsat,
Optatumque deis reserat clamore triumphum
175 Et de divitibus nota est victoria celo.

through his body a hellish poison, so that he is unable not to will evil; he knows no rest from wrongdoing, and honor cannot overcome his wickedness.

Ch. 6 The passage of Megaera and Death from the underworld into the mighty

5 "Subject to this Fury, he pursues his wonted course, while Megaera summons all the powers of hell. Whatever foul thing the world of Pluto produces, the teeming vices and the evil progeny of night are borne along in their mother's embrace and emerge from her bosom to sprinkle
o the dank waters of Styx over the drunken palace, where they are welcomed and lend their voice to all deliberations. But when all are sufficiently corrupted by their foul effluent, and the widespread taint has afflicted the whole world (for his wicked deeds ensure that no Dives will
5 evade Dis), Death, the evening of all our days, suddenly comes forth in her pallid robe, bearing a cypress torch kindled in waterless Phlegethon, to be laid on the pyre and adorn the breeze with its scent, as a final tribute to wealth. The night-owl, harbinger of doom, flies before, singing
o ominously of similar downfalls as Death draws on, together with the screech-owl, that priest of unlucky augury. Atropos, breaking the thread in the sweet prime of life, follows closely in the path of departing Fate. Weeping, Complaint and Mourning follow, and Clawing-at-the-
5 face, drenched with tears, Howling, the companion of funerals, dishevelled Hardship and Deprivation, tearing her hair, the torn blouse and the Honor of robes of mourning, their knots held fast by the comb of tightly clasped fingers.

"Death then grasps the robe of state and lays bare the hidden body,
o plucks the scepter from the right hand, the crown from the head, and relegates the despoiled monarch to the Stygian strand. Victorious, she causes funereal trumpets to resound through the court; an agent of divine justice, she makes the heavens throb with loud music, announc-
5 ing clamorously that this triumph is pleasing to the gods. A victory over wealth is acknowledged by heaven.

Cap. 7 Exclamacio in divicias

O subito lapsurus apex! o pendula rerum
Ardua, precipitem gravius factura ruinam!
O mundi lugubris honos et debile robur,
Divicie, Fati dubio quassabile flatu!
180 Haut procul a mentis oculo ventura recedat
Illa dies, quam clausa Dei prudencia differt
Occultamque videt, que tandem cognita regum
Mordeat excessus penamque excedere crimen
Vindicet et laqueis doleant crudescere regna.
185 Nec solio parcet superum clemencior urna
Nec penam redimes, quod mundum polluit, auro,
Cum – trabea tandem cessura moribus – ignis,
Quem Flegeton sudat, gemmarum diluet ignes
Vernabitque deum solio trabeata casarum
190 Sobrietas, tandemque dato fulgebit in ostro
Gaudebitque – velit Dominus! – vitale Iohannes
Eternare iubar, roseis ardere corone
Sideribus, quam non odium, non forcior etas,
Immo nec invidie rabies suspecta venenis
195 Excuciat, vitemque metet, quam plantet, honestas."

Cap. 8 Oracio Diogenis de contemptu mundi

Hic subicit nec amara timens nec dulcia sperans
Diogenes, fixus animo, sed mobilis ede
"Si quicquid gemino Phebus complectitur arcu,[3]
Imperio stringas, tumulo non maior humandus
200 Occidis et tandem, cui non suffecerat orbis,
Magnus Alexander parve non sufficit urne.
Si Paridis forme rosei precelleret oris
Gloria nec vultus macule nubesceret umbra,
Occiduus sol ille perit floremque iuvente
205 Vel fati cesura terit vel lima senecte.
Si prelustre genus, si regius ortus adusque
Innumeros decurrat avos, non sanguinis illa
Lux addit meritis; patrem dediscit in ense
Neptanabi proles,[4] matremque absolvit in armis.
210 Si fame radies titulis insignis et alto
Nomine gemmescas, anime non tergis olentes

Ch. 7 An outcry against wealth

"O pinnacle destined for sudden ruin! Your steep and precarious height makes the headlong fall yet harder. The world's riches are a sad glory, a fragile bulwark, shaken by the random winds of Fate. Let that coming day not seem far off to the mind's eye, that day which the hidden wisdom of God holds in store and ponders in secret, but which, revealed at last, will assail the excesses of kings, exacting penalties that exceed their crimes, until they lament that royal power is a fate worse than bondage.

"No merciful decree of heaven will spare the throne, nor may you pay the penalty with that gold which pollutes the world, when royal power at last succumbs to virtue, when the fire which Phlegethon pours forth consumes the blaze of your jewels. Then the sobriety of the cottager will shine in royal splendor on a divine throne. Then, God willing, Johannes himself will glory in the gift of a purple mantle and rejoice at the eternally living radiance that flashes from the glowing stars of a crown which no hatred, no time of violence may remove. Then will honor reap what it sows, a harvest which not even the hateful malice of envy may blight."

Ch. 8 Diogenes' oration on scorning worldly things

Next spoke Diogenes, who neither feared hardship nor yearned for pleasure, steadfast in mind, but of no fixed abode: "Though you should subject to your dominion whatever Phoebus' double arc[3] encompasses, you will not be too great for a tomb when you die. In the end great Alexander, for whom a world was not enough, was himself not enough to fill a small urn. Though the glory of your flourishing beauty surpass the fairness of Paris, and no trace of a blemish mar your face, this sun too is doomed to set, and either a sudden blow of fate or the file of old age will efface his youthful bloom.

Though you be of noble birth, though you trace your royal heritage through countless ancestors, an illustrious heritage does not enhance your merit: the son of Nectanabus[4] disavowed his patrimony with his sword, and absolved his mother by force of arms. Though you gleam with the emblems of renown and the splendor of a lofty title, you may not wipe away the foul-smelling vices that lurk beneath the sweet odor

Sub fama redolente notas, nam mentis inumbrat
Laudis oliva rubum, nec spinam pectore vellis.
      Si quicquid Socratis exundat fama, capaci
215 Hauseris ingenio, nichil est hausisse, tuumque
Insipidum scire est, nisi quod condivit honestas,
Nec morum redimit cumulata sciencia dampnum.
      Si longo senii fastidia traxeris evo
Nestor et ad quarti numerus processerit annos
220 Limitis,[5] exiguam sub morte crepuscula lucem
Claudunt et sedes superest suprema sepulcrum.
      Si toto physice lucteris robore, lucis
Continuasse moras, stamen tamen Atropos evi
Rumpit et in mortem non est prescriptio vite,
225 Producitque dies sed non medicina perhennat.
      Si quicquid Tirius accendit murice pecten
Aut Sidonis acus, nature simia, Serum
Velleribus fecunda parit, si quicquid ubique
Vestis abest, habeas, uni toga sufficit una.
230 Si quicquid gremio nutrit Rea, lactat in undis
Nereus aut Bachus pressa vomit ebrius uva,
Affluat, et precio cultuque arrideat ori
Copia, quo turges, uterum non amplius imples.
      Si varie sedes, si sit populosa domorum
235 Turba tibi, si mille lares, si milia, sola
Te capit una domus et frustra nanus in astra
Turribus accedis, casula contentus Amycle.''

Cap. 9 Oracio Socratis de commendacione Diogenis, Cratetis et Democriti

      Vix ea, cum Socratis surgens facundia verbo
Continuat verbum, reliquos affatur et ora
240 Sermonemque simul socias convertit ad aures:
      ''Hec rigui virtus cynici, quam nulla soluti
Polluit ebrietas luxus. o sobria pransi
Letaque ieiuni sacies! o rara verende
Maiestas casule soliumque volubilis aule
245 Doliolum, cuius patula fore ianua numquam
Limine nodatur, non obiectura frequenti
Hostia convive nec mandatura repulse
Dedecus occursu; fervorem, frigus, utrumque

of fame. The olive tree of praise overshadows the thicket of the mind, but
you cannot remove its thorns. Though you should drink in with
15 capacious understanding all that redounds to the glory of Socrates, it is
nothing to have done this, your knowledge is vain, unless it be tempered
by virtue. No amount of knowledge can redeem a ruined character.
Though you be a Nestor, protracting by longevity the tedium of old age,
20 though the number of your years extend to four figures,[5] the feeble glow
of your evening will be enveloped by death. The final resting place is the
tomb. Though you strive to prolong your time of life by all the powers of
medicine, Atropos will still break the stem of life, and there is no
25 prescription against death. Medicine can prolong our days, but not
make them last forever.

"Though you should possess all the cloth that the Tyrian shell has
illumined with its purple dye, whatever design the Sidonian needle,
aping nature, has bestowed on the cloths of China, or whatever
garment is anywhere to be found, a single robe is still enough for each of
30 us. Though you should be amply possessed of everything to which the
womb of mother Rhea gives life, all that Nereus nurtures with his tides,
or drunken Bacchus spews forth from the wine press; though such an
abundance of costly delicacies should grace your mouth that you swell
to bursting, your belly will be none the fuller. Though you possess
35 several dwellings, or a cluster of houses filled with retainers, though you
have a thousand homes, or thousands, a single house can still contain
you. It is vain, dwarf that you are, to raise your towers to the stars,
when Amyclas' hut is all you need."

Ch. 9 Socrates' speech commending Diogenes, Crates and Democritus

Scarcely had he ended when the lofty eloquence of Socrates added his
words to the other's, addressing the rest of the company and adapting
40 his words and expression to their friendly ears:

"Behold the virtue of the weeping Cynic, which no wanton drunkenness defiled. His are the sober, happy sufficiency of a frugal meal, and
the spare dignity of a dwelling small yet venerable. A little cask is the
45 throne of his portable court, whose wide entrance is never barred; its
doors do not shut out a throng of would-be dinner-guests, nor convey
by their closing an insulting message of rejection. It avoids the evils of

Evasura malum nec conquestura molestas
250   Aeris esse vices, properanti terga periclo
Obicit, et verse faciem non verberat Austris
Eolus, imber aquis, nive bruma, vaporibus estas.
Magni sprevit opes,[6] curarum pondus, et aurum
Insidiis plenum, suspectaque munera leti
255   Horruit, intactus gladios ridere latronum
Maluit et iuguli vacuus servasse cruorem.
      Erubuit transisse modum, quod flumina ligno
Hauserat, et calicis digitos collegit in orbem,
Libandoque manus docuit servire fluento,
260   Omnifico facta Nature pocula torno.[7]
      Indolis activa placuit, passiva laborum
Paupertas, vicii declinativa, malorum
Ablativa, virum genitiva, dativa bonorum.[8]
      Flevit opum risus lacrima mordente, Platonis
265   Sidonio fastu corrupta cubilia mente
Et pede calcavit.[9] Nature fercula numquam
Fastidivit, olus pallenti maluit unda
Quam lingue faleris Siculum mollire tyrannum
Alter Aristippus,[10] vestiri cannabe liber
270   Quam trabea servus et se quam regibus uti
Integer, haut sapido pretexte lesus odore,
Uberius felix anime quam vestis in auro.
      Cum peteret voto studii Thebanus Athenas
Philosophus Crates[11] notumque potentibus agmen
275   Collegisset opes socias, dissuada Minerve
Pondera, mersit eas ne mersaretur ab illis,
Passus, ut expensis impensa pecunia pessum
Pessima pressetur, meritamque ut naufraga penam
Naufragii lativa ferat. cum tenderet illo
280   Isdem Democritus studiis accensus, avari
Sacra suosque deos, loculos, abiecit; avitos
Distribuit census, librisque extructa Minervam
Sorbuit, inserto consurgens mantica Phebo,
Plena sophismaticis set opum ieiuna, Camenis
285   Intumuit, gravida concusso Pallade dorso."[12]

50 both heat and cold, and never complains that changes of weather are troublesome. It turns its back at the onset of danger, that Aeolus' autumnal stormwinds, the spring rains, the snows of winter and the summer's heat may not strike its averted face.

"He spurned the great man's riches,[6] his burdensome worries, and his gold fraught with treachery. He recoiled from gifts, which carry the

55 threat of death, preferring to laugh unscathed at the robber's sword, and to preserve his throat uncut in freedom. Mortified at having transgressed his own rule and drunk water from a wooden cup, he formed a

60 circular bowl of his fingers, and taught his hands, a goblet fashioned on the all-creating lathe of Nature, to assist him in drinking.[7] Poverty pleased him, as being active in disposition, passive in enduring hardship, and declinative of vice – ablative of evil, genitive of manliness, dative of virtue.[8]

65 "The tears he shed rebuked the jests of wealth, and in thought and act he trampled on the bed of Plato, decadent in the pride of its Sidonian hangings.[9] He never rejected Nature's food, and chose to soften a bit of cabbage with clear water, rather than mollify a Sicilian tyrant with delicacies, like Aristippus.[10] He preferred to be a free man dressed in

70 coarse cloth, rather than a slave in a royal robe; to be true to himself, rather than to kings. Never compromised by the rich aura of a purple robe, he was more abundantly blessed in the riches of mind than in those of dress.

"At the time when the Theban philosopher Crates was sailing to Athens in order to study, he had assembled a company of the sort well

75 known to great men: a body of riches, a burden incompatible with Minerva's service. He cast it overboard, rather than be drowned by it, preferring that money, an evil thing oppressive to spend, should sink under its own weight, that a force so productive of shipwreck should suffer the shipwreck it deserved.[11]

80 "Democritus, too, when he came to Athens inspired by the same zeal for learning, first cast away his riches, the shrines and idols of the greedy man. He gave away his ancestral estate, and his knapsack, stuffed with books, swollen by the infusion of Phoebus, drank its fill of Minerva. Full of wisdom, albeit poor in worldly goods, it waxed great in

85 the Muses, gifts, pregnant with Pallas as it bounced against his back."[12]

Cap. 10 Oracio Democriti quod divicie non sunt habende nisi ut expendantur

Hec ubi, Democritus: "Nullum placuisse merentur,
Que Styga pro fructu pariunt, hec omnia tractu
Duratura brevi, nimias mentita carenti
Delicias, illumque minus factura beatum,
290 Cui magis accedunt. reprimantur vota, sitisque
Extinguatur opum, nec clauso pectore census
Ardor agat rimas. opibus tamen omnis in omnes
Omnia posse potest, per eas suspectus ab hoste
Extorquetur amor, nodoque adversa ligantur
295 Insolido, censuque nefas suasura fugatur
Pauperies. liceat, est ipsa pecunia sanctis
Accipienda viris, licite quesita, datores
Magnanimos habeat et dantibus affluat, arche
Non inserta diu, rara et brevis hospita, numquam
300 Incola, nec turpe loculi questura sepulcrum.
     Collige sparsurus, mete que discrecio dextre
Seminet et summum dandi prudencia nomen
Germinet et meritis fructum producat in astris.
Invidiosa Titi[13] sit dextera, munera tanto
305 A simili sparge. quo dives splendeat astrum
Esse puta munus, oblitam dona memento
Amisisse diem. loculos signasse ruborem
Inferat et, census que pondere sudat, hanelet
Distribuendo manus. fudit Fortuna, refundat
310 Dextra; nec ardorem dandi respectus avari
Congelet. ille tibi Romani maximus auctor
Muneris occurrat, immo quem fausta dedere
Tempora Normannis,[14] qui dandi sidere mundo
Et superis fulget, cui, qua non prebuit, hec est
315 Visa nefasta dies; ille est, cui Copia cornu
Fundendique vicem ieiuno tradidit orbe."

Cap. 11 Oracio Ciceronis de prodigalitate vitanda

Hic Cicero[15] verbis instantibus ora resolvens:
"Dando tamen prefige modum, substringe solutos
Muneris excursus, iusto moderancia fine
320 Temperet expensas cedatque improvida ceci

Ch. 10 Democritus' oration: riches should be possessed only to be spent

When the speech had ended, Democritus spoke: "The riches which bear damnation as their fruit cannot buy pleasure. All such things will last for a short time, offering a false image of boundless delights to him who lacks them, but making a man less happy the more he possesses. Be all such wishes rebuked, and the thirst for wealth extinguished. Let not the burning desire for property crack the vessel of the spirit.

"It is true that by means of wealth it is possible for anyone to gain anything from anyone: through wealth an uneasy love is extorted from one's enemy, and opposed forces are linked by its untrustworthy bond. The poverty which draws one into wrongdoing is banished by property. Be it right, then, that money, legitimately acquired, be employed by virtuous men, making them magnanimous donors. But let it be amassed only by those who will give it back, not as a thing to be stored in chests, but as a brief and infrequent guest who must never settle, or be relegated to the sordid tomb of a coffer.

"Gather only to distribute, reap only what your prudent hand may sow again: such wise husbandry will produce the lofty title of donor, and bear the fruit of a heavenly reward. Let the hand of Titus[13] himself seem grudging as you bestow your gifts in accord with his great example. Think of a gift as a star that makes a rich man shine, and remember that you have wasted the day on which you forget to give. May you blush to have sealed up a moneybag, and convert the labor of bearing the burden of wealth to a zeal in giving it away. What Fortune grants, let your hand grant anew. Let not the concerns of the greedy man cool your ardent desire to give.

"Be mindful of that great exemplar of the bounty of Rome, still more of him whom a blessed day bestowed upon the Normans.[14] His generous star shines upon earth and heaven, and he considers that the day on which he has not made a bequest is profaned. To him Abundance has entrusted the office of showering forth her fruits on a starving world."

Ch. 11 Cicero's oration on avoiding prodigality

Then Cicero[15] gave forth these earnest words: "Yet establish a limit for your giving; control the flowing forth of your bounty, and let moderation keep your expenditure within proper bounds. Avoid the reckless drunkenness of blind excess, and confine your indulgence

Ebrietas luxus, moderandi limite dandi
Luxuriem precinge, pati largicio frenum
Noverit et, quantum permittit copia, funde
Largus, in exhibitis habiti modus arbiter esto,
325 Meta sit expense dandique auriga facultas.
　　　Luxus opum consumit opem, dandique potestas
Carpitur et carpit. non est insania maior
Quam, quod posse cupis, niti non posse. daturus
Et dans esse nequis, si luxum consulis. ille
330 Hoc illo perimit; dare, quod manus ebria spargit,
Ire datum tollit. sumptu consumeris, urges,
Quod doleas, spernis hodie, quod crastinus optes.
　　　Prodige, de pleno vacuum concludis, amarum
De sapido, de luce lutum, de Cesare Codrum,
335 Ludibrium de laude, nichil de quolibet. istud
Prodiga prodigium novit manus, amplius equo
Amplificans sumptus, habitisque licencius utens
Quam liceat; Natura petit, Fortuna ministret.
　　　Carptor opum vilescit inops. dum divite dextra
340 Dat, redolet; post munus olens mendicat ubique,
Inveniens nusquam. queritur, dum querit, amaros
Non prescisse dies, cum dulcibus usus amico
Fideret in Fato. pudet illis esse pudori,
Quos dives decuit, fusi reminiscitur eris
345 Amissique piget et opes fluxisse, refluxum
Non habuisse dolet, Fati resilire favorem
Ingemit et vellet – Fortuna dante – dedisse
Parcius et dextre male precavisse sinistram
Devovet et sero, quem leserit alea, ludi
350 Penitet elususque manum, qua luserit, odit."

Cap. 12 Oracio Plinii quid sequatur ex luxu

　　　Talibus annectit redolenti Plinius ore:
"Prodigus es, sequitur: eris indigus. huius Egestas
Est vicii vindex, meritaque ulciscitur ira
Pauperies luxum, tenui contracta cubili,
355 Panniculo sordens, ventri ieiunia longo
Indicens odio; Cereris Bachique recedunt

within the limits of well regulated giving. Teach your largesse to submit
to restraint, and issue gifts no larger than your resources permit. Let
25 moderation govern your displays of wealth, and let your means be a
charioteer to guide your giving and spending.

"Excess in the use of wealth consumes wealth; the capacity to give
both feeds on it and is diminished by it. There is no greater madness
than striving to make yourself unable to do what you wish to do. If you
30 practice excess in giving, you cannot continue to give. Such excess dies
by its own act: the gifts that a drunken hand strews abroad take away
the power of giving. By such expense you consume yourself, doing
eagerly what you regret, and making light today of what you will long
for tomorrow.

35 "Prodigal, you create emptiness out of fullness, bitter out of sweet,
murky gloom from light, a Codrus from a Caesar, mockery from praise,
nothing from anything. The prodigal hand can produce this sole
prodigy: the expansion of expense beyond reason, and the use of
possessions with illicit licence. Nature asks one way of life, Fortune
provides another.

"He who pares away the substance of his wealth becomes worthless
40 in his poverty. His scent is sweet as he gives with lavish hand, but
afterwards he becomes a stinking beggar, everywhere seeking, nowhere
rewarded. As he begs he laments that Fate does not shorten his bitter
days, he who, while he enjoyed life's sweets, trusted Fate as a friend. He
is ashamed to be an object of shame to those to whom, when wealthy,
he seemed a fitting companion; he remembers his squandered money,
45 repents of having lost it, and grieves that when wealth has flowed away
there is no flowing back. He bemoans the fleeting favor of Fate, wishes
that Fortune had granted him the ability to give more sparingly, and
would sacrifice his left hand to have been forewarned of the wickedness
50 of his right. Too late does he whom the dice have ruined regret having
played; only when he has lost does he come to hate the hand that made
the cast."

Ch. 12 Pliny's oration on the consequences of excess

To these words Pliny added his graceful words: "If you are a prodigal, it follows that you will become poor. Want herself is the scourge of
this vice, and excess is avenged by the righteous wrath of Poverty,
55 crouching in its narrow bed wrapped in foul rags, crying out against
hunger in protracted fits of anger. Ceres and Bacchus cease their

Accessus soliti, stomacho succedit inani
Egra Fames ardensque Sitis, vacuumque rapine
Instruit et dextram, qua fuderit omnia, furto.
360 Dampnat et ere manus alieno polluit, omne
Pro modico suasura nefas, clausisse bilingues
Ingeniosa dolos, ut, qua sibi deficit, alter
Supplementa ferat. omni, quo pauper habundet,
Limite procedit et primi rursus inundat
365 Diluvium luxus solitumque refluctuat equor
Et manus ad dandi revolat, quem noverat, estum.
    Cura prodigitur dando qui prodigit. eris
Creditor occurrit: gravis, urgens, improbus, acer
Impaciensque more, repetendi prodigus, ire
370 Largus, avarus opum; tantoque protervius heret,
Quo magis eris eges, quo plus sub mole terentis
Lederis usure. pulsat, ferit, instat oportet.[16]
Quod petit, ut solvas, nec solvere sufficit arche
Aut loculi macies. quid ages? te pessimus ille
375 Undique divellit; et dandi si qua reliquit
Primus amor, dantur; sed eo dilacio dono
Venit emisque moras, sed, qui prius institit, idem
Maturat reditum dolor, interrupta quievit
Rixa, sed ad tempus, redit in fervore tumultus
380 Asperior maiorque furor. mors sola dolores
Sopitura venit, latura beacius esse
Et miseris optata quies; solacia pene,
Que vita est, mors pena parit. respirat egestas
Mortis in amplexu, viteque molestia leto
385 Tollitur et vulnus curatur vulnere, pena
Pena, dolore dolor. ut te tot, prodige, tandem
Eruat adversis, ut tot pulsantibus obstet,
Supremi metuenda venit clemencia fati.
    Parcius a loculis expense audacia surgat
390 Ad census contracta modum, ne debita mensi
Devoret una dies, mensisque ligurriat anni
Suffectura more. si qua est improvida, non est
Sepe datura manus. nemo nisi parcus habebit,
Unde diu largus effundat muneris urnam,
395 Solaque munifico laudes cautela perhennat.''

accustomed visits, and faint Hunger and burning Thirst take over the empty stomach. Want teaches one to steal, condemns the hand that had once provided all things to thievery, and defiles it with the money of others. She persuades one to any wrongdoing for a small gain, and ingeniously hides her duplicitous wiles, so that when her own means fail another's may supplement them. She travels every path by which a pauper may grow rich, until the flood of former luxury rises again, the sea flows in as of old, and the hand quickly reverts to the familiar pouring forth of gifts.

"He who is prodigal in giving is visited by a prodigal array of worries. The moneylender visits him, grim, importunate, persistent, aggressive, impatient of delay; prodigal of petitions and lavish of anger, but covetous of his money. He clings to you shamelessly so that you may become still more needy, harassed still further by the grinding weight of his usury. He knocks, pounds, intrudes; you must pay what he asks,[16] though the emaciation of your purse and coffers is not sufficient to do so. What are you to do? He is a besetting evil that tears at you from every side. If the old love of giving has left you anything, this too is given. But while this gift puts him off and buys time, the same affliction that had formerly troubled you returns all too quickly. When his wrangling was suspended there was quiet, but soon the shouting returns, grown harsher in its intensity and rage. Only the coming of death can lay these sorrows to rest, bringing a happier condition and a long-awaited rest from misery. The penalty of death provides a solace for the suffering that is life. Poverty finds refreshment in the embrace of death, the trouble of life is removed by death. One wound is cured by another, pain is eased by pain, suffering by suffering. The fearful advent of the last day seems merciful to the prodigal, in that it frees him at last from so many ills, shields him from so many cruel blows.

"Therefore let expense issue less boldly from your purse, and keep within the limits of your resources. Let not a single day consume what should suffice for a month, or a month lick up delicacies that should suffice for a whole year. The hand that gives improvidently will not be able to give long. No one who is not frugal will be able to maintain for long the flow of generous gifts from his urn. Only foresight can ensure an enduring reputation for munificence."

Cap. 13 Oracio Cratetis de aule incommodis

Interea dubio versans in pectore Crates
Quando mersit opes,[17] longum meditatus: "En" inquit
"En memini, loculos odi, mundumque daturas
Fortune contempno manus. erroribus ortum
400 Divicie prestant et opes delicta tuentur,
Libertasque datur viciis et semina culpe
Prefecunda iacit, nec non altissima fati
Nulla venit sincera dies, maiorque potestas
Sevius a ludo Fortune leditur et plus
405 Solliciti quam pacis habet, semperque beatos
Altius, adversis labor inclemencius urget.
    Nulla quies aule! circumvenit improbus aulam
Curarum populus, vexat congesta laborum
Turba potestates, alienativa quietis
410 Agmina concurrunt, regni custodia, iuris
Sollicitudo minor, tractanda negocia, cause,
Iudicis examen, lis decidenda, querele,
Pauperis instantis pulsacio crebra, rogantis
Importuna manus, precibusque interflua rixe
415 Asperitas, quam pigra parit dilacio recti.
    Rarus ibi sompnus. vigilate tedia noctis
Indolitura dies equitantis vexat ocellum.
Semita delicti, culpe via, strata reatus,
Methodus inferni, Stygis orbita, limes Averni;
420 Nugarum lituus, falsi tuba, tibia ficti,
Buccina rumoris: denso strepit aula tumultu.
Altiloquus quatit astra fragor tollitque soporem
Et superis, fessasque Iovis ferit arduus aures.
Undique garritur: hic verbum supprimit, ille
425 Erigit; hic lingue tumidus tonat, ille susurrat;
Hic socium tangit, vicium mordente cachinno,
Publicat ille scelus, gravius ledente susurro.
    Ille movet rixas, hic corripit; ille flagello
Vapulat, hic lingua; contempnitur ille vel illa,
430 Prevalet is vel ea. raro tamen elicit aula
Eloquio laudes et se vix aulicus offert
Laudandi studio; sepelit, quod novit honestum,
Denudat vicium, meritum sub criminis umbra
Occulit et fame picturam moribus aufert.

Ch. 13 Crates' oration on the ills of the courtier's life

Meanwhile Crates was anxiously mulling over the day when he had cast his wealth into the sea.[17] "Yes" he said, after long reflection, "yes, I remember well. I detest riches, and I scorn Fortune's hand though it should offer me the world. Riches are an occasion for error, and wealth only makes good our crimes, giving free rein to vice and sowing the all too fertile seeds of wickedness. No day is without trouble, even when our fortune has attained its highest point. Those whose power is greater are assailed the more fiercely by Fortune's whims; they know more of trouble than of peace, and the burden of wealth itself troubles the favored few more deeply and harshly than adversity.

"There is no rest at court! An unruly mob of troubles throng the halls, a dense crowd of tasks assail men of power, armies hostile to peace charge toward them: affairs of state; petty legal difficulties; treaties to be negotiated; cases at law; judicial inquiries; disputes and complaints to be resolved; the relentless harassing of the desperate pauper; the importunate hand of the plaintiff; the entreaties interspersed with the harsh sound of anger to which the slow dispensation of justice gives rise.

"Sleep is rare for the courtier. His days must suffer the lingering effects of wakeful nights. The eye of the errant knight is distracted by the path of sin, the road of wrong-doing, the highway of guilty deeds – a route that leads to the underworld, a winding way to the Styx, a passage to Avernos. The court resounds with a continual tumult: the clarion call of petty quarrels, the trumpet of falsehood, the pipes of deception and the great horn of rumor. The clash of loud voices shakes the firmament, robs the very gods of sleep, and scales the heights to assail the weary ears of Jove. There is chattering everywhere. When one stops speaking, another begins. One speaks out in inflated language, another mutters. One man criticizes his companion, laughing as he censures his vicious conduct. Another exposes a crime in the whisper that inflicts a more serious wound. One man provokes a quarrel, another takes it up; the first strikes a blow, the other lashes back with his tongue; one or the other is put down, one or the other prevails. Only rarely is the eloquence of the court called forth in praise, and scarcely ever does a courtier put himself forward out of a desire to praise another. He conceals what he knows to be honorable, and reveals what is vicious, covers over merit with the suggestion of wrongdoing, and thereby robs another's character of its reputable appearance.

435   Hic scelus antiquum memorat, gaudetque relatum
      Non solus scivisse nefas, nullique pudendum
      Commisisse pudet, socii submurmurat aure
      Laudantis facinus, avidoque in crimina verbo
      Iactitat hic factum, deliberat ille futurum.
440   Non faleris, non felle vacat fecunda malorum
      Lingua parens, omnisque pluit facundia nugas.
          O male felices, quorum nec purpura morbos
      Nec loculus curat, nec opes suprema morantur
      Fata, nec ad nervum revocatur mortis harundo.
445   Dives apud Ditem veniam non impetrat auro,
      Nec cupide vendit Cereris gener auctius evum.
      Non parcit trabee subeunti Cerberus, illum
      Nec regni gladius nec mitre cornua terrent.
      Non homines humana beant; similemque beato
450   Forma, genus, pretexta facit – virtusque beatum."

Cap. 14 Oracio Senece de glorie contemptu

      "Sentit idem Crates, quod sentio, novimus aulam"
      Altitonantis ait Lucani patruus, ille
      Quo Nero defuncto quam vivo maluit uti.[18]
          "Optima paupertas possessio! Iulius orbem
455   Sorbuit et sompnum vacui laudavit Amicle.[19]
      Fulgor opum cecat. Fortuna miserrima, quid sit,
      Est homini factura fidem: quid possit in alto,
      Cernit in oppresso; quo fructu prospera rident,
      In lacrimis adversa vident; quo gloria tollat,
460   Inferiora docent; an virtus nana Gigantum
      In superos esset et debeat esse timori
      Iupiter, an possit deitas impune lacessi,
      Encheladi tandem rabies extincta probavit
      Et probat, iniectam quociens demugit ob Ethnam,
465   Alternatque latus humero nervoque sonanti,
      Aut manibus niti dorsoque assurgere temptat.
          Occubuit temere surgens Titania virtus
      Et caret optato presumens gloria fine.
      Tollo pedem fixumque ligo, nam lubricus ille
470   Est locus, accessu facilis gressuque relato
      Difficilis, raptisque Nothis elacio turget
      Et subito quevis tumet excellencia vento
      Et tenui novit illabi gloria rima.

435   "Here too men recount their own past misdeeds, and each rejoices that he is not the only one who knows the wickedness he reports. No one is ashamed to have committed shameful acts, each confides his guilt to the ear of an ally sure to praise them, and while one boasts of what he has done, in words that show his eagerness for crime, the other ponders

440 what he will do. The tongue, that teeming parent of evil, has no lack of ornate and poisonous words, and bestows its eloquence on every sort of meanness.

    "Cursed in their very happiness, no purple robe or store of wealth can minister to their disease; wealth will not delay the coming of the

445 final day, and the mortal arrow cannot be recalled to the string. Dives for all his gold will find no favor with Dis; Ceres' son-in-law will not sell an extended lease on life; Cerberus does not spare those who descend in stately robes, nor does the royal sword or horned mitre terrify him.

450 Mortal things cannot make mortals truly happy. Beauty, noble birth, robes of office can make one seem blessed, virtue alone makes one blessed."

Ch. 14 Seneca's oration on scorning glory

    "Crates' feelings are my own, for we know the court," says the uncle of high-thundering Lucan, he whom Nero appreciated better dead than

455 alive.[18] "The best of all possessions is poverty! Julius devoured the whole world, yet praised the slumber of the pauper Amyclas.[19] The gleam of wealth makes us blind. The worst of ill fortune is to place one's trust in mortal powers. Only when cast down does one see how little power one had when on high; weeping adversity sees the fruits that

460 make prosperity smile for what they are. To be cast down is to learn how glory exalts us. Only when the madness of Enceladus was finally extinguished did he gain proof that the strength of Giants was dwarfed by that of the gods, that Jupiter was indeed to be feared, that his godhead could not be attacked with impunity. And he proves it still,

465 whenever he groans because Aetna has been heaped upon him, turns himself over with creaking joints and muscles, or tries to stretch out his arms and arch his back.

    "The strength of the Titans, rising to heights of folly, was cast down, and their presuming ambition failed to achieve its goal. I turn my steps

470 away and hold fast to my course, for the place is treacherous; it is easy to enter and difficult to retrace one's path. Elation is puffed up as it snatches at the winds, and every sort of excellence is enlarged by their sudden blast; the love of glory can enter our minds through the merest fissure.

Cap. 15 De Alexandro

Altius ingenio raptus quam corpore, mundos
475   Innumeros potuit animo numerasse suosque
Pitagoras superos; stupidus narrante dolebat
Magnus Anaxarcho nec aperto lingua dolori
Defuit et morbum gemitu testatus hanelo:
'Ha miser!' exclamat 'vacuos rectoris inhermes
480   Tot video mundos, michi nondum serviat unus,
Nec mea dignatur casa mundus sceptra, nec unum
Exequasse Iovem Pelleis glorior armis.'[20]
O nimis excurrens presumptio, nescia votis
Ambicio preferre modum, que sola iubendi
485   Anxia diis solis regnantibus invidet orbem.
Fixum non habuit successum gloria: Magnum
Parvula, qui mundos siciebat, sorbuit urna.

Cap. 16 De morte Homero

Questio, quam predo fluvialis movit, Homero
Institit ad mortis lacrimas, nervosior ultra
490   Quam que Meonii posset succumbere lucte.
Plus equo doluit vulgo vilescere, fame
Laudibus incisis inconsolanter adaucte
Iacturam gemuit, qui non est passus, ut ampli
Nominis arduitas modica pro parte labasset,
495   Nec tulit, ut nomen tenui nubesceret umbra."[21]

Ch. 15 Alexander

175   "Borne aloft in imagination, if not in body, Pythagoras' mind was capable of comprehending innumerable worlds, each with its gods. Stupefied by Anaxarchos' account of him, the great Alexander felt the pangs of sorrow; he did not lack words to express his grief openly, and revealed his suffering in a painful groan: 'Wretch that I am,' he cries,
180 'for I behold so many worlds, unprotected and lacking rulers, but as yet not a single world owes service to me; not even the world where I dwell acknowledges my scepter, nor can I claim the glory of having made myself the equal of even a single Jove by force of Pellaean arms.'[20]

   "O unrestrained presumption, ambition incapable of setting a limit to
185 its hopes, so tormented by the desire to command that it envies a world ruled only by its gods. But glory attains no certain result: a little urn consumed the great Alexander, who had thirsted for entire worlds.

Ch. 16 The death of Homer

   "A question put to Homer by fishermen, a problem that proved too
190 knotty to yield to his efforts, drove the Maeonian bard to mortal sorrow. He grieved beyond measure at appearing commonplace to common people, mourned inconsolably the decline of his lofty reputation through this diminution of the chorus of praise. He could not endure that the loftiness of his glorious name be diminished by the least
195 amount, nor permit his dignity to be clouded by the slightest shadow."[21]

Liber Septimus

Cap. 1 Quam diligenter audiat Architrenius philosophos loquentes

Rivos eloquii prono succedere cursu
Et videt et mentis bibit Architrenius ore,
Et riguas capitis et cordis inebriat aures,
Dumque bibendo sitit, nec sentit ydropicus unde
5 Congestos calices, nisi fesso vase bibendi
Continuetur item. vix respirarat, et ecce
Iam decimum rursus eiusdem pocula Bachi
Pectoris a plena Simachi gener extrahit urna,
Nec de divitibus timet integrasse querelas.

Cap. 2 Oracio Boecii de potentum inclemencia

10 "O meritos extrema pati, quos ardua tollit
Ala potestatis, quorum clemencia numquam
Hospita divertit, sed mortis larga tyrannis,
Iustorum risura neces, factura flagello
Quod pietatis erit. ha nulla potencia rebus
15 Oppressis tranquilla venit, non sumit ab illa
Pauper opes vel opem. gravis est flexisse favorem
Inferius, qui summa potest; aciesque laborat
Ardua, pressa videns. raro, qui surgit in aulam,
Respexisse casam placido dignatur ocello.
20 Spernit hanelantis animi suspiria, surda
Preterit aure preces, lacrimis insultat easque
Ridet habere dolos, clamosaque pectora planctu
Exaudire vetat, gemitusque adversa loquentes
Vix recipit vultu, faciem pallore minantem
25 Horridiore fugit, domitas regnante repellit
Paupertate genas, fluidos merore tumenti
Nauseat ore sinus, senio rumpente solutos.

Book Seven

Ch. 1 How intently Architrenius listened to the philosophers' speeches

Architrenius perceives how the streams of eloquence pursue one another in an even course; the mouth of his mind drinks them in, and intoxication flows through the ears of head and heart. His thirst stems
5 from what he drinks, and in his dropsical state he does not notice how the succession of steadily accumulating goblets is maintained, save when his own vessel grows tired from drinking. Scarcely has he caught his breath when lo, Symmachus' son-in-law for a tenth time fills the goblet with the same wine from the brimming urn of his heart, and bravely carries forward the complaint against the wealthy.

Ch. 2 Boethius' oration on the harshness of rulers

10 "Deserving of the most extreme punishment are those whom the soaring wings of power bear aloft, yet whose mercy is never shown in the sheltering of guests. The tyrant is generous only with death, laughs at the destruction of good men, performs his acts of mercy with a whip.
15 Power never presents itself in a gentle way to the oppressed: the poor man derives from it neither aid nor riches. It is difficult for one who commands the heights to direct his favor to those below; beholding the downtrodden, one strives to ascend yet higher. Rarely does one who has attained the court deign to look back in a kindly way at the cottage.

20 "Power ignores the sighs of the exhausted spirit, turns a deaf ear to prayers, mocks at tears and laughingly suggests that they are a stratagem. It refuses to hear the loud cries of the complaining spirit, barely acknowledges the sobs that tell of adversity, flees the face whose pallor
25 bespeaks the horrors of its existence, rejects the cheek whose bloom has been overcome by the tyranny of poverty, sickens at the sight of garments damp with overflowing grief or tattered with age.

Non iuvenum cautela minor, non fracta senectus,
Non levior sexus, quam longa intorsit egestas,
30 Non oris ferrugo movet, non sordida vultus
Ariditas, non cura genis scriptura senectam,
Non exesa fames maciesque domestica leto,
Non quicquid Siculos posset movisse iuvencos.[1]
   Pauperis haut umquam fatum lugubre potentis
35 Extorquet lacrimam, tenuis fortuna beatos
Nescit in affectum tenuem flexisse, minorum
Dampna minus maiora movent, soliique facultas
Non meminit fragmenta case, non sarcit hiantes
Paupertate sinus, non egri exterminat oris
40 Attritam maciem, vacui non expedit usum
Pauperis; angustis sacies angustior aule
Plenius ad plenos opibus venit, ipsa potestas
Extorquet sibi cuncta dari, maioraque magnis
Accedunt, peiora bonis; si pluris habundes,
45 Dantis plura feres, – si quis caret, ipse carebit.
Maior opum maiora capit, maioris egenti
Fit minus et querit manus errantissima dantis,
Non qui plus egeat, sed qui plus possit habere.
   Dantis apud dextram non intercedit honestum,
50 Non anime vernantis odor, non impetrat ipsis
Proxima diis virtus, nec fame cognita morum
Canicies, nec fixa gravi constancia vultu,
Nec corrosa genas, marcenti livida labro
Religio, non fracta malis nulloque tumultu
55 Flexa voluptatis, animi vallata rigore.
   De tot divitibus nulli datur uncia Codro.
Dilapidantur opes, gula sic disponit et ultor
Luxus avaricie, violens exactor honesti,
Lenaque nec morum minus exactiva libido."[2]

Cap. 3 Oracio Xenocratis de libidine

60   Ad suprema gemit Xenocrates verba, nec ultra
Protrahit excitum reticendi lingua soporem:
   "Ecce malum, quo cuncta dolent, quo terra laborat,
Quo superi languent, quod Tartara movit et ipsum
Sepe Iovem torsit; quicquid vel surgit ad Euros
65 Vel cadit ad Zephyros, quicquid vel despicit Arthos

The powerful are not moved by the spectacle of unprotected youth, or enfeebled old age, or feminine frailty tormented by longstanding
30 want; nor by the blighted complexion, the face withered and streaked with dirt, the worry that inscribes the cheeks with the signs of age; nor by wasted hunger, the leanness that seems to dwell with death; nor by things that would move Sicilian bullocks to pity.[1]

35 Never does the pauper's grim fate exact a tear from the powerful, his meager lot cannot draw them to the slightest show of feeling. The greatest disasters of insignificant people are insignificant; he who possesses a throne does not notice the destruction of a cottage, mend
40 garments torn open by poverty, eliminate the worn, emaciated appearance of the sick, or provide for the needs of utter destitution. The abundance of the court is penurious toward those in penury, generous to those of generous means, for power takes pains to bestow all things on itself. The greater gifts are bestowed on the great, the lesser ones on
45 the just. The more amply you are endowed, the more of such gifts you will receive. If one is in need, his need will continue. The great man receives the greater portion, while he whose need is greater receives less. So erratic is the hand of the giver that he asks, not who is most in need, but who can claim to possess the most.

50 "Honor does not intercede to guide the hand of such donors, nor the springlike freshness of the pure spirit. Virtue, that godlike quality, gains no favor here, nor the ripeness of character that fame acknowledges, nor the grave countenance of firm constancy, nor religion, with her worn face and dull and withered lips, unbowed by misfortune, unmoved
55 by any tumultuous desire, secure in her strength of spirit.

"Out of such riches, not a penny is bestowed on Codrus. Instead wealth is squandered as gluttony decrees, and luxury, the avenger of avarice, who violently demands honor as her price, and lechery, a bawd equally adept at extorting virtue."[2]

Ch. 3 Xenocrates' oration on lust

50 At these last words Xenocrates gave a groan, and his tongue prolonged no further its reticent slumber: "Here is an evil which all things suffer, beneath which the earth labors and the gods lose their power, which stirs up Tartarus and has often tormented Jove himself. Whatever
55 rises in the East or sinks in the West, whatever the North Pole beholds or

Vel Nothus abscondit, urtica libidinis urit.
    Castra pudicicie furor hic predulcis amara
Obsidione ligat, facula contentus et arcu,
Fracturusque levi votorum pondera risu.
70 Huius in amplexu vis plectitur, huius ab usu
Treicii morbi[3] manavit abusio, cuius
Tracem peniteat frustra, cum iudicis urna
Venerit et fornax, si quos non coxerat ante
Orpheus, eterno mores coctura camino.
75 Hora nimis properata malis, sed tarda beatis,
Cum tandem Cresi fracto diademate sceptrum,
Quod feret orbigene dextre clemencia, Codrus
Induet et nostri Iovis ampla palacia paucos
Accipient, nec erit, populus quod peccat, inultum.
80   Hec satis est; hucusque licet meminisse profanam
Morfosin, infaustum Nature Prothea, Tracum
Thesiphonen; audire ipsum michi fascinat aures
Osque loqui, maculatque sacram conceptio mentem.
Quod decet, id sermo sapiat, fugiatque loquela,
85 Quod Natura fugit; satis est tetigisse, quod oris
Inquinat officium nec conciliatur honesto.
Est satis ad vires in nostra pericula dandas
Coniuga Nature mundo concessa libido,
Quantum prolis amor et sacra iugalia poscunt.
90   Ha Cipri rabies, quam dulci pace salutat,
Quem sibi venatur hominem, primoque propinat
Dulce, sed ex dulci tandem concludit amarum.
Sic est blanda Venus, sic, quos melliverat ante,
Edidicit fellire favos, sic ultima taxo
95 Toxicat et verna veniens hiberna recedit.
Quam placida mentis oculos omnemque soporat
Nube diem, dum clausa sacri sub pectoris aula
Fervet et irriguum fontem dessicat honesti
    Tucius est gelida vitam glaciasse sub Artho,
100 Quam semel in preceps flexa racionis habena
Lothofagos Veneris libasse et pocula Circes.
Tucius estifere radiis ardere Sienes,
Quam cesto posita Veneris sudasse camino.
Tucius indomitis animam fudisse lacertis
105 Herculis et Siculo rursus mugire iuvenco,
Quam iecur omnicremo fricuisse libidinis igne.

the South conceals from us, burns with the nettle of lust.

"This madness, surpassingly sweet, holds the forces of chastity under a bitter siege, content to fight with mere torches and bows, yet able to overcome the force of prayer with a gentle smile. Its power is derived from embracing, and from this practice stems that abuse known as the Thracian disease.[3] For this let Thracian Orpheus repent in vain, when the urn and fire of the Judge shall be at hand to blast in eternal fire whatever such habits Orpheus himself has not already purged. The hour is coming, too quickly for the wicked, too slowly for the blessed, when the diadem of Croesus will finally be broken, and Codrus will assume that scepter which a world-creating hand wields in mercy. The spacious palace of our Jove will admit the few, and the sins of the many will not go unavenged.

Enough of that. It is right to have said this much about the profane mutation, the ill-omened transformer of Nature, the Thracian Tisiphone. To hear such things and speak of them is an enticement to ears and lips, but to reflect on them taints the purity of the mind. Let our speech express what is fitting, and let our utterance shun what Nature herself shuns. It is enough to have touched on a thing which defiles the office of the lips and cannot be reconciled with decency. Suffice it to say of these powers bestowed to our peril, that lust has been granted to the world as Nature's partner, to perform what the love of offspring and the rites of marriage require.

"O madness of the Cyprian goddess! The man whom she pursues greets her kindly, and at first she offer him sweet delight, but in the end bitterness comes of this sweetness. So enticing is Venus that she has learned to make bitter those honeycombs which she had first endowed with honey, until it is finally as poisonous as the yew berry, and what had begun as spring ends in winter. How peacefully she makes drowsy the eyes of the mind, and steeps the day in cloud, while within our breast the chamber of the spirit grows hot with passion and dries up the brimming fount of honor.

It is safer to expose one's life to the frozen north than once to have cast aside the rein of reason and tasted Venus' lotos-food and the goblets of Circe. Safer to burn under the rays of the hot Egyptian sun than to unbuckle and sweat in the furnace of Venus. Safer to risk one's life in the invincible grip of Hercules, or make the Sicilian bull roar once again, than to roast one's liver in the all-consuming fire of lust. Scarcely can I

Vix ullo reprimo lacrimas adamante, quod ista
Blanda fames, quod grata sitis, quod mulcebris ardor
Carnem consumat, animam bibat, urat utrumque.
110   O vere studio degentibus optima vite
Forma foret supraque deum secreta viderent,
Hec nisi trabs oculis obiecta studentibus esset.
At sub sideribus deitas decisa beatis,
Non exacta datur, minor est quam plena bonorum
115 Integritas, raroque venit sincera venustas.
       Combussit Frigium pastorem, Pergama, Grecos
A Veneris surgens faculis amor, ignis et ira.[4]
       Canduit Alcides Veneris Nessique veneno
Et Veneris Nessi conclusit in ignibus ignes,
120 Dum quos interula teneros vestivit amores
Vestiit interitu, temere dum credidit hosti,
Et fuit Alcide, Nesso, sibi Deianira
Raptoris dolitura dolo: rogus, ultio, pena.
Alciden pudeat, quod eodem pollice pensum
125 Antheique necem – nunc vir, nunc femina – nevit.[5]
       Novimus ut Circes gremium molliret Ulixem,
Penelopes rigidos cum nemo flecteret arcus.
       Hoc sale, sal hominum, Salomon insulsus amari
Demeruit, morem quod amaro gessit amori.
130   Infractum Samxona Venus confregit et ipsum
Forcia rumpentem molli certamine rupit.
Occidit ad Colcon ortus Sulmone, Corinna
Dum male delituit velati nominis umbra.[6]
       Sed quid in immensum cedit labor? ut quid abyssum
135 Metior? incertas nullus definit harenas
Calculus et numerus vaga vix amplectitur astra.
Nulla dolos Veneris capit area, nulla dolendi
Sufficiunt exempla modis, ubi vulnus in alto
Sedit et igne Venus nocuit nervoque Cupido.
140   Ha Venus imperii, quod nullos excipit annos,
Quo senii lascivit hiemps, inflexa virorum
Mollescit gravitas, iuvenum calor uritur, annis
Solvitur integritas teneris, quo mollior etas,
Ductilis in cunctas species, transumitur usus
145 In geminos, dum mas nubit vel femina ducit.
       Ha Venus, ad nutum trahis omnia numina celi,
Astra moves alioque rotas errore planetas;

find the sternness to restrain my tears while this pleasant hunger devours our flesh, this gratifying thirst drinks up our spirit, this soothing fire burns both together.

10   Truly the life of those dedicated to study would be the best of all, and they would behold the mysteries of the gods on high, if this beam did not obstruct their scholarly vision. But here, far below the blessed stars, divinity is diminished: a full measure is not granted to us, the integrity

15 even of just men is less than perfect, and untainted beauty of spirit is rarely seen.

"Love, fire and wrath, arising together from the torch of Venus, destroyed the Phrygian shepherd, Pergama, and the Greeks.[4] Alcides burned with the poison of Venus and Nessus, and Venus' fires ended in

20 those of Nessus. Deianira, foolishly trusting her enemy, wrapped her beloved in the shirt of Nessus, and in so doing wrapped him in death; because of the guile of her ravisher, she was soon to mourn for Alcides, Nessus, and herself: for Hercules' pyre, for Nessus' revenge, for her own suffering. Let it be Alcides' shame that with the same hand he both plied

25 the distaff and wrought the death of Antaeus – a woman at one moment, a man the next.[5]

"We know how soothing for Ulysses was the embrace of Circe, while none could bend Penelope's rigid bow. The salt of the earth, Solomon, was so insipid as to let himself be loved in the same clever way, and so

30 gave himself to love of a bitter kind. Venus conquered the unconquerable Samson, using a tender kind of warfare to break that strength which could break strong bonds. He who was born at Sulmona died at Colchis, for his Corinna could not conceal herself beneath the shadow of a veiled identity.[6]

35 "But why have I embarked on so vast a task? Why do I seek to measure the abyss? As no reckoning can account for the infinite sands, no number comprehend the wandering stars, so no space can contain the wiles of Venus, no example do justice to the deceitful ways in which, when the wound is deep, Venus assails us with fire, Cupid with his bow.

40 "Venus' dominion exempts not even the elderly: the winter of age grows wanton, the unbending gravity of manhood is softened, the hot blood of youth burns, and even the purity of tender years is undone. Our

45 malleable age, lending itself to behavior of all kinds, adopts ambiguous customs, for males give themselves, and women take them, in marriage.

"Venus, you subject all the powers of heaven to your will, cause the stars to move and send the planets whirling on strange journeys. You

Accendis gelidam sine fratris lampade Pheben
Mutato cohitu; quin totus inardeat isto
150 Sidere, Mercurius non temperat astra galero;[7]
Iustius ipsa tuo percussa Cupidine Martis
Lederis amplexu; per te turbatus oberrat
Sol oculus mundi, respirat Martius ardor
Languescens ardore tuo, suspirat ad Arthon
155 Iupiter et fixam radios declinat ad Ursam.[8]
Fax tua Falciferi glaciem liquat. ecce superne
Religio sedis caveat sibi, si quis utrisque
Axibus ulterior latuit deus, imminet hostis,
Quem vix afficiat omnis satis impetus, in quem
160 Fulminis et tonitrus omnis natura laboret.
   Nec tamen hac miror iecur incandescere flamma,
Quod gula fermento Veneris corrumpit; honusta
Plus equo sacies Cipreum ventilat ignem
Idalioque rogo stomachi succendit abyssum
165 Et luteo renes iubet exundare fluento,
Talis enim tales effundit aquarius imbres."[9]

Cap. 4 Invectio Pitagore contra ingluviem

Sermones hucusque trahit; Samiusque loquendi
Reliquias lingue facundo pectine texit:
   "Aerie regionis opes, opulenta profundi
170 Vitrea regna dei, quicquid prelarga beato
Dulce dedit Natura solo, cur perditis omne
Obsequium prestare gule? cur gloria mense
Lascivit tot lauta cibis? o perdita luxus
Ambicio, cui tota suis elementa laborant
175 Deservire bonis, immo coguntur ad omnem
Delicias vomuisse famem dapibusque potentes
Explicuisse sinus. o compressura ciborum
Omne genus, nulloque gule suppressa libido!
   Cura quidem cunctis animantibus instat et unus
180 Anxius ardor inest, fragilis ieiunia vite
Quesito posuisse cibo; sed nescia rerum
Luxuries servasse modum, diffunditur ultra,
Quam licet, et libitum liciti transformat in usum.
   O sacies nullo violata libidinis estu,
185 Augustis augusta viris angustia, felix

set Phoebe afire, she who is so cold when her brother's lamp is absent,
50 by a new conjunction. Mercury indeed is wholly aflame for this star,
and his helmet no longer contains his radiance.[7] You yourself, fittingly
stricken by your own Cupid, suffer the harsh embrace of Mars; the Sun,
the world's eye, unsettled by you, strays at large; the fire of Mars pants
55 and grows weary in fiery desire for you; Jupiter sighs for the Pole, and
directs his rays toward the steadfast Bear;[8] your torch melts the icy chill
of the Scythe-bearer. Yes, let the sacred power of the heavenly region be
watchful, and any further deity who lurks between the two poles, for an
enemy is at hand whom all your power can scarcely affect, against
60 whom a universe of thunder and lightning might be spent in vain.

"And yet I do not wonder that the liver burns with this flame, when
gluttony adulterates it with the ferment of Venus; an appetite immoder-
ately indulged fans the Cyprian flames, makes the belly grow hot with
65 desire for the Idalian pyre, and commands the loins to discharge their
murky stream, for such an Aquarius pours forth such showers."[9]

Ch. 4 Pythagoras' inveighal against Gluttony

Xenocrates carried his discourse to this point, and Samian Pythagoras fashioned the remainder, weaving it in artful language: "The riches
70 of the regions of the air, the gleaming richness of the realm of the
highest God, all the delights that most bountiful Nature has bestowed on
this blessed earth: why do you sacrifice all this to offer service to
gluttony? Why does the splendor of the table run riot, garnished with so
many kinds of food? How ruinous is the ambition of luxury, for whom
75 all the elements are at pains to provide, nay are compelled to spew forth
delicacies for every appetite, and expand the bellies of the great with
feasting! A greedy lust that nothing can suppress, it seeks to force
together every kind of food. To allay the hunger of our frail existence by
80 seeking out food is a care that impends on every living thing; this one
anxious desire is present in all. But this luxury, unable to set a limit on
its consumption, goes far beyond what is fitting, and lets desire usurp
the office of decency.

85 "O simple sufficiency unsullied by the lustful seething of greed! Noble
austerity of noble men! Happy abundance of poverty, which makes life

Copia paupertas, factura beacius evum
Deposito luxu parituraque secula rursus
Aurea – calcato, quod mundum ferreat, auro.

Cap. 5 Conquestio eiusdem de nova vestium petulancia[10]

Hec doleo, sed adest iterum dolor, altera mentem
190 Non minor urget acus, animo subtexitur egro
Pena, labor gemitum vomit intimus, alta serenum
Pectoris in nubem premit indignacio, vestis
Ambicione nova nudaque libidine cultus
Secula dissolvi; veterum vilescit amictus
195 Religio, rerumque placet petulancior usus
Succumbunt antiqua novis, circumfluit orbem
Luxuries, folio levitatis cedit honestum
Maturusque rigor, ridetur sobria vite
Simplicitas, morumque viros infancia mollit.
200 Pronius ad vestes huius sollercia maior
Temporis inspexit, proprio male sedula dampno
Et temere sollers, urbano rustica cultu.

Cap. 6 Quod mundus exundet viciis, et de VII sapientibus qui in Grecia moribus et sciencia floruerunt

Quid moror? est mundus res immundissima,[11] labis
Alveus, exundans viciis, ut nubibus aer,
205 Equor aquis, celum radio, caligine tellus,
Fructibus autumpnus, ver floribus, estibus estas,
Frigoribus bruma, nitro Pharos, India nardo,
Cameleonte Friges, basiliscis Affrica, Nilus
Ypotamis, Ganges hebenis, sturionibus Helle,
210 Tartara tormentis, Styx nocte, Megera venenis,
Sedicione furor, gemitu dolor, ira tumultu,
Fulmina terrore, Mars ictibus, alea rixis,
Garrulitate merum, Venus igne, Cupido sagittis,
Ingluvies luxu, gula sorde, bitumine venter,
215 Curia fabellis, fora litibus, histrio nugis,
Pelex blandiciis, lupa questu, lena susurris,
Fastu nupta, socrus odio, livore noverca,

more blessed by casting luxury aside, and gives birth once again to an age of gold, while treading underfoot that gold which turns the world to iron!

Ch. 5 The same philosopher complains of a new wantonness in dress[10]

"I grieve over these things, but grief visits me again, for another point no less sharp goads my thoughts; deep in my weary mind there is pain, an inner struggle that pours forth in sobs, a deep-seated indignation that oppresses my peace of mind under a dark cloud. For our age has abandoned itself to a new ostentation in dress, a naked lust for finery. The concern of olden times for decent attire is scorned, and a new and more wanton practice is in favor. Ancient customs yield to new ones; luxury overruns the world, and stern, mature dignity has yielded the place of honor to fashions as changeable as a leaf in the wind. The life of sober simplicity is mocked, and childish customs enfeeble grown men. These times devote their most serious attention to dress, sinfully eager, recklessly at pains to bring ruin upon themselves, boorish in their very urbanity.

Ch. 6 The world teems with vice. Seven wise men renowned in Greece for character and learning

"Why should I say more? The world itself is the basest of worldly things,[11] a perilous pit as overflowing with vice as the air with clouds, the sea with water, heaven with light, earth with darkness, autumn with fruits, spring with flowers, summer with heat, winter with cold, Egypt with soda, India with nard, Phrygia with chameleons, Africa with basilisks, the Nile with hippopotami, the Ganges with ebony, the Hellespont with sturgeons, Tartarus with torments, Styx with night, Megaera with poisons, madness with mutiny, grief with sobbing, wrath with confusion, thunderbolts with terror, war with blows, gaming with quarrels, wine with talkativeness, Venus with fire, Cupid with arrows, gluttony with luxury, greed with foulness, the belly with waste, the court with gossip, the forum with debate, an actor with trifles, a mistress with enticements, a prostitute with haggling, a bawd with whispers, a bride with haughtiness, a father-in-law with hatred, a step-mother with envy, Chance with uncertainty, Fortune with guile,

Sors dubiis, Fortuna dolo, velamine Fatum,
Spe miser, opposito felix, utroque Iohannes.[12]
220   Cleobolus Lycios, Mitylenen Pitacus auxit
Consiliis, Sparte Philon[13] illuxit, Athenis,
Sol hominum, Solon, Periandro summa Corinthi
Paruit et valuit Bias famulante Priene.
Hos sibi cum magno gaudet peperisse Talete
225   Grecia, quos senior sapientes iactitat etas.
Mundus ne titubet, ne cecus et invius erret,
Hos habeat servetque duces; stillabit Ulixem
Lingua, senex Pilius[14] animi purgabit amurcam."

Cap. 7 De lamentacione Architrenii propter penam eternam ex vite immundicia secuturam

Dixerat. et fuso gemitu precordia rumpit
230   Et querulo planctus tonat Architrenius ore:
"Hoc miser, hocne salo semper iactabere, numquam
Sirenes poteris has declinasse tuoque
Per modicum servire Iovi? poterisne sub axe
Tartareo calicem mortis gustasse perhennem?
235   Quis poterit volvisse tuum revolubile pondus,
Sisyphe? quisve polos et eosdem Ixionis axes
Circinet et tociens uno nugetur in orbe?
Viscera quis reparet tociens peritura?[15] quis undis
Perditus impendat operam, quam perdat ut undas?
240   Quis tociens lusus pomi cedentis inane
Mordeat et siciat, in quo fit naufragus, amnem?
O quam triste sedet ad nigri iudicis urnam
Concilium, dum iura movet firmissima Minos,
Dum superum vindex cunctis excessibus equat
245   Penas et rigido leges exasperat ore!
Heu quam terribilis iudex immobilis,[16] heu quam
Difficiles Minos, Radamantus et Eacus umbris!
Quam dubio fluitat animus terrore metuque
Contrahitur, quociens meditanti pectore fundo
250   Cochiti lacrimas Flegetonteosque caminos.
Heu quis Titanum laqueos communicet? heu quis
Suspenso poterit vitam suspendere saxo?
Dira sibi triplex hominem partitur et omnes
Distrahit humanos affectus, facta, loquelas:

Fate with obscurity, Misery with hope, happiness with its opposite, Johannes with both.[12]

20 "Cleobolus enriched Lycia with his wisdom, and Pittacus Mitylene; Chilo[13] brought light to Sparta, and Solon, the sun of humankind, to Athens; the ruling house of Corinth gave birth to Periander, and Bias grew to manhood in the bosom of Priene. It is the joy of Greece to have 25 borne these men, along with great Thales, men who in ancient times were extolled as wise. If the world is not to falter, or wander blindly and at random, it must acknowledge and cherish these guides. Then language will be distilled into Ulyssean utterance, and the wisdom of the old man of Pylos[14] will clear away the dregs of the mind."

Ch. 7 Architrenius' lament over the eternal punishment that must result from the uncleanness of our life

Pythagoras had ended. Architrenius broke into a burst of sobbing, 30 and in plaintive tones uttered this lamentation: "Wretched man, must you be forever tossed about on this ocean? Will you never be able to turn away from these Sirens, and offer due service to your God? Are you 35 capable of drinking the cup of perpetual death in the depths of Tartarus? Who is able, O Sisyphus, to turn your ever-returning rock? Who can turn Ixion's axle-tree, and let himself be mocked by whirling again and again in the same circle? Who can keep restoring entrails that must be so often destroyed?[15] Who is so abandoned as to devote himself to 40 drawing water in order to lose it again? Who that has been so often mocked by the elusive fruit can keep snapping at air, and thirsting for a river in which to drown himself?

"O how grim is the council that sits about the urn of the dark judge, while Minos imposes his unalterable decrees, and the supernal avenger 5 assigns punishments to all our transgressions, his face impassive as he exerts the harsh power of his law! Alas, how terrible is that unyielding judge,[16] how hostile toward the shades are Minos, Rhadamanthus and Aeacus! How my soul quavers in uncertain terror, how it shrinks in fear 10 whenever I present to my reflecting mind the tears of Cocytus and the fiery furnace of Phlegethon! Who, alas, could share the bondage of the Titans? Who could allow his life to hang suspended from a hanging rock? The three Furies divide a man among themselves, and reduce all 15 human beings to feelings, deeds and words. Allecto defiles the precincts

255 Inquinat Allecto serve presepia mentis
Affectusque pios, sacrumque forinsecat ignem;
Iuris precipitat equum in declive Megera
Errantesque manus enormibus implicat actis;
Thesiphone linguas agitat scelerumque palude
260 Inficit eloquii currus auriga loquendi.[17]
        Nativum video iam caligasse serenum
Involvique diem tenebris, quem Iupiter annis
Commisit teneris; divum deus optimus ille
Corporee purum casule commiserat ignem.
265 Sed iam nubifera fumi pallescit in umbra,
Native sacras animas mundique minoris
Sidera noctiferum sepelit caligine peplum.
Criminis obnubor tenebris, hiis intus opacor
Noctibus, hoc ledor oculos, hoc lippio cepe,
270 Hee sorbent animam Syrtes, hiis pectus hanelat
Pestibus, hoc mortis sub pondere vita laborat,
Hiis rotor in preceps Furiis, hec vincula pessum
Os homini sublime trahunt, ne patria visat
Sidera, nec superos oculis et mente salutet;
275 In declive caput trahitur, ne glorier umquam
Affectum superis animo mandasse benigno."

Cap. 8 Oracio Taletis de timore Domini

        Conquestiva Tales exhaurit dicta, propinquus
Sede, querelanti reserasse domesticus aurem:
        "Quisquis es, hunc nostre ciatum libato Minerve.
280 Parce puer lacrimis, fletus agnosce virilem
Dedecuisse genam. pudor est hoc imbre rigorem
Immaduisse virum; lacrime planctusque loquuntur
Degeneres animos, riguumque facillima flendi
Femina pectus habet didicitque cadentibus ultro
285 In lacrimis clausisse dolos, reserasse dolores.
        Ianua virtutum purumque Aurora sciendi
Allatura diem et, quo primo acceditur astris,
Cardo: timor Domini, sine quo fraudatur in omni
Proposito votum, nulla est statura potestas
290 Ad subitum lapsura nichil, non purpura murum
Divitibus prestat, nec sontem protegit auri
Ambiciosa lues, et nullo pro aggere surgit

of the obedient mind, and dispels the sacred fire. Megaera causes the
sense of right to decline, and involves our hands in terrible acts.
60 Tisiphone, taking over the reins of speech, drives the tongue and the
chariot of eloquence through the swamp of wickedness.[17]

"I see that the clarity of my nature has grown dim, that shadow has
obscured that daylight with which Jupiter endowed my tender years.
For that best of gods installed his purest fire in my humble bodily
65 dwelling, but now it is dimmed by the shadow of a smoky cloud: the
shroud of night has obscured the sacred powers of the little world of my
nature, burying its stars in darkness. I am blinded by the shadows of
sinfulness, dwell inwardly in the darkness of night. This onion mars my
70 vision and makes me blear-eyed, these are the quicksands that absorb
my spirit, this the plague that makes me gasp for breath. My life labors
under this burden of death, I am hurled about by these Furies. These
chains draw a man's uplifted gaze toward the earth, lest he behold his
75 native stars, and acknowledge the gods in thought and vision. So too
my head is bowed low, that I may never rejoice to have offered my love
to the gods in a spirit of peace."

Ch. 8 Thales' oration on the fear of the Lord

Thales, seated close by, took in these plaintive words, lending the ear
of an intimate friend to the lamentation. "Whoever you are, accept this
80 goblet of our wisdom. Cease your tears, my boy, realize that weeping
does not become the face of a man. It is shameful to dampen one's
manly dignity with such a shower. Tears and laments bespeak a
degenerate spirit; it is woman, so readily inclined to weep, whose breast
85 is ever damp, for she has learned to conceal her wiles in falling tears,
and make known her grievances.

"The gateway to virtue, the Dawn which will bring on the clear day
of knowledge, the key principle whereby one begins to approach the
stars, is the fear of God. Without this, prayer for any undertaking is
90 worthless; no power is so stable that it may not suddenly collapse into
nothing; no purple splendor can confer immunity on the wealthy; nor
the evil habit of currying favor with gold protect a guilty man; and a
surrounding pile of riches will afford no man protection by serving as

Circumfusus opum cumulus nullumque tuetur.
Sceptri nulla salus, si quo mandaverit ictum
295 Iupiter, haut iaculo cogit lorica repulsam,
Nec clipeo telum galeaque repellitur ensis.
      Pone leves animos, temereque audacibus obsta
Principio votis et, cui parere necesse est,
Sollicitus sollersque time, nam cuncta videntem
300 Nil celasse potes, nec eum, qui totus ubique
Excubat, evades. et qui Deus omnia novit,
Falli non poterit. Iovis insopita lucerna
In tenebris lucet, secreti conscia, clausum
Non sinit esse nefas; non occultatur opertum
305 Ypocrisi crimen nec sub lodice sepultum
Zoi chai sichen,[18] indignas sole Micenas
Sensit,[19] adulterio nodatam Ciprida Marti
Sol superum vidit, mense conviva cruente
Arguit Archadicum, nec eum mansueta fefellit
310 Oris ovis mentisque lupus: vultusque recepit
Cognatos animis, totus fera factus, aperto
Mentis in ore lupo, ne pectore blandior esset
Vultus, utroque fera, faciem mens seva cruentam
Sumpsit et humano iugulo polluta tyrannis.
315   O quem nulla fides mundi tutatur, in omni
Robore quassari facilis, nullaque reniti
Libertate potens, nec – solo nomine felix –
Inter opes sensurus opem, timuisse potentem
Cuncta necesse puta. nam quo venisse voluntas
320 Oderit, ipse trahet supreme calculus urne,
Vindictamque pati Iovis inconcussa potestas
Cogit, et extremam tandem non differet iram."

Cap. 9 Oracio Biantis quod Deus sit totis intimis diligendus

Vix ea, cum Bias simili de fonte propinat:
"Ecce time, quo tutus eris, solidusque timendum
325 Amplectatur amor, totis enitere votis
Dilecto placuisse Iovi, cui sufficit omni
Gracia pro merito. satis est ad premia dantis
Accipientis amor; nec gratis prestita doni
Inquinat alterni precio, munusque relato

his fortress. The scepter itself will not be secure: when Jupiter has
)5 determined to strike, no breastplate withstands his javelin, and his spear
and sword cannot be warded off by shield or helmet.

"Cast idle thoughts aside, recklessly confront the author of things
with bold prayers, yet make every effort to live in fear of one whom it is
)o necessary to obey. For you can conceal nothing from one who sees all
things, nor elude one who keeps watch in all places; and a God who
knows all cannot be deceived. The light of Jove shines undimmed amid
the shadows, knows all secret places, and will permit no wicked act to
)5 remain hidden. The veiled crime of hypocrisy is not hidden from him,
nor the "ah, my life and soul"[18] shrouded in a coverlet. He knew that
the Mycenaeans were unworthy of sunlight[19] and, sun of heaven as he
is, he saw Venus fettered to Mars in adultery. Invited to a bloody feast,
:o he accused Arcadian Lycaon, and neither the mild sheep's face nor the
wolfish mind deceived him. Lycaon received a face akin to his thoughts,
becoming wholly bestial, his wolfish mind proclaimed openly in his
countenance; lest his face seem gentler than his spirit, both were made
savage, and the cruel mind, the tyrant spirit polluted by human bloodshed, took on a bloodthirsty aspect.

:5 "O you whom no trust in worldly power may protect, so easily
shaken for all your strength, powerless to stand firm despite your
unconstrained power; you who, happy only in name, can never know
security though surrounded by riches, know that all things must finally
,o live in fear of a higher power. For where your own will is loath to go, the
sentence of the urn of heaven will drag you; the unassailable power of
Jove compels the enduring of retribution, and in the end he will not
withhold his anger."

Ch. 9 Bias' oration on the duty to make God the
sole object of our deepest love

Scarcely had the speech ended when Bias proffered a draught from a
similar source: "See, and be fearful of that wherein you are secure,
5 embrace with steadfast love him whom you must fear, and strive in all
your prayers to be pleasing to that Jove whom you love, and whose
grace is sufficient to reward all deserving. The love of the recipient of
this grace is sufficient reward for the bestower, and he will not taint the
generosity of his giving by exacting the price of a gift in return; he does

330 Munere non vendit, absolvit libera dono
     Dona relativo. nec, quod dedit, auferet auctor
     Muneris et predo. nulli data gaudia leva
     Invidie tollit, ut eodem nunc sit avarus,
     Quo nunc largus erat. pleno sua munera cornu
335 Plus cumuli quam vallis habent, munusque volenti
     Exhilarat dextra, nec vultus pondere doni
     Gracia succumbit. tot dantem dilige! si qua
     Magna dedit, maiora dabit. meritisque tot unum,
     Dilexisse, refer. qui se tibi poscit amari,
340 Non sibi, totus ama. non est, quod prosit amato
     Collaturus amor, sed amanti. dilige, si te
     Non odisse velis. mundum seseque daturus,
     Hiis ut ametur, emit. non est deceptus amator,
     Qui recipit quod amat, superum conviva futurus
345 Eternamque Stygis non descensurus in Ethnam.
          Dilige, dilecti grato venare favorem
     Numinis obsequio, partum tenuisse labora
     Immotumque liga, mentis fervore refixum,
     Ne labet, astringe; ne gracia sumpta relabi
350 Diminuive queat, habitam servare voluntas
     Obsequiosa potest. cupidis attende volentis
     Imperio votis, animos impende iubenti.
     Mandati ne differ opus, ne langueat actu
     Gracia dilato, placitura citacius urge,
355 Ne meritum perdas; nam suspendisse volentem
     Est meruisse minus. maturo nitere facto,
     Plenius ad meritum presens quam crastinus imples."

Cap. 10 Oracio Periandri quod Deus colendus est

     "Non satis est" inquit Periander "tercia sume
     Pocula, de nostro placeat sorbere fluento.
360 Tange precum laudumque lyram, geminaque Tonantem
     Sedulitate lita. superum cultura loquatur
     Te celi cupidum; complecti numina mente
     Et toti nupsisse Deo. ne flecte tenendos
     Hic vigiles sensus et ei servire memento,
365 Quo solo regnare potes. ne cetera tollat
     Cura, Deum cura. quecumque negocia tractes,

30 not sell his favor in return for favors, his free bestowal absolves us of the need to reciprocate, and the author of this gift never turns robber and snatches away what he has given. From none does he take away with grudging hand the joys he has bestowed, or grow covetous at one moment of that with which he had been generous at another. The gifts 35 from his full horn partake more of the hill than of the valley. To give with willing hand is his joy, and the grace of his countenance is undiminished by any amount of giving.

"Love him who gives so much! Though he has bestowed great gifts, he will grant still greater ones. In return for so many favors, offer the 40 one gift of love. Love him totally who demands to be loved for your sake, not for his own. The love to be offered is one that benefits not the beloved, but the lover. Love him, unless you would show hatred toward yourself. He has redeemed the world and would give us his very self, that he may be loved by us. The lover who thus obtains the thing he 45 loves is not deceived, for he will come to partake of the feast of the gods, and will never descend to the eternal fires of Styx.

"Love, then, and pursue the favor of the beloved power by that obedience which pleases him; strive to retain what he has bestowed and hold it fast; cling tightly to it with eager mind, lest it elude you; for an obedient will can preserve the grace it has obtained so that, once 50 granted, it may not be diminished or pass away. Acknowledge his rule with the eager prayers of a submissive heart, apply your mind to his commands, and perform the task assigned you without delay. Let not his grace grow weak in you through delay, but do at once what will be 55 pleasing to him, lest you squander his favor. For to have deferred what one would do is to have proven less worthy of favor. Seek to act while the time is ripe, for you will prove more fully deserving by immediate than by deferred actions."

Ch. 10 The Oration of Periander on the duty of offering worship to God

"This is not enough," declared Periander. "Drink a third time, and 60 deign to accept this draught from my stream. Strike the lyre of prayer and praise, and propitiate the Thunderer with redoubled zeal. Let your worship of the gods make plain that you are eager for heaven, that you have embraced the divine powers in spirit, and given yourself wholly to God. Do not allow your mind to stray from constant awareness of him, 65 and be mindful of the need to serve him through whom alone you may come to rule. Let no other concern draw you away, but concern yourself

Providus ad superos oculum mentemque reducas.
   Nam vacat humanis studiis impensa, nichilque
Est lucri latura dies et inutilis exit
370 Exclusi secura Dei, cui vivere soli
Est toti vixisse sibi; sine numine frustra
Est operosa manus, studio marcescit inani
In vacuum tractura moras, sterilisque laborat
Actio, que nulla superis pro parte ministrat.
375   Que nocuos lesura tonat, que fulmina tractat,
Sit semper suspecta manus, non parcit inultis
Criminibus: tonitruque minas et fulmine penas
Mandat et ad Stygias urget properancius undas,
Quos Flegeton exasset aquis, Cochitus adustis
380 Elixet lacrimis, habeatque Ixionis axis
Quos rotet eternum, versentque reductile pondus
Sisyphium, penamque levent consorcia pene,
Communisque minus habeat iactura querele.
   Impermixta malis bonitas Iovis omne timeri,
385 Omne coli meruit. solida virtute cavendum
Luctandumque puta, ne quid deliret in illam
Error ad offensam; pudeat offendere, quem te
Offendisse pudet, illumque lacessere, cuius
Libertas est summa iugum, cui cedere pondus
390 Maiestatis habet, cui mendicare potestas,
Servire imperium, flere est non flere, dolere
Non dolor est, mors absque mori, sitis absque sitire,
Esuriisse cibus et ei parere iubentis
Est habuisse vicem, levibusque occurrere votis
395 Accurrisse deis, animoque excludere mundum
Inclusisse Deum, fierique a corporis umbra
Sidus, et optatum superis annectere civem.
   Nec minus invigiles inconcussoque rigore,
Si potes, evincas, ne vite larva coloret
400 Ypocrisis mendas, virtutum littera, prava
Pectoris interpres – utinamque incognita claustro
Et mitre et baculo! – vultus cautela professi
Mentis honestatem, verum occultare diserta,
Simpliciter falsum factura probabile, culpe
405 Occulto patrona dolo, pictura reatus,
Celatura notam; vultusque reconditur umbra
Mente latens ignotus homo, superumque favorem

with God. Whatever tasks you must undertake, be careful to draw your eyes and thoughts back to the higher powers. For time given to human pursuits is idle; a day from which God is carelessly excluded brings no
70 reward and issues in nothing. To live only for him is to live most completely for oneself. In the absence of divine favor the hand exerts itself in vain, falls into useless pursuits, spends long hours on nothing; any activity will prove sterile that makes no provision for the gods.

75 "Be ever fearful of his hand whose thunder threatens wrongdoers, who wields the lightning, for he does not suffer crimes to go unavenged. He declares his menace in thunder, his punishments in lightning, and drives swiftly to the Stygian shores those who are to burn in the waters
80 of Phlegethon, whom Cocytus is to steep in boiling tears, whom the wheel of Ixion is to claim and whirl about eternally, those who will roll the ever returning rock of Sisyphus, and alleviate his suffering by sharing it, that a common disaster may provide less occasion for lamentation.

85 "Untainted by evil, the goodness of Jove is wholly to be feared, wholly reverenced. See that you remain steadfast in virtue, cautiously on guard lest some reckless error offend against that goodness, and think it abhorrent to give offense to him to whom it would be abhorrent to offend you, or provoke him whose yoke is the highest freedom: to
90 submit to him is to partake of majesty, to beg at his hand is power, to serve him is to rule. To weep before him is to weep no more, to grieve is not grievous, to die is not to die; to thirst for him is to be without thirst, to hunger for him is to be nourished, to obey him is to become one who
95 commands, to run to him in swift prayer is to be quickly among the gods. To banish the world from your mind is to install God there, to be turned from a shadowy body to a star, and to join oneself to the cherished company of the heavens.

"Be no less alert and unyielding in firmness and you may be able to
00 ensure that the surface of life does not become a mask for the deceits of hypocrisy, the mere letter of virtue, a corrupt representation of the mind; would that it were unknown to the cloister, the mitre, the pastoral staff! The carefulness of a face that asserts the honesty of the mind within, well schooled in concealing the truth, rendering falsehood
05 plausible by its seeming frankness, lending a legitimacy to crime by hidden guile, embellishing guilt, concealing the marks of infamy. The man whose true mind lurks unknown is protected by the veil of

Excipit et mundi recipit, lucratus honores,
Dum simulat mores et morum nomine mundum
410 Deceptus deceptor emit, perditque superne
Delicias mense. verum tollatur inane
Ypocrisis velum, munde sincera choruscet
Integritas vite. refert fallentis in auro
Occultasse lutum, fraudisque iniuria stagnam
415 Palliat argento. reverencior esto nichilque
Deliquisse velis, Davumque a pectore tolle,
Nec vultu mentire Numam.[20] concordia vultum
Affectumque liget; pudeatque abscondere culpam,
Quam pepulisse potes, illumque accersere testem
420 Delicti, quem nulla latent, oculisque sopori
Occultis occulta videt, nullisque tenetur
Obicibus, quem nulla tenet distancia, visus.
    Est tamen, ut viciis mens obluctata ruinam
Declinasse nequit et nervo saucia labi
425 Cogitur in labem, nec vincere libera frustra
Carnis hanelat opem, certaminis impos, inhermis
Victa cadit, cecidisse dolet; sed dulce cadenti
Est vicii pondus, blandaque indagine cingit
Torquendas animas carnis mansueta tyrannis."

Cap. 11 Oracio Philonis de occultandis delictis

430 Hic Philon: "Viciis quociens victoria cedit,
Fas esto latuisse nefas, tenebrisque notatam
Dissimulasse notam, clausaque excludere mundi
Excubias culpa, cynicosque evadere morsus
Et satire serras, Flaccique eludere ludum
435 Insipidosque sales.[21] nam si sordere necesse
Est animam, sacius est munde parcere fame
Nec vite maculis oculos lesisse bonorum.
    Pullulat in vulgi facinus vulgata voluptas
Derivatque notam, dum plebis ceca libido
440 Imbibit aure scelus. sunt internuncia culpe
Scire, videre, loqui; scelerisque audacia multo
Crescit in exemplo, surgitque impune reatus
A simili, notumque trahit contagia crimen.
    Hec rerum dominis caveat sollercia, Fame
445 Deludens oculos. horum nota lacius orbem

appearance as he lays claim to divine favor and accepts the favor of the world, buying honor by feigning good character.

410 "Yet even as he garners worldly success in the name of virtue, this deceiver is deceived, for he is rejecting the delights of the heavenly feast. Let the insubstantial veil of hypocrisy be removed, and the simple integrity of the uncorrupted life shine forth, and it is evident that murky deception has covered itself in gold, that the cruelty of fraud has cloaked 415 its foulness in silver. Be reverent therefore, and seek never to transgress; banish Davus from your heart, and inscribe no false image of Numa on your countenance.[20] Let there be agreement between face and feeling, and think it shameful to conceal the guilty act which you might have repudiated by invoking that witness of your guilt from whom nothing is 420 hidden. He sees in the depths of his vision things too deep for us in our drowsy state, and as no amount of distance can keep him from us, so no obstacle can restrict his vision.

"And yet it is true that the mind assailed by vice cannot withstand 425 ruin; its strength is enfeebled and it is forced into decline. No longer in command, powerless to defend itself, it yearns in vain for succor from the flesh, and falls, a helpless victim, yet grieves at having fallen. But the burden of vice seems sweet to it as it falls: the mild tyranny of the flesh binds in a sweetly beguiling way those spirits that will suffer its torments."

Ch. 11 The oration of Chilo on the need to conceal our misdeeds

430 Here Chilo spoke: Whenever the victory is ceded to vice, it is right to keep the wrong hidden, to cover the evidence of infamy in darkness, and conceal the guilty act from the watchful eyes of the world, in order to evade the carping cynic and the barbs of satire, and escape the mockery, 435 the insipid wittiness, of the satirist.[21] Though it is inevitable that the spirit be defiled, it is right to be sparing of the untainted reputation, and not offend the sight of good men with the imperfections of the life.

"When a carnal sin is made public, it branches out, becomes a common state of sin, and spreads its infamy abroad; when the blind, 440 lustful mob takes in the news of the crime, knowledge, observation and word of mouth assume the role of go-betweens; sin grows more bold when it has an abundance of examples, and guilt thrives secure when it has a precedent: a well known crime is like an infectious disease.

"This concern to evade the scrutiny of Rumor should keep men of 445 power on their guard. Their faults, too widely known, pollute the world

Inquinat exemplis. populi delicta regentis
Absolvit facinus, maiorum forma minores
Pressius informat, avidusque in funera morbus,
Quo caput elanguet, reliquos depascitur artus;
450 Prelatique parit labis consorcia labes.
   At sceptri facinus latebris caret, ardua nubis
Excedunt latebras, nulla pretexitur umbra
Imperii sidus, noctisque excludit amictum
Principis illa dies, fama penetrante trahuntur
455 Regnorum secreta palam, scelerique potentum
Lux adhibet lucem, nec molli purpura sordes
Occulit in ruga. culpe latuisse volenti
Maiestas peccantis obest, maiusque videri
Maiorum facinus consuevit et auctior auget
460 Gloria delictum, nec sic censura togatos
Ut regni trabeas, plebi minus aspera, mordet.
   O igitur, quem nulla facit pretexta beatum,
O miser in letis: tibi delituisse negatur
Deliquisse nega! viciorum terge lituras
465 Nec labem sincerus habe, stabilemque nefandis
Pone modum votis morum candore nivescat
A vicii mens pura luto, mundique favorem
Extorque meritis, accensaque pectore virtus
Ferveat; hec anime tenebris intacta lucerna
470 Splendeat exterius, nullo dilanguida fumo.
   Nec permitto nefas. sed quem cecidisse necesse est,
Occulto nutasse volo scelerisque latendo
Evasisse notam. prave ne intellige, si quid
Instruit ad mores; non ultra sedulus esto,
475 Quam licet, interpres. temere volat ocior equo
Impetus ingenii, distortaque littera culpe
Promittit veniam, scelerisque occasio surgit
Ex male distinctis. nostris sollercia simplex
Accedat monitis, animo quid araverit auctor,
480 Indecepta videt. ponat presumptio lime
Lectorisque vicem, studii demencia ceca
Desinat erroris auctorem querere, si qua
Imperat enodis servandos pagina mores."
   Dixit; adhuc patula stetit Architrenius aure,
485 Eloquiique fores tacito Philone resolvit.

by their example. The transgressions of rulers absolve crime in general;
the pattern of great men's lives exerts a shaping influence on those of
lesser men. Like a raging, deadly disease which, when the head has
50 grown feeble, feeds on the rest of the body, the lapse of a prominent
figure spawns a communal decline.

"But the crimes of the ruler cannot be hidden; they stand out high
above the shadowing clouds. No darkness cloaks the star of ruling
power; the bright day of a prince rejects the mantle of night. Thus the
55 secrets of rulers are dragged into the open by probing rumor, and the
radiance of majesty serves to illumine its guilt. Foul deeds can not hide
themselves in the soft folds of a purple robe; the very dignity of the
sinner prevents his sinful impulses from remaining hidden. The crimes
60 of great men will always appear greater, and their larger glory only
enlarges their fault. Public opinion, less severe with common people,
does not tear at the humble toga as it does the kingly robe.

"Thus for you whom sumptuous trappings cannot make truly
happy, you who are wretched amid your good fortune, there can be no
concealment. Therefore let there be no sin! Wipe away the taint of your
65 vices, be pure and admit no weakness, impose a firm control on your
impious desires. Let your mind, purged of the taint of vice, gleam with
the candor of virtue, lay claim to the world's favor by your good actions,
70 and let the fire of virtue infuse your spirit. Let your soul's lamp shine
forth, untainted by shadow, dimmed by no smoky cloud.

"I do not condone wrongdoing. But I urge that whoever is forced to
fall should keep his weakness secret, and avoid notoriety by concealing
his crime. Do not read a wicked meaning into anything that promotes
75 morality, and be no more zealous a critic than the situation allows. The
impulses of human understanding are random and overhasty; a twisted
version of the facts can give rise to an acceptance of sin, and the
occasion for wrongdoing arises from situations badly defined. See that
those of rude understanding are provided with sound advice, for they
80 will see without error what authority has engraved in their minds. The
would-be moralist may lay aside his file, and cease to search for the
original malefactor in a mad excess of blind zeal, where there exists a
page that unambiguously enjoins the upholding of moral law."

85 He had spoken. Architrenius still sat with open ear, but as Chilo fell
silent, he opened the gates to his own eloquence.

Liber Octavus

Cap. 1 De commendacione antiquitatis et mundi negligencia circa mores

"Omne bonum veterum labiis distillat, et imbres
Pegaseos senior etas exundat et orbi
Ubera centenni puero distendit, honesti
Lacte fluens nutrix; nec maturatur – anilis
5 Criniculo, mente puerescens – mundus, et aucto
Corpore non adhibent crementum moribus anni.
Lactativa bibit veteris precepta Minerve,
Nutritiva parum. nam vix libata vomuntur
Pocula, nec prosunt, que nunc data nausea reddit,
10 Nec satis auricula vigilas, si pectore dormis.
    Area delicti, scelerum domus, excipit omnes
Mens hominum sordes. has egessisse paludes
Virtutis vis nulla potest, viciique revelli
Non didicit ruscus. paciatur cetera tolli,
15 Spina tamen restat; solidamque superbia sedem
Immota radice ligat truncoque recisa
Stirpe manet fixo. nichil est illime nec ista
Alcide potuit faculis arescere Lerna."

Cap. 2 Oracio Pitaci de mansuetudine appetenda et elacione vitanda

"At licet ista filix sit inextirpabilis" inquit
20 Pitacus "et nulli valeat succumbere falci,
Quin nocuo fetu populosa repullulet ydra,
Tu tamen assiduus anime luctare colonus.
Mollescant animi dulces, viciumque tumoris
Cedat, et asperitas nullo silvescat in actu
25 Obicibus ledens, inconsultique rigoris
Robora lentescant, assit clemencia sceptris

Book Eight

Ch. 1 In praise of ancient times, and on our own world's carelessness regarding morality

"All good doctrine flows from the lips of the ancients. It is an earlier age that gave rise to the Pegasean stream, and now distends its breasts, like a nurse abounding in the milk of virtue, to feed a world which, though centuries old, is still a child. For the world, though it shows the
5 outward signs of age, is childish in understanding, and does not mature. Though its body ages, the years do not bring an accompanying growth in moral wisdom. It drinks in the nutritive precepts of Minerva, but they provide little nourishment, for the drink is no sooner taken in than vomited forth. What nausea gives back the moment it receives it can do
10 no good; your ear cannot be sufficiently alert if the mind within is asleep.

"The mind of man is the place of transgression, the home of wickedness that admits every sort of foulness. No virtuous power can drain these swamps, no art can clear the dense thickets of vice. Though it be
15 granted us to remove the rest, these brambles will still remain. Pride, its roots immovably deep, remains firmly in its place, and though the trunk be cut away it remains fast rooted. No part of us is untainted, and this Lernaean monster cannot be burnt away by the torch of Hercules."

Ch. 2 Pittacus' oration on the duty of pursuing gentleness and avoiding vainglory

"But even granting that this bristle can not be plucked out," said
20 Pittacus, "and will yield to no blade, though indeed this Hydra may produce a whole tribe of baneful progeny, you must still fight zealously to reclaim your soul. That the mind's sweet enticements may be weakened, the vice of pride give way, the rough thickets of vice no longer
25 present a menacing obstacle to your actions, and the obduracy of ill-considered severity grow mild, let clemency, inseparable companion

Indivisa comes gladiique coherceat ausus
Micior et – iuris quantum permittit habena –
Imperio parcens, prohibens punire flagello
30 Deterrenda minis, fluvios exosa cruoris
Non lacrime, si quam regnis extorsit egestas
Et solium movere case, si quando potentum
Arentes oculos tenero compassio fletu
Impluit et latuit sceptro rorante tyrannis.
35 Corruit elatus, luci sublatus et umbris
Lucifer illatus, vanoque a numine venit,
Quo Numa devenit,[1] tumidusque inventus ab alto
Detumuit ventus, et Lucifer esse coactus
Letifer est factus,[2] astrisque parentibus orbus
40 Luteus in luteum[3] cadit, in pigrum impiger orbem.
Vicit in humano spolio Deus, exulis exul
Hospitis hospes erat, ad Ditis inhospita venit
Tartareasque fores celorum ianua, Christus,
Lucifer eternus, infractaque dextera fregit.
45 Ecce, quod amisit incauta superbia, celum
Maiestas submissa dedit, dominusque ministrum
Induit et meruit humilis vicisse potestas.
Fortius insudes humili mansuescere mente
Et placido vultu, socia dulcedine linguam
50 Affectumque riga. superum mundique favorem
Captet uterque favus, pacemque extorqueat orbis
Illa vel illa quies. animi depelle tumorem
Luciferique Nothos, tollatque superbia flatus
Precipites Boreamque suum, tumidique rigoris
55 Subsidat rabies et sola in pectore toto
Pax Zephyri vernet, florumque potencior illa
Pullulet aura crocos animeque superserat ortis.
Oderit ulcisci gladio censura. nec illum
Consulat in penam, nec eum tortore cruentet,
60 Quem liceat torquere minis; pudeatque regendos
Imperii fregisse iugo, semperque venenum
Et numquam fudisse favum, ferroque dolorum
Subsecuisse vias, crudisque extinguere morbos
Ignibus – alterutro levius curantibus herbis!
65 Tucior est regnis gladio tranquilla iubentis
Nec fraudis suspecta quies; hec mente favorem

of rulers, be at hand; let the boldness of the sword exercise control more gently and, so far as the force of law will allow, assert its authority
30 sparingly. Let it be forbidden to punish with the lash crimes which strong words should be sufficient to prevent, and let the flow of blood be deemed abhorrent – though not the flow of tears, if poverty has ever had the power to extort tears from kings, or the plight of the cottager affected the throne; if ever compassion has caused the dry eyes of the mighty to well up with tender weeping, or a tyrant been eclipsed by tears that bedewed his scepter.

35 "Proud Lucifer was overthrown, banished from the world of light and relegated to the shadows; from the seat of divine power he came to that empty place where Numa too has come.[1] Having been deemed too puffed up with pride, he dwindled as he descended from on high; having felt constrained as the bearer of light, he became the bearer of death.[2]
40 Banished from the starry realm of his birth, his brightness was cast into murky darkness;[3] his restless energy descended into the sluggish world.

"God, assuming human flesh, overcame him. An exile himself, he was the guest of an exile host. For Christ, the bearer of eternal light, came to the inhospitable realm of Dis, and his undaunted right arm
45 smashed open the gates of Tartarus to make them a gateway to heaven. Behold, submissive majesty restored that heaven which reckless pride had lost; the master put on the garb of the servant, and his power prevailed by humbling itself.

"Strive to be gentle, with unassuming spirit and peaceful counte-
50 nance. Let your words and thoughts be steeped in sweet sociability. Such twofold sweetness will win you the favor both of gods and men; the one gentleness and the other will reconcile the world. Rid yourself of the puffed-up spirit and windy thoughts of Lucifer, let pride withdraw her gusting blasts and northern chill; let the madness of unbending
55 haughtiness subside, and the vernal calm of Zephyrus take sole possession of your spirit, that its more efficacious breath may produce a rich flowering and strew the garden of your soul with blossoms.

"Let judgment think it hateful to enforce its decrees by the sword, and not seek this recourse in assigning punishment. Let no bloody
60 torture be visited on anyone whom it is possible to sway with stern warnings, and be it held shameful to destroy those who should be subject to the control of a governing power, to offer a drink that is always bitter poison, and never honey. Do not always carve out a path with the instruments of torment, and do not seek to purge every infection with harsh fire; far gentler than either of these are curative
65 herbs! Mild tranquillity, untainted by any suspicion of coercive betrayal,

Extrahit, hic lingua. feritas dirumpit amorem,
Mansuetudo ligat; hauritque incauta venenum
Effera maiestas vinoque ulciscitur enses,
70 Unaque tot flendi claudunt convivia rivos;[4]
Fictaque subridens iterat suspiria plebes,
Dum domini leto producit funera planctu
Et tenero sudant oculo velancia risum
Pectora, que modico pretexunt gaudia fletu.
75   Pax ad opus mandata rapit, stimulique potestas
Non perdit sub pace vicem; violenta trahuntur
Iussa minusque movent, segnesque ingrata ministros
Ingratosque trahunt, nec habent extorta volentem.
Est ubi mandatum violenta potencius urgent,
80 Servilesque docet animos servire flagellum;
Nec satis est mandantis amor, positoque voluntas
Mandativa iugo, precibusque innixa potestas.
Pollicitis instare vacat, mollire rigorem,
Blandiciis condire minas; sevire necesse est
85 Et virga mutasse preces, pressumque domandis
Inseruisse iugum. clemencia Cesaris auras
Verberat,[5] est tauro Phalaris mandanda voluntas.
At iuri precisa velis! premordeat equi
Lima voluntatem, quo solo invita trahatur
90 Leva potestatis gladio committere penam."

Cap. 3 Oracio Cleoboli de fortitudine

Hic Lycius: "Quicumque iubet, dulcescere raro
Edidicit, torquere potest, sed parcere nescit.
Imperii moles subiectos emolit. anceps
Hic gladius cladis est illativus, et ira
95 Principis in populos fulmen populatur et orbem
Hinc dominus pulsat, illinc Fortuna, Caribdis
Sevior inque bonos crudescens vipera. verum,
Si tumidum preseva tonet, si nauseet iras
Pectore flammato, vultu crudescat et axem
100 Torqueat in lacrimas, versumque exasperet orbem
Descendente rota, miseris oppone rigorem
Mentis inattrite, nubesque expelle sereno
Pectoris obiecti. veniat tutissima virtus

ensures a kingdom's safety better than the sword. The one elicits approval from the mind, the other only from the tongue. Brutality destroys the bond of love, gentleness strengthens it. Cruel majesty drinks poison unawares, and its violence is avenged with wine; in an
70 instant a feast closes off all the channels of tears.[4] The people, laughing inwardly, give forth repeated sounds of false grief as they perform the funeral rites for their deceased lord with due lamentation, and the breasts which conceal their smiles grow damp with tender weeping, cloaking their joy in a modest display of sorrow.

75   "It is peace that compels the carrying out of orders; power does not lose its influence by behaving mildly. Harsh commands are obeyed slowly and have less effect, for an inconsiderate master produces sluggish and unwilling agents: forced labor is performed unwillingly. For
80 when harsh commands impose the assigned task too forcefully, they teach the servant how to become deserving of the lash.

    "But it is not enough that he who commands be loving, that he make his will known without imposing force, making his power dependent upon persuasion. There is a time for relying on promises, for tempering one's firmness and concealing threats in sweet words. But it is also
85 necessary to grow angry, to substitute blows for appeals, and to impose the yoke firmly on those who must be tamed. Caesar's clemency proved futile;[5] such kindness will end in one's being consigned to the bull of Phalaris. But adhere strictly to the law! Let the file of equity so shape the
90 will as to ensure that the arm of power is drawn only reluctantly to impose its judgments by the sword."

Ch. 3 Cleobolus' oration on fortitude

    Here the Lycian spoke: "Those who command are rarely schooled in kindness: they can punish, but know not how to be sparing. The weight of ruling power grinds its subjects down; its double-edged sword
95 conveys the threat of slaughter, and the wrath of the prince assails his people like a thunderbolt. And as rulers attack the world from one side, Fortune, a Charybdis more savage than any serpent, rages against the good from the other. But however fiercely she thunders her proud taunts, however she spews forth rage from her fiery throat, though she
00 cruelly distorts her face and reduces all the earth to tears, or goads a whirling world to madness as her wheel pursues its descending course, withstand her with the firmness of a mind that suffering cannot wear down, and banish all clouds from the serenity of the spirit you display. Confront fortune in the full security of a virtue capable of evading the

Obvia fortune, fati evasura procellas
105 Naufragiique minas, ut non nisi prospera fiant
Fata. scias adversa pati! felicia numquam
Magnanimo desunt, animo fortuna virili
Omnis leta venit; fatum lugubre videri
Debilitas infirma facit. que sevius instant,
110 Materiam virtutis habent, certissima sunt hec
Argumenta viri; virtusque abscondita letis
Prodit in adversis, fatoque obscura sereno
Lucet in obscuro: dum voto accommoda fiunt
Omnia, noctescit, miserisque diescit, et umbram
115 Prospera virtuti faciunt, adversa lucernam.
    Ardua dum surgunt pendente Ceraunia fluctu,
Eversumque suas pelagus spumescit in iras,
Attollique fretum superis contendit et audax
Fluctus in astra volat lunamque extinguit et ipsos
120 Falciferos axes,[6] nunc trudit ad ultima navem
Tartara, nunc raptam superis nolentibus offert,
Nunc prora nunc puppe cadit, nunc surgit utroque
Sepe bibente ratis, trepida nunc claudicat alno
Luctanti cessura freto, dum pugnat et aure
125 Fluctibus et ponti, fervetque in funera toto
Mors armata mari: tunc remigis arte fruendum,
Tunc laus est vicisse fretum, tunc, si qua potestas
Est naute, fit tota palam, nec deside tutum
Est languere mora. venienti occurrere fato
130 Uniusque manu populi servasse salutem
Expedit, ut pelagi victorem fama coronet.
    Virtuti expediunt aditus adversa, virorum
Sarcina, torporis prohibens languescere sompno
Degeneres animos. nescit felicia virtus,
135 Mollibus utenti raro comes. induit omnem
Prosperitas labem, nulloque innoxia facto
Non sentit consueta nefas. temerarius ausis
Ignovisse solet, solidator criminis, usus.
    Qui flet in adversis, pueriles errat in actus
140 Et lacrimas perdit et famam polluit; auget
Litus arans adversa dolor nescitque rigorem,
Quo solidat Natura viros; doluisse dolenda
Non redimit, nec dampna levant, qui dampna queruntur.
Hic dolor elusas lacrimas serit, irrita mandat

105 storms of fate and their menace of shipwreck, that none but favorable
fate may befall you. Learn to accept adversity![6] Happiness never forsakes the great-hearted, and all fortune is favorable to a manly spirit. It
is faltering weakness that makes fate appear dismal. Those things that
110 bear hardest upon us provide the means for virtuous action and the
most decisive proof of a man's character. The virtue that lies hidden in
happy times serves us in adversity. Clouded over when fate smiles
serene, it shines forth when our fate is cloudy. When all things adapt
themselves to our wishes, it remains in darkness, but it shines forth in
115 times of sadness. Happy times reduce virtue to a shadow, but hardship
makes her its lamp.

"When the steep Ceraunian mountains pour forth their rushing
streams, when the storm-tossed ocean foams with rage, when the sea
struggles to reach the heavens, and its waves boldly assail the stars,
120 extinguishing the light of the moon and even the far-off Scythe-bearer;
when the sea thrusts the vessel down to the depths of Tartarus at one
moment, and at the next thrusts it aloft as an offering to the unwilling
gods: first the prow, then the stern is submerged; now the boat struggles
forward, continually awash at either end; now it staggers with creaking
timbers, nearly succumbing to the violent tide, and fights against the
125 surge of wind and water, while death itself takes up arms and rages over
the sea in search of victims. It is now that the oarsman's art must be put
to use, now it is praiseworthy to conquer the waves, now whatever
strength the sailor possesses shows plainly, and there is no safety for
those who languish in idleness. Now is the time for the hand of some
130 one man to confront the oncoming disaster and ensure the people's
safety, that fame may crown him victor over the sea.

"Hardship provides the occasion for virtue; it is a burden men must
bear, and forbids even degenerate spirits to languish in a drowsy torpor.
135 Virtue is unacquainted with happy times, and rarely attends those
whose situation is easy. It is prosperity that falls into disgrace, for none
of its actions are blameless, and it does not recognize the sinful state to
which it has accustomed itself. Thoughtless habit, accustomed to over-
looking its own shamelessness, strengthens the guilty impulse.

140 "He who weeps at hardship has strayed into childishness; he squanders his tears and taints his good name. Grief, plowing the barren
strand, increases its hardships, and never attains that firmness with
which Nature emboldens men. To grieve at one's grievous plight does
not make it better, and those who complain of their suffering do not
145 suffer less. Such grief strews futile tears, sows seed in vain, for the

145 Semina; nam sterilis nullaque puerpera messe
Fit seges et fallit vacuum cultura colonum.
Si miser es, spera! veniet felicior annis
Horula, meta malis. aperit solacia mestis
Fortune levitas, verni prenuncia plausus
150 Meroris presevit hiemps, preludit amaris
Mox latura favos, miseris Fortuna secundos
Adiectura dies; subitosque miserrima letis
Promittunt aditus, Fortune lubrica nescit
Mobilitas fixisse rotam, sceptroque minatur
155 Solaturque casas, varios fastidit honores
Cesaris et tandem solii spem mandat Amycle."

Cap. 4 Oracio Solonis circa prudenciam et vite optimam composicionem

Dixerat. at Solon: "Minor est precognita fati
Asperitas, adversa minus previsa flagellant.
Et quia Fortune laqueum prudencia solvit,
160 Semper ubique tibi caveas, teque omnis in omnes
Cautela eventus premuniat et tibi toti
Sis oculus totus; animi sollercia, lampas
Previa, noctifugam ferat insopita lucernam.
Hec tibi dictatrix operum cunctisque magistra
165 Prima rudimentis, ne qua ledatur honestum,
Invigilet, nulloque tibi non consulat actu.
Rem male provisam dubius manet exitus. alis
Evolat insolidis, si quem rapit impetus ausu
Non bene pennato; melior nisi navita clavum
170 Torserit et velo biberit prudencia ventos,
Tam mare quam mortem poture crederis alno.
Si datur indempnis voto dilacio, votum
Differ, ut inspicias. properatum velle volentem
Fraudat, et audaces maturo penitet ausi.
175 Tarda venit subitis successus gloria; dampnum
Precipitat, qui vota rapit; facienda diserte
Sunt studio tractanda more. festina iuventam
Plus redolent, previsa virum; precepsque volendi
Plurima presumit infancia, pauca secundat.
180 Circumspecta tamen oculo scrutante, labora
Impiger officii, nec honesto languidus actu;

yield is sterile and produces no harvest. Such farming leaves the farmer deceived and empty-handed.

"If you are unhappy, be hopeful! A happier time will come, an end to the hard years. The very capriciousness of Fortune affords comfort to
150 the sorrowful; the cruel winter of sorrow is itself a harbinger of the favor of spring, a bitter prelude to the sweets that will soon be at hand. Fortune is bound to bring a happier day to those in misery: the bitterest times are the surest promise of a sudden attainment of happiness. For Fortune, slippery and unstable, can never stay her wheel, and what
155 poses a threat to the ruler offers hope to the cottage-dweller. For she tires of the many honors bestowed on Caesar, and finally permits even Amyclas to hope for a throne."

Ch. 4 Solon's oration on prudence and the best way of ordering one's life

He had finished. But Solon followed: "The harshness of a fate fore-known is less severe; adversity strikes less cruelly when it is foreseen.
160 And since it is prudence that loosens the knots of Fortune, be always on your guard, take every precaution to protect yourself against every eventuality, and be for yourself a single all-seeing eye. Let the alertness of your mind, a forward-looking lamp, provide an unquenchable beacon to dispel the darkness. Let prudence prescribe your tasks and
165 teach you how to begin in all that you do; let her be watchful, lest your good name be damaged in any way, and let there be no undertaking in which she does not advise you.

"When a thing is badly planned, the outcome is uncertain. He who is caught up by impulse to an act of unfledged boldness flies on unsteady
170 wings. If prudence, the best of sailors, has not taken the helm and controlled the filling of the sail with wind, you have entrusted yourself to a vessel that is bound to drink its fill of sea-water and death.

"If what you seek to accomplish can be delayed without harm, defer it, so that you may consider it. To pursue what one hopes to do with haste is to betray one's hope. Those who act rashly soon regret their rashness; the glory of success is slow in coming for work too abruptly
175 begun. To snatch at what one wants is to bring on disaster. If a thing is to be done with skill, it must be done with a due regard for time. Haste is a property of youth, foresight of manhood, and infancy, impulsively grabbing at the many objects of its desire, accomplishes little.

180 "Look about you, then, with probing eye. Labor tirelessly at what you undertake, and never grow weary of honest toil. Do not allow your

Ignavo torpore veta mollescere nervos,
Nec sub fasciculo fascem laturus hanela.
Sordida, tersa minus, vulgo cognacior, absit
185   Cura, relinquatur aliis, aliena sit omnis
Actori paritura notam; vilescat oportet
Libertatis honor, serviles si induat usus.
　　　Est tamen ut, quociens locus aut vis temporis urget,
Maiorum deceant plebea negocia mores.
190   Quicquid ages, virtus illud premandet; et orsus
Perfice! nam cepti qui finem preterit errat,
Turpius admittens quam qui non inchoat; illud
Accusat levitas, hoc disquisicio recti
Excusare potest, opera nil ausa repenti,
195   Propositi longo trutinans examine metas.
　　　Si qua tamen cepisse pudet, clausisse pudori
Et culpe est, scelerumque licet rescindere cursus –
Imperfecta solent veniam delicta mereri
Et levius ledit, qui parcius institit, error.
200   Quas adhibes curas, vix interrumpe. laboris
Difficilem rursus capit intercisio nodum.
Fax, sopita nisi moveatur, mota soporem
Excitat in flammas vigiles – motuque remisso
Languet et amissos iterum vix integrat ignes.
205　　Crescat et in ramos virtus fundatur et alta
Evolet et penitus fixis radicibus orbem
Occupet, egregiis factis vulgata, tibique
Mane bono cumulet meliori vespere famam.
Assiduo fructu pariant hanc secula messem,
210   Nec nisi cum morum veniat lux crastina luce.
　　　Si qua tibi vicio sordet vicinia, labem
Effuge, ne spargant similes contagia mende.
Dilexisse bonos et eis devinctius uti
Innuit esse bonum; racioque probabilis urget
215   Esse malum coluisse malos. accedit eisdem
Unanimes nectens studiis devocio, blanda
Stringitur in simili convictus copula voto:
Et Marti Venus est et Marcia grata Catoni,
Nec Phariam Cesar refugit, Cornelia Magnum.
220　　Livoris pudeat rastro verrisse bonorum

sinews to grow soft in idle dullness, and if you aspire to bear the fasces, do not let a mere fascicle weary you. Put far away those base and
185 impure desires that are the property of the mob; let these be left for others, and have no part in anything that promises to bring censure on the doer. The honorable status of a free man must needs grow base if it involves itself in servile pursuits.

"But it may happen that when circumstances or the pressure of time require it, some plebeian task may be appropriate conduct for a noble
190 spirit. Whatever you do, let virtue prescribe it, and once embarked, bring it to completion. For he who omits to complete what he has undertaken commits an error more serious than he who does not begin. The one charge is a trivial matter to resolve, but the other can only be dismissed upon the discovery of a legitimate motive, a task not to be
195 rashly or hastily taken up, requiring a long and careful consideration of the object of the enterprise.

"If, however, one is ashamed of having begun some task, and it seems shameful and blameworthy to bring it to completion, one may declare the guilty undertaking null and void. Unaccomplished crimes are commonly treated indulgently, and a wrong action does less harm if its effect remains tentative.

200 "Whatever concerns may occupy you, avoid interruption. When a task is broken off it is difficult to grasp the problem a second time. A torch grows faint unless it is moved about; once moved it arouses its drowsy light into wakeful flames, but when movement ceases it grows faint and can scarcely remuster its wasted fires.

205 "Let your virtue flourish, let it spread its branches, grow tall and take over the whole earth with its deep-set roots; let its fame be spread abroad by your extraordinary deeds, and may it steadily increase your renown from good dawning to still better evening. May future ages
210 continue to produce such a harvest in unceasing abundance, and no day's light be unattended by the light of your good deeds.

"If proximity to vicious conduct causes you to appear tainted, flee from the danger, that those too like yourself may not spread the contagion of their error. To cherish the good, and engage yourself closely with them is a sign that you yourself are good, as there are
215 plausible grounds for arguing that he who cultivates bad companions is bad. The solidarity that binds those of like mind arises from common pursuits; the sweet bond of intimacy is made fast by a common desire: it is thus that Venus is pleasing to Mars, and Marcia to Cato, that Caesar does not reject Cleopatra, nor Cornelia Pompey.

220 "Think it shameful to seek to sweep away the splendid deeds of good

Magnificos actus. alienas auribus equis,
Non corrosivus, non invidus accipe laudes.
Sunt quos immeritus honor indignatur et illud
Non attingit humi serpens ignavia culmen,
225 Pigra, nec decedens, quem tollit gloria, monti.
Hii, quos erexit probitas, odere favoris
Non habitos plausus, aliis fluxisse dolentes,
Alteriusque favent animo successibus egro.
  Parce tue laudi! si quid bene gesseris, alter
230 Te tacito laudet; aliis dicenda, silendum
Est tibi, – nec vacua sunt laude silencia laudis.
Absit, ut a propriis iactandi gloria factis
Exeat et famam preco sibi polluat actor.
Plus egisse, loqui minus, id decet. amplior actis
235 Esto, minor tumidam solvat presumptio linguam.
  Absit, ut externi vicii te illesa voluptas
Ad scelus invitet, impunitumque timeri
Non perdat facinus. populus delinquere regum
A simili nolit. non est defendere culpam
240 Ostendisse malos; scelus est absolvere crimen
Crimine, nec magna redimunt exempla reatus.
  Sit tibi pro lima sapiens, auriga regendi
Pectoris excessus inhibens; suppresset habenam
Ad medium tendens, laterum vitando paludes.
245 Hic tibi sincere ferat exemplaria vite,
Hic precepta tuos domet in moralia sensus,
Hic paleas purgans excussos ventilet actus,
Albaque mundande tribuat tersoria menti.
  Prudentum speculo mores compone, disertos
250 Dilige, philosophis impende libencior aures.

Cap. 5 De subita morum mutacione circa Atticum Palemonem[7]

  Auribus hortatus bibulis hausisse peritos,
Quos habeat fructus, satis est monstrasse Palemo
Atticus, effusi suadente libidine luxus,
Qui non illecebris modo lascivire, sed ipso
255 Luxurie noto plebescere nomine vellet.

men with the rake of envy; be neither caustic nor envious, but accept praise of another with impartial ear. There are those who are angered by the spectacle of undeserved honor, though their own cowardice,
25 hugging the ground, does not approach these heights, too sluggish to attempt that mountain which glory has exalted. Such men hate those whom virtue has raised up, aggrieved that the favor and acclaim which they do not receive is visited on others, and lending only a faint-hearted approval to another's successes.

30 "Avoid self-praise! If you have done something well, let another praise it while you say nothing. It is right that others should speak and that you should remain silent. To leave one's own merit undeclared is not devoid of merit. Far be it that the glory of high praise should be withdrawn from your deeds, or that the author of them, by becoming his own herald, should mar his own reputation. To do much, to say
35 little: this is seemly. Be expansive in your actions, but do not presume to flaunt yourself in inflated speech.

"Let not another's unscathed pleasure in vicious conduct induce you to a guilty act; let not the fact that his crime goes unpunished allay your own fears. A people is not drawn to follow the guilty example of their
40 king, and to point out that there are malefactors is not to condone their wrongdoing. What is wicked is to give legitimacy to one crime be committing another; that it is great men who provide the example does not redeem their guilt.

"Let the wise man be your standard, a charioteer curbing the errant tendencies of your ruling spirit. Let his hand on the reins impose a
45 middle course, avoiding the mire on either side. Let the wise man provide you with the example of a pure life, let him conform your understanding to moral precepts, purge your thoughts of chaff, expose your actions to a winnowing scrutiny, and provide a white cloth to cleanse your mind.

50 "Order your character on the model of prudent men, cultivate the wise, and lend a willing ear to the philosopher.

Ch. 5 On the sudden transformation in the character of Polemo of Athens[7]

"To show what rewards may come to him who has been induced to drink in the words of the wise with thirsty ears, it is enough to cite the example of Polemo of Athens, who not only loved to pursue wanton
5 pleasures, seduced by the lust of unbridled pleasure, but relished the very notoriety of his reputation for wantonness.

Hic, matutinis Phebo candente caminis,
Morbida nocturne liquit dispendia cene,
Marcidus unguentis, sertis redimitus, honustus
Ora ligante mero, petulanti pictus amictu,
260 Aspectuque vagus, Xenocratis limen apertum
Cernit et accedit, plena sapientibus ausus
Consedisse domo, salibus risuque faceto
Divitis eloquii morsurus dogma; sed illum
Indignata virum gravitas matura recessum
265 Maturare iubet. Xenocratis sola morandi
Indulget veniam bonitas tranquilla, manuque
Pacis signa movet et – quod tractabat omisso
Propositi cursu – vires formamque modesti
Disserit, ut iuvenem, luxu qui sordet, honesti
270 Urat in affectus aliosque inflammet amores
Et vite in melius revocande spiret odorem.
      Nec mora, primicias capienti fronte pudoris
Erubet et molles habitus dampnasse Palemo
Sustinet, et vultus accusat purpura crimen.
275   Ecce voluptatum pudet et piget, ecce coronam
Decerpit capiti, leviumque insignia vellit,
Dispersaque comam serie conturbat et hirtam
Maturat tenero iuvenilem pectinis usu,
Effusasque manus inconsulteque vagantes
280 Contrahit et clamidis fugientibus inicit umbram.
      Succedente mora succedit gracia morum,
Inque dies cedit Venus accedente venusto,
Rectificatque virum declivem regula virtus,
Philosophumque facit facundia philosophantis,
285 Socraticosque bibit Xenocratis alumpnulus imbres.

Cap. 6 Quod Architrenius Naturam viderit in loco floribus prelascivo, et de Nature habitu eminenti et comitatu eiusdem

      Sic loquitur Solon et prona funditur urna
Eloquii torrens, non arescente loquendi
Equore nec liquidis intermiscente paludes.
Proclives oculos levat Architrenius: instar
290 Sideris ardescens mulier spectatur et igni
Lacius educto rutilum procul explicat orbem,

"As gleaming Phoebus was pursuing the path of morning, Polemo was leaving the unwholesome excesses of an all-night banquet, reeking of oil, crowned with garlands, full of wine which impaired his speech, and adorned with gaudy robes. His unsteady gaze fell on Xenocrates' open door, and he approached, making so bold as to take a seat in a house filled with wise men, and mock the teachings of their rich eloquence with jests and idle laughter. The company, their gravity outraged, ordered him to make a hasty withdrawal, but the peaceable good nature of Xenocrates himself granted him permission to stay. Making a peaceful gesture with his hand, and departing from the subject under discussion, he spoke to him about the power and character of moderation, in order to kindle in this young man, so tainted by excess, an attraction to honor, to make him burn with another sort of love and inspire him to a sense of the need to redirect his life in a better way.

"At once Polemo blushes, his forehead receiving the first tokens of his shame, and as his flushed face declares his sense of guilt, he agrees to destroy his effete garments. Indeed he feels shame and disgust for all his pleasures, snatches the crowning garland from his head, tears away all the tokens of frivolity, shakes out the scattered locks of his hair and by the delicate exercise of the comb disposes its youthful bushiness in a mature way. He draws back his hands, outflung and moving at random, and compels them to flee to the shadow of his cloak.

"As his resistance gives way, the appeal of morality takes its place, and Venus yields, day by day, as its charm gains the ascendancy. The rule of virtue rectifies the fallen man, the charm of philosophizing makes him a philosopher, and he becomes Xenocrates' little nursling, imbibing draughts of Socratic wisdom."

Ch. 6 Architrenius beholds Nature, in a place luxuriant with flowers. Nature's noble attire and her companions

Thus Solon spoke; the flood of eloquence poured forth from his inclining urn, a tide of discourse that neither ran dry nor interrupted its steady flow with stagnant pools. Architrenius raises his downcast eyes: a woman glowing like a star appears before him. Her brilliance, flashing forth on every side and casting a circle of radiance far abroad, lends a

Ingeminatque loci radios; nam Vere marito
Pregnativa parit rosulas et lilia Tellus,
Splendoresque serit alios fecundula florum
295   Flora, perhennantis iubar effusiva diei.
Non hiemis fecem queritur tersissima veris
Area, nec recipit Zephirus consorcia brume.
Hec mulier vultu roseo phebescit, ephebis
Defecata genis, senio matura, virentis
300   Servat adhuc laurum faciei, temporis evo
Non minor, ut Pilios longe precesserit annos.
Non marcente cuti vetulatur fixa iuvente
Floriditas, anus est etas faciesque puella,
Nec speculum longi nebulescit temporis umbra.
305   Preminet in specie maiestas, sobrius oris
Matronatur honos; levitatem nulla fatetur
Porcio nec quatitur gestu petulante, gravescit
Tota, brevisque suum non perdit fimbria pondus.
Illasciva sedet, quovis reverenda, chorusco
310   Imperiosa throno, quem lactea crine coronat
Turba senum, domine genibus minor. ardua sedes
Est illos equasse pedes, plenaque licemur
Nobilitate dee summum contingere calcem.
Innituntur humo cancellatisque sedentes
315   Cruribus insternunt pro pulvinaribus herbas.
    Miratur solito magis Architrenius, ardet
Agnovisse deam; novitas blanditur et urit
In desiderium. de qua Solone docenti
Ut primum didicit, quod erat Natura, citato
320   Advolat excursu, fletum derivat, adulte
Leticie testem, comitatu gaudia dulci
Producunt lacrime. venit, affandique negatur
Copia, de mundo Genesi texente loquelam.

Cap. 7 Sermo Nature de obsequio quod mundus homini exibet et situ eiusdem et motu[8]

"Omnigene partus homini famulantur, eique
325   Et domus et nutrix ancillaque, machina mundi,
Omne bonum fecunda parit, maiorque minori
Obsequitur mundus. tibi discors unio rerum
Eternum statura cohit, fractoque tumultu

twofold splendor to the place, for Earth, made pregnant by the bridegroom Spring, brings forth rosebuds and lilies, while Flora, modestly
95 prolific, spreads abroad the splendors of other blooms, her bounty like
that of an endless spring day. The immaculate face of this Spring is not
troubled by the dregs of winter, nor must Zephyrus endure the company
of frost.

This woman, Phoebuslike in the rosy glow of her face, has the
00 unblemished cheek of youth, though ripe in years. She preserves the
freshness of a flourishing complexion, though her span of life has not
been short and she has far surpassed the age attained by Nestor. By no
wrinkling of the skin does she appear aged; the bloom of youth inheres,
and though her age is an old woman's, her face is a young girl's. The
05 traces of a long lifetime do not cloud her mirror. Majesty is the dominant
effect of her beauty. The sober dignity of her face is matronly; none of
her features conveys any hint of levity or is disturbed by a wanton
gesture. Her dignity is complete: even the brief fringe of her garment
never departs from its downward posture. Grave, revered by all, she sits
10 in majesty on a gleaming throne, about which the throng of white-
haired old men, whose height does not reach the knees of their mistress,
form a circle. (To follow in their footsteps will afford us a precarious
vantage-point, and the boundless nobility of the goddess will permit us
to stand at her feet.) They lower themselves to the ground, and sitting
15 with crossed legs, make the grass serve them in place of cushions.

Architrenius is amazed beyond measure, and longs to approach the
goddess. The novelty of her appearance beguiles him and he burns with
desire. As soon as he learns by the prompting of Solon that this is
20 Nature, he rushes headlong toward her, summons forth weeping to
witness the fulness of his happiness, and a company of tender tears
attends his joy. A rush of words emerges, but is stayed, as Genesis
herself prepares to discourse about the universe.

Ch. 7 Nature's speech on the service that the universe offers to man. The structure and motion of the universe[8]

25 "Creatures of every kind attend on man. For him this universal frame
is home and nurse and handmaid. The greater world obeys the will of
the lesser, bringing forth every good in its fertility. It is for you that that
the union of its discordant parts coheres in eternal stability, that peace

Pax elementa ligat. gaude tibi sidera volvi
330 Defigique polos, mundique rotatilis aule
Artificem gratare Deum, dominumque ministro
Erexisse domum, cuius molicio summum
Actorem redolet. excelsi dextera tantis
Dotibus excoluit opifex opus, omnia posse
335 Disputat illud eam; nec enim decisa potestas
Est ea, qua numquam lapsurus volvitur orbis
Raptibus eternis, totusque volubilis axem
Circuit immotum, paribusque rotatibus actam
Precipitat speram, dum sola immobilis ima
340 Pondere vergit humus, nullo conamine surgens,
Se nulla levitate rotat, centroque coheret
Impaciens motus, medio pigrescit in axe
Infima, si veteres verum cecinere. moderne
At melior, famosa minus, sollercia pubis[9]
345 Vel nichil est imum vel quelibet infima; mundus
Ne labet, immenso circummordetur inani.
    Terra vicem puncti recipit collata supremo,
Unde modum terre visus punctum estimat, unde
Fraudari radios positis procul imputat astris.[10]
350   Terre forma teres, teretisque supernatat unde
Curva superficies, terramque amplectitur arcu
Imperfecta maris – prohibenti litore – spera,
Que medium centri contingit cuspide mundum.
    Ardenti spolio vestitur sidere celum
355 Multifidaque face tenebris occurrit et orbi
Exibet excubias oculis populosior Argus.
Astra pluunt radios et caligantibus usum
Lampadis indulgent et pessum nata superne
Flamma peregrinat, sordentibus hospita tectis.
360   Contrahitur terre stella globus arcior. illum,
Visa minor, superat astri rota plenior; infra
Sunt Cytherea, soror Phebi, Cyllenius ales.[11]

Cap. 8 De duplici stellarum genere

    Scinditur in geminum stellans genus. altera fixus
Impetus astra movet, error premit altera flexu
365 Multivago torsisse vias; interque planetas
Falce senex, sceptroque Iovis, Marsque ense choruscat;

has put down the conflict of the elements and united them. Be glad that
30 the stars revolve for you, while the poles stand firm. Give thanks to God,
the maker and ruler of this whirling court, the universe, for having
established such a home for his minister, whose very composition hints
at his supreme author. The shaping hand of that lofty being has
35 endowed his handiwork with such gifts that it declares his omnipotence;
for that power is unlimited through which the universe is turned
unfalteringly with eternal force, and all circles in rotation about an
unmoved axis, that power which impels each sphere to move in a
40 constant orbit, while earth alone, unmoved, is borne downward by its
weight. Powerless to raise itself, and lacking the buoyancy to rotate, it
rests at the center of things, incapable of movement, the inert low point
on the central axis, if what the ancients sang is true. But the astuteness
45 of our modern youth,[9] though less renowned, is superior. Either the
creation descends to nothingness, or there is some lowest level of being.
Lest the world should fall away, it is surrounded by a boundless void.
The earth fulfils the function of a centerpoint in relation to the heavens;
from on high the viewer deems the earth no larger than a point, and
blames the distant placement of the stars for having deceived his
sight.[10]
50   The earth is round in form, and the curving surface of the rounded
ocean swims over it. The sphere of ocean, incomplete because of the
intruding landmass, embraces the earth in its arc, and its center point
corresponds to the center of the earth.
55   "The sky is clad in a blazing array of stars, and challenges the
darkness with this many-faceted torch, and keeps watch over the world,
as abundantly eyed as Argus. The stars rain down their light, and grant
the use of their lamps to those in darkness. Born in heaven, their fire
descends to walk abroad, a welcome guest in lowly dwellings.
60   "The globe of the earth is more limited in size than a star. The circle of
a star, though it appears smaller, far exceeds it, though Cytherea, the
sister of Phoebus, and the winged Cyllenian are smaller.[11]

Ch. 8 The two kinds of stars

"The starry race is divided into two kinds. A fixed course governs the
movement of one kind, while the other is compelled to pursue a random,
65 winding course of continual change. Among the planets, light flashes
from the scythe of aged Saturn, the scepter of Jove, and the sword of

Sol arcum, Cytharea facem, Cyllenius arpen
Et Phebe pharetram venandi fervida gestat.
   Astri Luna vicem Phebi mendicat ab astro,
370 Sideris obscuro naturam eliminat orbe,
Iacturam redimit et Solis imagine Solem
Induit et dampnum fraterna lampade pensat;
Parte iubar recipit, partem ferrugine texit,
Nec Stigium perdit partim Proserpina peplum.
375 Nunc tamen et toto fraudatur luminis usu,
Cum Phebi radios terre ferit obvia nubes
Et caput aut caudam[12] Lunamque intercipit umbra
Et soror a fratris vultu declinat amato,
Totaque sulphureo nubit Proserpina Diti.
380   Nec minus et fratris homini iubar invidet, arcens
Obiectu radios, noctem mentita reciso
Luminis excursu; visusque excussus, ut axes
Phebeos feriat, lunari offenditur orbe,
Nec placitam celeri defigit harundine predam.

Cap. 9 De quorundam circulorum celestium descriptione[13]

385   Figit utrumque polum, paribusque utrumque diei
Respicit equator spaciis, mundique tumorem
Dividit et partes in spera maximus equat.
   Nec minor obliquo signorum circulus arcu
Ad Boream surgit et ad Austrum vergit, et illum
390 Equator mediumque secat, mediusque secatur.
   Nec minor et medie qui nocti ascribitur orbis,
Dimidiumque diem metiri dicitur, arcu
Stante, ceniz capitum mundique supermeat axes.
   Nec minor et medius medium partitus utrumque
395 Percutit axe ceniz, visus finitor, orizon
Et Styga cum superis communi limite nodat.
   Linea solsticii[14] mundi curvatur ad axes
Orbe paralello, Phebi sensura recursus,
Proxima fit capitum vel distantissima puncto.
400   Et tamen equator directo figit in orbe
Solsticium, quo cernit Aren[15] simul Arthon et Austrum;
Deprensum est hunc esse locum, tumor ille duobus
Solsticiis[16] ardet totidemque recessibus[17] idem

Mars; the Sun brandishes his bow, Cytherea her torch, the Cyllenian his curved blade, and Phoebe, that avid huntress, her quiver.

70 "The Moon borrows the luminous property of a star from the star of Phoebus; though her dark orb does not possess this property of stars by nature, she makes good this failing, and assumes a sunlike appearance by imitating the Sun, offsetting her own defect by borrowing her brother's light. In one part she receives his light, while cloaking another in dusky darkness (for Proserpina never wholly forsakes her Stygian 75 mantle), yet at certain times she is wholly denied the use of light, when the mass of the earth obstructs Phoebus' rays, and its shadow intercepts the Moon's light at the head or tail of its path,[12] so that the sister is withdrawn from the sight of her beloved brother, and Proserpina gives herself up to the reeking darkness of Dis.

80 "But she also withholds her brother's light from mankind, concealing his rays by intruding herself, and creating a false night by cutting off the flow of his light. As the beam of our vision goes forth, aiming to strike the center of Phoebus' circle, it is obstructed by the orb of the Moon, and its swift arrow does not reach its intended target.

Ch. 9 A description of certain celestial circles[13]

85 "The Equator defines the two Poles, and looks upon each during an equal interval of daylight. It cuts across the world's swell at its widest point, and divides its sphere into equal parts. The circle of the Signs, no less great, rises in the North and bends its slanting course toward the 90 South. The Equator intersects it at its midpoint, and is intersected by it at its own. No smaller is the circle of the Meridian, which is used to calculate the midpoint of night and divide the day in half by its steady circle, encompassing the Zeniths and the equatorial poles. Nor is that 95 circle smaller which is divided in half by the Meridian, and whose poles mark the midpoint between the two Zeniths – the Horizon, which sets a limit to sight, and draws the heavens and the Stygian realm together at a common border. The line of the Solstice[14] intersects the Poles in its circular course: it registers the recurring shifts of the sun, and is at one time close to the Zenith point, at another far from it.

100 But the Equator, too, where Aren[15] beholds both the North Pole and the South, marks a solstice[16] in its own straight course. It has been determined that in this region the swelling earth grows hot at two of its solstices, while at the two withdrawals[17] the same region grows cold,

Friget et equator solem stacione reflectit
405 Equidiemque facit. etenim sol cogitur omni
Stare paralello, qui Cancri interiacet altum
Depressique situs caput Egocerontis;[18] et illa
Sunt loca, zodiacus ubi plus declinat ad Austri
Arturique polos et ab equatore recedit.
410   Amplior includit egresse cuspidis orbem
Area zodiaci, quo sol raptatur ad ortum
Ingenito motu, centroque amplectitur arcum,
Nunc terre propior, nunc elongatus,[19] et augis
Figitur in Geminis et pigra rotatur ad ortum
415 Fixis tarda comes in eisdem raptibus astris.

Cap. 10 De eis que accidunt ex varia posicione orizontis[20]

Dividit innumerus speram declivis orizon,
Augeturque dies Cancri, contraque minorem
Deprimit Egoceron, quanto est erectior Arthos
Fit brevior brevior et maior maior, eamque
420 Nox recipit formam, similique revolvitur arcu.
Hic situs est declivis, ubi producitur absque
Nocte dies Cancri, nec nox contractior arcu
Languet in opposito, surgitque Aurora diei
Promissura facem, sed non latura, vel instans
425 Cogitur esse dies; nam idem complectitur ortum
Punctus et occasum, superisque revolvitur orbe
Dimidio Phebus, Thetidisque recolligit undis
Surgentes radios, pascitque soporibus artus
Insompnes alias, udisque cubilibus ardet.
430   Est ubi nox piceo mensem non vestit amictu,
Est ubi per geminos eadem non texitur umbra,
Est ubi Luna tribus fraterna lampade pallet,
Est ubi bis duplici Sol insopitus hanelat,
Est ubi per quinque Phebi vigil excubat ignis,
435 Est ubi sex solito caret hospite mater Achillis.[21].
Nec minus extendi brume contingit ad arcus
Oppositos noctes, totoque rotabitur anno
Una una cum nocte dies. ubi meta videnti
Sternitur equator et mundi figitur axe
440 Indeclive ceniz,[22] mediique est nulla diei

until the Equator turns the Sun back to its stable path and again creates an equidies. For the Sun is compelled to dwell in every latitude that lies between the high point of Cancer and the zenith of low-lying Aego-ceron.[18] And these are the places where the Zodiac inclines most toward the North and South Poles, and withdraws most from the Equator,

"Insofar as the Sun is drawn toward its rising by its own inherent motion, a broader portion of the Zodiac encompasses its eccentric course, and makes its orbit conform to its center.[19] Passing close to the earth at one moment, it withdraws from it at another. At its apogee it is located in Gemini, and returns slowly to its rising-point, a sluggish companion to those stars that are fixed in constant orbits.

Ch. 10 Things which occur because of the changing position of the Horizon[20]

"The shifting Horizon divides its circle in innumerable ways. Daytime is increased in Cancer, whereas Aegoceron's burden makes it shorter; and in proportion as the Polestar ascends, the shorter grows shorter, the longer longer, while Night assumes a corresponding form and passes through a similar cycle. At the point of extreme deviation, daytime in Cancer is prolonged by the absence of night, while at the opposite extreme night is just as long: Aurora appears, promising the lamp of daylight but not producing it, or else day is reduced to an instant; the same point of time embraces both rising and setting. Phoebus is borne through the heavens in a diminished orbit, and draws his beams back to the depths of Thetis even as they rise, craving sleep for those limbs which are sleepless in other regions, and eager for his watery bed.

"There is a place where for a month night does not spread her pitchy mantle; another where her shadow is not cast for two months; one where the Moon is dimmed by her brother's lamp for three months; one where the Sun labors without slumber for twice two months; one where the watchful fire of Phoebus keeps vigil for five months; and one where Achilles' mother[21] is deprived of her accustomed guest for six.

"Nor are the frosty nights any less protracted at the opposed poles, where the cycle of an entire year consists of a single day and a single night. At the point where the extended plane of the equator marks the limit of sight, and an unshifting zenith is defined by the axis of the earth,[22] there is no Meridian line, nor anything such as would divide

Linea vel quevis, situi cuicumque diurnam
Partitura moram, Boree quia subiacet; illa
In longum regio non tenditur, omnibus ipsa
Lacior, occiduis numquam decurritur astris.

Cap. 11 De ortu signorum[23]

445 Semper ab Eoo consurgit cardine mundus
Axibus immotis, signorumque erigit orbem,
Errantesque trahit stellas, totumque revolvit
In paritate more, nec idem mutatur eodem
Mutatove situ, nec surgit segnior arcus
450 Quam cadat oppositus, et Cancri semper in ortu
Egoceron vergit; et rursum, si qua propinquant
Frixei[24] capiti vel Libre signa, paresque
Interhabent arcus, neutrum deductius ortu
Surgit, et Astream qui Chelas[25] impetus urget,
455 Hemoniique moras idre sibi vendicat ultor.[26]
        Omnibus hoc speris; sed qua directus orizon
Ustam cingit Aren, equalis dirigit ortus
Zodiaci quartas, tropicas ubi flectit habenas
Sol, noctique diem punctis finalibus equat.
460 Quilibet hic arcus equales protrahit ortu
Occasuque moras, oriturque equaliter omne
Opposito signum. nam Libre suscipit horas
Portitor Elleus, nec Tauro Scorpio cedit,
Permittitque Chiron[27] gemino sua tempora fratri;
465 Egoceron Cancro par enatat, Urna Leoni;
Erigonesque[28] moras equant dispendia Piscis.
Equis a tropico spaciis distancia surgunt
Tractu signa pari, tropicoque propinquius ortum
Plenius extendit et Libra tardior exit
470 Scorpius, Erigone Cancer, Vectore[30] Lacones.[29]"

the day into regular periods in other places, for it lies at the very north. This region is not defined by longitude, and its latitude is greater than at any other place. The stars that pass over it never set.

Ch. 11 The rising of the Signs[23]

45   "The motion of the heavens on their unmoving axis always arises from the eastern portal. Here rises the circle of the signs, here the wandering stars are drawn forth. The whole firmament revolves at a uniform rate; nothing is changed from its constant state, nor does its
50   location change. One portion of the circle does not rise more slowly than the opposing portion declines; Aegoceron always touches the horizon as Cancer appears. Likewise the signs that border the Phrixean[24] or Libra, maintain equal intervals between them; none moves forth too tenta-
55   tively from its rising. The same force drives both Astraea and Chele,[25] and the avenger of the Hydra[26] adopts for himself the pace of the Haemonian Archer.

   "This is true for all the spheres. But where the horizon centers on burning Aren, when the Sun guides his teams away from the Tropics, and makes day equal to night in extent, an equal rising governs the
60   sections of the Zodiac. Here every portion of the circle will enjoy an equal interval of rising and setting, and every sign will arise in exact correspondence to its opposite. The ferrier of Helle claims the same portion of time as Libra, and Scorpio yields nothing to Taurus. Chiron[27]
65   allows the twin brother his due interval, Capricorn floats aloft like Cancer, the Urn like the Lion. The time allotted to Pisces equals that of Erigone.[28] The signs arise at an equal distance from the tropic, and in an identical path. In proportion as their rising is closer to the tropic the interval is extended. Thus Scorpio emerges more slowly than Libra,
70   Cancer more slowly than Erigone, the Spartans[29] than the Carrier."[30]

Liber Nonus

Cap. 1 De admiracione Architrenii super verbis Nature

"Mirari faciunt magis hec quam scire, rudisque
Ingenii non est" ait Architrenius "astris
Intrusisse stilum vel, que divina sigillant
Scrinia, deciso dubii cognoscere velo.
5 Trans hominem sunt verba dee. miracula cecus
Audio, nam lampas animi subtilia pingui
Celatur radio, nec mens sublimia visu
Vix humili cernit, nec distantissima luce
Fumidula monstrat. tamen hec ut maxima credam
10 Maiestas dicentis agit; celumque legentem
Miror et ignotis delector et aure libenti
Sollicitor, si magna loquens maiora loquatur."

Cap. 2 De residuo ortus signorum

Interea ceptum Genesis non segnior urget,
Sermonisque rota properante diucius addit:
15 Qua vero inclinat speram declivis orizon
Deprimiturque Nothus,[1] ibi quarta citacior exit,
Quam caput alterutro Frixeum limite claudit.
Tardior ad Libre caput est, pariterque remotis
A tropico signis, celerem rapit ocius ortum,
20 Cui magis accedit trepidantis portitor Elles.
Pisce magis Libra surgendi protrahit arcum,
Egoceronte Chiron, Tauro Leo, Scorpius Urna.
Egoceronta sequens declivi contrahit arcus
Orbe moras ortus,[2] rectoque[3] diucius instat
25 Segnicies signi, recipit contraria Cancri
Posteritas: rectumque citus superevolat ultor
Alcide,[4] sperisque piger declivibus exit.

Book Nine

Ch. 1 Architrenius' amazement at Nature's words

"These things create wonder rather than knowledge," said Architrenius. "It is not for the rude intellect to impose a pattern on the stars, or rend the veil of doubt and learn what divine caskets keep sealed. The words of a goddess are beyond human understanding. I hear of such miracles as if blind, for the lamp of my mind obscures subtle matters by its dull light. My mind can scarcely discern sublimity with its lowly gaze, its smoky little lamp cannot reveal things so remote. Nevertheless the majesty of the speaker compels me to believe these great utterances. I marvel at your reading of the heavens, take delight in things unknown, and wait eagerly with ready ear, should she who speaks of great matters speak of matters still greater."

Ch. 2 What remains to be said about the rising of the Signs

Even as he speaks, Genesis, unflagging, presses on, racing still further on the whirling wheels of speech: "But where the circle of the horizon is tilted, and the southern region is thrust downward, there the portion of the Zodiac, which the head of the Phrixean Ram confines with its double boundary[1] emerges more swiftly. The pace is slower near the region of Libra, and for those signs equally distant from the tropic, while a sign takes its rise more swiftly that is located closer to the bearer of trembling Helle. Thus Libra protracts her upward movement longer than Pisces, Chiron longer than Aegoceron, Leo than Taurus, Scorpio than the Urn.

"Those signs that follow Aegoceron along the slanting path[2] reduce the time of their ascending arc, and on the upright circle[3] they move forward more gradually. Those signs that follow Cancer experience the opposite effect: the attacker of Alcides[4] flies swiftly over the upright circle, but is slow to depart from the inclined. If you were to take

Tempora si sumas una, quibus elicit ortus
Oppositos arcus, recto labuntur in orbe
30 Tanta ut declivi; nec segnius una Lacones[5]
Hemoniumque simul quam quevis spera revolvit.
Proximitate quibus tropicus accedit eadem,
Accidit illud idem; nam quantus pignora Lede
Elevat et Cancrum, visus ubi limitat Arthos,[6]
35 Tantus ubi Borea surgenti vergit orizon.
    Nec cicius, qua fervet Aren mundique tumorem
Occupat, excurrunt signi cuiuslibet una
Ortus et occasus sumpti quam, qua eminet Arthos
Occuliturque Nothus, unde in declivibus ambos
40 Si simul annectas, directo fiet in orbe
Alterutri duplum.[7] nam qua raptissima torret
Ardua Libra ceniz, signo properatur ad ortum
Occasumque pares; et eodem tempore, visum
Quo fugit, Ideam Ganymedes detegit Urnam.

Cap. 3 Quod signa apud quosdam oriuntur inversa[8]

45 Qua magis a fixo Boreali distat orizon
Quam tropicus Cancri, qua nescia vere remitti
Equora bruma ligat, oriuntur versa caduntque
Signa: priorque venit quam Piscis portitor Elles,
Posterior Tauro Frixeus, Piscibus Urna.
50 Haut secus opposita vergunt: Libraque sequenti
Scorpius inversus decumbit, ad equora Libra
Virgine descendit prior hospita, Virgo Leone.

Cap. 4 De porcione terre que tota et sola secundum Alfraganum[9] inhabitatur

Circulus equidiem librans, Austrumque colurus[10]
Qui secat et Boream, Zephyri sub cardine mundum
55 Auroreque ligant, quartisque equaliter orbem
Sectio distinguit, et fixo stante coluro
Scinditur ad rectos terre fixissimus orbis.
Iunctior Arturis habitatur quarta; situsque
Reicit humanos extremi frigore limbi
60 Oppositoque gelu torpescit inhospita paulo
Ulterius Tyle, quam despicit hora Bootes.

together the lengths of time required for the rising of opposed signs, as
30 much time will elapse in the upright circle as in the inclined. One circle
does not revolve the Spartans[5] and the Haemonian more slowly than
the other. The same movement governs those signs which draw equally
close to the tropic; for whatever the angle to which the children of Leda
35 and Cancer rise where the northern Pole defines the limits of sight,[6] the
same angle is attained when the horizon shifts with the elevation of the
Pole.

"The rising and setting of any given sign do not run their course
more swiftly where Aren burns, placed as it is at the swelling center of
the world, than where the Pole is at its height and the southern region is
40 hidden. Thus if you were to combine the two movements in the inclined
circuit, it would amount to twice the amount of one or the other in the
upright circle.[7] For at the Zenith where Libra, at her height and moving
swiftly, grows hot, the length of rising and setting is identical for each
sign; Ganymede displays his Trojan urn for the same period that he
evades our gaze.

Ch. 3 The Signs appear in reverse order in certain regions[8]

45 "Where the Horizon diverges from the fixed northern Pole further
than the tropic of Cancer, where ice locks up oceans that never know
the release of spring, the Signs rise and set in reverse order. The
Phrixean bearer of Helle comes before Pisces and after Taurus, and the
50 Urn follows on Pisces. And the setting of their opposite signs is no
different: Scorpio falls backwards with Libra following;Libra descends
into the welcoming ocean before Virgo, Virgo before Leo.

Ch. 4 On that portion of the earth which, according to Alfraganus,[9] is solely and fully inhabited

"The circle which determines the equidies and a colure[10] which
intersects both the southern and northern Poles, contain the world
5 within its eastern and western boundaries. Their intersection divides the
world into quarters, for the unvarying circumference of the earth is
intersected at right angles by the fixed position of the colure. One
quarter that borders on the Arctic is inhabited. At its upper limit the cold
forbids human habitation; a little beyond Thule, the border of the
10 inhospitable terrain over which Bootes lowers, the earth grows hard

Quod riget eterna glacie, curtatur ad Arthon
Orbe paralello. quarte pars cetera tractu
Micior incolitur Boreali limite Sclavos
65 Metatura sinus, ut fama fante fatetur
Filius Admeti;[11] Zephyrique a follibus equor
Verberat occiduum, qua nomine celsius Athlas
Quam dorso erigitur; Eous limes ad Eurum
Finibus exit Acin,[12] ubi Gades[13] orbis habena
70 Fixit Alexander, cuius famosior aram
Yppanis attollit medioque opponitur orbe
Gadibus Alcide – si fas est credere, fama
Quod scivisse putat; sed ad Austrum porrigit Indos
Et sicientis Aren sepelit sub sole recessus,
75 Que medios signat in adusto limite[14] fines
Oppositisque pari discedit Gadibus arcu.

Cap. 5 De inequalitate dierum naturalium et arcu diei et arcu noctis

Sol iubar astrifugum mundum circummeat et, quo
Dimidius candet,[15] geminum complectitur ortum
Nocte sua comitata dies; verum incipit ille,
80 Terminat ille diem. sed nec mensura diebus
Omnibus una facit, distinguitur illa, nec omnes
Par mora distendit, cum nec rapiantur ad ortus
Tractu signa pari, nec in equo permeat equos
Tempore Sol arcus orbis, qui cuspide mundi
85 Centratur, medium dum terre immobile centro
Percutit et summo distinguitur orbita signis.
Volvitur in mundum mundoque revolvitur orbe
Pene paralello Phebus, nam signa relatas
Declinant obliqua vias; arcusque diei
90 Dicitur, occasum qui claudit et exerit ortum,
Oppositusque moras nocturne limitat umbre.[16]
Et quia maiores declivis spera diei
Suscipit ad Borean arcus, stratique minores
Amputat hora Nothi, Borealis crescit, ad Austrum
95 Contrahitur devexa dies; hec plenior, illa
Equidie brevior brumalibus evolat horis.

with resistant frost. The region which is fixed in perpetual ice is termi-
nated at the Pole by the colural circle.

"The milder remaining portion of this quarter is inhabited; along its
65 northern border it has been assigned as a haven for the Slavs (as the
slave-boy of Admetus could attest, if report be true[11]). A sea driven by
the bellows of Zephyrus pounds the western coast, where Atlas stands,
loftier in name than in elevation. The orient region extends to the east as
70 far as the territory of Acin,[12] where world-ruler Alexander founded his
own Cadiz.[13] At his famous Hypanis he raised an altar, a counterpart,
halfway round the world, to Hercules' altar at Cadiz – if it is right to
believe what Fame deems to be certain knowledge. India extends to the
south, and hidden from sight is the distant region of Aren, thirsting
75 beneath the hot sun, which marks the mid-point of the burning path,[14]
and is equidistant from the two Cadizes.

Ch. 5 The inequality of the natural day. The arc of day and the arc of night

"The Sun, whose radiance puts the stars to flight, moves around the
world, and where he shines for half the time,[15] a day, accompanied by
80 its night, spans two sunrises, for one rising begins each day and the
other concludes it. But a single standard of measure does not suffice for
all days; one is distinct from another, and all do not endure for an equal
length of time, since the Signs are not drawn to their rising always by
the same path, and the Sun does not move through a given arc in the
85 same time, even when its course is oriented to the Zenith of the
firmament, when its rays strike directly on the unmoving center of the
earth, and its orbit at its highest point emerges from the circle of the
Signs.

"Phoebus revolves now in opposition to the firmament, now is
revolved by it in an almost parallel orbit, for the signs descend obliquely
90 along a closely related path. What is called the "arc of day" concludes
with sunset and opens out at sunrise, and the opposing arc defines the
limits of the darkness of night.[16] And because the slanted circle attains a
larger diurnal arc in northern regions, while in the sprawling southern
region the days are cut short, the day grows longer toward the Boreal
95 region, and is diminished in its southward descent. The northern day
grows larger than the equidies, while the frosty hours of the southern
day become brief and fleeting.

Cap. 6 De ecentrico et motu epicicli in eo et de circulo Draconis et de motibus planetarum[17]

Circulus ecentris egressa cuspide mundum
Non figit medium, complectitur orbita terram
Et mediam centro quam totam circuit exit.

100 Volvitur ecentri brevior epiciclus in orbe
Excluditque solum, superos succinctus ad axes,
Vectorisque sui cuspis non deserit arcum.
    Zodiaci nullo tractu declinat ab orbe
Cuspide concentris mundo; scinditque Draconis[18]

105 Circulus ecentrem, quisquis declinat ad Austrum
Sidereosque boves. et qua transitur ab orbe
Signorum ad Boream: caput est ea sectio, nodus
Oppositus cauda, per quam vergente planeta
Ad Nothon urget iter, nautarum plaustra relinquens.

110   Fertur ad Auroram pariter festina planete
Cuspis in orbe brevi;[19] brevis eluctatur ad ortum
Cuspis in ecentri, sed et hunc Draco volvit eodem
Segnior ecentrem, fixis non ocior astris.
    Ad Zephyrum mundo non obvia Cynthia cuspis

115 Serpit in orbe brevi; preceps excurrit eodem
Impetus ecentris, cui parvo cuspis in orbe
Concentri rapitur mundo, motusque Draconis
Non alio raptat egresse cuspidis orbem
Ecentremque bigam, sed eadem segnior urget.

120   Reptat in occasus omni Proserpina centro,
Solus in ecentri mundo brevis obviat orbis.
Non secus et Stilbons rapitur, si ecentris agatur
Cuspis in occasus, infixe cuspidis orbe,
Qui minor angusto sic cuspide distet ab arcu,

125 Ut procul a medio mundi secat orbita mundum.
Nec minus et Stilbons comes est et Cynthia fixis
Sideribus, fixeque trahunt utrumque Draconem,
Qui rotat ecentrem secum torpentibus astris.

Ch. 6 The eccentric circle and the motion of the epicycle within it. The circle of the Dragon and the motions of the planets[17]

"An eccentric orbit, whose center has shifted, does not center on the midpoint of the world; its orbit embraces the earth, but departs from the center of that body which it encompasses. A smaller epicyclical revolution is contained within the eccentric orbit and this rejects the earth, bound to the greater circle as its axis, and its center never strays from the arc of the circle that determines its motion.

"The concentric circle is never drawn to deviate from the orbit of the Zodiac with the earth as its center; the circle of the Dragon[18] intersects the eccentric orbit whenever it sinks to the south and the starry oxen. And where it is crossed by the northward course of the circle of the Signs, that intersection is called the Head; the opposite point is the Tail, through which the path of a descending planet leads southward, leaving behind the Wagon known to sailors.

"Each planet is borne at the same swift rate to the east in its epicyclical motion,[19] but the circling body struggles to attain its rising point in its eccentric orbit. The sluggish Dragon, however, moves in an eccentric circle at the same rate, never slower than that of the fixed stars. Cynthia, independent of this cosmic pattern, glides westward in her epicyclical course; her eccentric movement proceeds equally swiftly. Her sphere in its modest orbit is governed by the earth as its center, and the motion of the Dragon does not so affect her eccentric movement as to place its shifted center elsewhere, but sluggishly impels her along a constant path.

"Proserpina creeps toward her setting wherever her orbit is centered, but only in its eccentric movement does her brief orbit resist the influence of earth. Mercury is borne along in the same way, when his eccentric course is drawn toward its setting; though the center of his circle is dislocated, his motion does not diverge from its narrow path enough to draw his orbit far from its center at the center of the earth. Mercury and Cynthia are likewise companions to the fixed stars, and these determine the movement of both in respect to the Dragon, who impels their eccentric movement by his own in relation to the slow-moving firmament.

Cap. 7 De retrogradacione et stacione et progressione planete a zodiaco versus Austrum et Septentrionem[20]

Retrogrados nescit errores Cynthia; nusquam
130   Stat biga cum Phebi curru contraria mundo.
Impetus errantis fit progressivus in orbe,
Quem rotat ecentris, quociens vicinior augi
Precipiti luctatur equo; retrogradus infra
Augis in opposito, dum stellis exit Eois
135   Occiduasque petit, mundoque citacior illas
– Oppositos inter motus staturus – hanelat.
    Ad Boream numquam signorum surgit ab orbe
Mercurius, contraque Venus non vergit ad Austrum;[21]
Luna, Iovis, Mavors et iniquus Falcifer: Austri
140   Nunc secreta petunt, nunc sidera tarda Bootis.
Cuspis in ecentri defertur Delia nusquam
Devia, zodiaci numquam declivia mutat.
    Ecce creatoris quid maius dextera mundo
Indulsisse queat homini? cui sidera volvit,
145   Continuat lucem, fervoribus obicit umbram,
Alternoque gelu sicientem submovet estum
Et noctis sompnique vices fomenta laboris
Adicit et noctis sepelit dispendia sompno.

Cap. 8 Quod Architrenius Nature genibus obvolvitur

"Quam procul eloquii fluvius decurret et aures
150   Influet exundans" ait Architrenius "utre
Iam duplici pleno? satis est hausisse referto
Vase, nec auricule pelagi capit alveus undam."
Hec fatus rumpitque moras pedibusque loquentis
Irruit et genuum demissos complicat artus
155   Et cubitos sternens iunctis iacet infimus ulnis.

Cap. 9 Oracio Architrenii ad Naturam

"Hoc nichil, immo minus nichilo, dea, respice! fletus
Fonticulos, stagna lacrime, meroris abyssos
Extenues et plena malis vivaria sicces.
    Torqueor et planctus animi tormenta fatetur
160   Garrulus et morbi latebras suspiria clamant.

Ch. 7 The retrogradation, stasis and progression of the planets to the north and south of the Zodiac[20]

30   Cynthia knows nothing of retrograde wandering; never does her team come to a standstill with Phoebus' chariot, resisting the influence of the earth. The pace of a wandering planet is progressive in the orbit that its eccentric motion pursues; whenever it draws close to its apogee, it must struggle with its impulsive steeds; at the perigee of its retrograde,

35   inward movement, when it leaves the eastern stars and seeks those that have set, it pursues them more swiftly than the firmament, though it will come to a standstill between its two opposing motions.

Mercury never ascends northward beyond the circle of the Signs; Venus in contrast never diverges to the south.[21] The Moon, Jove, Mars,

40   and the wicked Scythebearer seek the hidden regions of the South at one moment, the slow-moving stars of Bootes at another. The cusped Delian never varies her eccentric course, never alters in relation to the declivity of the Zodiac.

"Behold! What greater thing could the Creator's hand have done than to bestow the world on mankind? For whom does He move the

45   spheres, renew the light of day, dispel the darkness with warming beams, intersperse the parching summer with intervals of cold, provide the diversions of night and sleep to alleviate his toil, and bury the idle hours of darkness in slumber?"

Ch. 8 Architrenius embraces the knees of Nature

"How much longer," says Architrenius, "will this river of eloquence

50   run on, filling my ears to overflowing though the sack has already been filled twice over? Enough has been poured out when the jar is full; the little vessel of my ear cannot contain an ocean." And having said this he waits no longer, but rushes toward the speaker's feet, embraces her

55   knees, then throws himself flat on the ground and lies on his folded arms.

Ch. 9 Architrenius' prayer to Nature

"Look, O Goddess, upon this nothing, nay less than nothing! Diminish these fountains of weeping, these pools of tears, the abysses of misery; dry up these ponds that teem with evil. I am tortured; my

60   speaking grief declares the torments of my mind, my sighs proclaim the disease that lurks within. My tears are not feigned. The spring rain is

Nec lacrima fraudo; veris a nubibus imber
Solvitur et nimbos oculi pluit intima nubes,
Ducitur ex animo luctus, certissima flendi
Causa subest et vera movent adversa querelas
165 Nam tot inexhaustis anima languente procellis
Concucior, totusque dolor circumfluor omni
Peste, quod in lacrimas Phalarim siccumque moverem
Democritum, scopulosque novus suffunderet humor.
Sic mundi Boreis agitor, sic Syrtis harena
170 Naufragor humane, sic impacata Caribdis
Me sorbet, sic Scilla freto latrante flagellat.
Hiis michi naufragiis peregrino Tartara fletu
Compassura reor et flecti posse Megeram
Suspicor et sevos alias mansuescere crines.[22]
175 Omnis in hoc casu feritas admissa nocendi
Cederet, inflexi pietas adamanta rigoris
Molliret, precepsque Iovis lentesceret Ira.
        Compaterisne tuam scelerum, Natura, flagellis
Affligi sobolem? que sic in pignora pacem
180 Maternam turbavit hiemps? odiumne noverce
Matris amor didicit? o dulces ubera numquam
Exhibitura favos! heu pignora semper amarum
Gustatura cibum! pietas materna rigorem
Induit et scopulis Prognes induruit Ino.
185   Sed quid ego dubito, luctusne refundere culpam
In matrem liceat? matrem vexare querelis
Exhorret pietas. prohibet reverencia matris,
Imperat ira loqui; rabies in turpia solvit
Ora, pudorque ligat. sed iam declino pudoris
190 Imperium, maiorque michi dominatur Erinis.
Torrenti – fateor – ire non impero: de te,
Pace tua, Natura, queror.[23] tibi supplicat omnis
Maiestatis apex et nobis semper avarum
Obliquas oculum, nulla dulcedine clausas
195 Scis reserasse manus. homo preda doloribus evum
Tristibus immergit, nec amicis utitur annis,
Nec fruitur letis, nec verna vescitur aura.
Humanos statui numero strinxisse reatus,
Sed metam desperat opus, nec finis apertum
200 Principium clausisse potest; nam cedit harene
Turba malis, humana quibus demencia bellum

given forth by clouds, and a cloud within makes showers rain from my
eyes. My grief is wrung from the heart, the plainest reasons for weeping
165 give rise to it, and real hardships provoke my lamentation. For I am
assailed in my weary breast by so many unrelenting storms, I flounder
in utter misery amid such disease, that I might move Phalaris or
dry-eyed Democritus to tears, and cause an unwonted moisture to
suffuse the very rocks. So beaten am I by the chill wind of the world, so
170 cast adrift on the sand of a man-made desert, so implacable a Charybdis
draws me down, so loudly do Scylla's straits assail me. Even Tartarus, I
am sure, would weep in compassion for my outcast condition amid such
misfortunes; Megaera, I think, might be swayed, and her fierce locks[22]
175 learn a gentler manner. All savage things would give over their hurtful
wickedness, confronted with such a plight, pity would soften the hardness of the most unbending rigor, and the precipitate anger of Jove
himself would grow mild.

180   "And can you, Nature, allow your offspring to be tormented by the
scourge of wrong? What winter storm has so aroused your motherly
gentleness against your charges? Has a mother's love learned a step-
mother's hatred? Alas that your breasts will no longer impart their
honeyed sweetness! Alas that your charges must henceforth taste only
bitter food! Motherly compassion has cloaked itself in severity, and Ino
has grown as hard as unyielding Procne.

185   "But what am I to do? I doubt whether it be right to place the blame
for my suffering on my mother: filial devotion shrinks from assailing a
mother with complaints. But what reverence for a mother forbids,
wrath commands me to declare. Anger gives rein to foul speech, though
190 modesty resist it. I must now reject the rule of modesty, for the Fury who
dominates me is too strong. I must admit that I cannot stem the tide of
my wrath.

      "By your leave, O Nature, my complaint is of you.[23] The crowning
glory of your realm entreats you, yet you always turn a grudging eye
195 upon us, and can never treat us with openhanded kindness. Man, a prey
to hardship, lives his life immersed in misery; he knows no favorable
years, enjoys no delights, never feels the breeze of spring. I resolved to
set a number on the instances of human guilt, but to thus limit them
200 was a hopeless task. No end could have been imposed once a beginning
had been made, for the vast quantity of the sands must yield to that of
the wicked means by which human madness makes war against the

Indicit superis, divumque et fulmen et iram
In se cogit homo. Lipares Iovis eicit ignem
Dextra magis candens ira quam fulmine, vindex
205   Hostibus exoptans veniam, tonitruque minanti
Parcit, et admissos clemencia prepedit ictus,
Audacesque facit scelerum dilacio pene.
        Tolle, parens, odium! tandem mansuesce, novercam
Exue, blanda fave! morum bona singula mater
210   Possidet, et nato nec libra nec uncia servit."

Cap. 10 De responsione Nature et promissione subsidii

        Dixerat et verbum lacrimarum reppulit estus,
Et stetit opposito singultus obice lingua.
At dea: "Nec matris feritas est illa, nec illa
Fellificor taxo. semper tibi sedula grates
215   Et meritum perdo; gratamque, ingrate, bonorum
Indulsi saciem, misero felicia fudi
Non merito, donumque tenes donoque teneris.
Sollicitis hominem studiis limavit et orbem
Officiosa dedit, cumulato larga favore
220   Nostra Iovi bonitas cognata et cognita. numquam
Plenior exhibuit veram dilectio matrem.
Non egresco datis, dare non fastidio, rerum
Continuans partus, nec rumpit dextera fluxum
Muneris incisi, nec dandi rustica donum
225   Diminuit torpendo manus; sed dona minoris
Credis, ubi dono est plus quam contenta voluntas.
        Occulit ubertas precium, saciesque sapori
Derogat et tenuat accepti copia grates.
At quia sedulitas homini mea servit eique
230   Fundit opes et opem, meriti secura, malorum
Radicem fodiam, morbos a sedibus imis
Eiciam. paucis – cupias scivisse – docebo.
        Iam lacrime deterge lutum, limoque remoto.
Post tenebras admitte iubar. rorancia mores
235   Ubera nutricis senio lactandus hanelas,
Annosusque puer nec pectore canus ut annis,
Imberbique senex animo. iam debita menti
Canicies aderit et maturabitur intus,
Ne viridis putrescat homo, dabiturque petenti

gods. Man has drawn their wrath and lightning upon himself. Jove's
own hand has hurled the fire of Vulcan, his wrath hotter even than the
205   thunderbolt. But the avenger, wishing to be lenient toward his enemies,
curbed his thundering menace, and warded off with clemency those
blows which he permitted, until his deferral of punishment made men
bolder in crime.

"Withdraw your hatred, O Parent, grow mild at last, put off step-
motherly cruelty and be gentle and kind. A mother's nature should
210   possess every good quality, and not deal with her child in terms of
pounds and pennies."

Ch. 10 Nature's reply and her promise of assistance

He had said this much when a flood of tears prevented further
speech, and his tongue grew still, confronted by a barrier of sobbing. But
the goddess replied, "This cruelty is not your mother's, and no such
215   poison embitters me. Though I am ever zealous on your behalf, I gain
neither thanks nor reward. I have graced you, ingrate, with an abundance of delightful gifts, and showered happiness on your undeserving
wretchedness. All that you possess is my gift to you, and it is through
my gift that you are sustained.

"Our goodness, closely akin to Jove's, and sanctioned by him,
fashioned man with wearisome labor, and in our abundant largesse we
220   willingly bestowed the universe upon him. Never did a more loving act
reveal the true mother. And my power to give has not grown feeble, nor
am I grudging in my gifts. Constantly bringing new creatures to birth,
my hand never interrupts the pouring forth of its bounty, and no
225   laziness or clumsiness in its bestowal diminishes its value. But you
consider that an inferior gift by which your wishes are more than
fulfilled. Abundance appears of less worth, what is plentiful loses its
savor, and a bounteous gift reduces the gratitude of him who receives it.
230   But since it is my constant care to be of service to man, to shower him
with my wealth and succor with no concern for reward, I will dig out
the root of these evils, cast out the disease from your innermost being,
and offer a brief lesson; take pains to understand what I say. Wipe away
the stains of your tears, and when their taint is gone, let light enter in
235   place of shadow. In your old age you still long to be nursed with the
stream of moral wisdom that flows from your nurse's breast; though full
of years you are a mere boy, hoar in age but not in spirit, an old man
with the mind of beardless youth. Now your mind will assume the
white-haired gravity that befits it, and grow inwardly mature, rather
240   than rotting while still green. To him who seeks it a sweetness will be

240 Dulce, quod ad saciem siciens delibet alumpnus,
Quo puer ex animo sordensque infancia cedat.

Cap. 11 De sanctione Nature in rerum genituris

Sanctio nostra virum sterili marcescere ramo
Et fructum sepelire vetat, prolemque negantes
Obstruxisse vias. commissi viribus uti
245 Seminis et longam generis producere pompam
Religio nativa iubet, ne degener alnum
Induat aut platanum, semper virguncula laurus,
Aut salicem numquam parienti fronde puellam,
Aut si qua est vacuo folio vel flore pudica.

Cap. 12 De ancille amplexibus aspernandis

250 Nec facit ad sapidos amplexus nubile multis
Ancille gremium. variis hec bobus aratur
Terra nec indecores scit fastidire colonos.
Vulgi cimba rapax, carpentum vile, palustri
Accurrit populo, vix plena inviscerat alno
255 Vectorem quemcumque ratis, nauloque frequenti
Quot capit expilat. iteratis omnia carpit
Navigiis, usuque vices impendere gratis
Dememinit longo, nulloque innaufraga fluctu
Occumbit, tumidam ridens concussa procellan.

Cap. 13 De adulterio devitando

260 Turpis adulterii labes! redimicula morum
Vellit et obscuram trahit in contagia famam,
In varias suspecta neces, preciumque pudendi
Hospitis a loculo Nature malleus exit
Et Lachesis gemino succiso pollice, Parcis
265 Tollitur una colus, laribus depellitur exul
Amittitque Venus vacuos exclusa penates,
Arentique vado solitam sitit alveus undam.

granted which the eager nursling may taste until satisfied, and which will clear your mind of immaturity and the decayed remains of childishness.

Ch. 11 Nature's decree concerning procreation

"Our decree forbids man to wither on the barren bough, bury his talent in the ground, or prevent conception by blocking its channels. 245 Natural religion bids a man exercise the seminal power entrusted to him and give rise to a long procession of offspring, lest he remain ever virgin like the laurel, be reduced to the state of the barren alder, the plane-tree, the maiden willow whose boughs never bear, or any other plant so chaste as to be devoid of leaf or blossom.

Ch. 12 The embraces of maidservants are to be avoided

250 "But the body of a maidservant which has performed a wife's office for many men, does not make for pleasurable embraces. Such ground is plowed by oxen of all sorts, and does not know how to reject the crudest of farmers. Her skiff is greedy for a crowd; her common carriage serves a 255 filthy clientele; she will somehow force into her full vessel any steersman whatsoever. And however many she takes on board, she fleeces them all by her frequent tolls, robbing them of everything over the course of repeated voyages. Over her long career she has forgotten how to give a free performance. Immune to shipwreck, she never founders in the waves, but smiles as she is buffeted by the rising storm.

Ch. 13 Avoid adultery

260 "The foul disgrace of adultery plucks away the girdle of good character, and afflicts an already tainted reputation with diseases that lead to ruin in various ways. As the price of a shameful night's lodging the hammer forsakes its natural pouch, its twin is cut away by the hand of 265 Lachesis, and the distaff, too, is severed by the Fates. Venus is driven from her abode into exile, and forced to abandon her barren chambers, while the channel of the river grows dry and thirsts for its wonted stream.

Cap. 14 Persuasio Nature ut Architrenius ducat uxorem

Rumpe moras thalami, maturo contrahe! sunt hec
Illativa thori. solido nectatur oportet
270 Connubium nodo, riguo dum flamma iuvente
Fervet adhuc succo, nondumque infundit aniles
Brumula prima nives, nec vellera verticis albent
Crine pruinoso, nec serpit ruga, senecte
Verior interpres, ubi crispo fimbria vultu
275 Pallet et in facie numeratur Nestoris annus.
     Est michi dilecta nivei signata pudoris
Clave nec attrito marcens virguncula flore,
Iam vicina thoris, culmo solidata iuvente
Primaque lanigere texens velamina pubi,
280 Blanda comes thalami sapidoque tenellula tactu;
Obnubit splendore diem, noctisque profunde
Peplum siderei vultus carbunculus urit.
     Cum sit adulterii promptissima lena, Diones
Pronuba corrupte, Venerisque ancilla solute
285 Gloria, sollicito species suspecta pudori,
Non tamen hec recipit alienos innuba nexus,
Nec Ledea tenet animos, Lucrecia vultum,
Solaque Penelopen gremio gerit, ore Lacenam.[24]
     Flammativa viri sunt omnia, prona medullis
290 Inseruisse faces, hilarem factura iuventam
Iocundumque senem: longo Moderancia nobis
Cognita convictu, rerum cautissima, morum
Ingenio felix, Virtutis filia, natu
Nobilis et thalamos meditanti nubilis anno,
295 Pulchra – pudica tamen[25] – dabitur tibi, sacra ligabo
Federa, que nulla caveas diffibulet etas.
Ipsa quidem vicii pravos exosa susurros,
Haut immunda pati poterit consorcia, semper
Expavit tetigisse picem. contagia toto
300 Pectore declines, alioquin vincula rumpet
Coniugii, passum maculas non passa maritum.

Ch. 14 Nature persuades Architrenius to take a wife

"Defer no longer the nuptial rites, but marry in good season, for these are matters that belong to marriage, and it is proper that your marriage
270 should be made firm by a strong bond while the flame of youth still warms your blood; while no early winter has yet showered you with the snows of age, and the fleece of your head does not gleam with white frost; while wrinkles, a surer sign of age, have not yet crept forth, the
275 fringe around your pinched cheeks has not become white, and the years of Nestor cannot be read in your face.

"There is a maiden, dear to me, protected by the key of pure chastity, a maiden whose virgin flower is unwithered, She is ready for marriage, sustained by the sturdy plant of youth, and putting forth the first fleecy
280 growth of puberty. She will be a sweet companion in the marriage-chamber, delicately soft to the appreciative touch. Her splendor dims the light of day and the gemlike glow of her starry face burns through the mantle of the darkest night. Though the most persuasive of procuresses should present herself, the very matron of honor of corrupted love, the
285 most brilliant of the handmaids of dissolute Venus, that race whom anxious chastity so mistrusts, this maiden would never accept the embraces of a stranger. She does not harbor a Ledaean spirit behind the face of Lucretia; in her heart she is a very Penelope, though her face is the Spartan's.[24]

"Her every feature is well adapted to arouse a man and infuse his
290 marrow with fire, promising joy to youth and pleasure to old age. She is Moderation, well known to me from long intimacy, prudent in all things and blessed with a keen moral sense. As the daughter of Virtue she is of
295 noble birth, and of an age to consider the marriage-bed. Beautiful yet chaste,[25] she will be yours, and I myself will tie the sacred knot which, you may be sure, no length of time will undo. For she so detests the lewd whisperings of vice that she will never consent to any impure relations; she has ever shuddered at the thought of touching pitch. Keep your
300 mind wholly free of any taint of fear lest she ever break the bond of marriage, for she will never admit a husband who could admit the thought of such foulness.

Cap. 15 De cesto, cingulo Veneris

Nupta tibi ceston Veneris dabit. ille Diones
Baltheus, illa tuos precinget fascia lumbos.
Incudis studio sponse lucratus amorem,
305 Lennius hanc cocto solidavit sedulus auro,
Follibus eluctans vigiles excire caminos.
Non minus ardescens Lipares quam Cipridis igne,
Dum Venus emollit operam mirando laborem.
Dum tamen insudat operi manus, oscula morsis
310 Lingua rapit labris plus quam fabrilia. vultu
Sit licet obscuro, claudo pede, basia carpit
Dulcia nec plure saturantur adultera melle
Nec, Pari, plus Frigiis poteras pavisse Lacenam.

Cap. 16 De celatura eiusdem facta a Vulcano

Sollicito quedam digito celavit, amata
315 Dictantis rapiente vicem, manuumque Minervam
Spectatrix acuit et cotis suscipit usum,
Ingenii supplens laudato coniuge vires.
Hic vomit Ypolitus animam, ne Phedra pudorem
Sorbeat, intactus generis morumque noverce.
320 Expositum Phyrnes gremio vinoque perustum
Nulla Xenocratem Venus ebriat, innuba nusquam
Integritas nutat;[26] scorti luctamina ridet
Indomitus, frigetque mero candente libido.
Non potitur Lais dubio Demostene,[27] nec quem
325 Moverat evellit, perdendo prodigus auro
Non emit amplexus; thalamos qui vendit, ementem
Fallit, et emptorem mox penitet empta voluptas.
Inguina Democritus castrat,[28] sexumque virilem
Exuit et neutrum recipit, fratresque togatos
330 Detogat et Veneris geminum depellit avito
Mancipium tecto, lumbique incendia ferro
Ingelat et nervi succisus apocopat usum.
Renibus antiquo Pharius de more sacerdos
Excubat et palme de fronde cubilia sternit
335 Et sibi secretus alios latet incola phani,
Feminee labis vacuus, temereque vaganti
Non sitit aspecte speciei nectar ocello.

Ch. 15 The girdle of Venus

"Your bride will present you with the girdle of Venus. Let this Dionean belt, this band, gird your loins. The Lemnian smith, laboring at
305 the anvil to purchase the love of his spouse, carefully fashioned it from molten gold, straining with the bellows to heat his ever-glowing forge, and growing hot with both Liparean and Cyprian fires, when Venus lightened his labor by marvelling at his handiwork. Even as his hand
310 applied itself to the work, his mouth was snatching from her delicious lips kisses that were far from artificial. Though his face was blackened, and his gait halting, he fed on these sweet kisses; the kisses of adulterous love are no more steeped in honey, nor could Paris' Phrygian kisses have tasted sweeter to Helen.

Ch. 16 The engraving done by Vulcan on the girdle

315 "With careful hand he carved certain figures, while his beloved took on the office of dictation. By looking on she sharpened the skill of his hands, and performed the function of a whetstone, making her husband's artistic powers greater by praising them.

"Here Hippolytus pours forth his spirit lest Phaedra consume his chastity, remaining unviolated by one who was stepmother both to his
320 family and to his virtue. Though he is subjected to the embrace of Phryne and stimulated by wine, no power of Venus can intoxicate Xenocrates.[26] His virgin integrity never wavers, and he laughs, unaffected by the efforts of the harlot, his lust remaining cool even as the wine grows hot. Lais cannot overcome wavering Demosthenes;[27]
325 though she had moved him, she does not drag him down, and he who was so prodigal in squandering his gold will not buy her embraces. For she who sells her bed deceives the buyer, and pleasure that is purchased soon makes the buyer ashamed. Democritus cuts off his private parts,[28]
330 abandons the male sex and becomes neuter. He divests the robed brothers of their male robes, banishes Venus' twin servants from their ancestral home, quells with cold steel the fire in his loins, and cuts short the work of that organ by severing it. By ancient custom the priest of Isis
335 sleeps out of doors, and spreads himself a bed of palm fronds, secluding himself from mankind and living concealed in the sacred precincts. Free of the contamination of women, he never thirsts, with wantonly roving gaze, for the sweet sight of a comely body.

Cap. 17 De monili quod nupta fuerat delatura

Ipsa pudicicie testem castique monile
Argumenta thori, pectus clausura, retruso
340 Intrusore feret, prohibens ne iuncta dehiscant
Limina, neve sinus vilescat ianua, quovis
Trita viatore nec, quo delectet honestos
Coniugis attactus, oculus delibet adulter.
Pectoris hic nodus signis intexitur. Artis
345 Me – fateor – vincente manu, pictura pudicam
Predicat, et sacrum perhibent exempla cubile.
  Hic animo victrix, lecti Lucrecia ferro
Dedecus excusat; riget expectator Ulixis
Penelopes arcus; navem plus Claudia morum
350 Quam manuum virtute movet;[29] religatque solutum
Marcia nupta fide thalami, non carne Catonem.
  Prima sacerdotis vice Flacci dedicat uxor
Idalie sacrum, monitis instante Sibilla.[30]
  Frustra Meoniis[31] vates sub Apolline fati
355 Precinit ambages; precio Cassandra negato
Nec pactum recipit thalamo sed pectore Phebum,
Plenaque non tollit gremio sed mente magistrum.
  Risus et lacrimas sponsi partitur, utroque
Iuncta comes fato, nec deserit integra fractum
360 Ysicratea virum;[32] consors immota pericli
Ut thalami, regis nusquam secura suique
Metridatis, fragiles bellis accommodat artus:
Loricata latus, alienis degener armis
Exulat in clipeos, strictos peregrinat in enses,
365 Belligeros transumit equos, sexumque virili
Occulit in cultu, galeato mascula crine.
  Mausole, viva tibi dat Mausolea, virumque
Artemesia bibit;[33] quos pavit aromate, sponsi
Sorbet amans cineres, sparsumque in melle maritum
370 Haurit utrumque favum, nec fatis federe rupto
Connubium servat uteri thorus alter et una
Coniugis est coniunx tumulus, pira, piramis, urna.

Ch. 17 The necklace which the bride will wear

"As further attestation of her purity and the chastity of her bed, the
340 bride will wear a necklace, clasped about her breast to fend off any
intrusion, preventing the joined portals from gaping open, so that access
to her bosom may not seem an easy matter, a path to be trod by any
wayfarer, and so that what attracts the honorable caresses of a husband
may not gratify the eye of the adulterer.

345 "This band about her breast is worked with images. I must confess
that the artist's hand has captured me, and his representation proclaims
me chaste. His other examples enforce the sanctity of the marriage-bed.
Here the unconquered mind of Lucretia absolves herself by the sword
from the dishonor of her bed. Penelope's bow remains unbent, awaiting
350 the return of Ulysses. Claudia causes a ship to move by the power of her
virtue rather than her arms.[29] Marcia rejoins her sundered bond with
Cato, devoted to marriage in her fidelity, though not in carnal union.
The wife of Flaccus before all the others performs a priestlike office in
dedicating a temple to Venus, as the Sibyl's warnings had enjoined.[30] In
355 vain does Cassandra the priestess of Apollo sing to the Maeonians[31] of
the windings of fate. Having refused Apollo's offer, she receives him not,
as agreed, in her bed, but in her breast, suffering him not to fill her
womb, but to instruct her mind. Hypsicratea shares both the laughter
and the tears of her spouse, an inseparable companion in good times
360 and bad.[32] She remains loyal to her husband in defeat, a companion as
steadfast in time of danger as in the marriage-bed. Lest she ever be
separated from her royal husband Mithridates, she teaches her frail
body the arts of war. Clad in armor, unfit for the strange business of
365 fighting, she is an exile amid the clash of arms, strays among drawn
swords, rides a charger and conceals her sex in male garments, manlike
with her hair bound by a helmet. Mausolus, your Artemisia provides
you with a living mausoleum by drinking you.[33] For she lovingly
swallows the ashes of her spouse, which she has preserved with spices,
370 and consumes her husband mixed with honey (both equally sweet to
her). Thus fate cannot sunder their bond: her stomach, a secon
marriage-bed, preserves their marriage, and she is at once her husband's wife, tomb, pyre, monument and urn.

Cap. 18 De loculo puellari et contentis in eo

Hoc feret, inque tuis vigilabit zonula lumbis
Excuba, ne morum penetret lascivia murum.
375 Florida picture precio vernante brevemque
Ampla puellarem loculum demittit, amoris
Nuncia laturum sponse munuscula sponso
Clauditur in dando: lecti concordia, pacis
Fedus, amicicie nodus, correctio voti,
380 Integritas recti, virtutis serrula, morum
Lima, rigor mentis, maiestas oris, honesti
Pondus, habena modi, scelerum succisio, culpe
Meta, Minerva boni, medii via, methodus equi,
Mundicie pecten, vite fragrancia, fame
385 Gracia, solamen miseris, cautela secundis."

Cap. 19 De contractu coniugii et dote

Dixit. et a lacrimis redit Architrenius, egra
Mesticie caligo fugit nec lecior umquam
Federis instanter nodum petit. illa capacem
Consilii laudat, optata citacius urgens.
390 Curia contrahitur, legitur locus, apta iugandis
Omnia tractantur; producitur ultima virgo
Phebigero plus quam prefulgentissima vultu.
Dos datur a nupta: vigil observancia recti,
Casta quies lingue, facundia passa soporem,
395 Eloquii pondus, os in sermone pudicum,
Fece carens pectus, mens labis inhospita nevo,
Munda domus cordis, anime laudanda supellex
Pacis amor frater, germana modestia nupte,
Iuris norma comes, pietas vicina favori,
400 Arra pudor morum, fidei dilectio pignus,
Fame sponsor honos, maiestas nominis obses,
Spes pugil adversis, dubiis fiducia pugnans,
Consilii libra, resecans censura reatus,
Nestoris examen, polientis lima Catonis,
405 Sollicitudo fori, solidi cautela senatus,
Illimis bonitas manuum mundescere curis,
Circumcisa loqui studiose tersa voluntas,
Maior egestate, minor exundante facultas.

Ch. 18 The maiden's purse and what it contains

"This she will bring, and her girdle will stand guard over your loins,
375 watchful lest wantonness penetrate the barrier of virtue. From this
broad belt, sumptuous in the springlike richness of its decoration, there
depends a girl's modest purse, to bear those little gifts which betoken the
bride's love for her husband. Included among these gifts are the union of
the marriage-bed, the promise of peace, the bond of affection, the
380 guidance of prayer, inviolable rectitude, the saw of virtue, the file of
good character, gravity of mind, dignity of bearing, a firm sense of
honor. She will bring you the curb of restraint, a divorce from wrongdoing, an end to guilty actions, an understanding of goodness, the path
of the mean, the pattern of justice, the comb of cleanliness, sweetness of
385 life, the grace of a good name, solace in time of sorrow and caution amid
good fortune."

Ch. 19 The marriage contract and dowry

She concludes, and Architrenius emerges from his weeping. The
sickly pall of misery is dispelled and happier than ever before, he
demands at once the bond of union. The goddess commends his acceptance of her counsel, and sets quickly to work to fulfil his hopes.
390 A counsel is convened, a site is chosen, and all things pertaining to
the union are arranged. At last the maiden is brought forward, her face
radiating a more than surpassing brilliance. The bride's dowry is
presented: a constant adherence to the right; a modest softspokenness; a
395 fluency which allows intervals of rest; a capacity for grave eloquence; a
mouth pure in its choice of words; a breast devoid of foul thoughts; a
spirit that rejects any marks of dishonor; a heart that harbors purity; an
admirably well-stored mind; peace, the brother of love, and modesty,
sister to the bride herself; sound precept, the companion of justice; duty
400 which attains to favor; a sense of shame, earnest of good character;
affection, the token of trust; honor, the upholder of reputation; dignity,
surety for one's good name; hope, the foe of adversity; assurance, at war
with doubt; balanced judgment; severity in restraining guilt; the reflec-
405 tiveness of Nestor; the acumen of keen-minded Cato; a leader's concern
for the common weal; the prudence of a united senate; a spotless
goodness that remains unsullied by worldly affairs; a careful concern to
speak briefly and concisely, in a style that avoids excessive plainness yet
never becomes fulsome.

Cap. 20 De donacione et instrumentis musicis

A tenui sponso tenuis donacio: dantur
410 Obsequium carnis, anime tractabilis usus.
Connubii tandem solidatur nodus. et ecce
Leticiam spargit, solempnis prodiga plausus,
Solis opus cythara, studium Iyra Mercuriale,
Dulce Pharo sistrum, requies pastoris harundo,
415 Canna vocans sompnos, faciens syringa sopori,[34]
Lite graves aule, iocundula nabla querelis,
Folle chorus rauco,[35] petulanti cymbala tactu,
Pauper avena sono, modulatu fistula dives,
Buccina scabra modos, veterum sacra tympana sacris,
420 Tibia vulgaris, regina fidicula cantu,
Murmur honusque tuba, lituus citator edendi.

Cap. 21 De avibus verba usurpantibus

Nec minus et mima nemorum circumsonat ales
Et modulos crispat nativi pectinis arte:
Ruris alauda chelys, lyricen Philomena rubeto,
425 Per vada cantor olor, cithareda per equora Siren,
Corvus 'ave' dicens, homo lingue psitacus usu,
Pica salutatrix, lasciva monedula fando,
Turdula prompta loqui, facundo gracculus ore,
Et quecumque stilum valet usurpasse loquendi.

Cap. 22 De ancillis sponse

430 Sponse lecta manus, thalamis ancilla: ministrant
Virginis integritas, vidui castracio lecti,[36]
Matrone gravitas, levitas immota puelle,
Simplicitas vultus, redolescens oris honestas,
Tuta fides lecti, nupte Venus invia culpe.

Cap. 23 De clientela pro diversis officiis obsequenti

435 Ordo clientele varius discurrit, ubique
Servit et ad vota famulatum sedulus explet:
Firma viri virtus, teneri timor intimus anni,
Cura senectutis, operum passiva iuventus,

Ch. 20 The bridegroom's gift and the wedding music

410 From the frail bridegroom, a meager contribution: obedience in fleshly appetite and a spirit willing to be guided are his gifts. At last the bond of marriage is made firm, and lo! music, full of festive celebration, spreads joy abroad: the Sun-god's lute; the Mercurial art of the lyre; the rattle, so dear to the Egyptian; the flute, pastime of shepherds; the 415 cane-pipe, which gives rise to drowsiness, and creates an inlet for sleep;[34] the pipes that sound so stern in battle; the harp, so pleasing in its lament; the organ with its coarse bellows;[35] the wantonly tinkling cymbal; the meager sound of the oaten flute; the pan-pipe, so rich in its melodies; the war-trumpet with its harsh strains; the tymbrel, hallowed 420 by ancient rites; the common bone-flute and the regal song of the cithern; the tuba's growling burden; the clarion which announces proclamations.

Ch. 21 Birds appropriate the power of speech

The winged pageant of the surrounding groves is no less musical, warbling melodies with natural artistry: the lark, lyre of the country- 425 side; the nightingale, lyrical among the thorns; the swan, songster of the shallows; the Siren, carolling across the deep; the raven, crying "Hail!"; the parrot, manlike in his power of speech; the magpie's cheerful greeting; the lewd chough; the chattering thrush; the fluent jackdaw; and every bird that can assume the appearance of speech.

Ch. 22 The bride's attendants

430 A chosen band of attendants ready the bridal chamber: inviolate virgin-ity; the abstinence of an unshared bed;[36] matronly dignity; a maiden's steadfast delicacy; modesty of demeanor; a countenance redolent of honor; sure fidelity to the marriage-bed; a conjugal love immune to wickedness.

Ch. 23 The retainers who performed various offices

435 A varied array of retainers bustle about, assisting everywhere, and eagerly performing their duties on command: strong manly virtue; the inner doubts of tender years; the concerns of age; youth capable of accomplishment; a hand cautious in its giving, but prompt to reward

Dandi cauta manus, meritorum dextra beatrix,
440 Dona modus librans, inhibens prudencia luxum,
Expense racio, reminiscens calculus asses,
Sollers auricula, viciis inapertus ocellus,
Pesque reformidans molli iuvenescere passu,
Lascivaque timens dematurescere culpa.

Cap. 24 De ferculis in nuptiis Architrenii et Moderancie

445 Tempus adest mense, quam mundo Copia cornu
Sarcinat; et morum locupleti funditur urna:
Sobrietas mense, sacies angusta paratus,
Ventre minor potus, epuli contracta libido,
Pauca petens guttur, combustio nulla palati,
450 Mansuetudo gule, stomachi tranquilla Caribdis,
Limes in effusis, dapis artans meta volumen.

Cap. 25 Quod Fortuna favit nuptiis

Respicit et blandis epulas percurrit ocellis
Et vultus adhibet animi cum melle favorem
Sors inopum vindex, regum Tuchis ulta tumores,
455 Rannis opum terror, Nemesis suspecta tirannis,
Casus agens mitras, tribuens Fortuna curules.
O data vel raro vel nulli fercula, solis
Degustanda viris! o felix mensa, Catoni
Forsitan et nostro vix evo nota! beatis,
460 Immo beativis, indulge sumptibus. absit
Meta deum clausura dapes, connubia Virtus
Sanctiat et dempto convivia fine perhennet.

Hic igitur suspendo stilum. procedere ruptis
Erubeo mensis, quarum producere tempus
465 Non breviasse decet. metari prandia nolo,
Que Deus assiduo faciat succedere gustu,
Nec sacie nutet epulandi fixa voluptas.
O longum studii gremio nutrita, togati
Ingenii proles rudis et plebea, libelle,
470 Incolumis vivas, nec te languescere cogat

440 merit; a restraint that weighs the value of each gift; a prudence that
curbs luxury; reasonable expenditure, and an accounting of moneys
disbursed; an attentive ear; an eye undistracted by vice; feet fearful of
appearing too youthful by the lightness of their step, and wary of
lapsing from maturity by straying into wantonness.

Ch. 24 The banquet at the wedding of Architrenius and Moderation

445 The time for feasting is at hand. Plenty has heaped the board with a
seemly abundance, and poured from an urn well filled with virtues:
sobriety at table; a modest sufficiency of dishes; less drink than the belly
can bear; a restrained desire for rich food; a throat whose demands are
450 modest, and a palate that does not burn with greed; moderateness of
appetite; peace in the Charybdis of the guts; a limiting of expenditure
that sets a limit on the quantity of dishes.

Ch. 25 Fortune blesses the marriage

There is one looking on who surveys the feast with kindly eyes, and
matches the favor in her expression with the sweetness of her thoughts:
Fortune, the random and mutable power that protects the poor and
455 avenges the pride of kings, the Rhamnusian scourge of wealth, the
Nemesis so feared by tyrants, the power that effects the falls of rulers
and the distribution of high office.

O feast so rarely granted, if at all, to be enjoyed by a few chosen men!
O blessed board, familiar perhaps to Cato but in our age almost
460 unknown! Vouchsafe them your blessed, nay your beatifying abundance! Let that term be far off which will bring to an end this feast of the
gods; let Virtue hallow their marriage and perpetuate their feasting
without end!

465 Here, then, I stay my pen. I blush to go further after interrupting a feast
whose duration it were more fitting to prolong than curtail. I am loath
to set a limit to a meal which, God willing, will so prolong their eager
appetite that the pleasure in feasting will be constant, and not grow
drowsy with satiety.

O little book, nursed so long at the breast of study, O rough and
470 low-born offspring of the mind of a common man, may you survive

Invidie morsus, quo morbificante bonorum
Febricitat nomen et eo tortore modernis
Egrescit titulus. forsan, tibi si qua favoris
Uncia debetur, peplo livoris amicta
475 Non poterit venisse palam, dum sorbeat auras
Vivificas auctor. ortum lux illa Iohannis
Sumat in occasu, sol ille a funeris urna
Surgat, inextincto semper spectabilis igne.
Sub fati tenebris me noctescente, diescat
480 Hic liber et fame veterum feliciter annos
Equet, in eternum populis dilectus et ultra!

intact, and may the carping of envy never make your voice grow faint. For envy's baneful power blights the reputations of good men, and through its cruelty the renown of modern writers languishes. It may be that if you are deemed worthy of some scrap of favor, it must come
475 shrouded in the cloak of envy rather than appearing openly, since the author still breathes the breath of life. Let this light, then, dawn as Johannes' light is setting, let this sun rise from his funeral urn, and let its undimmed fire be beheld forever. As I enter the dark night of shadowy
480 fate, let this book emerge into daylight: let it know a favor as enduring as the fame of the ancients, and be cherished by all people to eternity and beyond!

Notes to the text

Prologue

1 The prologue appears in fewer than half the manuscripts, often in a later hand than the text, provides only the most obvious information in a stereotypical form, and hence can hardly be by Johannes. As Schmidt observes (p. 117) it is important mainly as evidence that the *Architrenius* was well known in the schools of the thirteenth century.

2 The opposition of "ferment" to pure (*azymus*, literally "unleavened") feeling echoes I Corinthians 5.7.

3 Matthew 19.6; Mark 10.9.

4 Three manuscripts provide the marginal gloss "Architrenius: archos; princeps; trenos: lamentum." Architrenius is the prince of sorrows or archweeper, and in providing the title for Johannes' poem his name conforms to the twelfth-century fashion of ornate titles loosely derived from Greek: *Didascalicon*, *Cosmographia*, *Policraticus*, *Metalogicon*. The custom is noted à propos of the *Architrenius* by Gervais of Melkley, *Ars poetica (ed. Gräbener), p. 94*.

Book One

1 The reference is to the bridging of the Hellespont and the canal dug through the Athos peninsula as preparation for Xerxes' campaign against Greece in 480. Cp. Walter of Châtillon, *Alexandreis* 6.188–91. The opening two words, "Velificatur Athos," echo Juvenal, *Satires* 10.174, where these events are also recalled, and show Johannes identifying his stance with that of the ancient satirist. Gervais of Melkley observes à propos of this phrase that the pentasyllable is a distinguished beginning for a hexameter line (*Ars*, p.210); of the opening two lines he notes that they illustrate a "paradigmatic" placement of exemplary material, designed to achieve a strongly hortatory effect, and that such an effect is enhanced by the figure of hypozeuxis, whereby each of a series of clauses has its own subject and verb (pp. 36, 151).

2 *togato*, as a gloss in MS D explains, denotes people of ordinary civilian status as opposed to members of the equestrian class or *trabeati*. Cp. Johannes' concluding reference to his poem as a product "togati / Ingenii," 9.468–69.

3 *succentus*, which I have translated as "lower note," is a musical term which denotes an accompaniment or second part; cp. Martianus Capella, *De nuptiis* I.II.

4   Amyclas, the poor boatman of Lucan, *De bello civili* 5.520ff., is a stock
figure for poverty in twelfth-century school-poetry; cp. 2.224; 6.237, etc..

5   I.e. Phaeton; cp. 5.24–30.

6   *Acin* or *Atin*, used loosely to signify the eastern limit of Johannes' world (as
Athlas in the same line signifies the far west), seems to denote a city in the region
corresponding to the province of Sind in modern Pakistan. On the complex
history of the term and Johannes' possible sources for it, see Schmidt, Intro
duction, pp. 73–76, and his note on this line. "Acin" and Atlas are used to
define the eastern and western limits of the inhabited world in 9.66–73.

7   Gervais of Melkley complains at length about the *dura transumptio* (i.e.
difficult metaphor) in *olore* (lit. "swan") *senecte*. Since what is in question is the
candor or whiteness of a surface, he considers that *nix* or *lilia* would be
preferable to *olor* as the metaphorical vehicle (*Ars*, pp. 136–37).

8   The opposition of *libri*, "books," and *librae*, "pounds" in the monetary
sense, or the "scales" used to weigh money and goods, is a commonplace; see
Schmidt.

9   The fullest account of the chastizing of Zoilus that Johannes is likely to have
known occurs in Vitruvius, *De architectura* 7, praef. 8, though Alexander does
not appear there. In MS Q, a gloss that is clearly derived from the anecdote in
Vitruvius assigns the rebuke of Zoilus to Alexander.

10   This rather abruptly digressive sentence refers to the conquest of Britain by
the Trojans under Brutus, the first of Johannes' numerous allusions to the
legendary history best known from the *Historia regum Britanniae* of Geoffrey of
Monmouth.

11   Walter of Coutances, newly named Archbishop of Rouen, to whom the
poem is dedicated. The first letters of the first eight books of the poem form the
acrostic VVALTERO. (The first letters of the final lines of these eight books form a
corresponding IOHANNES.) See Schmidt, pp. 14–15 and above, Introduction, n.
1. For a detailed review and assessment of Walter's career, see William Stubbs,
ed. *Chronica Magistri Rogeri de Houedene* (Rolls Series 51), Vol. 3 (London,
1870), pp. lix–ciii.

12   Johannes' suggestive use of *lares* to evoke the powers that govern the inner
life (cp. line 322 below) is discussed by Paul Piehler, *The Visionary Landscape*
(London, 1971), pp. 87–89; see also Owen Barfield's review of this book,
Medium Aevum 42 (1973), pp. 88–90. Johannes also uses the term as a simple
metonymy for "chambers" of whatever kind; see, e.g., 3. 61.

13   This concise Stoic formulation is based on the speech in which Lucan's Cato
repudiates the worship of transcendent Gods by declaring "Jupiter est, quodcumque vides, quocumque moveris" (*D.b.c.* 9.580).

14   Except where noted, the source of this bizarre catalog is Books 6 and 7 of
Pliny's *Natural History*. Much of Pliny's lore appears also in Solinus' *Collectanea
rerum memorabilium*, and some also in the *Etymologiae* of Isidore. Johannes
seems to have worked directly with both Pliny and Solinus (Schmidt, pp.
67–68).

15   Pliny (7.69) cites Cornelia as evidence that it is bad luck to be born with the

genitals closed ("concreto virginali"). Schmidt notes that Johannes may have impressionistically conflated this detail with Pliny's story about the father of the Gracchi (7.122). Two snakes of different sexes were discovered in the house, and when an oracle declared that he would live if the female snake were killed, he replied "No, kill my snake: Cornelia is young and still able to bear children." On the hammer as an image for the male organ or testicles, J. N. Adams, *The Latin Sexual Vocabulary* (Baltimore, 1982), p. 43, cites only the twelfth-century Latin comedy *Lydia*, but hammer and anvil appear as an image of sexual union at several points in the *De planctu naturae* of Alan of Lille.

16 Much of the point of this passage is in the application of the terms *ducere*, "to take in marriage," properly used of the bridegroom, and *nubere*, "to put on the marriage-veil," properly used with specific reference to the bride.

17 As Schmidt notes, Johannes here refers to the "astrological geography" which considers each region of the earth to be subject to the influence of a particular constellation. As it happens, Libra is associated with North Africa, and several manuscripts give "Libie" in place of "Libre."

18 On Gemagog and his battle with Corineus, see Geoffrey of Monmouth, *Historia* 1.16. On Corineus, see below, 5.385–429 and n. 15.

19 This incident, reported by Solinus, *Collectanea* 1.91, does not appear in Pliny.

20 A gloss in MS Q explains this puzzling passage by asserting that Rufinus, whom Claudian censured, was a virtuous man, while Stilicho, whom he praised, was in fact the enemy of Rome. But this probably reflects an attempt to make sense of Johannes' lines, rather than a considered judgment on the political subtleties of Claudian's poetry. Johannes' own reading of Claudian seems less systematically ironic, but he is clearly aware that the point of Claudian's elaborate praise and invective has little to do with the actual characters of the two men; his is a poetry of ornate and ambiguous surfaces and so, Johannes seems to suggest, an appropriate vehicle for that description of the house of Venus which he himself does not provide.

21 The apparently proverbial association of joined eyebrows with ill nature is noted in a gloss in MS v.

22 The play on "rubric," the term for the heading of a chapter or major division of a text, which was commonly written in red lettering, is part of an elaborate medieval metaphorics based on scribal practice. See below, Book II, n. 2; and E. R. Curtius, *European Literature and the Latin Middle Ages* (New York, 1953), pp. 315–16.

23 A gloss in MS v explains this as a reference to the practice of young women who bite their lips to make them red.

24 I.e. the constellation Leo, considered in astrological geography as governing Asia (see note 17 above).

Book Two

1   The implications of archetypal purity in this description are enhanced by the echo of Bernardus Silvestris, *Cosmographia* 1.1.56, where Noys, the wisdom of God is depicted as presiding over "an empty court," since God has not yet decreed the initial union of form with primordial matter.

2   As *pagina* (tr. "skin") indicates, the image is of a sheet of parchment, scraped with pumice to provide a clear and smooth surface for writing.

3   C. Fabricius Luscinus, Roman statesman and military hero, was consul in 282 and 278 B.C. (hence the reference to the fasces in line 177). He was a proverbial figure for poverty and austerity; cp. 2.391; 5.288.

4   C. Atilius Serranus, was summoned from his farm to Rome, where he served as consul in 257 and 250 B.C. He is paired with Fabricius in *Aeneid* 6.844; Claudian, *In Rufinum* 1.201–02, *De quartu consulato Honorii* 414–15.

5   I.e. which should be served in a sauce or broth.

6   *Baccis* is Johannes' preferred rendering of the name of the countrywoman Baucis. See 2.395–480, and Ovid, *Metamorphoses* 8.610–724.

7   Codrus, in twelfth-century poetry a stock figure for poverty (see 3.54; 6.334; 7.56), seems to represent the fusion of two traditions. A Codrus is named repeatedly by Vergil (*Ecl.* 5.11; 7.22, 26) and Juvenal (*Sat.* 1.2; 3.203, 208) as a bad, and in Juvenal's account also an impoverished poet. (Modern editors have emended the name of Juvenal's victim to "Cordus," but Johannes undoubtedly knew him as Codrus.) A second tradition names Codrus as the last of the kings of Athens (11th c. B.C.). When the Dorians invaded Attica, and the Delphic oracle declared that they would be victorious if Codrus' life were spared, he went forth disguised as a peasant and provoked a fatal quarrel with a Dorian, thereby saving Athens. See Valerius Maximus, *Facta et dicta memorabilia* 5.6. ext. 1.

8   *Memphis*, "the man of Memphis," i.e. Ptolemy.

9   On *Aren*, the name assigned by Arab astronomers to an imaginary city located on the equator, see Schmidt, pp. 74–75, and his long note.

10   The Colures are two imaginary circles, intersecting at the poles, one of which passes through the points in Cancer and Capricorn that mark the solstices, the other through the points in Aries and Libra that mark the equinoxes.

11   M. Licinius Crassus Dives (d. 53 B.C.), a Roman general and political ally of Julius Caesar, and a man of immense personal wealth (he reappears at 5.491 as one of the generals of the army of Avarice), was killed in battle by the Parthians. According to Florus, *Epitoma* 1.46(3.11).11, the Parthians sent his head to their king, who had it filled with molten gold, but medieval accounts suggest that he was made to drink the gold while still alive. See below, 5.288, 491; Valerius Maximus 9.4.1; Bernardus Silvestris, *Cosmographia* 1.3.237–38; Alan of Lille, *Anticlaudianus* 2.227–28.

12   As Homer's Ajax is lord of the seven-fold shield; cp. Ovid, *Met.* 13.1–2. Schmidt sees the English Ajax as a type ("der ungestüme Engländer"), but a

personal reference may be intended. Charles Hutchings, "L'Anticlaudianus d'Alain de Lille. Étude de chronologie," *Romania* 50 (1924), pp. 10–11, suggests that the characters of Nero, Midas, Ajax, Paris, and Davus in Alan of Lille, *Anticlaudianus* 1.169–81 represent Henry II and his four sons. Ajax would correspond to Richard Coeur-de-Lion.

13   The Cistercians, still at the height of their influence a generation after the death of St. Bernard of Clairvaux (1153).

14   Pliny 6.23.80, and Solinus 52.17, cite reports of two islands at the mouth of the Indus river, Chryse and Argyre, whose mines, as their names suggest, produced only gold and silver.

15   Lines 488–92, in which Paris ceases to be a city and becomes a sort of Paradise, recall the elaborate encomium on the natural endowments of Italy that concludes Pliny's *Natural History* (37.201–04).

Book Three

1   I.e. water.

2   Geta and Birria are the names of slaves in comedies of Terence, borrowed by the twelfth-century authors of elegiac comedies, and appropriated by Latin school-poetry generally to denote low or buffoonish types. See also 5.342; and the reference to "Davus" at 3.341.

3   The phrase *musica vincla* recalls Bernardus Silvestris, *Cosmographia* 1.1.22.

4   See Euclid, *Elementa* 10, Appendix 27.

5   Hegesias of Cyrene (early 3rd c., B.C.) was apparently an advocate of suicide, and was banished from Alexandria because of his teachings. Johannes' vivid picture embellishes the very brief account in Valerius Maximus 8.9. ext. 3.

6   I.e. dialectic, the art that distinguishes truth from error.

7   On Grammar as the "nurse and mother" of the Arts (whence the *cunis* of line 173), see John of Salisbury, *Metalogicon* 1.13.

8   If *transicio* denotes the transitive relation between nouns or pronouns, as in Priscian, the grammatical rules here set forth would seem to be false. Two nominatives (*recta*) can only be related by equivalence, and any relationship between a nominative and a word in a different case (*obliquum*) is in some sense transitive. See Priscian, *Institutiones* 14.14–15, cited by Schmidt; also 13.25–26; 17.153–55. Has Johannes perhaps deliberately scrambled the student's grammatical knowledge as a way of indicating the fatigue described in the following chapter?

9   By "mute babbling" I have tried to suggest the punning effect of *infancia*, speech which is at once unspoken and like that of a preverbal child.

10   I take the "line of Libra" to be the equinoctial, the circle which passes through the signs of Libra and Aries, and which thus provides a fixed point in relation to which the hour of sunrise can be estimated at other times of year.

11   The robber Sciron was killed by Theseus. Neither earth nor ocean would admit his bones, and they were transformed into rocky cliffs. See Ovid, *Met.* 7.443–47.

12 Sinis was also a robber killed by Theseus. He bent pine-trees to the ground, tied his captives to their tops, and then released them, catapulting the victims into the air. See Ovid, *Met.* 7.440–42.

13 Phalaris was a Sicilian tyrant for whom was made a brazen bull in which his enemies could be roasted alive. See below, 8.87; 9.167; Valerius Maximus 9.2. ext. 9; and on the cruelty of Phalaris, Cicero, *De officiis* 2.7.26.

14 Syrtis (lit. "sand-bank") commonly denotes an area of shoals off the north coast of Africa; cp. 9.169.

15 Like Geta and Birria, the name of a slave in Roman comedy, and of a ne'er-do-well in Horace, *Sat.* 2. 7; cp. 5.334; 7.416; and see Schmidt, for twelfth-century references to his ugliness and vile habits.

16 A city in India, the birthplace of Bacchus.

17 Schmidt sees this phrase as referring to Phoebus in his double aspect, as Sun and as god of wisdom, but other interpretations are clearly possible.

18 By "actor" here Johannes may signify the courtier who abandons his own character to adopt the self-serving role of flatterer. The equation of the client or courtier with the actor, common in Roman satire, is developed by John of Salisbury; see, e.g., *Policraticus* 3.4, 8.3.

Book Four

1 Pella, in Macedonia, birthplace of Alexander the Great.

2 *Aux* or *augis* is the term used by the ninth-century Arab astronomer Al-Farghani or "Alfraganus," Johannes' chief source for astronomical data, to denote the apogee of a planet. Hence the *oppositio* or *oppositum augis* is the perigee.

3 The *quadratura* is one half of one of the Moon's hemispheres, hence the phase described is half-moon.

4 My translation assumes that the mountain is reintroduced as subject at the midpoint of line 16. It would perhaps be possible to construe "partem . . . vergit" as referring to the moon, but *arduus* in 18 must refer to *mons*, and the use of the enclitic -*que* to link the two clauses suggests that they have a common subject.

5 See Ovid, *Heroides* 5.25–30.

6 On the *cinnamolgus*, a legendary bird that makes its nest in the cinnamon tree, see Pliny 10.97; Solinus 33.15; Isidore 12.7.23.

7 The notion of a "thirsting" peach (*persicus*) no doubt involves a play on *persiccus*, "very dry." The "rain of Bacchus" may refer to a method of preserving peaches in wine, or mixing their juice with wine. (Pliny, 23.132, recommends the latter.)

8 I am willing to leave for future study the question of just what six varieties of pear are referred to in lines 46–51. The pear hallowed with the name of Regulus in 46 is presumably, as Schmidt notes, the "pirum Sancti Reguli" cited in R.E. Latham *Revised Latin Word List* (London, 1965). That in 47, named for the hollow of the palm, is probably the *volema* of Vergil (*Georg.* 2.88) and Pliny (15.16.56), tentatively identified as "pound fruit" in the Rackham-Jones edition

of Pliny. DuCange cites a *pirum angustiae* and gives its French name as "poire d'angoisse"; this must be the pear associated with "materna angustia" in 48; in both cases the womb-like shape of the fruit must have suggested the association. (DuCange notes that the name seems to be derived "a vulgari notione.") For the pear of 49, sponsored by Augustus, Schmidt cites Valerius Cordus, *Historia plantarum ac stirpium* (Strassburg, 1561), p. 178, who names a *pirum Augusti* which ripens *tempestive* in the month of August. The pear fathered by Robert in 50 is glossed in MS x as "pere Robert." Various varieties named by Pliny are identified by French editors with the "poire de St. Jean," presumably the pear baptized by "another John"; but I have found no evidence that this other is the Evangelist rather than the Baptist, as Schmidt suggests, and Johannes may simply intend to denote a "John" other than himself.

9   Perhaps the whortleberry.

10   Though *caelestis homo* suggests a particular figure, I take the phrase as referring generally to the Titans, born of the union of Earth and Sky.

11   In translating I have ignored the metaphor, an enormous bird brooding on the mountain-top, in order to convey what I take to be its tenor.

12   The language and imagery of 227–29 recall Bernardus Silvestris, *Cosmographia* 1.1.39–40.

13   In MS x this passage is glossed as "commendacio maioris Britanniae", but while a later encomium on King Henry II (5.85–93) seems straightforward enough, in the present context it is likely that Johannes' praise of the culture of his court is at least partly ironic.

14   This gesture, part of the stock in trade of Ovid's attentive lover (*Ars Am.* 1.151), becomes standard courtly behavior in medieval satire; cp. the early thirteenth-century *De palpone et assentatore* 271–74, in *The Latin Poems commonly attributed to Walter Mapes*, ed. Thomas Wright (London, 1841), p. 114; and on the subject of 376–410, see also Alexander Murray, *Reason and Society in the Middle Ages* (2nd ed., Oxford, 1985), pp. 107–09.

15   The argument of this chapter closely resembles that of Boethius, *De consolatione philosophiae* 2, pr. 8.

Book Five

1   See Horace, *Epistles* 1.3.19; Phaedrus, *Fabulae Aesopiae* 1.3.

2   Isidore, *Etymologiae* 12.2.30, describes the ape as *facie foeda*. Solinus, *Collectanea* 27.56, speaks of apes that daub their eyes with birdlime, copying the deliberately deceptive gesture of a man and thereby rendering themselves easy to capture.

3   The elephant's rare and secret matings and its avoidance of promiscuity, reported by Pliny, 8.5.12–13, together with the sluggishness of the sexual nature of the male, become a standard topic in bestiaries. See *Physiologus latinus, Versio Y*, ed. F.J. Carmody (University of California Publications in Classical Philology 12.7, 1941), p. 117; *Theobaldi "Physiologus"*, ed. P. T. Eden (Lieden, 1972), pp. 64–65.

4 See Ovid's account of Phaeton's flight, *Met.* 2.176–77.

5 Pyrrhus, son of Achilles and ravisher of Andromache, supposed to have founded in Epirus a kingdom which took its name from Molossus, his son by Andromache.

6 For the anecdote of Aristotle's allowing his pupil to publish certain writings of his on rhetoric, see Valerius Maximus 8.14. ext. 3.

7 See Schmidt for other twelfth-century plays on *ara*, "pigsty," and *ara*, "altar."

8 *Dux*: "general" in war and "duke" in peace.

9 The black and white sails refer most obviously to the habits of Benedictine and Cistercian, but there is perhaps a reminiscence also of the ominous significance of Theseus' neglecting to change the sails of the vessel in which he returned from Crete after slaying the Minotaur, which led to the death of Aegeus.

10 The focus and even the subject of this difficult passage are hard to determine. I have assumed that *novissima* (165) and *prima* (166) refer to stages in the spiritual history of mankind, that mankind itself is the subject of *deligit* in 167, that the *usum* of 167 is a life governed by pride and that *superbia* itself is the *una* of 168.

I have taken the next five lines as heavily ironical in tone: mutual toleration among spirits united by their common pride and self-interest is the closest "modern" equivalent to the ideal of the common life still perceptible in the description of the cloister in lines 132–39 of the previous chapter. It would be possible to translate the lines in a positive way, as affirming the power of peace and communal bonds to give stability to the lives of the weak and unstable. But the ironic emphasis seems to me to be underscored by the allusion in 169 to Juvenal, *Sat.* 2.47, on the "magna concordia" among those "molles animos" united by a common pursuit of debased sexual practices.

11 The reference to "northern" and "southern" regions of Heaven is ultimately based on Isaiah 14.13, where Lucifer is made to declare that he will place his throne "in lateribus Aquilonis." On this and related questions of heavenly geography, see Thomas D. Hill, "Some Remarks on 'The Site of Lucifer's Throne'," *Anglia* 87 (1969), pp. 303–11.

12 Though *lentescere* is perhaps ambiguous, my rendering of the line is prompted by Schmidt's citation of the monostich, "Redditur invalidus, nimium si tenditur, arcus," No. 26448 in Hans Walther, *Lateinische Sprichwörter und Sentenzen des Mittelalters* (5 vols., Göttingen, 1963–69).

13 On this passage see Catherine Klaus, "De l'Enfer au Paradis ... et retour, dans l'Architrenius de Jean de Hanville," in *Pour une mythologie du Moyen Age*, ed. Laurence Harf-Lancner, Dominique Boutet (Paris, 1988), pp. 27–29.

14 *Ceraunia* is the name of a mountain range in Epirus. Johannes' association of it with *fluctus* may reflect a partial misreading of Lucan, *D.b.c.* 5.65off., where the huge waves of a sea-storm are described hyperbolically as threatening to dash Caesar's ship, not just against the rocky coast, but against the tops of the neighboring Ceraunian mountains. At 8.116 the "ardua Ceraunia" are associated with down-ward rushing streams.

15 *Phorcis* (gen. *Phorcidis*) identifies Scylla as daughter of Phorcus, best known as father of the Gorgons, but traditionally assigned various sea-monsters as progeny.

16 The Tagus, whose sands, like all the objects enumerated in the next few lines, were said to be gold.

17 The Macrobians, an Aethiopian people, were said to bind their criminals with chains of gold. See Solinus 30.10.

18 Schmidt notes that this reference is probably due to a misreading of Jerome's version of Eusebius' Chronicle, where the tomb of Bacchus is said to be visible at Delphi "iuxta Apollinem aureum," but is not itself said to be made of gold; *Chronicon Eusebii*, ed. Rudolf Helm (Eusebius, *Werke* 7.1, Leipzig, 1913), p. 54.

19 Ptolemy XIII, who drowned in the Nile in 47 B.C., was reported to have been wearing a golden breastplate. See Florus, *Epitoma* 2.13(4.2).60.

20 On Phoebus' gift to the Seven Sages, see Valerius Maximus 4.3.6.

21 Gervais of Melkley cites line 333 as an effective instance of *additiva correctio*, in that the point initially made by the opposition of *ara* to *auro* is clarified, and rendered progressively more meaningful, by the subsequent oppositions *liber-libra*, *numen-nummus* (*Ars*, p. 25).

22 On Corineus see Geoffrey of Monmouth, *Historia* 1.12–13, 15–16; and above, 1.286–87.

23 I.e. Hercules, whose youth is associated with the Argive town of Tiryns.

24 I.e. Cornwall.

25 On Pandrasus, see Geoffrey, *Historia* l.3–11.

26 See Geoffrey, *Historia* 2.8.

27 At this point Gawain's narrative abandons Geoffrey of Monmouth and becomes an elaborate compliment to John's patron, Walter of Coutances.

28 Rainfroy, the father of Walter of Coutances.

29 Avarice, here, as often in twelfth-century satire, associated with the papal court at Rome (Latium); see Murray, *Reason and Society*, pp. 74–75.

30 See Valerius Maximus 9.4.3.

31 See Valerius Maximus 9.4.2.

32 See Valerius Maximus 9.4. ext. 1.

Book Six

1 As Schmidt points out, Tylos with its perpetual spring cannot be identified with *Tyle*, the name Johannes employs twice (5.251; 9.61) to refer to the region known to ancient poets as Thule, the northernmost point of human habitation. Tylos seems rather to be the island so named by Pliny, 12.40 and Solinus, 52.49. Both report that the trees of this island never lose their leaves, which doubtless suggested to Johannes the perpetual springtime of lines 20–25.

2 The basis for associating Archytas of Tarentum with anger is an anecdote reported by Valerius Maximus, 4.1. ext. 1. Returning from a long sojourn with Pythagoras at Metapontum to discover that his overseer had neglected the

upkeep of his lands, Archytas refused to punish the man, fearing that his anger would make the punishment unjustly harsh.

3   I.e. the Sun's passage over both the known and the unknown hemisphere of the world.

4   I.e. Alexander.

5   The *Revised Medieval Latin Word-List* cites *limes c.* 1150 in the sense of "place in decimal notation."

6   As a gloss in x suggests, *Magni* may refer specifically to Alexander, as at 6.486; see the anecdote reported by Valerius Maximus, 4.3. ext. 4.

7   See John of Salisbury, *Policraticus* 5.17; Jerome, *Adversus Jovinianum* 2.14.

8   On the twelfth century's predilection for this sort of grammatical metaphor see Paul Lehmann, *Die Parodie im Mittelalter* (2nd edn, Stuttgart, 1963), pp. 49–54; and Jan Ziolkowski, *Alan of Lille's Grammar of Sex* (Cambridge, Mass., 1985), pp. 51–76.

9   See John of Salisbury, *Policraticus* 8.8; Jerome, *Adversus Jovinianum* 2.9.

10   See Valerius Maximus 4.3. ext. 4; Horace, *Epist.* 1.17.13–24. Horace, however, goes on to give Aristippus the better of his exchange with Diogenes.

11   See John of Salisbury, *Policraticus* 7.13; Jerome, *Adversus Jovinianum* 2.9.

12   See John of Salisbury, *Policraticus* 7.13; Valerius Maximus 8.7. ext. 4.

13   On Titus' generosity see Suetonius, *Titus* 8; John of Salisbury, *Policraticus* 3.14. His famous assertion that the day on which he did not make some donation was wasted, recalled at 306–07, is credited to Archbishop Walter (or King Henry) in lines 314–15 below.

14   Probably yet another tribute to Walter of Coutances but as Schmidt notes, perhaps a reference to Henry II.

15   Much of Cicero's speech and that of Pliny which follows it is drawn from the discussion of the use of riches in *De officiis* 2.54–55.

16   I have departed from Schmidt's punctuation, which conveys the misleading suggestion that the impersonal *oportet* is part of the sequence of parallel verbs *pulsat, ferit, instat.*

17   See above, lines 273–79.

18   Much of the argument of lines 451–60 can be traced to Seneca's *Epistulae morales* 31.10; 44.5–6; 76.16; 27.9; 4.11; 2.5; 18.8.

19   See above, Book I, n. 4, and Lucan, *D.b.c.* 5.526–31, where not Caesar but the narrator praises Amyclas' tranquillity.

20   See Valerius Maximus 8.14. ext. 2; John of Salisbury, *Policraticus* 8.5. Both identify the philosopher whose teaching Anaxarchus reports as Democritus.

21   See Valerius Maximus 9.12. ext. 3; John of Salisbury, *Policraticus* 2.26, 7.5. I take "predo fluvialis" as "river-plunderer," corresponding to Valerius' "piscatoribus." John speaks only of "nescioquam nautarum quaestionem."

Book Seven

1   Another reference to the bull of Phalaris. See Book 3, n. 12 above.

2   That is, the price of trafficking with lechery is the loss of good character.

3   For other twelfth-century examples of play on *usus* and *abusio* with reference to sodomy and pederasty, see Schmidt. As in the case of Alan's *De planctu naturae*, there is no way to determine the focus of Johannes' criticism here, though lines 70–86 suggest that a specific person or episode is implicated.

4   Gervais cites lines 116–17 as an instance of synthesis, or "hyperbaton ex omni parte confusum," a figure liable to be carried to "inexcusable" extremes, and even in this relatively clear instance misleading beause of the singular verb (*Ars*, pp. 82–84).

5   Gervais cites lines 118 and 124–25 as illustrating aspects of the "transumptive" or metaphorical use of diction. In 118 *veneno* is used literally (*proprie*) in respect to Nessus, metaphorically (*transumptive*) in respect to Venus. In 125, though the passage is corrupt in Gräbener's edition, the point is clearly that *nevit* is used in a similarly "equivocal" way in reference to *pensum* and *necem* (*Ars*, p. 138).

6   A gloss in MS x identifies Ovid's Corinna as "uxor Cesaris."

7   An echo of Statius, *Thebaid* 1.305, where Mercury dims his radiance in preparing to descend into Hades.

8   Ursa Maior, once the nymph Callisto whom Jupiter ravished and who was turned into a bear by Juno. She is *fixa* in that her constellation never sinks below the horizon.

9   An allusion to the identification of Aquarius with Ganymede, cup-bearer and favorite of Jove, a common figure for sodomy and pederasty in school-poetry.

10   On Pythagoras' concern over female dress, see Justinus, *Epitoma historiarum Philippicarum* 20.4; John of Salisbury, *Policraticus* 7.4.

11   On the word-play *mundus* / *mundanus*, see Schmidt.

12   I.e. Johannes is full of both hope and its opposite, fear.

13   Since the group Pythagoras has named are clearly the Seven Sages, "Philo," here and in Chapter 11 (430ff.) below, is Johannes' version of the name of the sage Chilo.

14   I.e. Nestor.

15   A reference to the giant Tityos, who was punished for assaulting the Titaness Leto or Latona was to lie stretched out on the floor of Hades, while two vultures tore at his liver. See Vergil, *Aeneid* 6.595–98.

16   Gervais cites line 246 as an instance of *leonitas* or internal rhyme, somewhat more "commendable" than the more extended exercise of 8.36–39 (*Ars*, p. 17; cp. below, Book Eight, n. 2).

17   As Schmidt notes, Johannes' characterization of the Furies recalls the common scheme in which Allecto represents unremitting anger, Megaera violent action, and Tisiphone hostile speech. See Fulgentius, *Mitologiae* 1.7.

18   See Juvenal, *Sat.* 6.195, where this phrase (ζωὴ χαὶ ψυχή) is cited as an example of Roman women's affected use in ordinary conversation of "bedroom Greek."

19   The sun turned back in its course after Atreus tricked Thyestes into eating the flesh of his own children; see Lucan, *D.b.c.* 1.543–44.

20 Numa, traditionally associated with the establishment of religious and political institutions, is a figure of wise governance; cp. 5.455.

21 Given Johannes' evident respect for Horace, as attested by his many borrowings and his use of him as a standard to rebuke the "presumption" of Persius (5.48), "Flacci" here should probably be taken as referring to satire in general (perhaps with a play on its literal meaning, "flabby," "flaccid," hence lacking in the force and firmness of effective satire)

Book Eight

1 See Horace, *Epist.* 1.6.27. Here again, as at 5.214–19, the juxtaposition of Lucifer with a figure from classical tradition has an oddly extenuating effect.

2 Gervais considers the *leonitas* of lines 36–39 "commendable," though carried too far (*Ars*, p. 17; cp. above, Book Seven, n. 13).

3 The effect of Lucifer's fall is conveyed in the Latin by an untranslatable play on *lūteus*, "golden," and *lŭteus*, "muddy," "dirty."

4 By effecting the death of the tyrant, the feast eliminates the many ways in which he had made his subjects weep.

5 See Velleius Paterculus, *Ad M. Vinicium libri (Historiae Romanae)* 2.57; John of Salisbury, *Policraticus* 8.7.

6 As Schmidt notes, the argument which follows recalls Seneca, *Epistulae,* 76.

7 See Valerius Maximus 6.9. ext. 1; John of Salisbury, *Policraticus* 8.9. The unusual length of the exemplary narrative points up its relevance to the experience of Architrenius.

8 The long discourse which follows, extending to 9.148, is based almost entirely on the translation by Johannes Hispalensis of the *Differentie* (i.e. "Chapters": in early printed editions the title is commonly *De rudimentis astronomie,* of Al-Farghani or "Alfraganus," (ed. F. J. Carmody, Berkeley, 1943; for a somewhat different Latin version, see *Il "libro dell'aggregazione delle stelle,"* ed. Romeo Campani, Collezione di opuscoli danteschi inediti o rari 87–90, Città di Castello, 1910).

I have also found useful the early thirteenth-century *Tractatus de spera* of Johannes de Sacrobosco (ed. and tr. Lynn Thorndike, *The "Sphere" of Sacrobosco and Its Commentators,* Chicago, 1949), pp. 76–142, a work which Johannes de Hauvilla could not have known, but which is largely based on Al-Farghani and provides less technical explanations (not always accurate) of most of the main features of his system that appear in the *Architrenius.* Three of the four chapters of the *De spera* in Thorndike's translation are reprinted with useful footnotes in *A Source Book of Medieval Science,* ed. Edward Grant (Cambridge, Mass., 1974), pp. 442–51.

9 If "modern youth" refers to anything more specific than the enterprise of twelfth-century natural science, which developed a cosmology based primarily on Platonic and Arab sources, it may denote Bernardus Silvestris, whose *Cosmographia* begins by depicting the immensity from which the universe first

emerged. For the "ancient" view that earth is the "lowest" of all things Schmidt cites Macrobius, *Commentarius in Somnium Scipionis* 1.19.11; 1.22.1.

10   On the relative smallness of the earth compared to any star, see Al-Farghani, *Differentie*, c. 4; Sacrobosco, *De spera*, c. 1.

11   See Al-Farghani, c. 22.

12   The two points at which the Moon's eccentric orbit intersects the plane of the Ecliptic, thus making possible an eclipse, are called the "head" and "tail" of the "Dragon"; see Al-Farghani, c. 28, Sacrobosco, c. 4.

13   The basis for this chapter is Al-Farghani, c. 5; cp. Sacrobosco, c. 2.

14   The "line of the solstice" described in 397–99 is one of the two "colures" (see above, 2.244–45 and n. 9); the other, which marks the equinoxes, intersects the solstitial colure at right angles at the poles.

15   On Aren see above, 2.243 and n. 8.

16   Johannes here seems to use "solstice" in a broad, literal sense as referring to any "standing" or "station" of the Sun (cp. *stacione* in 404), hence as denoting the equinoxes as well as the summer and winter solstices. Lucan refers to the Equator as the "circle of the high solstice" ("circulus alti / Solstitii"), *D.b.c.* 9.531–32; cp. Sacrobosco 3.

17   I.e. the summer and winter solstices, when the Sun's path is furthest from the Equator.

18   The rare epithet *Aegoceron* (*Egoceron*, cl. Latin *Aegoceros*) is Johannes' preferred name for the constellation Capricorn.

19   The Sun's speed is constant, but its orbit is eccentric, so that its rate of movement through the sky appears to vary. At its perigee its movement through the signs of the Zodiac seems accelerated, while at its apogee (*augis*) it seems to move at the same rate as the "fixed" stars. See Al-Farghani, c. 12; Sacrobosco, c. 4.

20   Most of this chapter is based on Al-Farghani, c. 7.

21   I.e. Thetis, the sea.

22   I.e. at the Pole.

23   This chapter and Chapter 2 of Book Nine are based on Al-Farghani, c. 10.

24   *Frixeus* is Johanne's name for the constellation Aries. Phrixus and Helle, children of the Theban king Athamas, fled from Thebes to Colchis, carried on the back of the ram of the golden fleece, to avoid the wrath of their step-mother Ino. Helle was drowned, and gave her name to the Hellespont. The same association is evoked by *portitor Elleus* in line 463 and *Vectore* in 470.

25   I.e. Virgo and Libra. Astraea, goddess of justice, is sometimes identified with Libra, but here with Virgo, as at Lucan, *D.b.c.* 9.535. *Chele* (literally "claws") refers to the "arms" of Scorpio, but since these extend into Libra, the term is also an epithet for this constellation; see Vergil, *Georg.* 1.33.

26   I.e. Cancer. When Hercules fought the Hydra, he was attacked by Cancer at the instigation of Hera. See Hyginus, *Astronomia* 2.23.

27   I.e. Sagittarius, already identified as Chiron by *Haemonius* ("Thessalian") in 455.

28   I.e. Virgo. Erigone, daughter of the Athenian noble Icarius, hung herself

out of grief for his death, and was transformed into a constellation. Her father became the constellation Boötes. See Hyginus, *Fabulae* 130. Erigone is identified with Astraea by Martianus Capella, *De nuptiis* 2.174.

29   I.e. the constellation Gemini. Castor and Pollux were the twin sons of the Spartan princess Leda.

30   I.e. the Ram, Aries. See above, note 24.

Book Nine

1   I.e. in the northern hemisphere. Nature here resumes her discussion of the rising of the zodiacal signs. Having devoted nearly all of 8.11 to the regularity with which the signs ascend and descend at the Equator, or "right" ascensions, she now discusses "oblique" ascensions, those that occur between the Equator and the Tropic, which are necessarily unequal.

2   I.e. in the region between the Equator and the Tropic.

3   I.e. the "right" or vertical course in which they ascend at the Equator.

4   I.e. Cancer; see 8.455 and note.

5   I.e. Castor and Pollux, the Gemini.

6   I.e. at the Equator.

7   Since the rate of ascent and descent in the "upright circle" (i.e. at the Equator) is the same.

8   See Al-Farghani, c. 7.

9   See Al-Farghani, c. 6.

10   This band is apparently neither of the Colures which make the points of equinox and solstice, though it resembles them in that it intersects the Equator at right angles (55–57). Al-Farghani (c. 6) invites us to "imagine" this circle, evidently as an ad hoc way of defining the habitable portion of the earth.

11   The *filius* (here in the broad sense of "boy" or "slave") is Apollo, whom Zeus compelled to serve as herdsman to King Admetus; see Ovid, *Ars Am.* 2.239–41. The point of the reference would seem to lie in the connection between Apollo's relegation to serfdom and the condition imposed on countless medieval Slavs.

12   See above, Book One, n. 5.

13   See Solinus 52.7.

14   See above, Book Two, n. 8.

15   I.e. at the Equator, where daytime and nighttime are equal.

16   On the "arc of day" and "arc of night" see Al-Farghani, c. 11.

17   See Al-Farghani, c. 12.

18   See above, Book Eight, n. 10, and Al-Farghani, c. 12.

19   This paragraph is based on Al-Farghani, c. 13.

20   See Al-Farghani, c. 15.

21   This paragraph is based on Al-Farghani, c. 18.

22   On Megaera's serpentine locks, see Vergil, *Aen.* 12.846–48.

23   Schmidt, p. 61, cites Lucan, *D.b.c.* 9.855, but Johannes' line also echoes Bernardus Silvestris, *Cosmographia* 1.1.55, and points up the broad parallel

between the two scenes. In the *Cosmographia* Nature had taxed Noys, the wisdom of God, with showing too little love toward her offspring, the still uncreated universe which as yet exists only in the form of chaotic primordial matter. Here, as in the *Anticlaudianus* of Alan of Lille, it is Nature who stands accused.

24   I.e. the face of Helen, daughter of the Spartan Leda. See above, Book 8, note 29.

25   The phrase "pulchra –pudica tamen" in 295 is twice cited by Gervais, first as an instance of the felicitous use of *tamen* to effect a simple *correctio* (cp. above, Book Five, n. 19, for the more complex *additiva correctio* of 5.333), and later as a successful instance of *adversatio* between two adjectives (*Ars*, pp. 17, 199).

26   See Valerius Maximus 4.3. ext. 3.

27   See Aulus Gellius, *Noctes Atticae* 1.8.3–6; John of Salisbury, *Policraticus* 6.23; Walter Map, *De nugis curialium* 4.3.

28   In the traditional story Democritus did not castrate, but rather blinded himself; see Cicero, *De finibus* 5.87; Aulus Gellius 10.17.1. Schmidt plausibly suggests that the basis for John's substitution of castration is Tertullian, *Apologeticum* 46.11, where Democritus is said to have blinded himself to avoid the stimulus to lust provided by the sight of women.

29   See Solinus 1.126; Jerome, *Adversus Jovinianum* 1.41.

30   See Valerius Maximus 8.15.12; Pliny 7.120; Solinus 1.126.

31   "Maeonians" is apparently intended as a reference to the Trojans, though the term perhaps refers to the Maeonian (i.e. Homeric; cp. 1.75) language in which Johannes may have imagined Cassandra's prophecies as having been uttered.

32   See Valerius Maximus 4.6. ext. 2.

33   See Valerius Maximus 4.6. ext. 1.

34   I assume a play on *syrinx*, in the double sense of a reed (or reed pipe) and syringe.

35   Probably, as Schmidt's note suggests, some smaller organ-like instrument.

36   As Schmidt notes, *castratio* must be intended as in some sense equivalent to *castitas*.

Selected bibliography

Primary sources

Architrenius, ed. Jodocus Badius Ascensius. Paris, 1517.
Johannis de Altavilla, *Architrenius*, ed. Thomas Wright, *The Anglo-Latin Satirical Poets and Epigrammatists of the Twelfth Century*. 2 vols., Rolls Series 59, London, 1872. Vol. I, pp. 240–392.
Johannes de Hauvilla, *Architrenius*, ed. Paul Gerhard Schmidt. Munich, 1974.

. . .

Alanus de Insulis (Alain de Lille), *Anticlaudianus*, ed. Robert Bossuat, Paris, 1955. Tr. James J. Sheridan, Toronto, 1973.
De planctu naturae, ed. Nicholas Häring, in *Studi medievali*, ser. 3, 19 (1978), pp. 797–879. Tr. James J. Sheridan, Toronto, 1980.
Al-Farghani ("Alfraganus"), *Differentie*, ed. F. J. Carmody. Berkeley, 1943.
[another version] *Il "libro dell'aggregazione delle stelle,"* ed. Romeo Campani, Collezione di opuscoli danteschi inediti o rari 87–90. Città di Castello, 1910.
Bernardus Silvestris, *Cosmographia*, ed. Peter Dronke, Leiden, 1978. Tr. Winthrop Wetherbee, New York, 1973.
Fulgentius, *Opera*, ed. Rudolph Helm, Leipzig, 1898.
Geoffrey of Monmouth, *Historia regum Britanniae*, ed. Edmond Faral in *La légende arthurienne: Études et documents*. 3 vols., Bibliothèque de l'École des Hautes Études 257–59, Paris, 1929. Vol. 3, pp. 64–303. Tr. Lewis Thorpe, Baltimore, 1966.
Gervaise of Melkley (Gervasius de Saltu Lacteo), *Ars poetica*, ed. Hans-Jürgen Gräbener. Forschungen zur Romanischen Philologie 17, Münster Westphalen, 1965.
John of Salisbury, *Entheticus de dogmate philosophorum* (*Entheticus maior*) and *Entheticus in Policraticum* (*Entheticus minor*), ed. Jan van Laarhoven, 3 vols., Leiden, 1987.
Metalogicon, ed. C. C. J. Webb, Oxford, 1929. Tr. D. D. McGarry, Berkeley, 1955.
Policraticus, ed. C. C. J. Webb, 2 vols., Oxford, 1909. A complete English version of the *Policraticus* exists in the form of two separately published volumes: Books 4, 5, 6 and parts of 7 and 8 make up *The Statesman's Book of John of Salisbury*, tr. John Dickinson, New York, 1927; Books 1, 2, 3

and the remainder of 7 and 8 are contained in *Frivolities of Courtiers and Footprints of Philosophers*, tr. Joseph B. Pike, Minneapolis, 1938.

Pliny the Elder, *Naturalis Historia*, ed. Karl Mayhoff, 6 vols., Leipzig, 1870–1906. English-Latin ed. and tr. Harris Rackham, W. H. S. Jones, D. E. Eichholz, 10 vols., Cambridge and London, 1938–63.

Solinus, C. Iulius, *Collectanea rerum memorabilium*, ed. Theodor Mommsen, Berlin, 1864.

Valerius Maximus, *Facta et dicta memorabilia*, ed. Karl Kempf, Leipzig, 1888.

Walter Map, *De nugis curialium*, ed. and tr. M. R. James, rev. C. N. L. Brook, R. A. B. Mynors, Oxford, 1983. Also tr. Frederick Tupper, Marbury Bladen Ogle, London, 1924.

Walter of Châtillon (Gualterus de Castellione), *Alexandreis*, ed. Marvin L. Colker, Thesaurus Mundi 17, Padua, 1978. Tr. R. Telfryn Pritchard, Toronto, 1986.

Secondary sources

Dufournet, Jean, "Relire le *De nugis curialium* de Gautier Map," *Le Moyen Age* 95 (1989), pp. 519–25.

Faral, Edmond, "Le Roman de la Rose et la pensée française au XIIIe siècle," *Revue des deux mondes* 35 (Sept. 1926), pp. 430–57.

"Le manuscrit 511 du 'Hunterian Museum' de Glasgow," *Studi medievali*, n.s. 9 (1936), pp. 18–119.

Francke, Kuno, "Der Architrenius des Johann von Anville," *Forschungen zur deutschen Geschichte* 20 (1880), pp. 473–502.

Gössmann, Elisabeth, *Antiqui und Moderni im Mittelalter. Eine geschichtliche Standortsbestimmung*, Munich–Vienna, 1974.

Hutchings, Charles M., "L'Anticlaudianus d'Alain de Lille. Étude de chronologie," *Romania* 50 (1924), pp. 1–13.

Jung, M.-R., *Études sur le poème allégorique en France au Moyen Age*, Romanica Helvetica 82, Bern, 1971.

Klaus, Catherine, "De l'Enfer au Paradis ... et retour, dans l'*Architrenius* de Jean de Hanville," in *Pour une mythologie du Moyen Age*, ed. Laurence Harf-Lancner, Dominique Boutet, Paris, 1988, pp. 27–42.

Ladner, Gerhart B., "Terms and Ideas of Renewal," in *Renaissance and Renewal in the Twelfth Century*, ed. Robert L. Benson, Giles Constable, Cambridge, Mass., 1982, pp. 1–33.

Latham, R. E., ed. *Revised Latin Word List from British and Irish Sources*, London, 1965.

Le Goff, Jacques, *Les intellectuels au Moyen Age*, 2nd edn, Paris, 1985.

The Medieval Imagination, Chicago, 1988.

Lehmann, Paul, *Die Parodie im Mittelalter*, 2nd edn, Stuttgart, 1963.

Lewis, C.S., *The Allegory of Love*, Oxford, 1936.

Liebeschütz, Hans, *Medieval Humanism in the Life and Writings of John of Salisbury*, Studies of the Warburg Institute 17, London, 1950.

Murray, Alexander, *Reason and Society in the Middle Ages*, 2nd edn, Oxford, 1985.

Payen, Jean-Charles, "L'utopie du contrat social dans l'*Anticlaudianus*," in *Alain de Lille, Gautier de Châtillon, Jakemart Giélée et leur temps*, ed. H. Roussel, F. Suard, Lille, 1980, pp. 125–34.

"L'utopie chez les Chartrains," *Le Moyen Age* 90 (1984), pp. 383–400.

Piehler, Paul, *The Visionary Landscape. A Study in Medieval Allegory*, London, 1971.

Simler, Joseph, *De Archithrenio duodecimi saeculi carmine*, Paris, 1871.

Takada, Yasunari, "The Brooch of Thebes and the Girdle of Venus: Courtly Love in an Oppositional Perspective," *Poetica* (Tokyo) 29–30 (1989), pp. 17–38.

Türk, Egbert, *Nugae curialium: Le règne d'Henri II Plantagenet (1154–1189) et l'éthique politique*, Geneva, 1977.

Uhlig, Claus, *Hofkritik im England des Mittelalters und der Renaissance. Studien zu einem Gemeinplatz der europäischen Moralistik*. Quellen und Forschungen zur Sprach- und Kulturgeschichte der germanischen Volker, N. F. 56, Berlin, 1973.

Wetherbee, Winthrop, *Platonism and Poetry in the Twelfth Century*, Princeton, 1972.

Wilks, Michael, ed. *The World of John of Salisbury*. Studies in Church History: Subsidia 3, Oxford, 1984.

Ziolkowski, Jan, *Alan of Lille's Grammar of Sex*, Cambridge, MA, 1985.

Index nominum

Note: The following list is keyed to the English translation. Italicized names occur only in the Latin text, and are represented in English by the terms with which they are joined. Names in brackets do not appear in the text, but identify figures who are mentioned only by way of paraphrase.

Achates 5.407
Achilles 4.238; 5.387; 6.1; 8.435
Achaean 1.100
Acin 1.81&n; 9.69
Acteus (Greek) 5.9
Admetus 9.66&n
Aeacus 7.247
Aegoceron (*Egoceron*, the constellation Capricorn) 8.407&n, 418, 451, 465; 9.22, 23
Aeolus 5.269; 6.252
Aetna 1.141; 2.344; 6.464; 7.345
Africa 7.208
Agamemnon (*Atrides*) 4.250
Ajax 2.303&n
Albion 5.412 (*v.* England, Britain)
Alcides 4.268, 271; 5.34; 7.118, 122, 124; 8.18; 9.27 (*v.* Hercules)
Alexander (*Magnus*) 1.95; 4.112; 6.201, 209&n, 253&n, 477, 486; 9.70 (*v.* Neptanabus)
Allecto 4.132; 7.255&n
Amyclas 1.53&n; 2.224; 6.237, 455&n; 8.156
Anaxarchus 6.477&n
Anchises 5.433
[Andromache 5.33]
Antaeus 5.427; 7.125
Antipodes 3.190; 5.248
Antonia 1.297
Aonian 1.48
Aquarius 7.166&n
Aquitanians 5.399
Arachne 4.215
Arcadian (Lycaon) 7.309
Archytas 6.28&n
Aren 2.243&n; 8.401&n, 457; 9.36, 74
Arescon 1.251

Argus 8.356
[Aries (constellation)] (*v.* Phrixean, Carrier, *Vector*)
Aristippus 6.269&n
Aristotle 3.97
Artemisia 9.368&n
Arthur 5.438; 6.2
Asia 1.109
Astraea (constellation) 8.454&n (*v.* Erigone, Virgo)
Athens 6.273; 7.221; 8.253
Athos (mountain) 1.1&n
Atlas 1.81; 4.148; 9.67
Atrides 4.240 (Menelaos), 250 (Agamemnon); 5.388
Atropos 1.188; 6.162, 223 (*v.* Parcae)
Attica 2.486
Augustus 4.49&n
Aurora 3.186, 222, 283; 8.423
Avernos 2.189; 5.71, 212, 424; 6.133, 419

Baucis (*Baccis*) 2.219&n, 396, 405, 440, 468
Bear (constellation) 7.155&n
Bellona 6.38, 93
Bias 7.223, 323
Birria 3.83&n; 5.342
Bithian 1.293&n
Bootes (constellation) 5.27&n; 9.61, 140
Britain 1.119; 4.291&n; 5.87, 413 (*v.* Albion, England)
Britons 1.159, 349
Brutus 5.407, 413
Busiris 3.308
Byblis 4.266

Cadiz 9.69&n, 72, 76